John Hanson Beadle

Life in Utah

The Mysteries and Crimes of Mormonism

John Hanson Beadle

Life in Utah
The Mysteries and Crimes of Mormonism

ISBN/EAN: 9783337339036

Printed in Europe, USA, Canada, Australia, Japan

Cover: Foto ©ninafisch / pixelio.de

More available books at **www.hansebooks.com**

LIFE IN UTAH;

OR, THE

Mysteries and Crimes of Mormonism

BEING AN EXPOSÉ

OF THE

SECRET RITES AND CEREMONIES

OF THE

LATTER-DAY SAINTS,

WITH A

FULL AND AUTHENTIC HISTORY OF POLYGAMY AND
THE MORMON SECT FROM ITS ORIGIN TO
THE PRESENT TIME.

BY

J. H. BEADLE,

EDITOR OF THE SALT LAKE REPORTER, AND UTAH CORRESPONDENT
OF THE CINCINNATI COMMERCIAL.

Issued by subscription only, and not for sale in the book stores. Residents of any district desiring a copy should address the publisher, and an agent will call upon them.

TORONTO, ONT.
PUBLISHED BY JAMES SPENCER, 65 COLBORNE STREET.
1872.

PREFACE.

AMERICA is the paradise of heterodoxy. All sorts of wild, strange and even abominable religions flourish unchecked, side by side, and generally without violent collision. The wild dreams of the fervid Oriental imagination; the vague shadowings of Gothic mysticism; the coarse materialism of French infidelity, and the ideal fancies of Greek and Asiatic, all the errors and worn out theories of the Old World, of schisms in the early Church, the monkish age and the rationalistic period, find here a free air, a fertile soil, a more congenial clime and a second native country, as it were, in which new and more luxuriant growths spring rapidly from the old and half dead stocks of pseudo-theology.

But the inventive American mind is not content merely with old errors, and the Yankee is nothing if not practical; hence we see that to every new or purely American phase of religious error, there is always tacked a feature of political power, communism of property, social license or moral perversion, a general revolt against accepted theories in law, medicine, marriage, government or social relations. Let the extreme tend which way it will, it is equally an extreme; whether of the anti-marriage Shakers, the celibate Harmonists, the wife-communists of Oneida, or the polygamous Mormons. All this is, perhaps, a necessary evil—an inevitable adjunct to a great good. In the perfect liberty of conscience guaranteed, the perverted or diseased conscience is equally free with the pure or healthy; and where every man is free to choose as he will, it is reasonable to suppose that many will choose but poorly. Like all good principles this liberty of conscience is strangely liable to abuse; but a careful examination will show, I think, that the present condition is far better, with all its evil outgrowths, than would be any aiming at repression. Repression is not unity. Suppose either of the prominent sects to be made the Established Church— if indeed the mind can possibly conceive of an Established Church in America—the Methodists, for instance; then would that Church at once lose many of its communicants; most people would avoid it to the farthest extent allowed by law, not from any particular hostility to that one Church, but simply because it *was* established.

We may, indeed, congratulate ourselves, that with such perfect liberty of choice so few have adopted beliefs at all dangerous either to the State or to society; for these last are the only questions with which we have a right to deal. But certain forms of belief cannot possibly confine themselves to speculative errors; the perversion of moral and ethical principles is too radical to be confined to the heart, and the hideous moral gangrene, starting from the soul and centre, works outwardly through the life in all manner of corruption, confusion and abomination. When the faith is perfectly inwrought, it cannot but show itself in acts, and with these the State has a right to deal. Perfect toleration is due to all beliefs, and these gross forms of error only demand attention when endeavoring, against the good of the State, to make a peculiar moral condition the general law for a whole people, and still more as laboring to radically pervert the Christian idea of marriage. If the experience of all civilized nations for three thousand years, and the best judgment of the best minds in law founded upon that experience, have proved any one fact more than another, it is that the marriage relation should be strictly regulated by law, that the State has an absolute right to prescribe the civil conditions accompanying and the civil rights resulting from it; and that the human passions, whether excited by mere lust or by religious fanaticism, must be controlled by positive law. It matters not if an individual esteem it his natural right to act contrary to express law, or if several individuals constituting a community believe it to be a religious right; they are equally subject thereto, and must take the legal consequence of disobedience. It is then a gratifying fact, that so few have adopted beliefs tending to pervert the marriage relation. Of the forty millions in America less than half a million are included in all of such sects. In this light liberty of conscience in America is almost a perfect success.

The vast majority of our people have founded their religious belief on theories not inimical to the public good; and the scores of varying sects which arise from year to year, generally do so only to run a brief and meteor-like race, and sink like dissolved exhalations in the bogs and mire of ignorance from which they arose. But occasionally we see one of these parasitic growths upon the body of religious freedom, which, from peculiar and special causes, extends its existence beyond what we would naturally look for; and a few, originally transplanted from Europe where the parent organization has long since expired, maintain a sort of sickly life through two or three generations in America. Of such are the Shakers from England, and the Harmonists from Germany. But where in contact with vital Christianity, they must sooner or later yield : their wild enthusiam is sufficient for rise and growth, but lacks the virtuous energy to direct and continue. To such, comparatively innocent and harmless, the public direct little attention. But there are a few, which manage to preserve a sort of isolation even in the midst of other sects, or in extreme cases, to get apart and aside, and maintain for a long period an independent existence. Of these none have attained to such prominence as the sect called Mormons. Having leaders at once sagacious and unscrupulous, they have long managed to avoid whatever contact would weaken their organization. We have seen them, from small and obscure beginnings, rise to a strength sufficient to create a local rebellion in Missouri; transplanted thence to Illinois, rise to a threatening power ; transplanted again, flourish rapidly for a while, and though now evidently on the decline, yet strong enough to create a difficult and delicate political problem, and like the Bohon Upas, overshadow a whole Territory with a deadly influence. Scattered through the nation Mormonism would be the weakest of all religions; collected into one Territory, and ruling there with almost absolute power, they present a painfully interesting problem. Comparatively, their numbers are trifling ; locally, they are of great importance. In the light of the principles here enunciated, and with perfect confidence in their correctness, this work has been prepared ; with a view to the better enlightenment of the American public on this question and, if possible, to make the duty of Government and people more plain, to set forth the most salient points in the progress of religious imposture, and to draw attention to a Territory rich in natural resources. It is believed that the work contains most of the material facts of interest in regard to Utah and the Mormons; whether of the climate and resources of the former, or the history, theology and peculiar social practices of the latter. The history of the sect is drawn from many sources : from their own works, from personal records of several who have spent many years among them, from evidence published by the State of Missouri, from official documents of States or the General Government, from previous compilations and other accredited sources. Of charges against the Mormons not fully proved, the statements for and against them have been equally presented. The same rules of evidence have been applied in summing up their history, as are held applicable in courts of justice. The author's opportunities for personal observation will be seen in the course of the work. The author is well aware of the many imperfections of the work, but does not seek to disarm criticism by a prefaced apology ; it is given as a compilation of testimony, on which the reader has the same privilege of passing judgment as the author has exercised on those before him. Whatever may be thought of the style in which they are presented, I trust many of the facts will be found interesting, and if the work should excite an intelligent interest among the American people, in regard to the affairs of Utah, it will have accomplished the dearest wish of the author.

J. H. B.

CORINNE, UTAH TERRITORY, *April 5th*, 1871.

CONTENTS.

CHAPTER I.
HISTORICAL.

Birth and early life of the Mormon Prophet—The original Smith family—Opinion of Brigham Young—The " peep-stone "—" Calling" of Joe Smith—The Golden Plates—" Reformed Egyptian" translated—" Book of Mormon" published—Synopsis of its contents—Real author of the work—"The glorious six" first converts—Emma Smith, "Elect Lady and Daughter of God"—Sidney Rigdon takes the field—First Hegira—"Zion" in Missouri—Kirtland Bank—Swindling and "persecution"—War in Jackson County—Smith "marches on Missouri"—Failure of the "Lord's Bank"—Flight of the Prophet—"Mormon War"—Capture of Smith—Flight into Illinois.. 21

CHAPTER II.
HISTORY FROM THE FOUNDING OF NAUVOO TILL 1843.

Rapid growth of Nauvoo—Apparent prosperity—" The vultures gather to the carcass"—Crime, polygamy and politics—Subserviency of the Politicians—Nauvoo Charters—A government within a government—Joe Smith twice arrested—Released by S. A. Douglas—Second time by Municipal Court of Nauvoo—McKinney's Account—Petty thieving—Gentiles driven out of Nauvoo—"Whittling Deacons" — " Danites" — Anti-Mormons organize a Political Party—Treachery of Davis and Owens—Defeat of Anti-Mormons—Campaign of 1843—Cyrus Walker, a great Criminal Lawyer—" Revelation" on Voting—The Prophet cheats the Lawyer—Astounding perfidy of the Mormon Leaders—Great increase of popular hatred—Just anger against the Saints..................... 48

CHAPTER III.

MORMON DIFFICULTIES AND DEATH OF THE PROPHET.

Ford's account—Double treachery in the Quincy district—New and startling developments in Nauvoo—Tyranny of Joe Smith—Revolt of a portion of his followers—The " Expositor"—It is declared "a nuisance" and "abated"—Flight of apostates—Warrants issued for Smith and other Mormons—Constables driven out of Nauvoo—Militia called for—Nauvoo fortified—Mormon war imminent—Governor Ford takes the field in person—Flight of the Prophet and Patriarch to Iowa—Their return and arrest—The Governor pledged for their safety—In his absence the jail is attacked — Death of the Smiths — Character of the Prophet— Comments.... 71

CHAPTER IV.

TWO YEARS OF STRIFE—EXODUS FROM ILLINOIS.

No Successor to the Prophet—David Hyrum Smith, the "Son of Promise"—Contest for the Leadership—Diplomacy of Brigham Young—Curious Trials—All of Brigham's Opponents " cut off "— Troubles Renewed—Fights, Outrages, Robberies and Murder— Another Election and more Treachery—Singular " Wolf Hunt"— Capture and Trial of Smith's Murderers—Of the Mormon Rioters—Failure and Defects of the Law—Further Outrages on Gentiles—Troubles in Adams County—The "Oneness"—The People of Adams Drive out the Mormons—Revenge by the Mormons— Murders of McBratney, Worrell, Wilcox, and Daubeneyer—Retaliation, and Murder of Durfee -The Mormons Ravage Hancock— Flight of the Gentiles—Militia Called, and Hancock put under Martial Law — The Mormons Begin to Leave Illinois — Fresh Quarrels—More Mormon Treachery—Bombardment of Nauvoo, and Final Expulsion of the Mormons...................................... 98

CHAPTER V.

FROM THE NAUVOO EXODUS TO THE MORMON WAR IN UTAH.

The *Via Dolorosa* of Mormon History—Through Iowa—Great suffering—"Stakes of Zion"—Settlement in Nebraska—"Mormon-Battalion"—Journey to Utah—Founding of Salt Lake City—Early accounts—Outrages upon California emigrants—Travellers murdered—Apostates "missing"—Dangers of rivalry in love with a Mormon Bishop—Usurpations of Mormon Courts and officers—Federal Judges driven out—Murders of Babbitt and Williams—Flight of Judges Stiles and Drummond—The Army set in motion for Utah—New officers appointed—Suspicious delay of the army—The "Mormon war begun."... 122

CHAPTER VI.

THE BLOODY PERIOD.

Sounds of war in Utah—Popular excitement—Fears of the disaffected—Attempted flight—Murder of the Potter and Parish families—Massacre of the Aiken party—Assassination of Yates—Killing of Forbes—Brigham "Turns loose the Indians"—MOUNTAIN MEADOW MASSACRE—Horrible Barbarity of Indians and Mormons—Evidence in the case—Attempt of Judge Cradlebaugh—Progress of the "Mormon War"—Delay of the army—Treachery or inefficiency?—Mormon Legion—Lieutenant General Wells—Brigham "Commands" the National troops to withdraw—Army trains destroyed—Lot Smith, the Mormon Guerilla—The "Army of Utah" in Winter Quarters—Colonel Kane again—Negotiations with Brigham—Governor Cumming "passed" through the Mormon lines—"Peace Commissioners"—Mormon Exodus—Weakness of Cumming—End of the War—Murders of Pike, the Jones's, Bernard, Drown, Arnold, McNeil, and others—A change at last...... 136

CHAPTER VII.

GENTILES IN UTAH.

A New Element—Livingston and Kinkead—"Jack-Mormonism at Washington"—Judge Drummond—M. Jules Remy—Gilbert and Sons — Heavy Trade — Later Gentile Merchants — Walker Brothers—Sales at Camp Floyd—"Crushing the Mormons"—Ransohoff & Co.—Mormon Outrages again—Murders of Brassfield and Dr. Robinson—Whipping of Weston—Evidence in case of Robinson—Outrages on Lieut. Brown and Dr. Williamson—Gentiles driven from the Public Land—Territorial Surveyor—Success of General Connor's Administration—The Government Returns to the Old Policy—Murder of Potter and Wilson—Horrible Death of "Negro Tom"—The Last Witness "put out of the Way"—"Danites" again—Murder each Other—Death of Hatch—Flight of Hickman—Forty-three Murders—Another change of Officials—Doty—Durkee—Shameful Neglect of the Government—Flight of the Gentiles—Comparative Quiet Again—A better Day—The Author Arrives in Utah.. 150

CHAPTER VIII.

FIRST VIEWS IN UTAH.

The real "American Desert"—No Myth—Bitter Creek -Green River—Lone Rock—Plains of Bridger—Quaking Asp Ridge—Bear River—A Mormon Autobiography—" Pulling hair"—"Aristocracy" on the Plains — "Mule-skinners" and "Bullwhackers" — The "Bullwhackers Epic"—Cache Cave—Echo Canon—Mormon "fortifications"—Braggadocio—Storm in Weber Canon—Up the Weber—Parley's Park—A Wife-stealing Apostle—Down the Canon—Majestic Scenery—First View of the Valley—The "City of the Saints." 166

CHAPTER IX.

TWO WEEKS IN SALT LAKE CITY.

Views of the City—Temple Block—Brigham's Block—Theatre—Immigrants — Mormon Arguments — Reasons for Polygamy—"Book of Mormon"— First Mormon Sermon—"Old" Joe Young—His Beauty (?)—His Sermon—Mormon Style of Preaching—Order of Services—First impressions rather favorable—Much to earn yet. 183

CHAPTER X.

TRIP TO BEAR RIVER AND RETURN.

Northward foot—Hot Springs — "Sessions Settlement"— Polygamy again—"Ephe Roberts' young wife "—Farmington—Kaysville — Three wives, and stone walls between — "Let us have Peace "—Red Sand Ridge—Ogden—Brigham City—Into the Poor District—Scandinavian porridge—English cookery—Rural life in Utah—Bear River, North—Cache Valley and the Canon—" Professor" Barker, the "Mad Philosopher"— A New Cosmogony— Mormon Science — "Celestial Masonry"—"Adam" redivivus— A Modern "Eve"—Folly and Fanaticism—Mineral Springs— The country vs. the city Mormon............ 201

CHAPTER XI.

THE CONFERENCE AND ITS RESULTS.

A Mormon mass-meeting—Faces and features—Great enthusiasm— A living "martyr"—A Mormon hymn—The Poetess—A "president" chosen—He recites the Church history—First view of Brigham—He curses the Gentiles—A "nasty sermon "—Coarseness and profanity—Bitterness of other speakers—Swearing in the pulpit—Exciting the people—Their frenzy and fanaticism— Hatred against the United States—Foolish bravado—The author gains new light on Mormonism — A subject to be studied — English and European Sects of like character—Division of the subject 214

CHAPTER XII.

ANALYSIS OF MORMON SOCIETY.

Difficulty at the outset—Extremes among witnesses—Prejudice on both sides—First impressions favorable—" Whited Sepulchres"— Classes of Mormons—Brigham Young ; imposter or fanatic ?—The dishonest class—The "earnest Mormons"—Disloyalty—Church and State Killing men to save their souls--Slavery of woman— Brigham the government—Prophecy against the United States— "War"—"Seven women to take hold of one man"—Another war expected—Blood and thunder in store for the Gentiles—" The great tribulation" about due—Popular errors—Witchcraft— "Faith-doctoring"—Zion in Jackson County, Missouri—Comfortable prospect. 223

CHAPTER XIII.

ANALYSIS OF MORMON THEOLOGY.

Its origin—A theological conglomerate—Mythology, Paganism, Mohammedanism, corrupt Christianity and Philosophy run mad— "First principles of the Gospel"—The five points of variance— Materialism—No spirit—A *god* with "body, parts and passions" —Matter eternal—No "creation"—Intelligent atoms—Pre-existent souls—High Times in the Spirit Worlds—Birth of Spirits— They hunt for "Earthly Tabernacles"—The "Second Estate"— Apotheosis—The "Third Estate"—"Fourth Estate"—Men become *gods*—"Divine generation"—Earthly Families and Heavenly Kingdoms—Did man come from the Sun?—"Building up the Kingdom"—One day as a thousand years—The time of the Gentiles about out—Great events at hand—"Gog and Magog," *et. al.*—Gentiles, prepare to make tracks—Return to "Zion," in Missouri—Christ's earthly empire—Great destiny for Missouri— Tenets from Christianity—Baptism a "Saving Ordinance"—Baptized twelve times—Office of the Holy Ghost—Strange fanaticism—Eclectic Theology—A personal *god*—The *homoousian* and the *homoiousian*—The *Logos* and the *Aeon*—Grossness and Vulgarity 239

CHAPTER XIV.

THEORETICAL POLYGAMY—ITS HISTORY.

Poetry of religious concubinage—Fanaticism and Sensualism—Two extremes—Origin of Polygamy—The great revelation—Its contradictions and absurdities—Mormon argument—Real origin— Beginning of Polygamy—A prostitute for religion's sake—Failures and Scandals—War in the Church—Stealing a Brother's wife—Furore in consequence—The *Expositor*—Its destruction— Death of the Smiths—Polygamy practised secretly and denied openly—Brigham's marriages—Nine years of concealment— Avowal at last—Argument in its favor—Demoralization in the English Church—A climax of unnatural obscenity—The "Reformation"—Temporary decline in Polygamy—Hostility of native

CONTENTS. xv

PAGE

Mormon girls—Outside influence—Difference of opinion—It dies hard—Spiritual wives—Mystery and abomination. 255

CHAATER XV.

PRACTICAL POLYGAMY.

Open evils and hidden sufferings--Miss S. E. Carmichael's testimony—Mormon sophistry—The sexual principle—Its objects—Theory and facts—Monogamist vs. Polygamist—Turk, Persian, and African vs. the Christian White—The same effects in Utah—Jealousy and Misery—Children of different wives—Cultivated indifference—Hatred among children—Brigham's idea of parental duty—Are the Mormon women happy ? — Submission and silence — Degradation of women—Mormon idea of politeness—Heber C. Kimball and his "cows"—"My women"—Slavery of sex—Moses and Mohammed outdone—Incest—Marrying a whole family—Robert Sharkey— Remorse and suicide—Uncle and niece—Bishop Smith and his nieces—Mixture of blood—Horrible crimes — Half-brother and sister — The Prophet "sold" —The doctrine of incest—"Too strong now, but the people will come to it"—Now openly avowed—Brothers and sisters to marry for a "pure priesthood"—Testimony of Wm. Hepworth Dixon—Father and daughter *may* marry—Effects upon the young—Infant mortality—Large average mortality—Fatal blindness—The growing youth —Demoralization—Youthful depravity—No hope for young men and women—Sophistry and madness—Ancient sensualism to be revived. 272

CHAPTER XVI.

THE MORMON THEOCRACY.

Absolutism—An ancient model—Three governments in Utah—Church officials—First President—First Presidency—" The worst man in Utah "—Quorum of Apostles—" The Twelve "—A dozen men with fifty-two wives—President of Seventies—Patriarch—"A blessing for a dollar"—Bishops—Division of the City and Territory—Their magisterial capacity—High Council—Judge and

xvi CONTENTS.

PAGE

Jury —Ward teachers — The confessional — The priesthood — Aaronic and Melchisedec—Evangelists—Secret police or "Danites"—Civil government only an appendage—Excessive power of the Mormon Courts—Perversions of law and justice—Organic Act defective—Federal Judges—Their weakness and disgrace—Verdict by ecclesiastical "counsel"—Verdicts dictated from the pulpit—Probate Judges really appointed by Brigham Young—Voting system—Marked ballots—"Protecting the ballot"—The Hooper-McGroarty race—Plurality of offices as well as wives—Tyranny of the Church—the Mormon vs. the American idea—The evils of which Gentiles complain.. 293

CHAPTER XVII.

RECUSANT SECTS OF MORMONS.

Repression not unity—Great break up at Nauvoo—Sidney Rigdon's Church—J. J. Strang—Cutler, Brewster, and Heddrick: "The Gatherers"—The "Truth-teller" — Lyman Wight in Texas— San Bernardino Mormons—Apostacy, Spiritualism and insanity— Brigham supreme in Utah—First Secession, the "Gladdenites"— Persecution and murders—Blood-atonement introduced—Second Secession, the "Morrisites"—War with the Sect—Massacre of the "Morrisites"—Governor Harding's adventure—General Connor protects the recusants—Soda Springs—Another Prophet— The "infant Christ"—Beginning of the Josephites—Emma and her sons—The "Re-organized Church"—First Mission—Mission of the "Smith boys"—Excitement at Salt Lake—Priestly lying— The Godbe Schism—Liberal principles—Hopeful indications— After Brigham, Who ? — Orson Hyde ?—Daniel H. Wells ?— George A. Smith ?—Probable future of the Church................... 309

CHAPTER XVIII.

GEOGRAPHICAL FEATURES.

Territorial limits—"Basins"—"Sinks"—"Flats"—Rain and evaporation—Elemental action and reaction—Potamology—Jordan— Kay's Creek—Weber—Bear River—Cache Valley—Timber—Blue Creek—Promontory—Great Desert—Utah Lake—Spanish Fork—

CONTENTS. xvii

PAGE

Salt Creek — Timpanogos — Sevier River—Colorado System—
Fish—Thermal and Chemical Springs — Healing Waters—Hotwater plants — Analysis by Dr. Gale —Mineral Springs—Salt
beds—Alkali flats — Native Salts — GREAT SALT LAKE — First
accounts—FREMONT — STANSBURY —Amount of salt—Valleys—
Rise of the Lake—Islands—Bear Lake—"Ginasticutis"—Utah
Lake—Climate—Increase of rain—Singular phenomena —Fine
air—Relief for pulmonary complaints.................................... 334

CHAPTER XIX.

MATERIAL RESOURCES OF UTAH.

Amount of arable land—Its nature and location—Increased rainfall—Causes—Probable greater increase—Mode of irrigation—
Aquarian—Socialism—No room for competition—Alkali—Some
advantages—Yield of various crops—"Beet sugar"—Sorghum
syrup—Mormon improvements (?)—Grossly exaggerated — True
Wealth of Utah—Mining and grazing—Bunch-grass—Mountain
pastures— Sheep and goats—"Fur, fin and feather"—Trapping
and hunting — Carnivora — Ruminants—Buffalo—None in the
Basin—Shoshonee tradition—Game, fowl—Amphibia—"Sandy
toad"—Serpents—Fish—Oysters in Salt Lake—Insects—"Mormon bedbugs"—Advantages from the dry air—Insectivora —
Crickets—Grasshoppers or locusts?—Indians of Utah—Rapid extinction—"Diggers"—"Club-men"—Utes—Shoshonees—Their
origin—Mormon theory—Scientific theory—Chinese annals—Tartars in America—Mormon settlers — Twenty-three years of
"gathering" — Much work, slow progress—Reasons—Inherent
weakness of the system—Great apostacy—Their present number — Exaggeration — Enumeration of settlements and population—Nationality—Total military force—Future of the Territory 353

CHAPTER XX.

MORMON MYSTERIES—THEIR ORIGIN.

The Endowment — Actors — Scenery and dress—Pre-requisites—
Adam and Eve, the Devil and Michael, Jehovah and Eloheim—
A new version—Blasphemous assumptions—Terrible oaths—Bar-
B

barous penalties—Origin—Scriptures Lost—Paradise and Eleusinian mysteries — "Morgan's Free-masonry" — The witnesses— Probabilities—Their reasons—Changes....................................... 372

CHAPTER XXI.

PRESENT CONDITION AND PROSPECTS.

Co-operation—The "bull's eye" signs—Inherent weakness of the system—Immediate effects on the Gentiles—Final result to the Saints—Founding of Corinne — Its bright prospects — Trip to Sevier—The deserted city—New Silverado—Mines and mining— A new interest in Utah—Rich discoveries—Hindrances—Grant's administration in Utah — Better men in the Revenue Department—Experience of Dr. J. P. Taggart—More "persecution"— The Judges—The Governor—Congressional Legislation—"Cullom Bill "—Probable effects—Guesses at the future—Another exodus—"Zion" in Sonora.. 387

CHAPTER XXII.

REDEEMING AGENCIES.

The Church—First attempt—Rev. Norman McLeod—Dr. J. K. Robinson—Second attempt, Father Kelley—Last attempt—The Episcopal Mission, success and progress—Sabbath School—Grammar School of St. Marks—A building needed—Mission of Rev. George W. Foote—Difficulties of the situation—Number and occupation of Gentiles—Political prospects—Gentile newspapers —The *Valley Tan*—The *Vedette*—The UTAH REPORTER—S. S. Saul, the founder—Messrs. Aulbach and Barrett—The author's experience — Principles advocated — Courtesy of the Gentiles— Conclusion... 405

LIST OF ILLUSTRATIONS.

1. Portrait of Brigham Young ................FRONTISPIECE.
2. Portrait of Joseph Smith........................ "
3. Portrait of Heber C. Kimball..................... "
4. Portrait of Hyrum Smith........................ "
5. Portrait of Orson Pratt........................ "
6. Portrait of Orson Hyde........................ "
7. Portrait of John Taylor........................ "

                                                            PAGE

8. Death of Joseph Smith.................................... 93
9. Four Wives.. 179
10. Mormon Temple being built in Salt Lake City............ 191
11. Scenes in the Endowment Ceremonies..................... 373

LIFE IN UTAH;

OR, THE

MYSTERIES AND CRIMES OF MORMONISM.

CHAPTER I.

HISTORICAL.

Birth and early life of the Mormon Prophet—The original Smith family—Opinion of Brigham Young—The "peep-stone"—"Calling" of Joe Smith—The Golden Plates—"Reformed Egyptian" translated—"Book of Mormon" published—Synopsis of its contents—Real author of the work—"The glorious six" first converts—Emma Smith, "Elect Lady and Daughter of God"—Sidney Rigdon takes the field—First Hegira—"Zion" in Missouri—Kirtland Bank—Swindling and "persecution"—War in Jackson County—Smith "marches on Missouri"—Failure of the "Lord's Bank"—Flight of the Prophet—"Mormon War"—Capture of Smith—Flight into Illinois.

JOSEPH SMITH, the founder of Mormonism, was born December 23rd, 1805, at Sharon, Windsor county, Vermont. His parents, Joseph Smith, Sen., and Lucy Mack Smith, belonged to the lowest grade of society, and, by the testimony of all their neighbors, were illiterate and superstitious, as well as indolent and unreliable. They could believe in the supernatural as easily as the natural; for they were as ignorant of the one as the other. These qualities seemed to descend upon the son by "ordinary generation;" but at an early age he showed that he far excelled all the rest of the family in a peculiar low cun-

C

ning, and a certain faculty of invention, which enabled him to have a story ready for any emergency.

In the year 1815, the Smith family removed to New York, and settled near Palmyra, Wayne county, where they resided ten years. Here young Joseph developed a remarkable talent for living without work, and at an early age adopted the profession of "Water Witch," in which calling he wandered about the adjoining country with a forked stick, or hazel rod, by the deflections of which, when held in a peculiar manner, he claimed to determine the spot where a vein of water lay nearest the surface. This had been a part of his father's business; but Joe was possessed of real genius, though of a peculiar kind, and soon struck into higher paths. He began to "divine" the locality of things which had been stolen, by means of a "peep-stone" placed in his hat, and by the same means to point out where hidden treasures lay. Almost innumerable are the stories of his youth, giving bright promise of future rascality. But many of them depend on little more than popular report, and we can only receive as authentic those events which rest upon the sworn testimony of reliable men who were his neighbors. After ten years' residence in Wayne, the family moved to the adjoining county of Ontario, and settled near the town of Manchester. Here, from pointing out the place for wells, Joe went to work digging them. While in this work for Mr. Willard Chase, a peculiar, round, white stone was found by him and the other workmen, which Joe took possession of and carried away, much to the regret of Mr. Chase's children, to whom it had been given as a curious plaything. This was afterwards the noted " peep-stone," in which Joe saw such wonders. Many of these statements are not very strenuously denied by the best-informed Mormons. They acknowledge, generally, that Joe Smith was of humble parentage, very poor and illiterate, and that he was for many years a "wild boy." Brigham Young is especially frank upon the subject, adding, in conclusion: "That the Prophet was of mean birth, that he was wild, intemperate, even dishonest and tricky in his youth, is nothing against his mission. God can, and does, make use of the vilest instruments. Joseph has brought forth a religion which will save us if we abide by it. Bring anything against that if you can. I care not if he gamble, lie, swear, and run horses every day, for I embrace no man in my faith. The religion is all in all."

Brigham is correct; the early character of the Prophet has little to do with the religion, *except* as determining the character and credibility of his evidence. Let us then examine briefly the origin of this new theology, present the main testimony; and, as impartial judges, hear the Prophet's account first. Many years after, when Mormonism was an established fact, Joseph gave the following account: At the early age of fifteen he became much concerned about the salvation of his soul, and at the same time a powerful revival of religion spread throughout Western New York. Joseph professed to be converted and his mother, sister Sophronia and his brothers, Samuel and Hyrum (so spelled by his father) joined the church. But when the revival ceased, a "great rush" took place among the ministers of various denominations as to who should secure most of the new converts; Joseph's soul was vexed, and he began to have serious doubts. In this frame of mind he opened the Bible, and his eye fell upon this text: "If any of you lack wisdom, let him ask of God, that giveth to all men liberally, and upbraideth not"—JAMES, Chap. I. v. 5. He, therefore, retired to a secluded thicket near his father's house, and knelt in prayer, supplicating the Lord to know "which of all the sects was really right." While praying, the entire wood was illuminated with a great light, he was enveloped in the midst of it and caught away in a heavenly vision, he saw two glorious personages and was told that his sins were forgiven. He learned also that none of the sects was quite right, but that God had chosen him to restore the true priesthood upon earth. Afterwards, he began again to doubt, and, being quite young, fell into sin, and it was not until September 23rd, 1823, that God again heard his prayers, and sent heavenly messengers to tell him his sins were forgiven. An angel visited him from time to time afterwards, instructing him in his duties, and finally informed him that in "the hill

Cumorah," not far from Manchester, certain Golden Plates were buried, containing an account of the settlement of America, before Christ. After several preliminary visits, on the 22nd of September, 1826, the Golden Plates were taken up from the hill Cumorah " with a mighty display of celestial machinery," and delivered by the angel to Joseph. His vision being cleared, at the same time, he saw a great concourse of devils struggling with angels to prevent the work. The plates were " of the thickness of tin, bound together like a book, fastened at one side by three rings which run through the whole, forming a volume about six inches thick." The record was engraved on the plates in "reformed Egyptian" characters, consisting of "the language of the Jews and the writing of the Egyptians." In the same box with the plates, were found two stones, "transparent and clear as crystal, the Urim and Thummim used by seers in ancient times, the instruments of revelations of things distant, past and future." When the news of this discovery spread abroad "the Prophet was the sport of lies, slanders and mobs, and vain attempts to rob him of his plates." He was ere long supplied with witnesses. Oliver Cowdery, David Whitmer, and Martin Harris, make the following solemn certificate :—

" We have seen the plates which contain the records; they were translated by the gift and power of God, for His voice hath declared it unto us, wherefore we know of a surety that the work is true; and we declare with words of soberness that an angel of God came down from heaven, and brought and laid before our eyes, that we beheld and saw the plates and the engravings thereon."

The testimony of these three is prefixed to all printed copies of the "Book of Mormon," for such is the name now given to the work. Oliver Cowdery was at that time a sort of wandering schoolmaster, rather noted as an elegant scribe. He assisted in translating the inscriptions on the plates, continued an active Saint for many years, and was finally expelled from the Church in Missouri, " for lying, counterfeiting and immorality." He led a rambling life for many years, and died a short time since a miserable drunkard.

Martin Harris was a credulous farmer who lived near the Smiths. He had imbibed the notion, so common in the religious excitement of that period, that "the last days were at hand," and mortgaged his farm for three thousand dollars, to pay for printing the first edition of the book. He continued with the Mormons till his means were exhausted, and having quarrelled with Joe Smith, in Missouri, returned to his old residence in New York. Of David Whitmer little is known. He dropped out of the Mormon community, in one of the "drives" in Missouri, and settled in that State. But the Prophet had other witnesses. Soon after, four of the Smiths, three of the Whitmers, and another witness, eight in all, testify as follows: "Joseph Smith, the translator, has shown us the plates of which hath been spoken, which had the appearance of gold; and as many of the plates as the said Smith had translated, we did handle with our hands and also saw the engravings thereon, all of which had the appearance of ancient work and curious workmanship."

According to Smith's account, he first met Oliver Cowdery, April 16th, 1829, and after convincing him of his divine mission, on the 15th of May following, John the Baptist appeared, and ordained them both into the Aaronic Priesthood, after which they baptized each other. In July following, the Golden Plates were shown the "three witnesses," and in that year the translation was completed. It was begun some time before, but suspended in July, 1828, from the singular circumstance that the wife of Martin Harris had stolen a hundred and eighteen pages of the manuscript. As afterwards appeared, the translators thought she intended to wait until they had supplied the stolen part, then reproduce the original, and prove that they did not literally correspond. But it seems they had credited her with more cunning than she possessed. She had bitterly opposed her husband in his venture upon the new speculation, and had burned that part of the manuscript he brought home, hoping thereby to put a stop to the work. She afterwards attempted, by legal proceedings, to prevent the disposal of his farm; but, failing in that, finally separated from him. The translation was then completed, Oliver Cowdery making most of the final copy. The "Book of Mormon" was first given to the world early in 1830, when three thousand volumes were published, under contract, by Mr. Pomeroy Tucker, then proprietor of a paper in the county. He has, within a few years, given to the world a valuable work on the "Origin and Progress of Mormonism," containing many interesting facts concerning the origin of the sect. The first proof-sheet of the work was given by Mr. Tucker, as a sort of curiosity, to his cousin Steve S. Harding, whom he styles "a fun-loving youth of that vicinity." Mr. Harding soon after removed to Indiana, and just thirty-two years afterwards, was appointed by President Lincoln Governor of Utah, whither he carried the proof-sheet, and presented it to the Church Historian.

The "Book of Mormon" was rapidly circulated, and attracted some comment. And at this point, a brief synopsis of this work is appropriate. It consists of a number of Books, named after their reputed authors—Book of Nephi, Book of Alma, Esther, Jared, etc. They contain the following history:

In the reign of Zedekiah, six hundred years before Christ, a Jewish family, with a few friends and retainers, left Jerusalem, being warned of God that a great destruction and captivity were at hand, and journeyed eastward in search of a "land of promise." After many wanderings, and the death of the Patriarch, they reached the sea, when Nephi, who had succeeded his father in the Patriarchate and Priesthood, was directed by the Lord to build a boat; and, furnished with a "double ball and spindle," which served the exact purpose of the modern mariner's compass. They embarked, and in due time reached the continent of America. Subsequent revelations have decided that they landed in Central America. There they increased rapidly; but a great schism arose, and one Laman, with his followers, refused to obey the true priesthood, for which they were cut off, cursed, and condemned "to be a brutish and a savage people, having dark skins, compelled to dig in the ground for roots, and hunt their meat in the forests like beasts of prey." But it was foretold that a remnant of them should, in time, "have the curse removed, and become a fair and delightsome people," who should "blossom as the rose, under the teachings of the Latter-day Saints." These were the Lamanites, the present Indians, while the Christian party were known as Nephites. The latter spread over all of North and South America, became rich and powerful, and built the cities of Zarahemla, Jacobbugath, Manti, Gidgiddoni, and scores of others, thus accounting for the numerous ruins found on this continent. They were ruled over successively by Nephi the First, Second, and Third, by Noah, Alma, Kish, Coriantumnr, and numerous other kings, and were successively instructed by a number of prophets. But the Lamanites increased likewise, and carried on almost perpetual war with the Nephites, till a great part of the land was desolate. According to this history, there have been no people of the Old World so warlike and blood-thirsty as these; and battles in which from twenty to fifty thousand were slain were of common occurrence. The Nephites were troubled, too, by "false doctrine, heresy, and schism;" the true priesthood was reviled; one man arose and preached Universalism, "that God would save all mankind at the last day," and others followed strange *gods*. An immense mass of the nation turned back and joined the Lamanites, and a band of robbers, under one Gadianton, desolated a large part of the land. At length prophets appeared and announced the coming of Christ, who, after he was crucified at Jerusalem, preached the Gospel in America. At the time of his death, this country, also, was shrouded in darkness; a mighty earthquake threw down the wicked city of Jacobbugath, opened great chasms and basins throughout the land, and the whole face of the country was changed. The Nephites accepted Christ at once; but, in a few generations, fell again into apostasy, and the Lord delivered them into the hand of their enemies. The mighty Chieftain Omandagus, whose rule was from the Rocky Mountains to the Mississippi, fought against the Nephites, and after him many others. Little by little, the Nephites were driven eastward, but made a stand near the shores of Lake Erie, and fought "till the whole land was covered with dead bodies." They made their final stand about 430, A.D., at the hill Cumorah, in Ontario County, New York, where the Lamanites came against them, and the battle raged till two hundred and thirty thousand Nephites were slain; the little remnant was captured, and only Mormon and his son Moroni escaped.

The various kings and priests had kept a record of their history, which Mormon now collected in one volume, added a book of his own, and gave them to his son. The latter finished the record, and buried the whole in the hill Cumorah, being assured of God that in fourteen centuries, a great Prophet should restore them to man. Such is the book, and Joseph's account of it. On such testimony alone there is sufficient cause to reject it, the book itself containing abundant internal evidence of a fraud.

Let us now glance at the opposing account. In the year 1812, a written work, called the "Manuscript Found," was presented to Mr. Patterson, a bookseller of Pittsburg, Penna., by the author, Rev. Solomon Spaulding. This gentleman was born in Pennsylvania, was a graduate of Dartmouth College, and for many years a Presbyterian minister; he fell into bad health, left the ministry, and finally died of consumption. The "Manuscript Found" was written by Spaulding as a historical romance, to account for the settlement of America, and he proposed to Mr. Patterson to publish it with a preface, giving an imaginary account of its having been taken from plates dug up in Ohio; but the latter did not think the enterprise would pay. Sidney Rigdon was then at work in the office of Mr. Patterson; the latter died in 1826, and what became of that copy of the manuscript is not known. Mrs. Spaulding had another complete copy; but in the year 1825, while residing in Ontario Co, N. Y., next door to a man named Stroude, for whom Joe Smith was then digging a well, that copy also was lost. She thinks it was stolen from her trunk. Thus far all is clear, and there is no particular discrepancy between the two accounts; but when the "Book of Mormon" was published, the widow and brother of Solomon Spaulding, and several other persons who had heard him read his work, forthwith claimed that the new publication was nearly identical with the "Manuscript Found," varying only in certain interpolated texts on doctrinal points. This claim was circulated abroad, and caused Sidney Rigdon to write a highly slanderous and abusive letter to the press, in regard to Mrs. Spaulding. Mormon historians say that Spaulding's book was a mere idolatrous romance, and that the whole story is the invention of Dr. Philastus Hurlbut, who seceded from the saints in Ohio, and "persecuted" Joe Smith in various ways. The widow's and brother's statement is supported by the evidence of Mr. Joseph Miller, Sr., now of Washington Co., Penna., who had often heard Spaulding read his work; by that of Mr. Redick McKee, who formerly boarded with the Spauldings, and by others who knew of the work. Space fails to set forth all the evidence presented in support of this view. Suffice it to say, that while it is of moral force sufficient to convince most minds, it is yet not such proof as would establish the fact beyond all doubt, or convict Smith and Rigdon of theft and forgery in a court of justice. If the proof were any less strong than it is, I would decide against the Spaulding claim, solely from the internal evidence of the book; for the style and matter are such as to raise a very strong presumption that it could not be the work of any man with intelligence enough for a minister, or of a graduate from Dartmouth College. But the true theory no doubt is, that the writing of Spaulding was taken by Smith, Rigdon, Cowdery and others, as the suggestion and idea of their work; but was greatly modified and interpolated by them, leaving sufficient characteristics to be recognized by the Spaulding witnesses, who were left solely to their memory for a comparison with the "Book of Mormon," recognizing what was in it, and forgetting much that was not included.

Of the "three witnesses" it is unnecessary to treat; their subsequent course shows what weight is to be attached to their testimony. The best evidence furthermore shows, that Sidney Rigdon was the prime mover in the fraud, and that Joe Smith was conveniently put forward as the Prophet.

The year 1830 ranks as number one of the Mormon era. Early in the spring, the "Book of Mormon" appeared, and on the memorable 6th of April following, the Mormon Church was organized near Manchester. Six members were baptized and ordained elders, viz :— Joseph Smith, Sr., Joseph Smith, Jr., Hyrum Smith, Samuel Smith, Oliver Cowdery, and Joseph Knight, all but the last two of the "original Smith family." The sacrament was forthwith administered, and hands laid on "for the gift of the Holy Ghost." On the 11th of April, Oliver Cowdery preached the first public discourse on the new faith, and the same month the "first miracle" was performed in Colesville, Broome Co., N. Y. On the first of June, the Church, which had meanwhile gained a few more Whitmers and some others, held its "First Conference" at Fayette, in Seneca Co.; and the same month Joe Smith was twice arrested, "on false charges," tried and acquitted. Meanwhile, on the 18th of January, 1827, he had married Emma Hale, daughter of Isaac Hale, of South Bainbridge, Chenango Co., N. Y.; and, in 1830, she was by special revelation, pronounced "Elect Lady and Daughter of God," afterwards more learnedly styled *Electa Cyria*. She became thoroughly disgusted at her husband's religion while in Nauvoo, and expressed no particular regret at his death ; she refused to emigrate to Utah, but apostatized and married a Gentile, and is rather popular as landlady of the old Mansion House, at Nauvoo. In August of 1830, Parley P. Pratt, a young Campbellite preacher, came on a visit especially to hear of the new faith, and was at once converted, and soon after, Sidney Rigdon appeared as a leading Mormon. Their own history states that he had never heard of Smith until this time. Soon after, Orson Pratt was baptized, and the new Church now had valuable material in its composition. The wild, poetical zeal of Parley, and the cool determination of Orson Pratt, the immense biblical knowledge and controversial skill of Sidney Rigdon, and the shrewd cunning of Joe Smith, were united in the work of propagandism, and converts multiplied. In October, missionaries were sent to the "Lamanites," and in December, Sidney Rigdon visited Joe Smith, and preached several times in the vicinity. In January, Smith and Rigdon proceeded to the latter's residence, near Kirtland, Ohio, preaching by the way. Rigdon had previously collected a band of nearly one hundred persons, who called themselves Disciples; mostly seceders from other denominations, holding to a literal and rapid fulfilment of the prophecies, very fanatical and looking daily for " some great event to occur." Many of these adopted the new faith at once, and a church of thirty was organized. "By revelation" of February 9th, the elders were commanded "to go forth in pairs and preach," and it was ordered they should dwell particularly upon the fact that "the last days were at hand."

This idea is one that has a great hold upon many minds. Nor is it confined to the ignorant; many intelligent men in every generation become impressed with the idea that "in *our* day the world has become *so* corrupt, that God Almighty is going to make a great change," and, in spite of the plain declarations of Scripture, fanatics will wrest the mild precepts of the Gospel, and force them to indicate that hell-fire and destruction are impending over everybody but their own particular sect. The Mormons began as Millenarians, and that of the maddest sort; but they did not preach that the world itself was to be destroyed, only that destruction was soon to fall upon all who did not embrace the new gospel. No particular time was set for this consummation, but it was understood to be imminent. Early in 1831, John Whitmer was appointed Church recorder and historian, and about the same time, the remaining New York saints came to Kirtland, which is set down in Mormon annals as the First Hegira.

On the 6th of June, the Melchisedek, or Superior Priesthood, was first conferred upon the elders, and soon after Joe Smith had a revelation that the final gathering place of the Saints was to be in Missouri. He set out the same month with a few elders, and, in the middle of July, reached Jackson County, Missouri, where another revelation was granted that this was "Zion which should never be moved," and the whole land was "solemnly dedicated to the Lord and His Saints." They began at once to build, and laid the first log in Kaw Township, twelve miles west of Independence. Another revelation, of August 2nd, fixed the site of the Great Temple "three hundred yards west of the Court House in Independence," which spot was accordingly dedicated by religious exercises, which were followed by a great accession of "gifts." On the 4th of August, another large party arrived from Kirtland, a "General Conference" was held in the "land of Zion," and another revelation vouchsafed to Joseph, that the whole land should be theirs, and should not be obtained "*but by purchase or by blood.*"

Just what was to be understood by that strange wording, it is now impossible to tell. The Mormons explain it ,very innocently, and the Missourians construed it to mean that the Saints would unite with the Indians and drive out the old settlers. Joe Smith returned to Kirtland the latter part of August, and soon after established a mill, store, and bank. The last was what was then denominated a "wild cat" bank, that is, it had no charter, and deposited no State bonds for security; but rested solely on the individual credit of the proprietors. As several wealthy men had come into the new organization, the notes of the bank circulated at par. Joseph Smith was made President, and Sidney Rigdon, Cashier. For the next five months, Joseph travelled and preached in the Northern and Eastern States, making many converts, who "gathered" either at Kirtland, or in Missouri. The elders sent out in February previous had met with tolerable success, and Samuel H. Smith, brother of the Prophet, had added greatly to the Church by converting Brigham Young. This noted personage was born at Whittingham, Windham Co., Vermont, June 1st, 1801. He had four brothers and six sisters, all of whom became Mormons. He was baptized in April, 1832, by Eleazer Millard, and soon after "gathered" at Kirtland. He was brought up on a farm, and learned the trade of a painter and glazier, which he followed till after his conversion to Mormonism. In him Joe Smith recognized one "born to rule," and his deep cunning and wonderful knowledge of the weak points in human nature soon gave him a leading position in the Church. In March, 1832, Joe Smith and Sidney Rigdon, while absent from home, were tarred and feathered by a mob, "for attempting to establish Communism, for forgery and dishonorable dealing," according to their adversaries; by their own account, "for the truth's sake," and this is set down as "the beginning of persecutions." Early in April, Joe Smith found it necessary to go again to Independence, Mo., where a sort of "Œcumenical Council" was held, and a printing office set up. In June, was issued the *Morning and Evening Star*, the first Mormon periodical, edited by W. W. Phelps. Joe Smith soon returned to Kirtland, and the latter part of the same year, Heber Chase Kimball was baptized into the Church. In February, 1833, Joe Smith finished his "inspired retranslation" of the New Testament, and soon after received a "revelation to square things in Zion." A quorum of three High Priests, Joseph Smith, Sidney Rigdon, and Frederick G. Williams, was organized as "Presidency of the Church," and they were at once favored with "visions of the Saviour and concourse of angels."

By the spring of 1833, the Mormons numbered some fifteen hundred in Jackson County, Missouri. They had taken virtual possession of Independence, where their paper was published, and were fast extending their settlements westward. The intense religious excitement which raged throughout the United States during the decade of 1820–30, which led to the wild phenomena of "jerks," and so-called religious exercises of howling, jumping, barking and muttering, seems to have left a precipitate of its worst materials in Mormonism. They daily proclaimed to the older settlers that the Lord had given them the whole land of Missouri; that bloody wars would extirpate all other sects from the country; that "it would be one gore of blood from the Mississippi to the border," and that the few who survived would be servants to the

Saints, who would own all the property in the country. As their numbers increased, arrogance and spiritual pride took possession of them; they proclaimed themselves "Kings and Priests of the Most High God," and regarded all others as reprobates, destined to a speedy destruction. In conversation with the Missourians, they never wearied of declaring that all the Churches established by the latter were "alike the creation of the devil," that they were under the curse of God, and all their members doomed, castaway Gentiles, worse than heathen, and unworthy of longer life. At the same time it does not appear that there were any more violations of law among them, than would be among the same number of very poor and ignorant people anywhere; but their general conduct was insufferable. In the first flush of their religious enthusiasm, they seem to have been governed by no ideas of moderation; they proclaimed through the country that it was useless folly for Gentiles to open farms, the Lord would never allow them to enjoy the fruits of their labor; they notified the workmen upon new buildings that they could never hope to be paid therefor, and generally proclaimed that in a very few months the Gentiles would have neither name nor place in Missouri.

The simple-minded Missourians listened with a vague wonder to their first predictions, then smiled at their confident boastings of superior purity and holiness; but soon their increasing numbers and arrogance awakened serious fears of the future. The Missourians, unaccustomed to the language of hyperbole in prophecy, interpreted their predictions to mean that the Saints themselves would be the ministers of God's vengeance, and smite the unbelievers; many were incensed against them for their language, and the public mind was greatly inflamed. In April, 1833, a number of Missourians came together in Independence, and decided that "means of defence ought to be taken," but determined upon nothing. The first June number of the *Morning and Evening Star* contained an intemperate article, headed, "Free People of Color," which excited the wrath of the old citizens against the Mormons, as "abolitionists," and was answered by a small pamphlet, headed, "Beware of False Prophets." As summer advanced, it appeared that the Mormons would be sufficiently numerous to carry the county at the August election, and this roused all the fears of the old settlers afresh. Without apparent concert, an armed mob of three hundred assembled at Independence, tore down the newspaper office, tarred and feathered several of the Saints, whipped two of them a little and ordered all to leave the county. Oliver Cowdery was started to Kirtland to consult with Joe Smith; but, during his absence, the Saints agreed with the citizens to leave Jackson County. On the 8th of October, W. W. Phelps and Orson Hyde presented a memorial to Governor Dunklin, of Missouri, praying for redress, to which that officer made answer, that they "had a right to the protection of the law, if they chose to stay in Jackson.". Emboldened by this, they refused to leave according to agreement, and the last of the month the mob again rose, burnt ten Mormons' houses and committed a few other outrages. The Mormons armed in turn, and fired into a portion of the mob, killing two; the whole body of citizens then arose against them, calling in aid from other counties, when the Mormons became panic-stricken and suddenly evacuated Jackson, crossing the Missouri River during the nights of November 4th and 5th into Clay County.

This first expulsion of the Mormons is a point upon which there has been much discussion. That the people of Jackson County were not justified in law is plain; but that they did exactly as the people of nine counties out of ten would have done, is equally plain. They seem to have been actuated much more by a fear of what the Mormons would do when they had the power, than by what they had done; and that those fears were well founded, is abundantly shown by subsequent events. The near vicinity of the Mormons was intolerable, and the settlers were determined they should leave. The mob allowed the Saints to carry their printing material to Liberty, Clay Co., where they soon after began to publish the *Missouri Enquirer*. They spread themselves over Clay and into Van Buren County; but were "persecuted" and annoyed in the latter so they made no great settlement.

Meanwhile, Joe Smith and a much more intelligent class of Mormons were building up Kirtland. July 2nd, 1833, Smith completed his "inspired translation" of the Old Testament, and soon after a printing press was set up in Kirtland, and the *Latter-Day Saints' Messenger and Advocate* established. "Old man Smith," the Prophet's father, was made Patriarch, and Bishop Partridge head of that branch of the Church. When the news of affairs in Jackson County reached him, Joseph "determined on war, and began at once to collect a small force." He soon had two hundred men, with whom he started westward; "marched on Missouri," according to Gentile history; "hoped to redeem Zion," according to Mormon annals. About this time, Joseph had another revelation "as to business," which will be found in the *Doctrine and Covenants* with the rest, which contained, among other directions, this remarkable passage:—" Behold, it is said or written in my laws: Thou shalt not get in debt to thine enemies. But, behold, it is not said at any time the Lord should not *take when He pleases*, and pay as seemeth to Him good. Wherefore, as ye are on the Lord's business, whatsoever ye do," etc. We need not be surprised, therefore, to learn, as we do from Joseph's Autobiography, that the people along the road were very hostile. Two days before starting, on May 3rd, the Conference of Elders, in Kirtland, repudiated the name of Mormons and adopted, for the first time, that of Latter-Day Saints; and we notice in Joseph's account that along the road they constantly denied the name of Mormons. These being the "last days," they were Latter-day Saints, as well as to distinguish them from the Saints of former days; the term Mormon, on the contrary, is supposed to be derived from the Greek Μορμον [*Mormou*], signifying a "horrible fright" or "bug-bear."

Joe and his "army" reached Missouri in the latter part of June, but while near the Mississippi, the cholera, then but just known in America, broke out in his camp, and in a few days twenty of the company died. Joe preached, prayed and prophesied in vain; his followers were panic-stricken at the horrible and unknown disease. He first attempted to cure it "by laying on of hands," but desisted with the remark, that "when the Lord would destroy, it was vain for man to attempt to stay His hand." An armed force which had meanwhile gathered in Jackson County, in anticipation of his coming, was scattered by a violent storm, and in a few days, the cholera having spent its force, the company reached Liberty. There was nothing to be done, and in a few days Smith returned to Kirtland. A quorum of twelve apostles was then organized, among them, Brigham Young and Heber C. Kimball. The former received the "gift of tongues," and was sent on a mission to the Eastern States, and in May, 1835, all the twelve left Kirtland on general missions. The ensuing August, there was a General Assembly at Kirtland, in which the "Book of Doctrine and Covenants," and the "Lectures on Faith," by Sidney Rigdon, were adopted as the rule of faith. About this time, a learned Jew, formerly Professor of Oriental tongues in New York, was connected with the Mormons, and on the 4th of January, 1836, a Hebrew professorship was established at Kirtland, Joseph Smith and several other leading Mormons entering upon the study. A Temple had been projected early in the settlement, which was completed and dedicated as the "House of the Lord," March 27th, 1836. This was their first temple, and its estimated cost, $40,000. Meanwhile, Governor Dunklin had attempted to have the Mormons again put in possession of their lands, in Jackson County, whereupon a committee of citizens from the latter met a committee of the Mormons, and offered the following:

"*Proposition of the people of Jackson County to the Mormons:*

"The undersigned committee, being fully authorized by the people of Jackson County, hereby propose to the Mormons, that they will buy all the land that the said Mormons own in the County of Jackson, and also all the improvements which the said Mormons had on any of the public lands in said County of Jackson, as they existed before the first disturbance between the people of Jackson and the Mormons, and for such as they have made since. They further propose, that the valuation of said land and improvements shall be ascertained by three disinterested arbitrators, to be chosen and agreed to by both parties. They further propose, that should the parties disagree in the choice of arbitrators, then —— is to choose them. They further propose, that twelve of the Mormons shall be permitted to go along with the arbitrators, to show them their land and improvements while valuing the same, and such other of the Mormons as the arbitrators shall wish to do so, to give them information; and the people of Jackson County hereby guarantee their entire safety while doing so. They further propose, that when the arbitrators report the value of the land and improvements, as aforesaid, the people of Jackson will pay the valuation, *with one hundred per cent., added thereon,* to the Mormons within thirty days thereafter.

"They further propose, that the Mormons are not to make any effort, ever after, to settle either collectively or individually within the limits of Jackson County. The Mormons are to enter into bonds to insure the conveyance of their land in Jackson County, according to the above terms, when payment shall be made; and the committee will enter into a like bond, with such security as may be deemed sufficient for the payment of the money, according to the above proposition, etc., etc."

The Mormons have always maintained that their later troubles were "solely on account of their religion," but that they were driven from Jackson County because "the mob desired to get possession of their lands." The above document certainly tends to disprove that charge. The foremost men in the county offered their personal security for the payment, but the Mormons rejected the proposition, on the ground that the Lord had said, "Zion should never be moved." The citizens of Jackson then became apprehensive that they would be attacked from Clay County, and stirred up those in the latter county who considered they already had cause to complain of the

Mormons; so they "requested" the latter, in May, 1836, to remove, which they did, this time settling in Carroll, Davis and Caldwell Counties. In the last named they founded the town of Far-West, and these counties being new and unoccupied, they prospered greatly for a while.

In June, 1837, the first organized foreign mission was sent to England, consisting of H. C. Kimball, Orson Hyde and W. Richards. On the 30th of July following, they baptized the first converts there, in the river Ribble, and the first confirmation of members was at Walkerford, August 4th. The first Conference of English Mormons was held in the cock-pit at Preston, the 25th of the following December.

In the autumn of the same year, the " Kirtland Safety Society Bank," engineered by Smith and Rigdon, failed, under circumstances which created great scandal, and the Prophet had a revelation to "depart for the land of Zion," in Missouri. Smith and Rigdon left Kirtland "between two days," and their creditors pursued them for a hundred miles; but in the language of Joseph's Autobiography, "the Lord delivered them out of the hands of their persecutors." They reached Far-West in March, and found a fearful schism raging in the Church. The authority of Joseph was unequal to the task of restoring order, and Martin Harris, Oliver Cowdery and one L. E. Johnson, were "cut off from the Church," while Orson Hyde, Thomas B. Marsh, W. W. Phelps, and many others apostatized and brought many serious charges against Joe Smith and other leaders. It was said they were plotting treason against the State, that they were conspiring with the Indians, that they were engaged in counterfeiting and cattle-stealing, and were attempting to establish a community of goods as well as wives. The dissenters stirred up the neighboring people against the Saints, and for purposes of defence and retaliation, the "Danite Band" was organized. They were first commanded by D. W. Patton, who took the name of "Captain Fearnot," and styled themselves "Daughters of Gideon." Afterwards they adopted their present name from the suggestion in GENESIS xlix. 17 : " Dan shall be a serpent by the way, an adder in the path, that biteth the horse's heels, so that his rider shall fall backward."

On the 4th of July, Sidney Rigdon preached what he called, "Sidney's last sermon;" in which he threatened Gentiles and apostates with violence, and declared that the "Saints were above all law." Troubles soon after arose in Davis County, at elections; the Mormons all voting one way secured control of the County; a general fight occurred at the August election in the town of Gallatin, in which a number were seriously wounded on both sides. For two months there were occasional fights all over Davis County, and the Mormons at length declared their "independence of all earthly rulers and magistrates." The Clerk of the County, a Mormon, was commanded by Joe Smith to issue no more writs against the Saints; and the Justice of the Peace in Gallatin was mobbed for entertaining suits against them. Scattering parties of militia began to assemble under arms in the neighboring counties, one of which, commanded by Captain Bogart, came to battle with a party of seventy Mormons and defeated them. Another party of Mormons attacked the militia near Richmond, in Clay county, and killed two of them; the latter returned the fire, killing "Captain Fearnot." The Mormons then rose *en masse* and drove out all the officers of Davis County not of their faith, and burned and plundered the town of Gallatin, another small village, and much of the surrounding country, driving out the inhabitants.

About this time, Brigham Young fled for his life to Quincy, Illinois. The troubles grew so extensive and complicated, that after many attempts to learn something definite from "the seat of war," Governor Lilburn W. Boggs called out fifteen thousand militia to restore order. The first detachment had a sort of battle with the Mormons in Carroll County, after which, Governor Boggs issued an order that the Mormons "should be expelled from the State," adding, "even if it was necessary to exterminate them." This is the celebrated "exterminating order," and Governor Boggs the "Nero" of Mormon historians. Another body of militia were fired upon by the

Mormons at Haun's Mill, and in revenge exterminated the whole Mormon party, variously estimated at from sixteen to thirty. Only two escaped alive. The Mormon forces then began to retreat on every hand, and finally united in the town of Far-West, where they were surrounded by a large militia force under Generals Doniphan, Lucas and Clarke, and compelled to surrender at discretion. Most of their plunder was recaptured and delivered to the owners, and the great body of the Mormons were released under a promise to leave the State.

Joe Smith, Hyrum Smith, and forty others were held for trial, and the militia officers forthwith organized a Court Martial and condemned several of them to be shot. But General Doniphan, a sound lawyer and brave man, by a firm use of his authority and influence, prevented this foolishly illegal action. The prisoners were taken before the nearest Circuit Judge and put upon trial " for treason, murder, robbery, arson, larceny, and breach of the peace." They could not well have been tried for more; but it seems by the evidence that many of them were guilty on most of the charges. They were committed to jail to await their final trial. The evidence in the case was printed by order of the Missouri Legislature, and presents a singular instance of how a few knaves may lead to their destruction a whole people, if sufficiently ignorant and fanatical. Comparative peace was restored, but the history of civil commotions shows that private revenge will seek such a period for its gratification, and in many neighborhoods fearful outrages were perpetrated upon individual Mormons by those who held a personal animosity against them. Their leaders had provoked a conflict for which the innocent suffered; and the most quiet and unoffending portion of the Mormons were hunted out and rudely hurried from their homes at the most inclement season of the year, often without a chance to supply themselves or dispose of their property, and much suffering was the result. They now numbered over twelve thousand, and in the month of December this large body began the journey into Illinois, which the most of them reached in January, 1839. They spread over the western counties wherever they could find food or employment, particularly about the town of Quincy, in Adams county; while many went as far east as Springfield, and others to St. Louis. They were everywhere received as sufferers for their religion, and to some extent for their "free-state" sentiments; for Illinois was just then beginning to be agitated by the anti-slavery excitement, and the Mormons had been driven from a slave State. The Missouri border had never been well spoken of, nor was it till long afterwards; and the Illinoisans rather seemed pleased with the opportunity of showing how superior they were to the "border ruffians." They regarded but little the Mormon statement that their religion was the only cause of trouble; in fact the more intelligent knew that such could not be the case; but they made haste to assume that the Mormons were "New York and New England Yankees, driven out as abolitionists," because the Missourians would not tolerate such sentiments. The people of Illinois, particularly of the western counties, knew little and cared less about differences of speculative theology. That portion known as the "Military Tract" had but lately come into market, and was settled very rapidly; the religious training of the people had not kept pace with the advance of their material interests, and a sermon to them was a sermon, whether preached by Arminian or Calvinist, orthodox Trinitarian or heterodox Unitarian. Perhaps they were not impious or sceptical; religion was "at loose ends," but there was always a sentiment in its favor, only Sectarianism was little understood, talked of, or cared for. In short the charity of these people was broad enough to cover all sects, and no man was persecuted or called in question for his religious belief. Under these circumstances they gave the Mormon people protection, and welcomed them to their homes and tables; they listened to the story of their wrongs with tears in their eyes; they grasped the outcasts by the hand, and swore to stand by them to the bitter end. Subscriptions were opened for them in many places; even the Indians, yet upon a near reservation, contributed liberally, and several sections made kindly overtures, and pressingly invited the fugitives to settle among them. They had not yet caught sight of the cloven foot of the monster, or seen its miscreated front.

The Missourians found, in the meantime, that they had "caught an elephant;" they had Joe Smith, his brother Hyrum, and forty others in jail on a multitude of charges; but many of the witnesses were gone, the trial would have been long and expensive, and it was probably the best policy to get them all out of the State in such a way that none would re-enter it, rather than condemn a few to the penitentiary. Accordingly, they were removed from place to place, loosely guarded, and, on the 15th of April, Joseph and a few others escaped from their guards, who were either drunk or pretended to be. They hastily made their way to Quincy, followed by the small remnant of Mormons which had been left at Far-West. The remaining prisoners escaped and followed soon after, and in the language of Governor Boggs' next message, "the young and growing State was happily rid of the fanatical sect;" but in the language of Mormon poetry,

" —— Missouri,
Like a whirlwind in her fury,
Drove the Saints and spilled their blood."

Early in May, Joe Smith went to Commerce, in Hancock County, Illinois, by invitation of Dr. Isaac Galland, from whom he obtained a large tract of land near the head of the Des Moines Rapids, and shortly had another revelation for his people to settle there. To a proper understanding of their future history, a brief sketch of the locality is necessary, which has been kindly furnished me by R. W. McKinney, Esq., present Postmaster at Nauvoo, who has resided in that vicinity since 1837:

"Hancock is a river county, washed on the west by the Mississippi for forty miles, taking into account the windings of the river. It was originally nearly all prairie, extending eastward in a direct line from Commerce twenty-five miles; high and rolling, with a soil of inexhaustible fertility, and with most of the timber fringing the streams along the eastern border. The western part of the county, bordering on the Des Moines Rapids, was alway a favourite spot of beauty to the voyager on the Mississippi; the eye was here relieved by a most inviting prospect, the river was fringed by low wooded hills, from which gushed clear and sparkling brooks, passing with low musical murmurs over their rocky beds, until they were finally lost in the 'Father of Waters.'

"But the early progress of Hancock County way anything but encouraging. While other sections of the State, with fewer advantages, and a less healthy climate, rapidly augmented in wealth and population, this remained almost a wilderness, and this by reason of uncertain titles.

"Hancock County, fair, healthful, and fertile, 'even as the Garden of the Lord,' was one of those unfortunate counties comprised in that afflicted section lying between the Illinois and Mississippi rivers, known as the 'Military Tract.' It had been set apart, by Act of Congress, as bounty land for the soldiers of the War of 1812; but few of them emigrated there, and nearly all of the patents, or 'soldiers' rights,' as they were called, were thrown upon the market for sale. This furnished, for a score of years, a rich harvest for speculators and land jobbers, and the 'Military Tract' became the 'happy hunting ground' of sharks and sharpers of every description. A race of 'bloated patent holders' was thus created, whose broad tract of wilderness land rivalled in extent the proudest dukedoms and baronies of the old world. It was against sound public policy to create such a land monopoly on the public domain; but much greater evils grew out of this thing, in the establishment of a conflict of titles, creating doubt and uncertainty, casting a shadow on every man's homestead who dared to erect it on the Tract, and driving away honest and enterprising settlers. A system arose in the East of forging patents, by having absent or deceased soldiers represented by others, and even by making duplicate copies entire without affidavit, or aid from the Land Office.

"In hundreds of instances there were three patents

upon the same section, with facilities to make a thousand, in fact, the entire Tract was eventually strewn with patents as thick as autumn leaves in an unbroken forest. So great grew the evils of this system, and from the non-payment of taxes by non-residents, that the Legislature of Illinois went to work to devise a remedy. But the legislators of new States are not generally very learned or capable statesmen, and the sharpers laughed at the idea of illiterate men thwarting the plans of men whose business it was to 'pierce the centre' of the most explicit statute. The Legislature having tried sharp and pointed statutes on the fraternity before, but without success, instead of tinkering and amending laws which 'John Doe, et al.,' had laughed at, tried the virtue of a more sweeping enactment. They enacted, in substance, that if any one held possession of land for seven years, under color of title, such possession should be proof of title conclusive against all the world, and that 'John Doe, et al.,' with their pockets full of patents, should be forever barred and excluded. When John Doe and his compeers took in the force of this statute, not a smile lit up their solemn countenances. They were caught at last. But everybody was disappointed by the final operation of the statute. It only created or attracted another 'swarm of flies, more hungry voracious, and pestilent than any that had preceded them; the heavens and the earth were darkened by their myriads, and no friendly swallow appeared to drive them away.'

"No sooner was the 'Delinquent List' exposed for sale for non-payment of taxes, than a crowd appeared in and around the Court House, hungry and haggard, the like of which had surely not been seen since Pharaoh's lean kind emerged from the river Nile. Here were congregated broken down tradesmen, tinkers and vagabonds; rough, roaring, swearing fellows, and smooth-faced, hypocritical, canting knaves, jostled each other, and mingled and commingled in the halls of justice, each one striving, with the few dollars he had contrived to save out of the general wreck by cheating his creditors, to retrieve his fortunes, and the result was a land-monopoly, more corrupt than any that had preceded it. The law had been aimed at the non-resident jobber, to compel the payment of taxes; but this unscrupulous crowd hurled it without mercy or discrimination at the heads of everybody; if it carried away the inheritance of the widow and orphan, it was all the same to them. The wise legislators stood aghast at the havoc they had innocently caused. They had 'called spirits from the vasty deep,' and, contrary to all past experience, they had come. These sharpers inspired general terror, and no wonder; for had the incongruous and villanous crowd made a descent into hell, the devil would have fled howling to the most retired and gloomy corner of his domain, leaving them to contend and squabble among themselves for a 'tax title' on his burning throne! It was now an indiscriminate fight on the 'Military Tract,' in which all sorts of persons, with all sorts of papers, documents, and titles, rushed to the conflict and couched their lances for the fray. In this hot contest the unsophisticated settler, not conversant with these matters, had but little show. He could much more readily, with the slightest possible assistance, 'read his title clear to mansions in the skies,' than so establish his claim to a single foot of land covered by 'soldiers' rights,' forged patents, and tax titles on the whole Military Tract.

"Fortunately, Hancock County was not altogether covered by these titles. The Act granted the soldier 'one hundred and sixty acres of land,' no less, no more. Hence, those quarters called 'fractional,' with less or more than one hundred and sixty acres, were subject to entry at the Land Office. These skirted the banks of the river and along the township lines of the whole county, and were rapidly taken up and settled before the arrival of the Mormons, at which time Hancock County contained a sparse population of several thousand. Owing to greater security of title, most of them were settled along the Mississippi. The Des Moines Rapids excited much attention as a favorable site. Among the conspicuous men who visited this section was General Robert E. Lee, then a Lieutenant of Topographical Engineers, in the employ of the War Department, for the purpose of making a survey of the rapids. His visit was in 1832, and he remained in the county the whole season, and was favorably known to all the old settlers, and much respected for his urbanity and gentlemanly bearing. It was then a favorite idea with some, that the Mississippi would in time be bridged at these Rapids, and that at no other place could a permanent structure be erected. Hancock was organized as a county in 1829, and the Capital permanently established a few years after at Carthage.

"Meanwhile the courts travelled around the country after the manner of a public exhibition, holding terms at such points as met the views of the lawyers, or perhaps where it was considered that law and justice were most needed. Among the lawyers who then practised in Hancock, were Malcolm McGregor, Archibald Williams and O. H. Browning; the former, a brilliant genius, died young, and the latter two have since become 'known to fame.'

"First in history was a Post Office at the Rapids, called Venice, but there was no town of that name. In the year 1834, Commerce was laid out by Messrs. Alex. White and James B. Teas; and shortly after a Mr. Hotchkiss, of New Haven, Conn., laid out Commerce City, just above the other town. All proved failures, but many still had confidence that this was *the* place for a great city in the future. Among the owners of the 'bottom land' was Dr. Isaac Galland, a man of *some* enterprise, who, immediately after the failure of Hotchkiss, opened a correspondence with Joe Smith, which resulted in an agreement that the latter should settle all his people near Commerce."

To the foregoing graphic sketch it is only necessary to add, that the Prophet purchased a small tract and received gratis a larger one; a convenient revelation was vouchsafed for the Saints to gather to this stake of Zion; they complied with rapidity, the plat of a great city was laid out and the Mormon star was once more in the ascendant.

48 LIFE IN UTAH; OR, THE MYSTERIES

CHAPTER II.

HISTORY FROM THE FOUNDING OF NAUVOO TILL 1843.

Rapid growth of Nauvoo—Apparent prosperity—"The vultures gather to the carcass"—Crime, polygamy and politics—Subserviency of the Politicians—Nauvoo Charters—A government within a government—Joe Smith twice arrested—Released by S. A. Douglas—Second time by Municipal Court of Nauvoo—McRinney's Account—Petty thieving—Gentiles driven out of Nauvoo—"Whittling Deacons"—"Danites"—Anti-Mormons organize a Political Party—Treachery of Davis and Owens—Defeat of Anti-Mormons—Campaign of 1843—Cyrus Walker, a great Criminal Lawyer—"Revelation" on Voting—The Prophet cheats the Lawyer—Astounding perfidy of the Mormon Leaders—Great increase of popular hatred—Just anger against the Saints.

A CITY rose as if by magic. Temporary in character as most of the buildings were, rude log houses or frame shanties, they served to shelter the rapidly gathering Saints. The first house on the new site was erected June 11th, 1839, and in eighteen months thereafter there were two thousand dwellings, besides school houses and other public buildings. The new city was named NAUVOO, a word which has no signification in any known language, but in the "reformed Egyptian" of Joe Smith's imaginary history, is said to mean "The Beautiful." The site was indeed beautiful, but not the most feasible they could have selected. Instead of locating immediately at the head of the Rapids, where there was a convenient landing at all seasons, they chose a spot one mile below, only approachable by steamboats at high water. The temporary structures, in no long time, gave way to more permanent buildings; improvements multiplied on every hand, and Joe Smith had almost daily revelations directing how every work should be carried on. Here, it was foretold, was to be built a great city and temple, which should be the great gathering place of "Zion," and central rendezvous of the sect, "until such time as the Lord should open the way for their return to Zion, indeed"—Jackson County, Missouri; and from here were to spread gigantic operations for the conversion of the world. One by one most of the Missouri apostates came creeping back into the Church; Orson Hyde was restored to his place as apostle, and was able to explain his apparent defection. A missionary board was organized, and arrangements perfected for foreign missions embracing half the world. On the 29th of August, Orson Pratt and Parley P. Pratt set out on a mission to England, followed, September the 20th, by Elders Brigham Young, H. C. Kimball, George A. Smith, R. Hedlock, and T. Turley. Brigham had been appointed "President of the Twelve Apostles" in 1836, in place of Thomas B. Marsh, the apostate. They landed at Liverpool, the 6th of April, 1840, and entered with zeal upon their work. Brigham assumed entire control of the enterprise, established various missions, baptized numerous converts, labored among the common people, preached, prayed, wrote and argued, lived hard, and travelled hundreds of miles on foot. May the 29th, 1840, he established and issued the first number of the *Latter-Day Saints' Millennial Star*, a periodical never suspended since. He organized a number of flourishing churches, and early in 1841 returned to Nauvoo, bringing with him seven hundred and sixty-nine converts. Shortly before this time, Sidney Rigdon had addressed a memorial to the Legislature of the State of Pennsylvania, praying for redress for the alleged losses of the Saints in Missouri, and calling upon the Congressional delegation from that State to move the General Government in their behalf; and in October, 1839, Joseph Smith, Sidney Rigdon, Elias Higbee and Orrin Porter Rockwell set out for Washington, delegated to seek redress. They reached the Capital, November the 28th, and were admitted forthwith to an audience with President Van Buren, who heard them through, and, according to their report, replied, "Gentlemen, your cause is just, but I can do nothing for you," adding, in undertone, "I should lose the vote of the State of Missouri." By his own account this last remark was, "The General Government cannot interfere in the domestic concerns of Missouri." Nothing resulted from either application; but the attention of the country was attracted to Nauvoo. The rapid growth of the city excited the wonder of eastern people, and numerous curiosity hunters, correspondents and tourists hastened to visit it. They were treated with extreme complaisance, and in their reports the city lost nothing of its wonders. In October, 1840, a petition with many thousand names was forwarded for an Act of Incorporation for Nauvoo, and about the same time Joe Smith had another revelation that the Temple must be commenced at once, and ground was broken therefor October the 3rd. The sudden and surprising prosperity of the sect attracted to them a number of ambitious and unscrupulous men, of whom four deserve particular notice.

Dr. Isaac Galland, was in the early part of his life, a notorious horse-thief and counterfeiter, belonging to the "Massac Gang," as it was called, on the Ohio river. He had then nominally reformed and moved into Hancock County, where he was, in 1834, a candidate for the Legislature, but was defeated by a small majority. Soon after, he came into possession of a large tract of land, and induced Joe Smith to settle on a part, with a view to enhancing the value of the rest.

Jacob Backinstos came to Hancock from Sangamon County, where he had got credit for a stock of goods, sold them, and defrauded his creditors; after which he came over to the Mormons seeking his fortune. His brother married a niece of Joe Smith, but Backinstos held off and took rank as a "managing Democrat," a sort of local politician. In this capacity he rendered some service to Judge Stephen A. Douglas, who, in turn, appointed him Clerk of the Hancock Circuit Court, this giving him great political power with the Mormons. By them he was at different times elected Sheriff and member of the Legislature, and continued a "Jack Mormon" to the end of the chapter.

"General" James Arlington Bennett was an adventurer of some talent, whose "range" was from Virginia to New York City, where he had an occasional connection with the press. He early wrote to Joe Smith, proposing a religious and political alliance, adding, with refreshing candor, "You know Mahomed had his *right hand man.*" Joe replied in a tone of good humored sarcasm, adding, however, a sort of offer for Bennett to visit Nauvoo.

The latter came soon after, and was baptized into the Church, but, not being trusted to the extent he desired, soon departed.

Dr. John C. Bennett was usually considered "one of the greatest scamps in the Western country." He was a man of real talent, some ambition, overbearing zeal, and all engrossing lust; at the same time rather good looking, of smooth manners and easy address. Besides, being a medical graduate and practising physician, he had acquired considerable military and engineering skill, and had been Adjutant General of the State of Illinois. He now brought his talents and rascality to an alliance with Joe Smith; for a year and a-half he was his intimate friend and trusted counselor, when, as has so often happened before, a beautiful woman set them at outs, and forever put an end to this touching friendship. These, and a score of others of like character, attached themselves to the rising sect, and became Joe Smith's unscrupulous tools and allies. As for the common Saints, the pliable mass, though not nearly so foolish and fanatical as in Jackson County, they were quite as obsequious, and worked steadily to build up the material interests of "Zion."

The missions in England, Wales and Scotland prospered greatly, and many thousands of foreign Saints arrived in Nauvoo; some remained, but the majority were scattered in settlements through the country, which the Prophet called "Stakes of Zion." They were not to rival the great city, but to be its feeders and tributaries. The swamp land adjacent to Nauvoo was drained, and the site rendered quite healthy; the rapids were surveyed by J. C. Bennett, and a wing dam projected, which was to make a commodious harbor in front of Nauvoo, and secure driving power sufficient to turn all the factory wheels of a vast commercial city.

These were the palmy days of Joe Smith; this was the "Golden Age" of Mormonism. The former was no more the wandering lad, with "peep-stone" and hazel rod, or the fugitive vagabond fleeing from Missouri rifles; he was at the head of a now consolidated and rapidly augmenting sect; he was courted and flattered of politicians; he was absolute ruler and main proprietor of a city already populous, and destined to be rich and powerful. Bright visions of future aggrandizement and wealth floated through his brain, and he confidently looked forward to the time when he should be virtual dictator of a powerful State. But into the very noon of this halcyon day floated the faint rumbling of a distant earthquake, and afar upon the political and social horizon appeared a little cloud, "no bigger than a man's hand," which stayed not till it darkened the whole heaven of the future, and dashed this proud fabric to the ground.

There now devolves upon me the narration of a change in public sentiment, swift and violent, almost without parallel in America; and the reader will learn with surprise that in a brief period hatred took the place of friendship, and the same people who had received the Mormons with gladness, were in hot haste to drive them out at the bayonet's point. The consideration of what caused this unprecedented change in public sentiment, and the intense hatred against the Mormons, presents some points of pertinent inquiry to politicians, and perhaps some lessons to religious sects. The various causes which led to the Mormon troubles in Illinois, and their final expulsion, may be grouped under three heads:

I. Criminal. II. Moral and Social. III, Political.

I, In the first, it may well be said, the Mormons were destined to experience, in all its bitterness, the force of the homely adage in regard to giving a dog a bad name. The Mississippi Valley, from St. Louis to Galena, had been for years unusually infested with reckless and blood-stained men. The whole of south-eastern Iowa, and much of north-eastern Missouri, was in a comparatively wild and lawless state; the "half-breed" tract of the former, from unsettled land titles and other causes, was appropriated as a refuge for and overrun by coiners, horse-thieves and robbers; and the latter section, adjacent, was little if any better. The law was enforced with slackness, or the combination of rogues was too great for the ordinary machinery of justice; people had but little confidence in courts and juries, and, in more atrocious cases than common, satisfied themselves with lynch law.

The islands and groves farther up the river, near Davenport and Rock Island, were the hiding places of regularly organized bands of marauders; as also were the bayous and hollows west of Nauvoo. The writer was but a boy, but remembers well the thrills of horror that ran through the West at the murder of Miller and Liecy in Lee County, Iowa, of Col. Davenport at Rock Island, of an entire family of five persons in Adams County, and others too numerous to mention. Long afterwards, while the writer was travelling through Hancock, Pike, and Adams Counties, no family thought of retiring at night without barring and double-locking every ingress; and the names of John Long, Aaron Long, Granville Young, Robert Birch, the Hodges and Foxes, and dozens of other murderers, were as common as household words.

To all that class the bad name given the Mormons in Missouri was so much capital, and it gathered around them, with the real vulture instinct. Hundreds of licentious villains, cut-throats, and robbers made their way into Nauvoo, were baptized into the Church as a convenient cover for their crimes, and made that their secret headquarters. Property stolen far up the river, or east of the city, was run through and concealed in the western bayous, or hastily disposed of to innocent purchasers, so that the owners generally found it among the Mormons. The criminals were, in many instances, traced directly to Nauvoo; but once within the charmed circle, all power to punish them was gone.

Their secret confederates were ready to "swear" them clear, and too often the cry of "persecution" was sufficient to mislead really honest Mormons, and cause them to defend one who, though really guilty, claimed the name of a Saint. Thus, while the Mormons could truly say there was less crime in Nauvoo than in most other cities of its size, it was still true that more criminals issued thence than from any other.

How many of the real Mormons were concerned in these depredations it is impossible to say, probably very few; but the fact remained that the criminals had most of them assumed the name of Mormons, that they were not thrust out and punished, and that the really innocent portion obstinately refused to entertain any charge against the guilty, making the Church a complete cover and exemption for crime. An angry people could not be expected to go into their city and discriminate between them; they struck blindly at the whole community, and thus while two-thirds of them were probably guiltless of crime, all suffered alike. In the outer settlements there was actual cause to complain of the foreign Saints; thousands of them had "gathered" in great haste and extreme poverty; they had nothing, and knew not how to rapidly accommodate themselves to their new pursuits, and at the same time very naturally refused to starve in a plentiful country.

Their doctrines virtually invited them to take what they needed, and they did.

As to the heads of the Church and their newly-acquired allies, enough has been said to show that much of their conduct was on the very border-line of rascality, if it did not altogether step over it.

II. Of the second class of causes, but little need be added to the history of polygamy, to be more fully recited hereafter. Of the ten thousand intrigues of Smith, Bennett, Rigdon and other leaders, it is useless to speak, except to give their public results. While the established denominations of Illinois were threatened, and her political stability endangered, her people were also shocked by the introduction of new, and, to them, revolting vices.

III. But the great cause of popular hostility, which finally led to the worst result, was the Mormon system of voting solidly, at the dictation of a few men.

They have always insisted on this principle, pretending that there would be no union in their Church, if the members were allowed to vote by individual will. Such a course must ever have one effect, to cause the Church to be regarded as a mere political entity, to be fought accordingly, and, in time, arouse the fiercest opposition. It will hardly do to say no Church has a *right* to so direct its vote, and yet, if persisted in, it must be a constant source of faction. Any such Church would constitute a dangerous power in a republican government; and would soon have arrayed against it all those who were defeated by its vote, all who failed to get its support, all who disdained to stoop to the arts necessary to obtain it, and all those who clearly saw the evil tendency of such a system. In two years after he entered Illinois, Joe Smith was absolute master of three thousand votes; practically, he might just as well have been allowed to cast so many himself. The offices of the County were in his gift; no man could hope to reach Congress from that district, without his favor, and it was highly probable, that, by the next election, his simple will would determine who should be Governor of the State.

Such power in the hands of a corrupt man, used with a singular perfidy, and in the interests of the worst clique ever assembled, would alone be almost sufficient to determine the people upon the expulsion of him and his fanatical sect. The particular situation, at the time, rendered this evil ten-fold more apparent. For the first time since its organization, the Whig Party had a fair prospect of carrying the State and the nation; but Illinois was doubtful.

If Henry Clay should again be the nominee of the Whigs, Kentucky, Louisiana and other Southern States were considered certain for that party, and, in certain very probable contingencies, Illinois would turn the scale one way or the other. It was quite certain the Mormons would, by 1844, give the casting vote in Illinois, and Joe Smith had perfect control of the Mormon vote. Such contingencies are liable to frequently occur in our politics, and henceforth set it down as an American axiom, that any Church assuming to cast its vote as a unit, for its own interests, under the dictation of its spiritual head or heads, is the deadly foe of our liberties, and justly an object of distrust and dislike to every lover of his country. With this digression, I resume the thread of history.

The "Harrison Campaign" of 1840 was in full tide, and the politicians gathered thick around Joe Smith. His people had been driven from a Democratic State by order of a Democratic Governor, and himself denied redress by a Democratic President; while his "memorial" against Missouri had been introduced and countenanced in the Senate of the United States by Henry Clay, and in the House by John F. Stuart, both Whigs.

He felt friendly to them, but, finding he had great power, determined to use it well, and took good care not to commit himself. When wined, dined, toasted, and feasted by managers of both parties, he stated, in general terms, that he felt no particular interest in politics; he had tried the Yankees of New York, and the "free soilers" of the Western Reserve, and had met with rough treatment; he had gone thence to the pro-slavery Missourians, and had met with rougher treatment; the Democrats had robbed him, and the Whigs refused him redress, and he had little confidence in either.

But there were certain things absolutely necessary for his city to receive from the Legislature, to protect him and his people from mobs, and the party that could most certainly give him these would obtain his support. This cheerful frankness was met by renewed protestations of respect and good-will, and both parties were eager to grant him favors.

After secret consultation with his counsellors at Nauvoo, Joe had a revelation to support the Whig ticket, which the Mormons did unanimously in 1840 and '41. In the Legislature of '40–'41, it became an object with the Democrats to conciliate them, and at that session Dr. J. C. Bennett came with a charter, mainly drawn up by himself and Joe Smith, for the incorporation of Nauvoo. The charter was referred to the Judiciary Committee, who reported favorably, the ayes and noes were called in neither house, and the charter passed without a dissenting vote.

The annals of ancient and modern legislation might be

searched in vain for a parallel to that Nauvoo Charter. It gave all the powers ever granted to incorporated cities, and gave them power to pass all laws "*not repugnant to the Constitution of the United States, or of this State,*" which was afterwards interpreted to mean that they might pass local ordinances, contrary to the *laws* of the State. It provided for a Mayor, four Aldermen, and nine Councillors, and established a Mayor's Court with exclusive jurisdiction in all cases arising under the city ordinances.

It also established a Municipal Court, to be composed of the Mayor as Chief Justice, and four Aldermen as associates, and gave this Court the power to issue writs of *Habeas Corpus*. And this not only to try the sufficiency of writs issuing from any other court, which is a power rarely granted a Municipal Court, but to go beyond that and try the original cause of action. Hitherto none but Judges of the Supreme and Circuit Court could issue such writs, and there were just nine persons in the State empowered to do so; but this Act at one fell swoop conferred it upon the five judges of this Municipal Court, and those the persons above all others most liable to abuse it. It also incorporated the militia of Nauvoo into a body to be called the "Nauvoo Legion," independent of all other militia officers in the State, except the Governor as Commander-in-Chief. It established a court-martial for this Legion, composed of the commissioned officers, entirely independent of all other officers, and in the regulations *not governed by the laws of the State!*

This Legion was to be at the disposal of the Mayor in executing the ordinances of the city. Another charter incorporated a great tavern to be known as the Nauvoo House. "Thus," says Governor Ford, "it was proposed to re-establish for the Mormons a government within a government; a legislature with power to pass ordinances at war with the laws of the State; courts to execute them with but little dependence upon the constitutional judiciary, and a military force at their own command, to be governed by its own laws and ordinances, and subject to no State authority but that of the Governor.

"The powers conferred were expressed in language at once ambiguous and undefined; as if on purpose to allow of misconstruction. The great law of the separation of the powers of government was wholly disregarded. The Mayor was at once the executive power, the judiciary, and part of the legislature. The Common Council, in passing ordinances, were restrained only by the Constitution. One would have thought that these charters stood a poor chance of passing the legislature of a republican people jealous of their liberties. Nevertheless they did pass unanimously through both houses. Messrs. Little and Douglas managed with great dexterity with their respective parties. Each party was afraid to object to them, for fear of losing the Mormon vote, and each believed that it had secured their favor. A city government, under the charter, was organized in 1841, and Joe Smith was elected Mayor.

"In this capacity he presided in the Common Council, and assisted in making the laws for the government of the city; and as Mayor, also, he was to see these laws put into force. He was *ex-officio* judge of the Mayor's Court, and chief justice of the Municipal Court, and in these capacities he was to interpret the laws which he had assisted to make. The Nauvoo Legion was also organized, with a great multitude of high officers. It was divided into divisions, brigades, cohorts, regiments, battalions and companies. Each division, brigade and cohort had its General, and over the whole, as Commander-in-Chief, Joe Smith was appointed Lieutenant-General. These offices, and particularly the last, were created by an ordinance of the Court-martial composed of the commissioned officers of the Legion.

"The Common Council passed many ordinances for the punishments of crime. The punishments were generally different from, and vastly more severe than the punishments provided by the laws of the State."

Elder Howard Coray, who was at that time a confidential clerk of Joe Smith's, states that he was present at the time Smith and Bennett were constructing this charter; that Bennett objected to certain clauses as being "too strong," to which Smith replied, "We must have that power in our courts, for this work will gather of all mankind; the Turk, *with his ten wives*, will come to Nauvoo, and we must have laws to protect him with these wives." Elder Coray, now a devoted Brighamite, at Salt Lake, advanced this to disprove the statement of Joe Smith's sons that their father did not establish polygamy. It merely proves, as will hereafter be shown, that he was in that practice long before the date of his pretended revelation.

It was, indeed, necessary for him to fence out the Missourians with strong ordinances, for his old enemies in that State were busy in scheme against him. In the fall of 1841, the Governor sent a requisition to Illinois for Smith's arrest, and after some evasion it was executed. A writ of *Habeas Corpus* was sued out before Judge S. A. Douglas, whose circuit embraced Hancock. On technical grounds Douglas released Smith, which the latter considered a great favor from the Democrats. Again, in 1842, Smith was arrested on a requisition, and this time forcibly rescued by his followers. The election of 1842 was approaching; the Whigs nominated Joseph Duncan for Governor, and the Democrats Thos. I. Ford. After an immense amount of wire-pulling, Joe Smith issued a proclamation to his people—there seems to have been no revelation this time—pronouncing "Judge Douglas a master-spirit," and commanding the people to vote the Democratic ticket. Ford was elected, and assumed the duties of Governor, late in 1842. He has embodied the official acts of his Administration in his "History of Illinois," and throughout this part of my narrative the quotations are from that work, unless otherwise credited.

The Democrats would almost certainly have carried the State without the Mormons; but in 1843, there was to be an election for Congressman in their district, and therein they were absolute. But the great reaction had set in, and the Mormons were fast becoming odious to the body of the people. After the political account, the reader will be interested in the anti-Mormon account, and I quote from the narrative of R. W. McKinney, Esq., before alluded to, a witness of the facts:

"The preaching of Mormonism was a greater success than could have been reasonably expected in so enlightened an age, and one to a great extent inclined to scepticism. A new spirit of emigration was excited, and every convert was urged to hasten to where he could gaze upon the divine face of the Prophet, and where the wealth of the Gentile world would flow in upon them. Two years had not elapsed since the first fugitives arrived at Nauvoo before the Mormons outnumbered the old settlers. The latter began to think they had enough for the present. None of the promised advantages had accrued from the settlement of the Mormons among them. They had created but little trade or commerce, had made no improvement of the rapids, had established no manufactories, erected no school-houses, organized no institutions for instruction, and made no provision for the support of the poor. They were pressed into Joe's service, and employed upon the erection of a temple of an order of architecture such as the world had never seen. They now assumed a haughty bearing and arrogant speech towards their old friends and protectors, and the latter were constantly sneered at as blind and erring Gentiles, whose steps were tending downward to the deepest pit of hell. The Saints were to possess the earth and the Gentiles be crushed beneath their footsteps. This doctrine had a fearful effect upon the common Mormon; he looked upon the old settler much as the followers of Moses and Joshua looked upon the Canaanites. If the earth was to be delivered to the Saints with the fullness thereof, why not take possession at once, or so much of it as to supply present wants? The old settlers began to feel that the inflated declarations of the Prophet meant something more than idle gasconade. Their cattle, which had pastured safely on the broad prairies, now failed to come up; their poultry took wings and flew away to some undiscovered country, never to return, and their barns and granaries were depleted with unheard of rapidity. If one visited Nauvoo in search of estrays, if by accident he peeped into the shambles or slaughter-pens of the Saints, he was rudely rebuffed as a disturber of the peace of Zion.

He was fortunate if he escaped arrest, and did not often escape annoyance. The Mormons prided themselves on their genius in devising modes of annoyance by which a suspicious stranger could be driven away without resort to violence; the Prophet had systemized annoyance, and reduced it to a science. He had organized clubs of loafers and boys into what he called 'whittling deacons.'

"They were composed of the lowest grade of vagabonds in Nauvoo, and were stationed around the streets and corners, armed with pieces of pine board and sharp dirk-knives, always ready for instant service. If a stranger were seen on the streets, the first thing was to find out if he were obnoxious. An experienced spy was placed upon his track, who followed him until it was ascertained what the stranger was. If he appeared hostile to the Saints, if he spoke disparagingly of the Prophet or his religion, 'the whittling deacons' were put at his heels.

"They would surround him with pine sticks and dirk-knives, and, whistling gravely, keep up a continual whittling, the shavings flying into the face and over the person of the obnoxious one, and the sharp knives being flourished dangerously close to his ears. If timid and nervous he retreated soon; but if he faced the music, the whittling was more energetic, the whistling louder and schriller, the knives approached closer and flashed more brightly, till his retreat was a necessity. Strange that a person who claimed to be commissioned as a Prophet, could have authorized such low and disgraceful work; but we have the authority of the Saints that it was Joe Smith's own invention, and was considered a brilliant stroke of genius. If the suspected person was contumacious and stood out against the 'whittling deacons,' his case was referred to a higher tribunal, the 'Danite Band.' The 'whittling deacons' were composed of Saintly loafers, this of Saintly ruffians. Many of them were outlaws, criminals who had fled from justice and who sought and received protection from Joe. No man was too deeply stained with crime to gain that protection, if the Prophet could use him. If a fugitive from justice proved a worthless and inefficient tool, he was given up with a great flourish of trumpets, and with glowing comments by the newspaper press as to what an orderly and law abiding people the Mormons were.

" Who ever heard of Joe Smith giving up Porter Rockwell, or that he ever lost any respect on account of his crimes. This lawless banditti went after the contumacious stranger with bowie-knives and Colt's revolvers. Their business was to terrify and insult him, to salute his ears with strange oaths and blasphemies, to menace him with threats of instant death and to flourish their deadly weapons in his face. But were there no police to appeal to ? These assailants were themselves the police, powerful only for evil. If the suspected was still fool-hardy enough to refuse to leave, his case was reported to a higher tribunal, who gave secret and mysterious warnings, written in mystic characters and stained with blood, which dropped in the way of the suspected, were found in his bed room, under his pillow or about his person. Dire was his fate if he disregarded this last solemn admonition. He would never again be heard from ; the mission of the 'destroying angel' was sudden, sure and complete.

" The Prophet's ambition and love of display had been sated by a shower of civic honors thrust upon him by the Corporation Act. His love of power and desire for vengeance were gratified by a review of his solid squares of infantry, his squadrons of cavalry and parks of artillery. He was the only man of his age beneath the rank of Grand Duke, that could summon a well-equipped army from his retainers. But he had other vices to gratify besides ambition and love of display.

" How to gratify his licentious desires became with him a great study. To overcome the virtue of his female followers and establish prostitution as a religious rite, he had a revelation. None of his compeers or successors could compete with him in revelations. His son Joe, who claims to be his legitimate successor, has been so reticent as to receive from the Brighamites, and deserve, the title of the ' dumb Prophet.' The elder Joe, had revelations on all sorts of subjects; building houses, ploughing lands and selling merchandise, and now authorizing him to seduce and degrade his female devotees. His elders were now instructed that the time had arrived when seven women should take hold of one man; that no woman could be saved unless united to a husband in a spiritual sense; that such union was enjoined by divine authority, and to resist it was to resist the ordinance of God. Here was the dilemma for the female Saint: she must succumb to a libidinous priest, or be sent to perdition; she must accept prostitution or damnation, and there was no escape. It was at first claimed that this connection was purely spiritual and platonic; but the admissions of incautious Saints, and the testimony of many women, soon left no doubt in any intelligent mind that the system was one of complete concubinage.

"The two young Smiths, who lately made a raid into Utah, denying that their father practised polygamy, ought to know, as every intelligent person does know, that the will of Joe Smith was absolute in Nauvoo, and all the councils, sanhedrims and priests in the city could never have established polygamy there, if he had but shook his little finger in opposition.

"The Mormons were not only introducing a new religion, but striving to introduce a new civilization; or rather laboring to abolish all civilization, and to re-establish a barbarism old as the infancy of the world. If an old patriarch, who lived immediately after the earth emerged from the deluge, through ignorance married a sister or an aunt, the Mormon assumed the same right. If another patriarch armed his numerous servants, and invaded the tented city of a rival, carried his wives and children into captivity, and drove away his sheep, cattle and oxen, it was a divine precedent which the Saint would do well to follow. As in those remote ages the whole people labored and toiled for the aggrandizement of their chieftain in erecting castles for his protection, or guarding the flocks and herds in which his wealth consisted, so the Mormon chieftain employed his retainers in the erection of a gorgeous temple. The anti-Mormons saw that the Mormons were industrious, and saw too that much of their labor was misdirected, and that they derived no benefit from it, more than the enslaved multitudes who toiled on the Egyptian pyramids in the traditional ages of the world. They saw that Hancock County, under the control of the dominant sect, was receding to the remotest and most barbarous ages of the world. They farther understood that the multitudes who lived in shanties, and worked without pay, were not likely to starve as long as they were taught that the earth, and all things therein, belonged to the Saints of the Lord. It was thought high time to impose some barrier to the further increase of the dominant Mormons. No one then thought of violence or war; there had been no lawless demonstrations prior to the Mormons' arrival, and, in justice to the old settlers, it should be noted there has been none since their expulsion. Every one considered that most of the evils resulted from the power vested in the Prophet by the Mormon Charter, and the creation of the Legion. It was, therefore, thought best to constitute a new political organization, uniting all anti-Mormons without regard to previous predilections, having for its object united opposition to the Mormons, and repeal of all the Mormon Charters, and disbanding of the Nauvoo Legion. A general mass-meeting was called, and was fully attended. Whigs and Democrats fraternized and rivalled each other in their zeal to rid the country of the growing incubus. But when it came to county nominations, unfortunately there were more aspirants than offices. Those who received nominations were content; but the rejected ones affected to consider themselves badly abused men. Among them were two who went right over with their influence to Joe Smith. The first was a Reverend Thomas Owens, a renegade Baptist preacher, and the other Jacob C. Davis, a lawyer, too indolent to labor or study, but the political oracle of the red-eyed loafers, who congregated together in the low groggeries of the town where he lived. This brace of worthies wended their way to Nauvoo, and informed the Mormon autocrat of the combination against him; but tendered him their sympathy and support, offering to run as the Mormon candidates for the Legislature. The Prophet chose Jacob Davis as his candidate for the State Senate, and Bill Smith, his own brother, and Thomas Owens, his candidates for the Lower House. The rest of the county ticket was filled out by the Prophet from his own Mormon tools.

"The issue was for the first time clearly drawn, the election in due time came off, and the Prophet was triumphant. He had elected everything on the county ticket. By this combination he had completely defeated the anti-Mormon move, and had for county officers his trusty friends, devoted to his interests. If his enemies chose to appeal from the decision of the polls, he was ready for them. His battalions were models of discipline, devoted to his service, numbered by thousands, and armed with an efficiency which distinguished no other troops in America. The walls of the Temple were progressing rapidly. The anti-Mormons looked upon the structure with many doubts and apprehensions. Everything the Mormons did was veiled in mystery. This structure resembled no church, its walls of massive limestone were impervious to the shot of the heaviest cannon. It had two tiers of circular windows, which looked, to the wondering Gentiles, very much as if they were port-holes for the manning of cannon. The building was near the centre of a square of four acres, to be surrounded by a massive wall ten feet in height, and six in thickness. This, the Mormons said, was for a promenade; the anti-Mormons would have told you, it could be constructed for no other purpose than a fortification, and one which would have stood a heavy bombardment without being breached.

"Another charter provided for the erection of 'a large hotel,' and it was denominated the 'Lord's boarding house.' to which a revelation is added, that Joe Smith and his heirs were to have 'a suite of rooms dedicated to their use forever.'

"It was the boast of Joe that this would be the great 'Mission House' of the world; that in its parlor he would entertain princes, kings, and emperors from Europe and

Asia, who would leave their distant homes to receive information and instruction from him in the new faith. So completely had Joe's head been turned, and so wild and visionary had he become, that it was not without reason that his wife, only a few years after his death, published a statement in the *Quincy Whig*, that she had no belief in his prophetic character, and considered his pretended revelations the emanations of a diseased mind. It may be some gratification to know that the apostolic dignitaries did not always agree among themselves, after the establishment of 'spiritual wifery,' in the distribution of female prizes. They had no dispute in polemic theology. The oracle Joe settled everything of that sort by immediate revelation. But when the face of a handsome female Saint was seen peering from under the curtains of an immigrant waggon, it was like throwing the apple of discord among the lascivious priests of the new religion; and however submissive the sacred college may have been to the settlement of a theological tenet, when the same oracle pronounced a verdict, in regard to a female prize, against one of them, his curses were loud and deep. In fact, this system was soon the means of destroying the Mormon unity right at home; the entering wedge that divided Nauvoo into factions, and gave the anti-Mormons a clue to success.

"The name of Cyrus Walker had long been conspicuous in western Illinois. He was an eminent lawyer, who had acquired a great reputation in Kentucky, where he came into competition with Ben Hardin, John Rowan and the Wickliffs. He was past middle life, and had never been a politician; but, in 1843, the Whigs needed a popular candidate, in the Hancock district, for Congress. There was no hope of his election unless Joe Smith and his followers could be manipulated, and thus balance the Democratic majority. Mr. Walker resided in the adjoining county of McDonough, and was thought to be just the man, as, in a long criminal practice, his mind had become a perfect storehouse of expedients, artifices and dodges. He was nominated, and accepted in the full belief that he was a match for the tricky Prophet. His chances were rather doubtful, as the Whigs had been most active in the anti-Mormon Convention. Owen and Davis, Democrats, had deserted to the Mormon camp; but no Whig had been guilty of such defection. But it was confidently anticipated Walker could out-general the commonplace Mr. Hoge, the Democratic candidate. Meanwhile the peace of the Mormon Zion was disturbed. Men who had toiled without remuneration began to murmur, and the families of those who went forth to preach the gospel, without 'purse or scrip,' often suffered greatly in their absence. Dr. John C. Bennett, to whose instructions the Legion owed its admirable drill and discipline, had not risen to that high rank in the Hierarchy which he fancied his talents entitled him to, and had been slighted in the distribution of female prizes. He had seceded, and was a conspirator against the Prophet, denouncing him with a bitterness born of imaginary slight and wrong. He travelled through the West, secured large crowds wherever he lectured, of all who were attracted by the disgusting details of Mormon depravity. But at the same time the Prophet was engaged in exposing and denouncing him; while he proved Joe to be immoral and licentious, the latter proved the same thing against him, and the community soon became satisfied that it was a quarrel between two great rascals, and they were not called upon to decide which was the greater. Joe had apparently forgotten all about the indictment still pending against him in Missouri; but Bennett had not, and, by his intrigues, a fresh requisition was issued, and Joe was arrested in Henderson county, at one of the 'Stakes of Zion,' some twenty-five miles from Nauvoo. But the officers soon found themselves surrounded by a detachment of the Nauvoo Legion, and the whole party was conducted in triumph to that city. The Municipal Court met to try the legality of the requisition, and the regularity of the proceedings, and Cyrus Walker was called upon for his opinion. Their judgment was in no wise controlled by his arguments; but his approval of such jurisdiction was of great value to Joe Smith. He was profuse in his thanks to Walker, and promised earnestly to support him. Walker fully believed that this settled every Mormon vote in his favor, was satisfied he need do nothing more, and returned home to study up the political questions of the day, and fit himself for his future duties in Congress.

"But there was some 'wire-pulling' going on of which he little dreamed; there was a great deal of running to and fro of 'managing Democrats' between Nauvoo and Springfield, and suddenly the Mormons were called in a mass meeting, the second day before the election, when Hyrum Smith arose and announced that he had just received a revelation from heaven, that the Mormons were to vote for the Democrat, Mr. Hoge! They were still in doubt till the Prophet arrived next day, when the whole voting population of Nauvoo again assembled to hear from him. He stated that he was not prepared to advise them with regard to election matters; he could only inform them that he had pledged his own vote to Mr. Walker, and would keep his pledge; but he had received no communication from the Lord on the subject; 'he had not seen the Lord, nor had he gone to seek the Lord about the matter. He was not disposed to call upon the Lord at the request or desire of any Gentile politician; if the Lord really wanted to see him, there was nothing to prevent His calling upon him. So far as he was concerned, the people might vote for Walker, Hoge, or the devil; it was all the same to him. But,' continued the Prophet, 'I am informed my brother Hyrum has seen the Lord, and has something to say to you. I have known brother Hyrum ever since he was a boy, and never knew him to lie. When the Lord speaks, let all the earth keep silent.' Thereupon brother Hyrum took the stand and boldly announced that he *had* seen the Lord, who had instructed him to support Mr. Hoge, 'and, brethren, you are all commanded to vote for Mr. Hoge, for thus saith the Lord God Almighty.' This short address of the Patriarch was no doubt the most powerful and convincing 'stump speech' ever delivered. When the count was rendered next day, Mr. Cyrus Walker had one vote, whilst Hoge's counted by thousands. It is difficult to realize that, in this enlightened age and most enlightened nation, any assembly could be found so deplorably ignorant as to be controlled by two such blackguard impostors, yet so it was; they listened to these blasphemous deceivers, as though God spoke from the heavens. Mr. Walker did not go to Congress. He withdrew forever from politics, devoted himself to his profession, and grew rich. He heard the result of the Nauvoo election with deep mortification. He had been a match for the shrewdest and most cultivated members of his own profession; he was now tricked and sold by a miserable impostor, beneath the notice of any respectable man. Mr. Walker retired to his bed on that night the most bitter, uncompromising and persevering anti-Mormon in the State of Illinois."

To this interesting recital it is only necessary to add a few facts from the official record. Early in May, 1843, Governor Lilburn W. Bogg, of Missouri, while sitting, in the evening, near an open window, was shot from without, and seriously wounded in the head. By the testimony of various apostates it appears, that Joe Smith had frequently foretold the "sudden vengeance of God on the Nero of Missouri," who had used the State troops to expel the Mormons; and that, about this time, Orrin Porter Rockwell was for some time absent from Nauvoo; and when Joe Smith was asked his whereabouts, he replied, with a laugh, "O, just gone to fulfil prophecy." On these and other statements, an indictment was found in Missouri against Smith and Rockwell, and soon after the officers of that State secured another requisition, from Governor Ford, for Joe Smith. He was arrested, and released by his own Municipal Court, with the advice of Mr. Walker, as already related. The agents of Missouri went forthwith to make application to Governor Ford, for a body of militia to enforce the writ, and Walker was sent by the Mormons, as their attorney, to resist the application. Governor Ford declined either to act at once, or to say how he would finally act; as he afterwards stated, because he was not clear as to his duty, and knew the politicians only wanted his decision to carry back to the Mormons. In this state of uncertainty the Mormon leaders sent "Jake" Backinstos to manœuvre at Springfield, and ascertain, if possible, what the Governor would finally do. Governor Ford was absent at St. Louis, and a prominent Democrat, in his interest at Springfield, gave the most solemn assurance, in the Governor's name, that the militia would not be sent against the Mormons, *if they voted the Democrat ticket.* Neither Governor Ford, nor any other responsible official knew aught of this promise in his name, till after the Mormons left the State. With this promise, Backinstos reached Nauvoo but two days before the election, with what result has already been seen. Such damning political treachery was not without due punishment. The Whigs now saw, with amazement, that the most solemn promises meant nothing from Joe Smith; the Democrats generally felt that a sect of such political power, for sale every day, and every hour in the day, and uncertain till the last hour of election, was no safe ally, and both parties awaked to the startling fact, that Joe Smith was actual dictator of their politics and chose their rulers. The anti-Mormon excitement was accelerated ten-fold, and ceased not till their final and complete expulsion from the State. And disastrous as was that expulsion, terrible as were the sufferings of individual Mormons, it is scarcely too much to say they richly deserved it, for this one act of perfidy and folly.

CHAPTER III.

MORMON DIFFICULTIES AND DEATH OF THE PROPHET.

Ford's account—Double treachery in the Quincy district—New and startling developments in Nauvoo—Tyranny of Joe Smith—Revolt of a portion of his followers—The " Expositor"—It is declared "a nuisance" and "abated"—Flight of apostates—Warrants issued for Smith and other Mormons—Constables driven out of Nauvoo—Militia called for —Nauvoo fortified—Mormon war imminent—Governor Ford takes the field in person—Flight of the Prophet and Patriarch to Iowa—Their return and arrest—The Governor pledged for their safety—In his absence the jail is attacked—Death of the Smiths—Character of the Prophet—Comments.

As from this point nearly everything connected with the Illinois history of the Mormons is official and political, I here take up Governor Ford's account :—

" It appears that the Mormons had been directed by their leaders to vote the Whig ticket in the Quincy, as well as the Hancock district. In the Quincy district, Judge Douglas was the Democratic candidate, and O. H. Browning the candidate of the Whigs. The leading Mormons at Nauvoo having never determined in favor of the Democrats until a day or two before the election, there was not sufficient time, or it was neglected, to send orders from Nauvoo into the Quincy district, to effect a change there. The Mormons in that district voted for Browning. Douglas and his friends, being afraid that I might be in his way for the United States Senate in 1846, seized hold of this circumstance to affect my party standing, and thereby gave countenance to the clamor of the Whigs, secretly whispering it about that I had not only influenced the Mormons to vote for Hoge, but for Browning also. This decided many of the Democrats in favor of the expulsion of the Mormons.

" No further demand for the arrest of Joe Smith having been made by Missouri, he became emboldened by success. The Mormons became more arrogant and overbearing. In the winter of 1843-4, the Common Council passed some further ordinances to protect their leaders from arrests, on demand from Missouri. They enacted that no writ issued from any other place than Nauvoo, for the arrest of any person in it, should be executed in the city, without an approval endorsed thereon by the Mayor; that if any public officer, by virtue of any foreign writ, should attempt to make any arrest in the city, without such approval of his process, he should be subject to imprisonment for life, and that the Governor of the State should not have the power of pardoning the offender without the consent of the Mayor. When these ordinances were published, they created general astonishment. Many people began to believe in good earnest that the Mormons were about to set up a separate government for themselves in defiance of the laws of the State. Owners of property stolen in other counties made pursuit into Nauvoo, and were fined by the Mormon Courts for daring to seek their property in the holy city. To one such I granted a pardon. Several of the Mormons had been convicted of larceny, and they never failed in any instance to procure petitions signed by 1,500 or 2,000 of their friends for their pardon. But that which made it more certain than everything else, that the Mormons contemplated a separate government, was that about this time they petitioned Congress to establish a territorial government for them in Nauvoo; as if Congress had any power to establish such a government, or any other, within the bounds of a State.

"To crown the whole folly of the Mormons, in the spring of 1844, Joe Smith announced himself as a candidate for President of the United States. His followers were confident that he would be elected. Two or three thousand missionaries were immediately sent out to preach their religion, and to electioneer in favor of their prophet for the Presidency. This folly at once covered that people with ridicule in the minds of all sensible men, and brought them into conflict with the zealots and bigots of all political parties; as the arrogance and extravagance of their religious pretensions had already aroused the opposition of all other denominations in religion. It seems, from the best information that could be got from the best men who had seceded from the Mormon Church, that Joe Smith about this time conceived the idea of making himself a temporal prince as well as spiritual leader of his people. He instituted a new and select order of the priesthood, the members of which were to be priests and kings temporally and spiritually. These were to be his nobility, who were to be the upholders of his throne. He caused himself to be crowned and anointed king and priest, far above the rest; and he prescribed the form of an oath of allegiance to himself, which he administered to his principal followers. To uphold his pretensions to royalty, he deduced his descent by an unbroken chain from Joseph the son of Jacob, and that of his wife from some other renowned personage of Old Testament history. The Mormons openly denounced the Government of the United States as utterly corrupt, and as being about to pass away, and to be replaced by the Government of God, to be administered by his servant Joseph. It is at this day certain, also, that about this time, the prophet re-instituted an order in the Church called the 'Danite Band.' These were to be a body of police and guards about the person of their sovereign, who were sworn to obey his orders as the orders of God himself.

"Soon after these institutions were established, Joe Smith began to play the tyrant over several of his followers. The first act of this sort which excited attention, was an attempt to take the wife of William Law, one of his most talented and principal disciples, and make her a spiritual wife. By means of his Common Council, without the authority of law, he established a recorder's office in Nauvoo, in which alone the titles of property could be recorded. In the same manner and with the same want of legal authority, he established an office for issuing marriage licenses to Mormons, so as to give him absolute control of the marrying propensities of his people. He proclaimed that none in the city should purchase real estate to sell again, but himself. He also permitted no one but himself to have a license in the city for the sale of spirituous liquors; and in many other ways he undertook to regulate and control the business of the Mormons. This despotism, administered by a corrupt and unprincipled man, soon became intolerable. William Law, one of the most eloquent preachers of the Mormons, who appeared to me to be a deluded but conscientious and candid man, Wilson Law, his brother, Major-General of the Legion, and four or five other Mormon leaders, resolved upon a rebellion against the authority of the Prophet. They designed to enlighten their brethren and fellow-citizens upon the new institutions, the new turn given to Mormonism, and the practices under the new system, by procuring a printing-press and establishing a newspaper in the city, to be the organ of their complaints and views. But they never issued but one number; before the second could appear, the press was demolished by an order of the Common Council, and the conspirators were ejected from the Mormon Church.

"The Mormons themselves published the proceedings of the Council in the trial and destruction of the heretical press; from which it does not appear that any one was tried, or that the editor or any of the owners of the property had notice of the trial, or were permitted to defend in any particular.

"The proceeding was an *exparte* proceeding, partly civil and partly ecclesiastical, against the press itself. No jury was called or sworn, nor were the witnesses required to give their evidence upon oath. The councillors stood up one after another, and some of them several times, and related what they pretended to know. In this mode it was abundantly proved that the owners of the proscribed press were sinners, whoremasters, thieves, swindlers, counterfeiters and robbers; the evidence of which is reported in the trial at full length. It was altogether the most curious and irregular trial that was ever recorded in any civilized country; and one finds difficulty in determining whether the proceedings of the Council were more the result of insanity or depravity. The trial resulted in the conviction of the press as a public nuisance. The Mayor was ordered to see it abated as such, and, if necessary, to call the Legion to his assistance. The Mayor issued his warrant to the City Marshal, who, aided by a portion of the Legion, proceeded to the obnoxious printing-office, and destroyed the press, and scattered the types and other materials.

"After this, it became too hot for the seceding and rejected Mormons to remain in the holy city. They retired to Carthage, the county-seat of Hancock County, and took out warrants for the Mayor and members of the Common Council, and others engaged in the outrage, for a riot. Some of those were arrested, but were immediately taken before the Municipal Court of the city on *habeas corpus*, and discharged from custody.

"On the seventeenth day of June following, a committee of a meeting of the citizens of Carthage presented themselves to me, with a request that the militia might be ordered out to assist in executing process in the city of Nauvoo. I determined to visit in person that section of country, and examine for myself the truth and nature of their complaints. No order for the militia was made ; and I arrived at Carthage on the morning of the 21st day of the same month.

"Upon my arrival, I found an armed force assembled, and hourly increasing, under the summons and direction of the constables of the county, to serve as a *posse comitatus*, to assist in the execution of process. The general of the brigade had also called for the militia, *en masse*, of the counties of McDonough and Schuyler, for a similar purpose. Another assemblage to a considerable number had been made at Warsaw, under military command of Col. Levi Williams.

"The first thing which I did on my arrival was to place all the militia then assembled, and which were expected to assemble, under military command of their proper officers. I next dispatched a messenger to Nauvoo, informing the Mayor and Common Council of the nature of the complaint made against them ; and requested that persons might be sent to me to lay their side of the question before me. A Committee was accordingly sent, who made such acknowledgements that I had no difficulty in concluding what were the facts.

"It appeared clearly, both from the complaints of the citizens and the acknowledgments of the Mormon Committee, that the whole proceedings of the Mayor, the Common Council, and the Municipal Court, were irregular and illegal, and not to be endured in a free country; though, perhaps, some apology might be made for the Court, as it had been repeatedly assured by some of the best lawyers in the State, who had been candidates for office before that people, that it had full and competent power to issue writs of *habeas corpus* in all cases whatever. The Common Council violated the law in assuming the exercise of judicial power; in proceeding *exparte* without notice to the owners of the property; in proceeding against the property *in rem;* in not calling a jury; in not swearing all the witnesses; in not giving the owners of the property, accused of being a nuisance, in consequence of being libelous, an opportunity of giving the truth in evidence; and, in fact, by not proceeding by civil suit or indictment, as in other cases of libel. The Mayor violated the law in ordering this erroneous and absurd judgment of the Common Council to be executed. And the Municipal Court erred in discharging them from arrest.

"As this proceeding touched the liberty of the press, which is justly dear to any Republican people, it was well calculated to raise a great flame of excitement. And it may well be questioned whether years of misrepresentation, by the most profligate newspaper, could have engendered such a feeling as was produced by the destruction of this one press. It is apparent that the Mormon leaders but little understood, and regarded less, the true principles of civil liberty. A free press, well conducted, is a great blessing to a free people; a profligate one is likely soon to deprive itself of all credit and influence by the multitude of falsehoods put forth by it. In addition to these causes of excitement, there were a great many reports in circulation, and generally believed by the people.

"Fortunately for the purposes of those who were active in creating excitement, there were many known truths which gave countenance to some of these accusations. It was sufficiently proved in a proceeding at Carthage, whilst I was there, that Joe Smith had sent a band of his followers to Missouri, to kidnap two men who were witnesses against a member of his Church then in jail, about to be tried on a charge of larceny. It was also a notorious fact, that he had assaulted and severely beaten an officer of the county, for an alleged non-performance of his duty, at a time when that officer was just recovering from a severe illness. It is a fact also, that he stood indicted for the crime of perjury, as was alleged, in swearing to an accusation for murder, in order to drive a man out of Nauvoo, who had been engaged in buying and selling lots of land, and thus interfering with the monopoly of the Prophet as a speculator. It is a fact also, that his Municipal Court, of which he was Chief Justice, by writ of *habeas corpus*, had frequently discharged individuals accused of high crimes and offences against the laws of the State; and on one occasion had discharged a person accused of swindling the Government of the United States, who had been arrested by process of the Federal Courts; thereby giving countenance to the report, that he obstructed the administration of justice, and had set up a government at Nauvoo, independent of the laws and Government of the State. This idea was further corroborated in the minds of the people, by the fact that the people of Nauvoo had petitioned Congress for a Territorial Government to be established there, and to be independent of the State Government. It was a fact also, that some larcenies and robberies had been committed, and that Mormons had been convicted of the crimes, and that other larcenies had been committed by persons unknown, but suspected to be Mormons. Justice, however, requires me here to say that, upon such investigation as I then could make, the charge of promiscuous stealing appeared to be exaggerated.

"Another cause of excitement was a report industriously circulated, and generally believed, that Hyrum Smith, another leader of the Mormon Church, had offered a reward for the destruction of the press of the 'Warsaw Signal,' a newspaper published in the county, and the organ of the opposition to the Mormons. It was also asserted that the Mormons, scattered through the settlements of the county, had threatened all persons who turned out to assist the constables, with the destruction of their property, and the murder of their families, in the absence of their fathers, brothers and husbands. A Mormon woman, in McDonough County, was imprisoned for threatening to poison the wells of the people who turned out in the *posse;* and a Mormon in Warsaw publicly avowed that he was bound, by his religion, to obey all orders of the Prophet, even to commit murder, if so commanded.

"But the great cause of popular fury was, that the Mormons, at several preceding elections, had cast their vote as a unit; thereby making the fact apparent, that no one could aspire to the honors or offices of the country within the sphere of their influence, without their approbation and votes.

"As my object in visiting Hancock was expressly to assist in the execution of the laws, and not to violate them, or to witness or permit their violation, as I was convinced that the Mormon leaders had committed a crime in the destruction of the press, and had resisted the execution of process, I determined to exert the whole force of the State, if necessary, to bring them to justice. But seeing the great excitement in the public mind, and the manifest tendency of this excitement to run into mobocracy, I was of opinion that, before I acted, I ought to obtain a pledge from the officers and men to support me in strictly legal measures, and to protect the prisoners in case they surrendered. I was determined, if possible, the forms of law should not be made a catspaw of a mob, to seduce these people to a quiet surrender, as the convenient victims of popular fury. I therefore called together the whole force then assembled at Carthage, and made an address, explaining to them what I could, and what I could not, legally do; and also adducing to them various reasons why they, as well as the Mormons, should submit to the laws; and why, if they had resolved on revolutionary proceedings, their purpose should be abandoned. The assembled troops seemed much pleased with the address; and, upon its conclusion, the officers and men unanimously voted, with acclamation, to sustain me in a strictly legal course, and that the prisoners should be protected from violence. Upon the arrival of additional forces from Warsaw, McDonough, and Schuyler, similar addresses were made, with the same result.

"It seemed to me that these votes fully authorized me to promise the accused Mormons the protection of the law in case they surrendered. They were accordingly duly informed that if they surrendered they would be protected, and, if they did not, the whole force of the State would be called out, if necessary, to compel the submission. A force of ten men was despatched with the constable to make the arrests, and to guard the prisoners to headquarters.

"In the meantime, Joe Smith, as Lieutenant-General of the Nauvoo Legion, had declared martial law in the city; the Legion was assembled, and ordered under arms; the members of it residing in the country were ordered into town. The Mormon settlements obeyed the summons of their leader, and marched to his assistance. Nauvoo was one great military camp, strictly guarded and watched; and no ingress or egress was allowed except upon the strictest examination. In one instance, which came to my knowledge, a citizen of McDonough, who happened to be in the city, was denied the privilege of returning, until he made oath that he did not belong to the party at Carthage, that he would return home without calling at Carthage, and that he would give no information of the movements of the Mormons.

"However, upon the arrival of the constable and guard, the Mayor and Common Council at once signified their willingness to surrender, and stated their readiness to proceed to Carthage next morning at eight o'clock.

Martial law had previously been abolished. The hour of eight o'clock came, and the accused failed to make their appearance. The constable and his escort returned. The constable made no effort to arrest any of them, nor would he or the guard delay their departure one minute beyond the time, to see whether an arrest could be made. Upon their return, they reported that they had been informed that the accused had fled, and could not be found.

"In the meantime, I made a requisition upon the officers of the Nauvoo Legion for the State arms in their possession. It appears that there was no evidence in the quartermaster-general's office of the number and description of the arms with which the Legion had been furnished. Dr. Bennett, after he had been appointed quartermaster-general, had joined the Mormons, and had disposed of the public arms as he pleased, without keeping or giving any account of them. On this subject I applied to General Wilson Law for information. He had lately been the Major-general of the Legion. He had seceded from the Mormon party; was one of the owners of the proscribed press; had left the city, as he said, in fear of his life, and was one of the party asking for justice against its constituted authorities. He was interested to exaggerate the number of arms rather than to place it at too low an estimate. From his information I learned that the Legion had received three pieces of cannon, and about two hundred and fifty stand of small arms and their accoutrements. Of these, the three pieces of cannon and two hundred and fifty stand of small arms were surrendered. These arms were demanded because the Legion was illegally used in the destruction of the press, and in enforcing martial law in the city, in open resistance to legal process, and the *posse comitatus*.

"I demanded the surrender also, on account of the great prejudice and excitement which the possession of these arms by the Mormons had always kindled in the minds of the people. A large portion of the people, by pure misrepresentation, had been made to believe that the Legion had received from the State as many as thirty pieces of artillery and five or six thousand stands of small arms, which, in all probability, would soon be wielded for the conquest of the country, and for their subjection to Mormon domination. I was of opinion that the removal of these arms would tend much to allay this excitement and prejudice; and in point of fact, although wearing a severe aspect, would be an act of real kindness to the Mormons themselves.

"On the 23d or 24th day of June, Joe Smith, the Mayor of Nauvoo, together with his brother Hyrum and all the members of the Council, and all others demanded, came into Carthage, and surrendered themselves prisoners to the constable, on the charge of riot. They all voluntarily entered into a recognizance before the Justice of the Peace, for their appearance at court to answer the charge. And all of them were discharged from custody except Joe and Hyrum Smith, against whom the magistrate had issued a new writ, on a complaint of treason. They were immediately arrested by the constable on this charge, and retained in his custody to answer it.

"Soon after the surrender of the Smiths, at their request I despatched Captain Singleton with his company, from Brown County to Nauvoo, to guard the town; and I authorized him to take command of the Legion. He reported to me afterwards, that he called out the Legion for inspection; and that, upon two hours' notice, two thousand of them assembled, all of them armed; and this after the public arms had been taken away from them. So it appears that they had a sufficiency of private arms for any reasonable purpose.

"After the Smiths had been arrested on the new charge of treason, the Justice of the Peace postponed the examination, because neither of the parties were prepared with their witnesses for trial. Meanwhile he committed them to the jail of the county for greater security. The jail, in which they were confined, is a considerable stone building; containing a residence for the jailor, cells for the close confinement of prisoners, and one larger room not so strong, but more airy and comfortable than the cells. They were put into the cells by the jailor; but upon their remonstrance and request, and by my advice, they were transferred to the larger room; and there they remained until the final catastrophe. Neither they nor I seriously apprehended an attack on the jail, through the guard stationed to protect it. Nor did I apprehend the least danger on their part of an attempt to escape. For I was very sure that any such an attempt would have been the signal of their immediate death. Indeed, if they had escaped, it would have been fortunate for the purposes of those who were anxious for the expulsion of the Mormon population. For the great body of that people would most assuredly have followed their Prophet and principal leaders, as they did in their flight from Missouri. I learned afterwards that the leaders of the anti-Mormons did much to stimulate their followers to the murder of the Smiths in jail, by alleging that the Governor intended to favor their escape. If this had been true, and could have been well carried out, it would have been the best way of getting rid of the Mormons. The leaders would not have dared to return, and all their church would have followed. I had such a plan in my mind, but I had never breathed it to a living soul, and was thus thwarted in ridding the State of the Mormons two years before they actually left, by the insane fury of the anti-Mormons.

"The force assembled at Carthage amounted to about twelve or thirteen hundred men, and it was calculated that four or five hundred more were assembled at Warsaw. Nearly all that portion resident in Hancock were anxious to be marched into Nauvoo. This measure was supposed to be necessary, to search for counterfeit money and the apparatus to make it, and also to strike a salutary terror into the Mormon people, by an exhibition of the force of the State, and thereby prevent future outrages, murders, robberies, burnings, and the like, apprehended as the effect of Mormon vengeance on those who had taken a part against them. On my part, at one time, this arrangement was agreed to. The morning of the 27th day of June was appointed for the march; and Golden's Point, near the Mississippi river, and about equidistant from Nauvoo and Warsaw, was selected as the place of rendezvous. I had determined to prevail on the Justice to bring out his prisoners, and take them along. A council of officers, however, determined that this would be highly inexpedient and dangerous, and offered such substantial reasons for their opinions as induced me to change my resolution.

"Two or three days' preparation had been made for this expedition. I observed that some of the people became more and more excited and inflammatory, the further the preparations were advanced. Occasional threats came to my ears of destroying the city and murdering or expelling the inhabitants. I had no objection to ease the terrors of the people by such a display of force, and was most anxious also to search for the alleged apparatus for making counterfeit money; and, in fact, to inquire into all the charges against that people, if I could have been assured of my command against mutiny and insubordination. But I gradually learned, to my entire satisfaction, that there was a plan to get the troops into Nauvoo, and there to begin the war, probably by some of our own party, or some of the seceding Mormons, taking advantage of the night to fire on our own force, and then laying it to the Mormons. I was satisfied there were those amongst us fully capable of such an act, hoping that in the alarm, bustle and confusion of a militia camp, the truth could not be discovered, and that it might lead to the desired collision.

"All these considerations were duly urged by me upon the attention of a council of officers, convened on the morning of June 27th. I also urged upon the council, that such wanton and unprovoked barbarity on their part would turn the sympathy of the people in the surrounding counties in favor of the Mormons, and therefore it would be impossible to raise a volunteer militia force to protect such a people against them. Many of the officers admitted that there might be danger of a collision. But such was the blind fury prevailing at the time, though not showing itself by much visible excitement, that a small majority of the council adhered to the first resolution of marching into Nauvoo; most of the officers of the Schuyler and McDonough militia voting against it, and most of those of the County of Hancock voting in its favor.

"A very responsible duty now devolved upon me to determine whether I would, as Commander-in-Chief, be governed by the advice of this majority. I had no hesitation in deciding that I would not; but on the contrary, I ordered the troops to be disbanded, both at Carthage and Warsaw, with the exception of three companies, two of which were retained as a guard to the jail, and the other to accompany me to Nauvoo.

"I ordered two companies under the command of Captain R. F. Smith, of the Carthage Grays, to guard the jail. In selecting these companies, and particularly the company of the Carthage Grays for this service, I have been subjected to some censure. It has been said that this company had already been guilty of mutiny, and had been ordered to be arrested whilst in the encampment at Carthage; and they and their officers were the deadly enemies of the prisoners. Indeed it would have been difficult to find friends of the prisoners under my command, unless I had called in the Mormons as a guard; and this I was satisfied would have led to immediate war, and the sure death of the prisoners.

"Although I knew that this company were the enemies of the Smiths, yet I had confidence in their loyalty and integrity; because their captain was universally spoken of as a respectable citizen and honorable man. The company itself was an old independent company, well armed, uniformed and drilled; and the members of it were the *elite* of the militia of the county. I relied upon this company especially, because it was an independent company, for a long time instructed and practised in military discipline and subordination. I also had their word of honor, officers and men, that they would do their duty according to law. Besides all this the officers and most of the men resided in Carthage; and in the near vicinity of Nauvoo; and, as I thought, must know that they would make themselves and their property convenient and conspicuous marks of Mormon vengeance, in case they were guilty of treachery.

"I had at first intended to select a guard from the County of McDonough, but the militia of that county were very much dissatisfied to remain; their crops were suffering at home; they were in a perfect fever to be discharged; and I was destitute of provisions to supply them for more than a few days. They were far from home, where they could not supply themselves. Whilst the Carthage company could board at their own homes, and would be put to little inconvenience in comparison.

"It is true also, that at this time I had not believed or suspected that an attack would be made upon the prisoners in jail. It is true that I was aware that a great deal of hatred existed against them, and that there were those who would do them an injury if they could. I had heard of some threats being made, but none of an attack upon the prisoners while in jail. These threats seemed to be made by individuals not acting in concert. They were no more than the bluster which might have been expected, and furnished no indication of numbers combining for this or any other purpose. Having ordered the guard and left Gen. Deming in command and discharged the residue of the militia, I immediately departed for Nauvoo, eighteen miles distant, accompanied by Colonel Buckmaster, Quartermaster General, and Captain Dunn's company of dragoons.

"After we had proceeded four miles, Col. Buckmaster intimated to me a suspicion that an attack would be made upon the jail. He stated the matter as a mere suspicion, arising from having seen two persons converse together at Carthage with some air of mystery. I myself entertained no suspicion of such an attack; at any rate, none before the next day in the afternoon; because it was notorious that we had departed from Carthage with the declared intention of being absent at least two days. I could not believe that any person would attack the jail whilst we were in Nauvoo, and thereby expose my life and the life of my companions to the sudden vengeance of the Mormons, upon hearing of the death of their leaders. Nevertheless, acting upon the principle of providing against mere possibilities, I sent back one of the company with a special order to Captain Smith to guard the jail strictly, and at the peril of his life, until my return.

"We proceeded on our journey four miles further. By this time I had convinced myself that no attack would be made upon the jail that day or night. I supposed that a regard for my safety and the safety of my companions would prevent an attack until those to be engaged in it could be assured of our departure from Nauvoo. I still think that this ought to have appeared to me to be a reasonable supposition. I therefore determined at this point to omit making the search for counterfeit money at Nauvoo, and defer an examination of all other abominations charged on that people, in order to return to Carthage that same night, that I might be on the ground in person, in time to prevent an attack upon the jail, if any had been meditated. To this end we called a halt; the baggage waggons where ordered to remain where they were until towards evening, and then return to Carthage.

"Having made these arrangements, we proceeded on our march, and arrived at Nauvoo about four o'clock of the afternoon of the 27th day of June. As soon as notice could be given, a crowd of the citizens assembled to hear an address which I proposed to deliver to them. The number present has been variously estimated at from one to five thousand.

"In this address I stated to them how, and in what, their functionaries had violated the laws. Also, the many scandalous reports in circulation against them, and that these reports, whether true or false, were generally believed by the people. I distinctly stated to them the amount of hatred and prejudice which prevailed everywhere against them, and the causes of it, at length.

"I also told them plainly and emphatically, that if any vengeance should be attempted, openly or secretly, against the persons or property of the citizens who had taken part against their leaders, that the public hatred and excitement were such, that thousands would assemble for the total destruction of their city and the extermination of their people; and that no power in the

State would be able to prevent it. During this address some impatience and resentment were manifested by the Mormons, at the recital of the various reports enumerated concerning them, which they strenuously and indignantly denied to be true. They claimed to be a law-abiding people, and insisted that as they looked to the law alone for their protection, so were they careful themselves to observe its provisions. Upon the conclusion of this address, I proposed to take a vote on the question whether they would strictly observe the laws, even in opposition to their Prophet and leaders. The vote was unanimous in favor of this proposition.

"The anti-Mormons contended that such a vote from the Mormons signified nothing; and truly the subsequent history of that people showed clearly that they were loudest in their professions of attachment to the law, when they were guilty of the greatest extravagances; and in fact, that they were so ignorant and stupid about matters of law, that they had no means of judging of the legality of their conduct, only as they were instructed by their spiritual leaders.

"A short time before sundown we departed on our return to Carthage. When we had proceeded two miles, we met two individuals, one of them a Mormon, who informed us that the Smiths had been assassinated in jail, about five or six o'clock of that day. The intelligence seemed to strike every one with a kind of dumbness. As to myself it was perfectly astounding; and I anticipated the very worst consequences from it. The Mormons had been represented to me as a lawless, infatuated and fanatical people, not governed by the ordinary motives which influence the rest of mankind. If so, most likely an exterminating war would ensue, and the whole land would be covered with desolation. Acting upon this supposition, it was my duty to provide, as well as I could, for the event. I therefore took the two messengers in custody back to Carthage, in order to gain time, and make such arrangements as could be made, to prevent any sudden explosion of Mormon excitement. I also despatched messengers to Warsaw, to advise the citizens of the event. But the people there knew all about it, and, like myself, feared a general attack. The women and children were moved across the river, and a committee despatched that night to Quincy for assistance. The next morning, by daylight, the ringing of the bells in the city of Quincy announced a public meeting. The people assembled in great numbers. The Warsaw committee stated to the meeting, that a party of Mormons had attempted to rescue the Smiths out of jail; that a party of Missourians and others had killed the prisoners to prevent their escape; that the Governor and his party were at Nauvoo at the time, when intelligence of the fact was brought there; that they had been attacked by the Nauvoo Legion, and had retreated to a house where they were then closely besieged. That the Governor had sent out word that he could maintain his position for two days, and would be certain to be massacred if assistance did not arrive by the end of that time. It is unnecessary to say that this entire story was a fabrication. The effect of it, however, was that by ten o'clock on the 28th of June, between two and three hundred men from Quincy, under command of Major Flood, embarked on board a steamboat for Nauvoo, to assist in raising the siege, as they honestly believed.

"Upon hearing of the assassination of the Smiths, I was sensible that my command was at an end; that my destruction was meditated, as well as that of the Mormons; and that I could not reasonably confide longer in one party or the other. I am convinced that it was the expectation that the Mormons would assassinate me, on the supposition that I had planned the murder of the Smiths. Hence the conspirators committed their act while I was at Nauvoo.

"It was many days after the assassination of the Smiths before the circumstances of the murder became fully known. It then appeared that, agreeably to previous orders, the *posse* at Warsaw had marched on the morning of the 27th of June, in the direction of Golden's Point, with a view to join the force from Carthage, the whole body then to be marched into Nauvoo. When they had gone eight miles, they were met by the order to disband; and learning, at the same time, that the Governor was absent at Nauvoo, about two hundred of these men, many of them disguised, by blacking their faces with powder and mud, hastened immediately to Carthage. There they encamped at some distance from the village, and soon learned that one of the companies, left as a guard, had disbanded and returned to their homes; the other company, the Carthage Grays, was stationed by the Captain in the public square, a hundred and fifty yards from the jail, whilst eight men were detailed by him, under the command of Sergeant Franklin A. Worrell, to guard the prisoners. A communication was soon established between the conspirators and the company; and it was arranged that the guard should have their guns charged with blank cartridges, and fire at the assailants when they attempted to enter the jail. General Deming, who was left in command, being deserted by some of his troops, and perceiving the arrangement with the others, and having no force upon which he could rely, for fear of his life, retired from the village. The conspirators came up, jumped the slight fence around the jail, were fired upon by the guard, which, according to arrangement, was overpowered immediately, and the assailants entered the prison, to the door of the room, where the two prisoners were confined, with two of their friends, who voluntarily bore them company. An attempt was made to break open the door; but Joe Smith being armed with a six barrelled pistol, furnished by his friends, fired several times as the door was bursted open, and wounded three of the assailants. At the same time several shots were fired into the room, by some of which John Taylor received four wounds, and Hyrum Smith was instantly killed. Joe Smith now attempted to escape, by jumping out of the second-story window; but the fall so stunned him that he was unable to arise, and, being placed in a sitting posture by the conspirators below, they despatched him, with four balls shot through his body.

"Thus fell Joe Smith, the most successful impostor in modern times; a man who, though ignorant and coarse, had some great natural parts, which fitted him for temporary success, but which were so obscured and counteracted by the inherent corruption and vices of his nature, that he never could succeed in establishing a system of policy which looked to permanent success in the future. His lusts, his love of money and power, always set him to studying present gratification and convenience, rather than the remote consequences of his plans. It seems that no power of intellect can save a corrupt man from this error. The strong cravings of the animal nature will never give fair play to a fine understanding; the judgment is never allowed to choose that good which is far away, in preference to enticing evil near at hand. And this may be considered a wise ordinance of Providence, by which the counsels of talented but corrupt men are defeated in the very act which promised success.

"It must not be supposed that the pretended Prophet practised the tricks of a common impostor; that he was a dark and gloomy person, with a long beard, a grave, and severe aspect, and a reserved and saintly carriage of his person; on the contrary, he was full of levity, even to boyish romping; dressed like a dandy, and, at times, drank like a sailor, and swore like a pirate. He could, as occasion required, be exceedingly meek in his deportment, and then again rough and boisterous as a highway robber; being always able to satisfy his followers of the propriety of his conduct. He always quailed before power, and was arrogant to weakness. At times he could put on the air of a penitent, as if feeling the deepest humiliation for his sins, and suffering unutterable anguish, and indulging in the most gloomy forebodings of eternal woe. At such times, he would call for the prayers of the brethren on his behalf, with a wild and fearful energy and earnestness. He was full six feet high, strongly built, and uncommonly well muscled. No doubt he was as much indebted for his influence over an ignorant people, to the superiority of his physical vigor, as to his greater cunning and intellect.

"His followers were divided into the leaders and the led; the first division embraced a numerous class of broken-down, unprincipled men of talent, to be found in every country, who, bankrupt in character and fortune, had nothing to lose by deserting the known religions, and carving out a new one of their own. They were mostly infidels, who holding all religions in derision, believed they had as good a right as Christ or Mahomet, or any of the founders of former systems, to create one for themselves; and, if they could impose it upon mankind, to live upon the labour of their dupes. Those of the second division were the credulous, wondering part of men, whose easy belief and admiring natures are always the victims of novelty in whatever shape it may come; who have a capacity to believe any strange and wonderful matter, if it only be new, whilst the wonders of former ages command neither faith nor reverence; they are men of feeble purposes, readily subjected to the will of the strong, giving themselves up entirely to the direction of their leaders; and this accounts for the very great influence of those leaders in controlling them. In other respects some of the Mormons were abandoned rogues, who had taken shelter in Nauvoo, as a convenient place for the headquarters of their villany; and others were good, honest, industrious people, who were the sincere victims of artful delusion. Such as these were more the proper objects of pity than persecution. With them, their religious belief was a kind of insanity; and certainly no greater calamity can befall a human being than to have a mind so constituted as to be made the sincere dupe of a religious imposture."

It were vain to attempt to describe the mingled feelings of grief and rage which agitated the people of Nauvoo, when the death of Joe Smith was announced there. All his errors and tyrannies seemed to be obliterated from their minds; he had "sealed the truth with his blood," and stood henceforth a sainted martyr. The spiritual wives of the dead Prophet filled the city with their cries, but his lawful wife Emma was quiet and resigned. When Joseph and Hyrum retreated across the river to avoid the constable first sent from Carthage, she had joined with the Apostle William Marks in writing them an indignant letter, in which she charged them as "cowardly shepherds, who had left the sheep in danger and fled." This statement rests upon the testimony of Joseph F. Smith, son of Hyrum, now an Apostle at Salt Lake, who adds : " When Joseph saw that letter his great heart almost bursted, and he said, 'If that is all my wife and friends care for my life, then I don't care for it,' and returned and gave himself up."

The whole people turned out, in deep mourning, and with every demonstration of grief, and the remains of Joseph and Hyrum were honored with a magnificent funeral. Joseph was thirty-nine, and Hyrum forty-four years old. In the short space of fifteen years Joe Smith and his coadjutors had brought forth a new Bible, ordained a new morality, established a new theology, and founded a Church with missions in half the civilized world. Organized in 1830, the Church, at the time of their death, numbered probably two hundred thousand throughout the world. The Mormons themselves claimed half a million. But they have probably never exceeded the former number since that time. Under the lead of Brigham Young they made tolerable progress for a few years, but are certainly losing in numbers at present. In the very germ of the new sect was planted a fatal principle of progress in evil, which, by its appeal to the vagaries and vices of men, gave a predisposition to rapid rise and the assurance of early decay. From a living and erring Prophet of personal prowess and prestige, the progress was regular and natural to intrigue, grossness and materialism ; materialism and sanctified lust necessitated polygamy, and polygamy has in the perfect order of nature proved the mother of incest and blood atonement. From the worship of a human demigod of passion, under a light and false mantle of religion, the descent was easy to the worship of only sensual forms and practices. There is nothing more surprising in it than in the progress from the serpent's egg to the deadly viper. Nor is it strange that the sect increased rapidly ; every century, and almost every generation, has witnessed the sudden rise of

DEATH OF JOSEPH SMITH.

a corrupt and law-defying sect; and modern society still presents ample materials. As like produces like, and everything its kind in nature, so the evil-hearted and credulous will be led to worse evil by any religion that does not convert and reform. The various sects, too, have lost much of that burning and aggressive vigor which distinguished their rise; and redemptive agencies have not, in all respects, kept pace with sinful allurement, and a fair field has been left for delusion. The minister in many cases still travels on horseback, while the devil goes by rail. With all the power of evangelical organization and gospel at work, Satan too often rides upon the whirlwind of popular passion, and subsidizes by trick and prejudice the very enthusiasm of man's nature.

The Methodists, who formerly prided themselves on a hearty simplicity and earnest work among the masses. have too often attained to the elegant conservatism of the Old Mother; they are in some places fixed almost in gilded formalism, and in others reduced to the prejudiced following after traditions of religion, both lacking much the kindling of the "fire from the altar." The Baptists, who were also the hardy pioneers, have so entrenched themselves about as to be separated from other denominations in sympathy, and almost from the world, leaving themselves open, at least, to the charge of following "the water-god of exclusive errorists." The Presbyterians, whose [universal suffrage should be peculiarly suited to the genius of our whole people, seemed to have struck but a certain class of quietly reserved tastes; and they appear to the world as much interested in preserving the authority of an ancient Confession of Faith as in vitalizing their republicanism for the conversion of the people. The Campbellites have developed a controversial spirit which may well be suspected of having gone beyond a mere zeal for the truth. The Episcopalians, with an organization essentially monarchical in form, looking to its dignitaries for authority and power, divided even here as to the policy of carrying this principle further, cannot yet be said to be fully naturalized as an American church. All have attained to a more formal, or sober and intellectual sort of religion. Nor should we quarrel with this, of itself. Intellectual men must have an intellectual faith ; a mere emotional experience is quite impossible to them, nor would it content them. Notwithstanding this, the Unitarians, a sect whose faith is more purely one of philosophy and taste, have shown little vitality in extending their bounds. There is still the great mass of men who will be content with nothing short of a simple religion, warmed with a generous enthusiasm ; and this, in the hands or under the direction of corrupt or crazy men, becomes a wild, fierce fanaticism. Not that religion should accommodate the vices of human nature ; but while it reforms them it should give virtuous direction to that enthusiasm which will otherwise rend and tear them. It is not at all too late for another successful delusion. Millions pant for novelty, for a personal *god*, for present light and prophecy, for something harmonious entirely with our own day and nation, more real, more tangible, not a mere matter of two thousand years of church erudition and history, grand as they are in the triumphs of an improving civilization.

In the midst of such excitement in the West came the impostor, and to the lowest manifestation of this want Mormonism was addressed. But Mormonism could never be a success in America, because it controverted the inherent American idea ; it turned back to sensualism for its inspiration, and to despotism for its model. Had it been founded on progressive instead of retrograde ideas, had it developed individuality and personal freedom, had it claimed a higher consideration for the feminine in creation, and a more perfect independence for woman, had it stepped forward, and not back, then it might have helped to reform all America, and founded a permanent, new order.

The religious public may then be re-assured ; Mormonism is not *the* religion or sect which is to play havoc among existing systems. But the signs of the times indicate a *new* or modified *phase of religion*. We will have a distinctly American Church. The Roman Empire Christianized made Roman Catholicism, which has been reformed, as its people have in the governments; Russia made the finished Greek system; Italy is Ultramontane Catholic; England has the Establishment; Scandinavia has the Lutheran Church; each nation has developed one central, theological and ecclesiastical idea, and we are not yet so fully completed and individualized, as to be without the same want and yearning. Perhaps one of the present sects will modify and *advance* to the needed place; or from the spirit of union in *many*, may come the ascendant and satisfying *one*. The Church of the future must be both intellectual and emotional; it must look to the future for its hope, and to our own land for its governing polity, and not to worn out systems which have proved too weak for earthly means; as truth is immortal it must look only for new developments of truth; it must *purify the marriage* relation, and recognize the political and social independence of woman; it must *believe* in sanctification, even if it does not claim to have obtained it, and it must make unceasing war upon every species of oppression, and every form of intemperance. Such a Church must have more truth than error, both in method and creed and, for it, a broad field is open.

But Mormonism was a mushroom growth upon a rich bed of decay, which sprang up merely because *something better was not planted*, but had no enduring root. It might flourish for half a century or more, upon the scum of vice in America, and the ignorance of Europe, but could enjoy at best but a sort of living death, and must soon wither and decay.

CHAPTER IV.

TWO YEARS OF STRIFE—EXODUS FROM ILLINOIS.

No Successor to the Prophet—David Hyrum Smith, the "Son of Promise"—Contest for the Leadership—Diplomacy of Brigham Young—Curious Trials—All of Brigham's Opponents "cut off"—Troubles Renewed—Fights, Outrages, Robberies and Murder—Another Election and more Treachery—Singular "Wolf Hunt"—Capture and Trial of Smith's Murderers—Of the Mormon Rioters—Failure and Defects of the Law—Further Outrages on Gentiles — Troubles in Adams County—The "Oneness"—The People of Adams Drive out the Mormons—Revenge by the Mormons—Murders of McBratney, Worrell, Wilcox, and Daubeneyer—Retaliation, and Murder of Durfee -The Mormons Ravage Hancock—Flight of the Gentiles—Militia Called, and Hancock put under Martial Law—The Mormons Begin to Leave Illinois—Fresh Quarrels—More Mormon Treachery—Bombardment of Nauvoo, and Final Expulsion of the Mormons.

THE hostility of the Gentiles suddenly relaxed, and a brief period of repose followed. But it was necessary to provide for the government of the Church. The theocratic polity had been fully established by Joe Smith, but no provision made for a successor. The Prophet had, it is true, laid his hands on the head of his eldest son Joseph, and ordained him a king and a priest in his stead, and but a short time before his death he stated, " the man was not born who was to lead this people, but of Emma Smith—then promising him an heir—should be born a son who would succeed in the Presidency, after a season of disturbance." This son named, from his father's direction, David Hyrum, was born at the Mansion House, on the 17th of November following. This is the "son of promise," whom thousands of Mormons still regard as the predestined leader, who is finally to bring them back to Jackson County.

But an immediate leader was needed. Many had revelations that Joseph would, like the Saviour, rise from the dead, and some reported that they had seen him coursing the air on a great white horse. But all these were finally condemned by the priesthood as "lying revelations." William Smith, the Prophet's only surviving brother, claimed the succession on that account. Sidney Rigdon, who was one of the First Presidency, from his peculiar relations to the Church, asserted the strongest claim. James Strang had an immediate revelation that he was to lead the people into Wisconsin. Lyman Wight received a divine order to go to Texas, and Gladden Bishop, John E. Page, Cutler, Hedrick, Brewster and others laid in their claims.

On the 15th of August, the Twelve Apostles, headed by Brigham Young, addressed an "Encyclical letter to all the Saints in the world," and the 7th of October, the Saints of Nauvoo and vicinity met in council to determine who should take control. Brigham had been absent in Boston, and Rigdon, very busy among the people, had succeeded in getting a special convention called; but Brigham arrived the very day of the meeting, and signally defeated Rigdon. The people voted that the government should for the present be in the "College of Twelve Apostles," which was in effect making Brigham chief ruler. The next day Brigham made a savage address against Sidney Rigdon, who, meanwhile, had a revelation that all the wealthy members were to follow him to western Pennsylvania, and establish a new "stake" for the others to gather to! Brigham then denounced Rigdon and all his revelations as from the devil, and moved that he be "cut off." Nearly a hundred voted in the negative, when it was immediately resolved they were in a spirit of apostacy and they were "cut off." It was then proposed and unanimously carried, that "all who should hereafter defend Rigdon should be cut off," which ended the so-called election. Rigdon took a small band to Pennsylvania, and most of the other aspirants also took off various sects, known in the Brighamite church as "Gladdenites," "Strangeites," "Brewsterites," "Cutlerites," "Gatherers," etc. Most of these sects have fallen to pieces. The *Times and Seasons*, a weekly periodical, had been established at Nauvoo soon after its settlement, and in the fifth volume may be found a full account of these curious trials.

Brigham Young now took entire control, hastened the completion of the upper rooms of the Temple, and hurried the people through their "endowments." These consist of a mystical ceremony representing the various stages in man's progress, during which the candidates are initiated and passed to the various degrees of the priesthood, and sworn to obey all orders of their superiors. The penalties for violation of these oaths are, according to the uniform testimony of various apostates, "having the throat cut," the "bowels slit across," the "heart plucked out," or the " blood spilt upon the ground," according to the several degrees. Brigham consolidated his power rapidly, but, by the opening of 1845, outside hostility again began to be felt, and the leaders secretly resolved to abandon Nauvoo.

The malcontents from the city, and those who had suffered, would run away to anti-Mormon neighborhoods, and stir up hatred against the Saints. Gentiles, who owned property near Nauvoo, found it practically worthless, for they could sell it to no other Gentiles; and in the county at large, where the Mormons settled around an old resident, his society was gone ; he could have no church nor school privileges ; he could not affiliate or be neighborly with the new comers, and often suspected them of trespass and constant annoyance. His land lost half its value, and the near presence of foreigners of the fanatic sect caused him to be forever on his guard. It became a settled conviction in the minds of the people that they could have no peaceful enjoyment of their property while the Saints remained. Gentiles combined in groups for society and protection, and the Mormons did the same at command of the Church, to which they were bound by such absolute oaths ; and this, of course, led to local and sectional hatred, which, among people who habitually wore arms, soon culminated in blood. Men became afraid to stir abroad, except in squads ; riots and regular skirmishes, amounting almost to pitched battles, took place ; blood was shed, lives were lost, and the exasperation of both parties was raised to the highest pitch. The Western press teemed with accounts of the enormities of Nauvoo, no doubt, greatly exaggerated, but still with considerable basis of truth. A horrible murder was committed in Lee County, Iowa, and the perpetrators were traced directly to Nauvoo. At least a dozen Mormons swore positively that the accused were in that city at the time of the murder; and yet so contradictory was their testimony and so plain the rest of the evidence, that the murderers, two brothers named Hodges, were convicted and hanged at Montrose, Iowa. It was whispered about that they would be rescued by a Mormon force, and nearly every man in southern Iowa, then but eighty miles wide, the rest to the Missouri being Indian country, attended the execution. This case excited all of Iowa as well as Illinois afresh against Nauvoo. Conspicuous among the journals of that period, in advocating the expulsion or extermination of the Mormons, were the *Sangamo Journal*, *Burlington Hawk-eye*, *Quincy Whig* and *Warsaw Signal*. At the same time, the executive of the State was accused openly of favoring the Mormons. Perhaps no fact in Mormon history so fully illustrates the blind unreason of the laity, or the corruption and treachery of the leaders, as their treatment of the Governor, Thomas L. Ford. He had been elected with the aid of their votes, and had always maintained that the crusade against them was only for political effect; he had been their friend in most difficult situations, and had even strained the facts to make a sort of excuse for them; he had done all that was supposed necessary to save the Smiths, and had risked his popularity and life to bring their murderers to punishment. And yet they are never weary of heaping abuse upon him, because he did not accede to other demands on their part; they generally accuse him of conniving at the murder of the Smiths, and heap execrations upon his memory. It must be remembered, that Governor Ford wrote his history the year after the Mormons left, that it is not so much a history of the State as a defence of his administration, that, politically, he was more of an enemy to the anti-Mormons of

Western Illinois than to the Mormons, and consequently inclined to make as favorable a showing as possible for the latter. With this comment, or caution rather, I return to his account:

"About one year after the apostles were installed in power, they abandoned, for the present, the project of converting the world to the new religion. All the missionaries and members abroad were ordered home; it was announced that the world had rejected the gospel by the murder of the Prophet and Patriarch, and was to be left to perish in its sins. In the meantime, both before and after this, the elders at Nauvoo quit preaching about religion. The Mormons came from every part pouring into the city; the congregations were regularly called together for worship, but instead of expounding the new gospel, the zealous and infuriated preachers now indulged only in curses and strains of abuse of the Gentiles, and it seemed to be their design to fill their followers with the greatest amount of hatred to all mankind, excepting the 'Saints.' A sermon was no more than an inflammatory stump speech, relating to their quarrels with their enemies, and ornamented with an abundance of profanity. From my own personal knowledge of this people, I can say, with truth, that I have never known much of any of their leaders who was not addicted to profane swearing. No other kind of discourses than these were heard in the city. Curses upon their enemies, upon the country, upon Government, upon all public officers, were now the lessons taught by the elders, to inflame their people with the highest degree of spite and malice against all who were not of the Mormon Church, or its obsequious tools. The reader can readily imagine how a city of fifteen thousand inhabitants could be wrought up and kept in a continual rage by the inflammatory harangues of its leaders.

"In the meantime, the anti-Mormons were not idle; they were more than ever determined to expel the Mormons; and, being passionately inflamed against them, they made many applications for executive assistance. On the other hand, the Mormons invoked the assistance of Government to take vengeance upon the murderers of the Smiths. The anti-Mormons asked the Governor to violate the Constitution, which he was sworn to support, by erecting himself into a military despot, and exiling the Mormons. The Mormons, on their part, in their newspapers, invited the Governor to assume absolute power, by taking a summary vengeance upon their enemies, by shooting fifty or a hundred of them, without judge or jury. Both parties were thoroughly disgusted with Constitutional provisions, restraining them from summary vengeance; each was ready to submit to arbitrary power, to the fiat of a dictator, to make me a king for the time being, or at least that I might exercise the power of a king, to abolish both the forms and spirit of free government, if the despotism to be erected upon its ruins could only be wielded for their benefit, and to take vengeance on their enemies.

"Another election was to come off in August, 1844, for members of Congress, and for the Legislature; and an election was pending throughout the nation for a President of the United States. The war of party was never more fierce and terrible than during the pendency of these elections. As a means of allaying the excitement, and making the question more manageable, I was most anxious that the Mormons should not vote at this election, and strongly advised them against doing so. But Col. E. D. Taylor went to their city a few days before the election, and the Mormons, being ever disposed to follow the worst advice they could get, were induced by him and others to vote all the Democratic candidates. Col. Taylor found them very hostile to the Governor, and on that account much disposed not to vote at this election. The leading Whig anti-Mormons, believing that I had an influence over the Mormons, for the purpose of destroying it, had assured them that the Governor had planned and been favorable to the murder of their Prophet and Patriarch. The Mormons pretended to suspect that the Governor had given some countenance to the murder, or at least had neglected to take the proper precautions to prevent it.

"In the course of the fall of 1844, the anti-Mormon

leaders sent printed invitations to all the militia captains in Hancock, and to the captains of militia in all the neighboring counties in Illinois, Iowa, and Missouri, to be present with their companies at a great wolf hunt in Hancock; and it was privately announced that the wolves to be hunted were the Mormons, and Jack Mormons.* Preparations were made for assembling several thousand men, with provisions for six days; and the anti-Mormon newspapers, in aid of the movement, commenced anew the most awful accounts of thefts and robberies, and meditated outrages by the Mormons. The Whig press, in every part of the United States, came to their assistance. The Democratic newspapers and the leading Democrats, who had received the benefit of the Mormon votes to their party, quailed under the tempest, leaving no organ for the correction of public opinion, either at home or abroad, except the discredited Mormon newspaper at Nauvoo. But very few of my prominent Democratic friends would dare to come up to the assistance of their Governor, and but few of them dared openly to vindicate his motives in endeavoring to keep the peace. They were willing and anxious for Mormon votes at elections, but they were unwilling to risk their popularity with the people, by taking a part in their favor, even when law and justice, and the constitution were all on their side— such being the odious character of the Mormons, the hatred of the common people against them, and such being the pusillanimity of leading men, in fearing to encounter it.

"In this state of the case I applied to Brigadier-General J. J. Hardin of the State militia, and to Colonels Baker and Merriman, all Whigs, but all of them men of military ambition, and they, together with Colonel William Weatherford, a Democrat, with my own exertions, succeeded in raising about five hundred volunteers; and thus did these Whigs that which my own political friends, with two or three exceptions, were slow to do, from a sense of duty and gratitude.

---

* A slang name applied to Gentiles who favor the Mormons.

"With this little force under the command of General Hardin, I arrived in Hancock County on the 25th of October. The malcontents abandoned their design, and all the leaders of it fled to Missouri. The Carthage Grays fled almost in a body, carrying their arms along with them. During our stay in the county the anti-Mormons thronged into the camp, and conversed freely with the men, who were fast infected with their prejudices, and it was impossible to get any of the officers to aid in expelling them. Colonels Baker, Merriman, and Weatherford volunteered their services if I would go with them, to cross with a force into Missouri, to capture three of the anti-Mormon leaders, for whose arrest writs had been issued for the murder of the Smiths. To this I assented, and procured a boat which was sent down in the night, and secretly landed a mile above Warsaw. Our little force arrived at that place about noon; that night we were to cross the Missouri at Churchville, and seize the accused there encamped with a number of their friends; but that afternoon Colonel Baker visited the hostile camp, and on his return refused to participate in the expedition, and so advised his friends.— There was no authority for compelling men to invade a neighboring State, and for this cause, much to the vexation of myself and others, the matter fell through. It seems that Colonel Baker had already partly arranged the terms for the accused to surrender. They were to be taken to Quincy for examination under a military guard; the attorney for the people was to be advised to admit them to bail, and they were to be entitled to a continuance of their trial at the next Court at Carthage; upon this, two of the accused came over and surrendered themselves prisoners.

"I employed able lawyers to hunt up the testimony, procure indictments and prosecute the offenders. A trial was had before Judge Young in the summer of 1845. The Sheriff and panel of jurors selected by the Mormon Court were set aside for prejudice, a new panel was ordered and elisors were appointed for this purpose; but as more than a thousand men had assembled under arms at the court to keep away the Mormons and their friends, the jury was made up of these military followers of the court, who all swore that they had never formed or expressed an opinion as to the guilt or innocence of the accused. The Mormons had one principal witness, who was with the troops at Warsaw, had marched with them until they were disbanded, heard their consultations, went before them to Carthage, and saw them murder the Smiths. But before the trial came on they had induced him to become a Mormon; and being much more anxious for the glorification of the Prophet than to avenge his death, the leading Mormons made him publish a pamphlet giving an account of the murder, in which he professed to have seen a bright and shining light descend upon the head of Joe Smith, to strike some of the conspirators with blindness, and that he heard supernatural voices in the air confirming his mission as a Prophet! Having published this in a book, he was compelled to swear to it in court, which, of course, destroyed the credit of his evidence. This witness was afterwards expelled from the Mormons, but no doubt they will cling to his evidence in favor of the divine mission of the Prophet. Many other witnesses were examined who knew the facts, but, under the influence of the demoralization of faction, denied all knowledge of them. It has been said, that faction may find men honest, but it scarcely ever leaves them so. This was verified to the letter, in the history of the Mormon quarrel. The accused were all acquitted.

"At the next term the leading Mormons were tried and acquitted for the destruction of the heretical press. It appears that, not being interested in objecting to the Sheriff or jury selected by a court elected by themselves, they, in their turn, got a favorable jury determined upon acquittal; and yet the Mormon jurors all swore that they had formed no opinion as to the guilt or innocence of their accused friends. It appeared that the laws furnished the means of suiting each party with a jury. The Mormons could have a Mormon jury to be tried by, selected by themselves; and the anti-Mormons, by objecting to the Sheriff and regular panel, could have one from the anti-Mormons. Henceforth no leading man on either side could be arrested without the aid of an army, as the men of one party could not safely surrender to the other for fear of being murdered; when arrested by a military force, the Constitution prohibited a trial in any other county without the consent of the accused. No one would be convicted of any crime in Hancock; and this put an end to the administration of the criminal law in that distracted county, government was at an end there, and the whole community was delivered up to the dominion of a frightful anarchy. If the whole State had been in the same condition, then indeed would have been verified to the letter what was said by a wit, when he expressed an opinion that the people were neither capable of governing themselves, nor of being governed by others."

Late in 1845, the Mormon Charters were revoked by the Legislature, which act that body evidently considered a cure for all the evils of Mormonism.

"Nauvoo was now a city of about 15,000 inhabitants, and was fast increasing, as the followers of the Prophet were pouring into it from all parts of the world; and there were several other settlements and villages of Mormons in Hancock County. Nauvoo was scattered over about six square miles, a part of it being built upon the flat, skirting and fronting on the Mississippi River, but the greater portion of it upon the bluffs back, east of the river. The great Temple, which is said to have cost a million of dollars in money and labor, occupied a commanding position on the brow of this bluff, and overlooked the country around for twenty miles in Illinois and Iowa.

"The anti-Mormons complained of a large number of larcenies and robberies. The Mormon press at Nauvoo and the anti-Mormon papers at Warsaw, Quincy, Springfield, Alton, and St. Louis, kept up a constant fire at each other; the anti-Mormons all the time calling upon the people to rise and expel, or exterminate, the Mormons.— The great fires in Pittsburg and in other cities about this time, were seized upon by the Mormon press to countenance the assertion that the Lord had sent them to manifest his displeasure against the Gentiles, and to hint that all other places which should countenance the enemies of the Mormons, might expect to be visited by 'hot drops' of the same description. This was interpreted by the anti-Mormons to be a threat by Mormon incendiaries to burn down all cities and places not friendly to their religion. About this time also, a suit had been commenced in the circuit court of the United States against some of the Twelve Apostles, on a note given in Ohio. The deputy marshal went to summon the defendants. They were determined not to be served with process, and a great meeting of their people being called, outrageously inflammatory speeches were made by the leaders; the marshal was threatened and abused for intending to serve a lawful process, and here it was publicly declared and agreed to by the Mormons, that no more processes should be served in Nauvoo. Also, about this time, a leading anti-Mormon by the name of Dr. Marshall, made an assault upon Gen. Deming, the Sheriff of the County, and was killed by the Sheriff in repelling the assault. The Sheriff was arrested and held to bail by Judge Young, for manslaughter; though, as he had acted strictly in self-defence, no one seriously believed him to be guilty of any crime whatever. But Dr, Marshall had many friends disposed to revenge his death, and the rage of the people ran very high, for which reason it was thought best by the judge to hold the Sheriff to bail for something, to save him from being sacrificed to the public fury.

"Not long after the trials of the supposed murderers of the Smiths, it was discovered on the trial of a right of property near Lima, in Adams county, by Mormon testimony, that that people had an institution in their Church called a " Oneness," which was composed of an association of five persons, over whom one was appointed as a kind of guardian. This one was trustee for the rest, was to own all the property of the association; so that if it were levied upon by an execution for debt, the Mormons could prove that the property belonged to one or the other of the parties, as might be required to defeat the execution. And not long after this discovery, in the fall of 1845, the anti-Mormons of Lima and Green Plains held a meeting to devise means for the expulsion of the Mormons from their neighborhood. They appointed some persons of their own number to fire a few shots at the house where they were assembled; but to do it in such a way as to hurt none who attended the meeting. The meeting was held, the house was fired at, but so as to hurt no one; and the anti-Mormons suddenly breaking up their meeting, rode all over the country, spreading the dire alarm that the Mormons had commenced the work of massacre and death.

"This startling intelligence soon assembled a mob, which proceeded to warn the Mormons to leave the neighborhood, and threatened them with fire and sword if they remained. A very poor class of Mormons resided there, and it is very likely that the other inhabitants were annoyed beyond further endurance by their little larcenies and rogueries. The Mormons refused to remove; and about one hundred and seventy-five houses and hovels were burnt, the inmates being obliged to flee for their lives. They fled to Nauvoo in a state of utter destitution, carrying their women and children, aged and sick, along with them as best they could. The sight of these miserable creatures aroused the wrath of the Mormons at Nauvoo. As soon as authentic intelligence of these events reached Springfield, I ordered General Hardin to raise a force and restore the rule of law. But whilst this force was gathering, the Sheriff of the County had taken the matter in hand. General Deming had died not long after the death of Dr. Marshall, and the Mormons had elected Jacob B. Backinstos to be Sheriff in his place. Being just now regarded as the political leader of the Mormons, Backinstos was hated with a sincere and thorough hatred by the opposite party.

"When the burning of the houses commenced, the great body of the anti-Mormons expressed themselves strongly against it, giving hopes thereby that a posse of anti-Mormons could be raised to put a stop to such incendiary and riotous conduct. But when they were called on by the new Sheriff, not a man of them turned out to his assistance, many of them no doubt being influenced by their hatred of the Sheriff. Backinstos then went to Nauvoo, where he raised a posse of several hundred armed

Mormons, with which he swept over the country, took possession of Carthage, and established a permanent guard there. The anti-Mormons everywhere fled from their houses before the Sheriff, some of them to Iowa and Missouri, and others to the neighboring counties in Illinois. The Sheriff was unable or unwilling to bring any portion of the rioters to battle, or to arrest any of them for their crimes. The posse came near surprising one small squad, but they made their escape, all but one, before they could be attacked. This one, named McBratney, was shot down by some of the posse in advance, by whom he was hacked and mutilated as though he had been murdered by the Indians.

"The Sheriff was also in continual peril of his life from the anti-Mormons, who daily threatened him with death the first opportunity. As he was going in a buggy from Warsaw in the direction of Nauvoo, he was pursued by three or four men to a place in the road where some Mormon teams were standing. Backinstos passed the teams a few rods, and then stopping, the pursuers came up within one hundred and fifty yards, when they were fired upon, with an unerring aim, by some one concealed not far to one side of them. By this fire* Franklin A. Worrel was killed. He was the same man who had commanded the guard at the jail at the time the Smiths were assassinated; and there made himself conspicuous in betraying his trust by consenting to the assassination. It is believed that Backinstos expected to be pursued and attacked, and had previously stationed some men in ambush, to fire upon his pursuers. He was aftewards indicted for the supposed murder, and procured a change of venue to Peoria County where he was acquitted of the charge. About this time also, the Mormons murdered a man by the name of Daubeneyer, without any apparent provocation; and another anti-Mormon, named Wilcox, was murdered in Nauvoo, as it was believed, by order of the twelve Apostles. The anti-Mormons also committed one murder.

---

* It has since transp'red that "Port" Rockwell fired the fatal shot; and the gun he used is still preserved as a triumphant relic, in Salt Lake City.

Some of them, under Backman, set fire to some straw near a barn belonging to Durfee, an old Mormon of seventy years; and then lay in ambush until the old man came out to extinguish the fire, when they shot him dead from their place of concealment. The perpetrators of this murder were arrested and brought before an anti-Morman justice of the peace, and were acquitted, though their guilt was sufficiently apparent.

"During the ascendancy of the Sheriff and the absence of the anti-Mormons from their homes, the people who had been burnt out of their homes assembled at Nauvoo, from whence, with many others, they sallied forth and ravaged the country, stealing and plundering whatever was convenient to carry or drive away. When informed of these proceedings, I hastened to Jacksonville, where, in a conference with General Hardin, Major Warren, Judge Douglas, and the Attorney General, Mr. McDougall, it was agreed that these gentlemen should proceed to Hancock in all haste, with whatever forces had been raised, few or many, and put an end to these disorders. It was now apparent that neither party in Hancock could be trusted with the power to keep the peace. It was also agreed that all these gentlemen should unite their influence with mine to induce the Mormons to leave the State. General Hardin lost no time in raising three or four hundred volunteers, and when he got to Carthage he found a Mormon guard in possession of the Court House. This force he ordered to disband and disperse in fifteen minutes. The plundering parties of Mormons were stopped in their ravages. The fugitive anti-Mormons were recalled to their homes, and all parties above four in number on either side were prohibited from assembling and marching over the country.

"Whilst General Hardin was at Carthage, a convention previously appointed assembled at that place, composed of delegates from the eight neighboring counties. The people of the neighboring counties were alarmed lest the anti-Mormons should entirely desert Hancock, and by that means leave one of the largest counties in the State to be possessed entirely by Mormons. This they feared would bring the surrounding counties into immediate collision with them. They had, therefore, appointed this convention to consider measures for the expulsion of the Mormons. The twelve Apostles had now become satisfied that the Mormons could not remain, or, if they did, the leaders would be compelled to abandon the sway and dominion they exercised over them. They had now become convinced that the kind of Mahometanism which they sought to establish could never be maintained in the near vicinity of a people whose morals and prejudices were all outraged and shocked by it, unless indeed they were prepared to establish it by force of arms. Through the intervention of General Hardin, acting under instructions from me, an agreement was made between the hostile parties for the voluntary removal of the greater part of the Mormons in the spring of 1846.

"The two parties agreed that, in the meantime, they would seek to make no arrests for crimes previously committed; and on my part, I agreed that an armed force should be stationed in the county to keep the peace. The presence of such a force and amnesty from prosecutions on all sides were insisted on by the Mormons that they might devote their time and energies to prepare for their removal. General Hardin first diminished his force to one hundred men, leaving Major William B. Warren in command. And this force being further reduced during the winter to fifty, and then to ten men, was kept up until the last of May, 1846. This force was commanded with great prudence and efficiency during all this winter and spring by Major Warren; and with it he was enabled to keep the turbulent spirit of faction in check, the Mormons well knowing that it would be supported by a much larger force whenever the Governor saw proper to call for it. In the meantime, they somewhat repented of their bargain, and desired Major Warren to be withdrawn. Backinstos was anxious to be again at the head of his posse, to goster over the country and to take vengeance on his enemies. The anti-Mormons were also dissatisfied, because the State force preserved a threatening aspect toward them as well as the Mormons. He was always ready to enforce arrests of criminals for new offences on either side; and this pleased neither party. Civil war was upon the point of breaking out more than a dozen times during the winter. Both parties complained of Major Warren; but I, well knowing that he was manfully doing his duty, in one of the most difficult and vexatious services, steadily sustained him against the complaints on both sides. Great credit is due General Hardin and Major Warren for their services, which had the happiest results, and prevented a civil war in the winter time, when much misery would have followed it.

"During the winter of 1845–'46, the Mormons made the most prodigious preparations for removal. All the houses in Nauvoo, and even the Temple, were converted into workshops; and before spring more than twelve thousand waggons were in readiness. The people from all parts of the country flocked to Nauvoo to purchase houses and farms, which were sold extremely low, lower than the prices at a sheriff's sale, for money, waggons, horses, oxen, cattle, and other articles of personal property, which might be needed by the Mormons during their exodus into the wilderness. By the middle of May it was estimated, that sixteen thousand Mormons had crossed the Mississippi and taken up their line of march westward; leaving behind them in Nauvoo a small remnant of a thousand souls, being those who were unable to sell their property, or, having none to sell, were unable to get away.

"The twelve Apostles went first with about two thousand of their followers. Indictments had been found against nine of them in the Circuit Court of the United States for the district of Illinois, at its December term, 1845, for counterfeiting the current coin of the United States. The United States Marshal had applied to me for a militia force to arrest them; but in pursuance of the amnesty agreed upon, and consequent considerations, I declined the application unless regularly called on by the President according to law. The arrest of the leaders would end the preparations for removal, and it was notorious that none of them could be convicted; for they always commanded evidence and witnessess enough to render conviction impossible. But with a view to hasten their removal they were made to believe that the President would order the regular army to Nauvoo as soon as navigation opened in the spring. This had its intended effect; the twelve with about two thousand followers immediately crossed the Mississippi before the breaking up of the ice. But before this, the deputy marshal had sought to arrest the accused without success.

"Notwithstanding but few of the Mormons remained behind, after June, 1846, the anti-Mormons were no less anxious for their expulsion by force of arms; being another instance of a party not being satisfied with success not brought about by themselves, and by measures of their own. It was feared that the Mormons might vote at the August election of that year; and that enough of them yet remained to control the elections in the county, and perhaps in the district for Congress. They, therefore, took measures to get up a new quarrel with the remaining Mormons. And for this purpose they attacked and severely whipped a party of eight or ten Mormons, which had been sent out in the country to harvest some wheat in the neighborhood of Pontoosuc, and who had provoked the wrath of the settlement by hallooing, yelling, and other arrogant behavior. Writs were sworn out in Nauvoo against the men of Pontoosuc, who were kept for several days under strict guard until they gave bail. Then, in their turn, they swore out writs for the arrest of the constable and his posse who had made the first arrest, for false imprisonment. The Mormon posse were no doubt really afraid to be arrested, believing that they would be murdered. This made an excuse for an anti-Mormon posse of several hundred men; but the matter was finally adjusted without any one being taken. A committee of anti-Mormons was sent into Nauvoo, who reported that the Mormons were making every possible preparation for removal; and the leading Mormons on their part agreed that their people should not vote at the next election.

"The August election soon came, and the Mormons all voted the whole Democratic ticket. I have since been informed by Babbitt, the Mormon elder and agent for the sale of Church property, that they were induced to vote this time from the following considerations:

"The President of the United States had permitted the Mormons to settle on the Indian lands on the Missouri River, and had taken five hundred of them into the service as soldiers in the war with Mexico; and, in consequence of these favors, the Mormons felt under obligations to vote for Democrats in support of the Administration; and so determined were they that their support of the President should be efficient, that they all voted three or four times each for a member of Congress.

"This vote of the Mormons enraged the Whigs anew against them; the probability that they might attempt to remain permanently in the country, and the certainty that many designing persons for selfish purposes were endeavoring to keep them there, revived all the excitement which had ever existed against that people. In pursuance of the advice and under the direction of Archibald Williams, a distinguished lawyer and a Whig politician of Quincy, writs were again sworn out for the arrest of persons in Nauvoo, on various charges. But to create a necessity for a great force to make the arrests, it was freely admitted by John Carlin, the constable sent in with the writs, that the prisoners would be murdered if arrested and taken out of the city. And now having failed to make the arrests, the constable began to call out the *posse comitatus*. This was about the 1st of September, 1846. The posse soon amounted to several hundred men. The Mormons, in their turn, swore out several writs for the arrest of leading anti-Mormons. Here was writ against writ; constable against constable; law against law, and posse against posse.

"Whilst the parties were assembling their forces, the trustees of Nauvoo being new citizens, not Mormons, applied to the Governor for a militia officer to be sent over with ten men, they supposing that this small force would dispense with the services of the civil posse on either side. There was such a want of confidence on all side, that no one would submit to be arrested by an adversary, for fear of assassination.

"In looking around over the State for a suitable officer, those upon whom I had relied in all previous emergencies having gone to the Mexican war, the choice fell upon Major Parker, of Fulton County. He was a Whig, and was selected partly for that reason, believing that now, as in previous cases, a Whig would have more influence in restraining the anti-Mormons than a Democrat.

"The posse continued to increase until it numbered about eight hundred men; and whilst it was getting ready to march into the city, it was represented to me by another committee that the new citizens of Nauvoo were themselves divided into two parties, the one siding with the Mormons, the other with their enemies. The Mormons threatened the disaffected with death, if they did not join in defence of the city. For this reason, I sent over M. Brayman, Esq., a judicious citizen of Springfield, with suitable orders restraining all compulsion, in forcing the citizens to join the Mormons against their will, and generally to inquire into and report all the circumstances of the quarrel. Soon after Mr. Brayman arrived there, he persuaded the leaders on each side into an adjustment of the quarrel. It was agreed that the Mormons should immediately surrender their arms to some person to be appointed to receive them, and to be re-delivered when they left the State, and that they would remove from the State in two months. This treaty was agreed to by General Singleton, Colonel Chittenden and others on the side of the Antis, and by Major Parker and some leading Mormons on the other side. But when the treaty was submitted to the anti-Mormon forces for ratification, it was rejected by a small majority. General Singleton and Colonel Chittenden, with a proper self respect, immediately withdrew from command; they not being the first great men placed at the head of affairs at the beginning of violence, who have been hurled from their places before the popular frenzy had run its course. And with them also great Archibald Williams, the prime mover of the enterprise, he not being the first man who has got up a popular commotion and failed to govern it afterwards. Indeed, the whole history of revolutions and popular excitements leading to violence is full of instances like these. Mr. Brayman, the same day of the rejection of the treaty, reported to me that nearly one-half of the anti-Mormons would abandon the enterprise and retire with their late commanders, 'leaving a set of hair-brained fools to be flogged or to disperse at their leisure.' It turned out, however, that the calculations of Mr. Brayman were not realized; for when Singleton and Chittenden retired, Thomas S. Brockman was put in command of the posse. This Brockman was a Campbellite preacher, nominally belonging to the Democratic party. He was a large, awkard, uncouth, ignorant, semi-barbarian; ambitious of office, and bent upon acquiring notoriety. After the appointment of Brockman, I was not enabled to hear in any authentic shape of the movements on either side, until the anti-Mormon forces had arrived near the suburbs of the city, and were about ready to commence an attack. The information which was received, was by mere rumor of travellers, or by the newspapers from St. Louis. And I will remark that, during none of these difficulties, have I been able to get letters and despatches from Nauvoo by the United States mail, coming, as it was obliged to do, through anti-Mormon settlements and Post Offices."

The Governor's account proceeds to state the efforts and failures to raise an additional force of militia to quell the disturbance; that, if any had been raised, it would have only operated to increase the excitement and the anti-Mormon force; that, it was his solemn conviction, no sufficient force could have been raised to fight in favor of the Mormons; that no force could have more than temporarily suppressed the difficulties, and such was the public prejudice against the Mormons, that, ten chances to one, any large force of militia which might have been ordered there would have joined the rioters, rather than fought in favor of the Mormons.

"The forces under Brockman numbered about 800 men; they were armed with the State arms, which had been given up to them by independent militia companies in the adjacent counties. They also had five six-pounder iron cannon, belonging to the State, which they had obtained in the same way. The Mormon party and their allies, being some of the new citizens under the command of Major Clifford, numbered, at first, about two hundred and fifty men, but were diminished by desertions and removals, before any decisive fighting took place, to about one hundred and fifty. Some of them were armed with sixteen shooting rifles, which experience proved ineffective in their hands, and a few of them with muskets. They had four or five cannon, rudely and hastily made by themselves out of the shaft of a steamboat. The Mormons and their allies took position in the suburbs, about one mile east of the temple, where they threw up some breastworks for the protection of their artillery. The attacking force was strong enough to have been divided and marched into the city, on each side of this battery, and entirely out of the range of its shot; and thus the place might have been taken without the firing of a gun. But Brockman, although he professed a desire to save the lives of his men, planted his force directly in front of the enemy's battery, but distant more than half a mile; and now both parties commenced a fire from their cannon, and some few persons on each side approached near enough to open a fire with their rifles and muskets, but not near enough to do each other material injury.

"In this manner they continued to fire at each other, at such a distance, and with such want of skill, that there was but little prospect of injury, until the anti-Mormons had exhausted their ammunition, when they retreated in some disorder to their camp. They were not pursued, and here the Mormons committed an error, for all experience of irregular forces has shown that, however brave they may be, a charge on them when they have once commenced to retreat, is sure to be successful. Having waited a few days to supply themselves with ammunition from Quincy, the Antis again advanced to the attack, but without coming nearer to the enemy than before, and that which, at the time, was called a battle, was kept up three or four days, during all which time the Mormons admit a loss of two men and a boy killed, and three or four wounded. The Antis admit a loss, on their side, of one man mortally, and nine or ten others not so dangerously, wounded. The Mormons claimed that they had killed thirty or forty of the Anties. The Anties claimed that they had killed thirty or forty of the Mormons ; and both parties could have proved their claim by incontestable evidence, if their witnesses had been credible. But the account which each party renders of its own loss should be taken as the true one, unless such account can be successfully controverted. During all the skirmishing and firing of cannon, it is estimated that from seven to nine hundred cannon balls, and an infinite number of bullets, were fired on each side, from which it appears that the remarkable fact of so few being killed and wounded can be accounted for, only, by supposing great unskilfulness in the use of arms, and by the very safe distance which the parties kept from each other.

At last, through the intervention of an anti-Mormon committee, of one hundred, from Quincy, the Mormons and their allies were induced to submit to such terms as the posse chose to dictate, which were, that the Mormons should immediately give up their arms to the Quincy committee, and remove from the State. The trustees of the Church, and five of their clerks, were permitted to remain for the sale of Mormon property, and the posse were to march in unmolested, and to leave a sufficient force to guarantee the performance of these stipulations.

"Accordingly the constable's posse marched in, with Brockman at their head, consisting of about eight hundred armed men, and six or seven hundred unarmed, who had assembled, from all the country around, from motives of curiosity, to see the once proud city of Nauvoo humbled, and delivered up to its enemies, and to the domination of a self-constituted and irresponsible power. They proceeded into the city slowly and carefully, examining the way, from fear of the explosion of a mine, many of which had been made by the Mormons, by burying kegs of powder in the ground, with a man stationed at a distance to pull a string communicating with the trigger of a percussion lock, affixed to the keg. This kind of contrivance was called by the Mormons a ' hell's half-acre.'

I

When the posse arrived in the city, the leaders of it erected themselves into a tribunal to decide who should be forced away and who remain. Parties were despatched to hunt for Mormon arms and for Mormons, and to bring them to the judgment, where they received their doom from the mouth of Brockman, who then sat a grim and unawed tyrant for the time. As a general rule, the Mormons were ordered to leave within an hour or two hours; and by rare grace some of them were allowed until next day, and in a few cases longer.

"The treaty specified that the Mormons only should be driven into exile. Nothing was said in it concerning the new citizens, who had, with the Mormons, defended the city. But the posse no sooner obtained possession, than they commenced expelling the new citizens. Some of them were ducked in the river, being, in one or two instances, actually baptized in the name of the leaders of the mob; others were forcibly driven into the ferry boats, to be taken over the river, before the bayonets of armed ruffians; and it is asserted that the houses of most of them were broken open, and their property stolen during their absence.

"Although the mob leaders, in the exercise of unbridled power, were guilty of many enormities to the persons of individuals, and though much personal property was stolen, yet they abstained from materially injuring houses and buildings. The most that was done in this way was the stealing of the doors and sash of the windows from a few houses by somebody; each party equally alleging that it was done by the other.

" The Mormons had been forced away from their homes, unprepared for a journey. They and their women and children had been thrown houseless upon the Iowa shore, without provisions or the means of getting them, or to get away to places where provisions might be obtained. It was now the height of the sickly season. Many of them were taken from sick beds, hurried into the boats, and driven away by the armed ruffians, now exercising the power of government. The best they could do was to erect their tents on the banks of the river, and there remain to take their chances of perishing by hunger, or by prevailing sickness. In this condition the sick, without shelter, food, nourishment or medicines, died by scores. The mother watched her sick babe, without hope, until it died, and when she sank under accumulated miseries, it was only to be quickly followed by her other children, now left without the least attention; for the men had scattered out over the country, seeking employment and the means of living. Their distressed condition was no sooner known, than all parties contributed to their relief; the anti-Mormons as much as others."

CHAPTER V.

FROM THE NAUVOO EXODUS TO THE MORMON WAR IN UTAH.

The *Via Dolorosa* of Mormon History—Through Iowa—Great suffering—"Stakes of Zion"—Settlement in Nebraska---"Mormon Battalion"---Journey to Utah---Founding of Salt Lake City---Early accounts---Outrages upon California emigrants---Travellers murdered---Apostates "missing"---Dangers of rivalry in love with a Mormon Bishop---Usurpations of Mormon Courts and officers---Federal Judges driven out---Murders of Babbitt and Williams---Flight of Judges Stiles and Drummond---The Army set in motion for Utah---New officers appointed---Suspicious delay of the army---The "Mormon war begun."

THE last of the Mormons was exiled from the State which had gladly received them seven years before, and we turn to their march through Iowa—the *Via Dolorosa* of Mormon history. A band of pioneers through Iowa left Nauvoo the 20th day of January, 1846, and the same day the High Council issued a circular announcing the general intention to leave. Early in February, several thousand Mormons crossed the Mississippi, many of them on the ice, and started directly west, along a line near the northern boundary of Missouri. They were divided into companies of ten waggons each, under control of captains, and this semi-military order was maintained throughout. As the spring advanced, many of the able-bodied men scattered to various places in Missouri and Iowa, seeking employment of every kind, and the remaining men, with a great band of women and children, pursued their way. In that climate and at that season, their sufferings were necessarily great. The high waters, wet prairie, damp winds, and muddy roads of spring troubled them worse than the frosts of winter, and sickness and death increased. "All night," says a woman who made the journey, "the waggons came trundling into camp with half frozen children screaming with cold, or crying for bread, and the same the next day, and the next, the whole line of march.

"The open sky and bare ground for women and children in February is a thing only to be endured when human nature is put to the rack of necessity, and many a mother hastily buried her dead child by the wayside, only regretting she could not lie down with it herself and be at peace."

On their way they established "Stakes," and when the weather had sufficiently advanced, enclosed large fields and planted them with grain for those who were to follow after. The most noted of these "stakes" were Garden Grove and Mt. Pisgah. They bridged the Nishnabatona, Nodaway and Grand Rivers, besides many smaller streams, and later, when the grass was grown, turned northward.

But the advance of the season seemed to increase the amount of disease; hundreds who had been frost-bitten and chilled during the winter died along the way, and the route was lined with graves. Still the zeal of the survivors sustained them, and the cruel ambition of their leader forced them on; and though many deserted and turned away to various Gentile settlements, a majority remained. As successive parties left Nauvoo, the trains were spread over a line of a hundred miles; but, during the latter part of the season they concentrated in the Pottawattomie country, extending up and down the Missouri from Council Bluffs. Here they built ferry boats, and a part crossed the river. Preparations for the winter were made on both sides; cabins were built, rude tents erected, and "dugouts," dwellings half under ground, constructed. Many young men went back to the States, and hired out to work for provisions, which were forwarded to the camp. According to other witnesses, a band of horse and cattle thieves was organized under the control of Orson Hyde, and a gang of counterfeiters sent into Missouri. In the July previous they had been visited by Captain James G. Allen, of the United States Dragoons, with whom Brigham Young entered into negotiations to furnish a battalion for the Mexican War. The Mormons were the more ready to enter this service, as they expected to be discharged in

California, where the Church then intended to settle. Five hundred men were enrolled in a few days, and proceeded to Leavenworth, where they were mustered into the service of the United States. An agent of Brigham Young accompanied them thus far and received twenty thousand dollars of their advanced bounty, which was understood to be for the support of their families during their absence. Several of them, since apostatized, testified that none of it was ever so appropriated. The battalion was placed under the command of Colonel Philip Saint George Cooke, and started forthwith on the noted overland march of General Kearny.

They marched two thousand and fifty miles to San Diego, California, passing through the mountains of southern Colorado and New Mexico, and across the "desert of death." One company of them re-enlisted for a short time in California, many apostatized and the rest made their way to Salt Lake City. The main body of the Saints meanwhile concentrated at what is now Florence, six miles north of Omaha, which they called Winter Quarters. There they built five hundred log houses, one grist mill, and several "horse mills;" there the Church was completely reorganized; the "Quorum of Three" re-established, and it was unanimously resolved that "the mantle of the Prophet Joseph had fallen on the Seer and Revelator, Brigham Young;" who was accordingly chosen to all the offices and titles of the dead Prophet.

On the eastern side of the Missouri, were still some two thousand waggons scattered in various camps, each bearing the name of its leader. Many of these names remain in the local nomenclature of that country, as Cutlers, Perkins, Millers, etc. At this time they were visited by Colonel (since General) Thos. L. Kane, of Philadelphia, who continued with them some time, crossed a portion of the plains with them, and figured extensively in an important period of Mormon history. Elder John Hyde, the noted apostate, says that Kane there embraced Mormonism, but this seems quite improbable. During the winter Orson Pratt, Parley P. Pratt, and John Taylor went on a mission to England, giving general notice to the Saints abroad, that the next "gathering place would be in Upper California." At a conference held before they left Nauvoo, to determine their destination, Lyman Wight had strongly urged Texas, John Taylor proposed Vancouver's Island, many were in favor of Oregon, and Brigham Young insisted upon California. They finally fixed indefinitely upon "some valley in the Rocky Mountains."

In accordance with this conclusion, the "Pioneer Band," a hundred and forty-three men, driving seventy wagons, under the command of Brigham Young, left Winter Quarters, April, 14th, 1847, and followed Fremont's Trail westward up the Platte River. West of the Black Hills, they diverged and followed a "trapper's trail" for four hundred miles, and from Bear River westward, laid out a new route through Emigration Canon to Jordan Valley.

The company entered the Valley July 24th, now celebrated as "Anniversary Day." They found willows and other scant vegetation about a rod wide along City Creek, and this stream they dammed, and dug an irrigating ditch. They planted a few potatoes, from which they raised enough that year to serve for seed for a large plat, though no bigger than chesnuts. They proceeded also to lay out a city, and in October, Brigham Young and a few others went back to Winter Quarters. The people had suffered greatly with cholera, fever, and inflammatory diseases, and the "Old Mormon Graveyard" at Florence contains seven hundred graves of that winter, of which two hundred are of children. Vast numbers had "fallen into apostacy," or turned away and joined themselves to recusant sects; and all their fair-weather friends had forsaken them. But the little remnant were at least consolidated in sentiment strengthened and confirmed together by mutual suffering, firm and self-reliant ; and something over four thousand made the journey to Salt Lake the following season. But the small party left in the valley had raised but a scant crop, and though the new comers had transported all the provisions they could, there was great scarcity. Every head of a family issued rations to those dependent upon him, and many children received, for months, " each one biscuit a day and all the *sego* roots they could dig."

Wolves, raw hides, rabbits, thistle roots, *segos*, and everything that would support life was resorted to. In 1849, a plentiful crop was raised, furnishing enough for food and a small surplus. February 20th, 1848, emigration from Great Britain was re-commenced, after a suspension of two years. On the 10th of November of that year, the inhabitants of Nauvoo were awakened at an early hour by a fire in the Mormon Temple, which was soon beyond their control and in a short time everything was destroyed but the bare walls. The city was largely occupied by a colony of Icarians, French Communists, under the lead of M. Cabet, and they had begun to refurnish the building for a social hall and schoolroom. The *Hancock Patriot* of that date gives a full account of the misfortune, showing conclusively that the building had been fired by an incendiary. "But it is," says the *Patriot*, "impossible to assign a probable motive. The destroyer certainly had less worthy feelings than the man who fired the 'Ephesian Dome.' Admit that it was a monument of folly and evil, it was at least a splendid and harmless one."

Many have since supposed that it was fired by an emissary from a rival city. The walls still stood in such perfect preservation, that nearly two years after the citizens determined to roof and finish it for an Academy; but on May 27th, 1850, a violent hurricane swept over Iowa and Illinois and prostrated the structure, leaving only a portion of the western wall, and now naught but a shapeless pile of stones marks the spot. Mormon annals give many interesting incidents of their first three years in Utah, but this record can deal particularly only with that portion of their history where they came in immediate contact with the Gentiles. For two years they seem to have had it all their own way; if there were Gentiles resident in Salt Lake City before 1849, they were "braves before Agamemnon," history makes no mention of them. Of course there were trappers and mountaineers who occasionally visited the city, and a few parties of emigrants passed that way even before the great rush of '49. Lieutenant Ruxton's "Life in the Far

West" gives an account of a visit to the new city, which is both amusing and romantic, and M. Violet, the French chief among the Shoshonees, visited the Mormon settlements soon after their establishment. For three years the Mormons devoted all their energies to developing the country and getting ready to live; their extreme poverty prevented their being either very enterprising in reaching out towards their neighbors, or particularly anxious to encroach on any one. Quite a number of Gentiles had met with them in various places on the plains and accompanied them some distance; but Colonel Thomas L. Kane, who made most of the journey with them, and witnessed their early efforts, has left the only account approaching to exactness of these early years. The great rush of gold hunters in 1849, was coeval with a season of plenty, and the associations seems to have been mutually beneficial to Mormons and pioneers, but none of the latter appear to have halted in "Zion." They were in too eager haste to gain the new Eldorado. As early as 1846 a few emigrants passed this way to the Pacific coast, and the latter part of that year one Hastings led a party by a new route south of the Lake, since known as "Hastings Cut-off."

It is estimated by those living at various military posts on the overland route, that from five to ten thousand emigrants from the United States had crossed to the Pacific coast before the discovery of gold. Fort Bridger had been occupied several years by Colonel James Bridger, the oldest mountaineer in that region, who had been engaged in the Indian trade there, and upon the head waters of the Missouri and Columbia since 1819. Early in 1849, General Wilson, newly appointed Indian Agent for California, passed through Salt Lake City, making a short stay, and late the same year ·Captain Howard Stansbury, of the United States Topographical Engineers, reached the city and remained till the next May. This officer, with his assistant, Lieutenant Gunnison, set out from Leavenworth, Kansas, on the 31st of May, 1849; travelling up the Blue River to its head, he crossed over to the Platte and followed the main emigrant route as far as Fort Bridger.

Thence he endeavored to find a more direct route to the head of the lake than the one usually followed by Fort Hall, in Idaho, which required a "northing" of nearly two degrees. In pursuance of this intention he followed the "Mormon Road" west to Bear River, then followed down that stream northward, six miles to Medicine Butte, from which he sought a route due west, but was obliged to turn again to the south and struck upon the head of Pumbars Creek, a tributary of the Weber.

From this hollow he passed over another ridge to Ogden Hole, long the *rendezvous* of the North-west Fur Company, on account of its fine range for stock in winter. From this place he passed out into the main valley, and from the "bench" north-west of Ogden, on the 27th of August, caught his first view of the Great Salt Lake. Thinking, as he stated, that his success depended somewhat upon the good-will of the Mormons, he visited Salt Lake City at once, and seems to have formed a very favorable opinion. He acknowledges the courtesy and assistance of the Mormons, "as soon as the true object of the expedition was understood." His party were probably the first Gentiles who ever spent more than a month or two in Salt Lake City. Late in 1849, or early in 1850, Messrs. Livingston and Kinkead, pioneer merchants, opened a store in Salt Lake City, and from the extent of their trade, the Saints seemed to have realized handsomely on their sales to the California emigrants.

Captain Stansbury completed his survey of the Great Salt Lake, and set out on his return to the States in August, 1850; and soon after an immense emigration appeared on their way to California. The association of the preceding year seems to have created great confidence, and nearly all these emigrants made a lengthy stay in the Mormon settlements. For three years the Mormons had been almost unheard of in the States, most of the prejudice against them had died out, and had the policy of the first year been pursued, mutual good-will would have been established on a firm basis and the settlement in Utah considered a real blessing.

But renewed prosperity, plenty and increasing numbers had produced their usual effects, arrogance, spiritual pride, and a desire to dominate over "the unbelievers," and numerous difficulties arose. Late in the season a large number of emigrants were persuaded that it was unsafe to continue the westward route at that season, and concluded to remain all winter among the Mormons. They represent that all was pleasant until autumn was too far advanced for them to leave even by the southern route, after which a series of merciless exactions began, and never ceased as long as the Mormon civil authorities could find pretences for bogus legal actions, or the emigrants had anything of which they could be stripped. Those who had hired out to work for Mormons were re-used their pay, and denied redress in the courts; if difficulties arose, fines of from one to five hundred dollars were imposed for the slightest misdemeanors; in all suits between Mormon and Gentile, the latter invariably paid the costs; they were openly reviled in court by the Mormon Judges, and in one peculiarly aggravating instance Justice Willard Snow boasted to Gentiles in his court that "the time was near at hand, when he would judge Gentiles for life and death, and then he would snatch their heads off like chickens in the door yard."

In one case an emigrant died near the Hot Springs, and his three companions buried him and proceeded on their way without notifying the city authorities. Complaint was made that some city ordinance had been violated; they were pursued, taken back to the city, and every dollar they had, as well as their waggon and all their stock, were taken to pay their fine and costs. Another Gentile was struck over the head with a board by Bill Hickman, and returned the blow, for which he was arrested and fined eighty dollars; the costs made up the amount to more than two hundred dollars, but as he had but little over half the sum, they kindly contented themselves with taking all he had, and let him depart. Many who had come in with a complete "outfit," finished their journey on foot. When these emigrants reached the general rendezvous on the Sacramento, they began to compare notes. And as each new comer added to the evidence, it was thought best to compile their statements to send to their eastern friends. Accordingly the affidavits of five hundred of them were selected, reduced to form, and, with their names appended, published and circulated generally in the East.

This book, of which a copy may be found in the State library at Sacramento, contains statements of facts which seem almost incredible, even with our present knowledge of Mormon law and its administration; but they rest on the sworn testimony of reliable men, who now reside in Tuolumne, Amador, Placer, Nevada, Sierra, and other mining counties of California.

This publication roused all the old bitterness of feeling against the Mormons, which was not a little heightened soon after by the shameless avowal on their part of polygamy and incest as features of their religion. Meanwhile, by the treaty of Guadaloupe Hidalgo, in 1848, all that section had passed from the dominion of Mexico to that of the United States, and early in 1849, the Mormon authorities called a convention "of all the citizens of that portion of Upper California lying east of the Sierra Nevada Mountains, to take into consideration the propriety of organizing a Territorial or State Government." This convention met at Salt Lake City on the 5th of March, 1849, and in a short session "ordained and established a *free and independent* Government, by the name of the STATE OF DESERET," fixed the boundaries of the new State and provided for the election of a Governor and all State officers. On the 2nd of July following, the Legislature of the new State met, elected a delegate to Congress, adopted a memorial also to that body, in which they set forth their loyalty, patriotism and material progress, population and other qualifications and asked for admission.

Congress, however, failed to see it precisely in that light, and on the 9th of September, 1850, passed an Act to organize the Territory of Utah, of which President Fillmore appointed Brigham Young Governor. In return for this courtesy, Brigham soon after preached one of his "live sermons," in which he said; "Why, when that time comes (the earthly reign of the Saints) the Gentiles will come begging to us to be our servants. I know several men, high in office in the Nation, who would make good servants. I expect the President of the United States to *black my boots.*" This was, to say the least, unkind of Brigham. At the same time, Lemuel C. Brandenburg was appointed Chief Justice; Perry E. Brochus, and Zerubbabel Snow (Mormon), Associate Justices; Seth M. Blair (Mormon), Attorney General, and B. D. Harris, Secretary. Thus the President had divided the offices pretty equally between Saint and Gentile. The officers did not reach Utah till July, 1851, at which time there were a few Gentiles resident in Salt Lake City, mostly carpenters and other artisans whose labor was just then in special demand, emigrants who had failed at that point on their way to the Pacific, and perhaps half a dozen California traders or cattle dealers. The new Gentile officers soon found themselves involved in difficulty; Judge Brochus rashly attempted to preach against polygamy, and, having his life threatened, soon after left the Territory, followed in 1852, by Secretary Harris, leaving the government once more in the hands of the Mormons. Brigham Young appointed his second counsellor, Willard Richards, to fill the vacant Secretaryship, the sole remaining Judge Z. Snow and the District Attorney being " good Mormons."

A few Spaniards, who had come into Utah from the South, were tried before Snow, and convicted " of buying Indian children for slaves," whether justly or not cannot now be determined. The Indians were taken from the Gentiles, and turned over to the " brethren," to make them, according to prophecy, " a fair and delightsome people." An Indian war soon after broke out, and occasional difficulties continued through 1852, '53, and '54. In place of the judges who had resigned, President Pierce appointed Judges Leonidas Shaver and Lazarus H. Reed; the former arrived in the fall of '52, the latter in June, '53. Judge Shaver was a " hail fellow, well met," and lived on the best of terms with the Mormons for some time, but at length a sudden quarrel occurred between him and Brigham Young. He occupied a room in a house belonging to Elder Howard Coray, but rented by a Mr. Dotson.

One night he retired in his usual health, and the next morning was found dead in his bed. The Church authorities ordered a thorough investigation, and the Coroner's jury of Mormons decided that he died of "some disease of the head." One physician gave it as his opinion, that the Judge had been greatly addicted to the use of opium, and died in consequence of being suddenly deprived of it; and this is the popular belief among the Mormons. Only one witness on this matter was ever examined in the States, and she gave it as her opinion that he had been poisoned, adding that she had heard Brigham Young say: "Judge Shaver knew too much, and he dare not allow him to leave the Territory." Being an apostate Mormon, her evidence may be true or untrue. The Mormons treated Judge Reed with marked courtesy, and after a stay of one year he left with an exalted opinion of them. He went to his home in New York, intending to return, but died very suddenly while there.

About this time, a young man named Wallace A. C. Bowman, a native of New York, arrived at Salt Lake from New Mexico, with a company of Spanish traders. He met Brigham Young and his "body guard" at Utah Lake, and, according to his companion's account, had some difficulty with the latter. On his arrival in the city, he was arrested by Robert T. Burton on several charges. He was kept in confinement several weeks, but no evidence appearing against him was released. He started east at once, but was shot and instantly killed in a cañon but a few miles from the city, "by Indians," according to the Mormon account; by Nerton and Ferguson, "Danites," according to the same witness above mentioned. As in that case, it is now impossible to tell which story is true. John F. Kinney, of Iowa, was appointed Chief Justice to succeed Reed, and George P. Stiles, Associate Justice; Joseph Holman, of Iowa, Attorney General, and Almon W. Babbitt, Secretary. In the spring of 1855, W. W. Drummond, of Illinois, was also appointed Associate Justice.

In the fall of 1854, Colonel Steptoe, with about three hundred men of the United States Army, reached Salt

Lake and spent the winter. At the same time quite a number of Gentiles, on their way to, or returning from, California, wintered in the city. It is now known that Colonel Steptoe had been secretly commissioned Governor of Utah, by President Pierce, but, being of an uncautious disposition, he attempted to practise polygamy on a free and easy plan, not approved by the Saints, the result of which was, that he was ingeniously trapped by two of Brigham's "decoy women," and, to avoid exposure, resigned his commission, and recommended Young's continuance in that office. Utah now began to be regarded as the "Botany Bay of worn-out politicians;" if a man was fit for nothing else, and yet had to be rewarded for political services, he was sent to Utah.

During all the period from 1852 to 1856 numerous "Gladdenites" and other apostate and recusant Mormons were frequently slipping away and crossing to California and Oregon ; and many of these parties, as well as trains of Gentile emigrants, were harassed in various ways, which could hardly be accounted for by Indian hostility. Almon W. Babbitt, having quarrelled with Brigham, started across the plains in 1855, and was murdered " by Indians who spoke good English;" and, of this case, Brigham said, "He lived a fool and died like a fool. When officers undertake to interfere with affairs that do not concern them, I will not be far off. He undertook to quarrel with me, *and soon after was killed by the Indians,*"

In 1852 Lieutenant Gunnison, M. Creuzfeldt, the botanist, and eight of their party, were massacred near Sevier Lake, by Indians, as then reported ; but, soon after, escaped apostates stated that it was done by " painted Mormons." In 1851 a Mr. Tobin came to Salt Lake with a party, and while there was quite intimate with Brigham's family. It is reported also that he was engaged to Brigham's daughter, Alice Young. He returned in 1856, but had some difficulty and left. His party was attacked at night on the Santa Clara, three hundred and seventy miles south, many of them wounded, and six of their horses killed ; but they escaped by abandoning their baggage.

Not an arrow was shot at them, their clothing was pierced by bullets, the wounds were evidently from the best make of rifles, and they all testify that the attacking party spoke English. Other parties of recusant Mormons were missed in Nevada; several emigrants from Missouri were last heard of near Salt Lake, and others had their stock run off, where it was reasonably certain there were no hostile Indians.

A recusant testifies that "one of the Missourians had boasted of helping to drive the Saints from Jackson County, and that he was kidnapped and murdered under the old mint, by John Kay and other 'Danites'" A young man in Cache Valley had a difficulty with the bishop, in regard to a girl whom the bishop wanted for a "plural wife." The young man was seized in a cañon by two men with blackened faces, and by them mutilated in an unspeakable manner. He afterwards went to San Bernardino, California, and died insane. A similar difficulty arose in a settlement on the Weber, and the young man was found dead, having received two shots in the back. One general difficulty exists in all these cases. The witnesses were all apostate Mormons. While the writer would not stigmatize a whole class, among whom he has many pleasant acquaintances, and which contains some thoroughly honest and reliable men, yet it must be confessed that, of those who have lived Mormons for a term of years, the outside world must always remain in doubt.

There were very few Gentiles in Salt Lake, their interests required that they should know nothing outside their business, and they generally took care to make no inquiry. Hence little definite and positive proof of the affairs of that period was laid before the Government; but these reports spread through the West and constantly increased the bitterness against the Mormons. Had the latter shown any willingness to throw light upon disputed points, their case would have a much better appearance. But their preaching constantly excited the people to greater hostility against the Government, and their courts and officers regularly thwarted every attempt of the Federal officials to inquire into reported crimes, or bring offenders to justice. In the fall of 1856, it became no longer possible for the Federal Judges to maintain the independence of their courts. The Mormons claimed that the Territorial Marshal should select the jurors for Federal courts, when doing Territorial business, instead of the United States Marshal.

Pending the decision of this question, James Ferguson, Hosea Stout, and other Mormon lawyers and officials, entered the court-room, with an armed mob, and compelled Judge Stiles to adjourn his court. Thomas Williams, a Mormon lawyer, who had an office with Judge Stiles, protested against this action, for which his life was threatened. He soon after tried to escape to California, but was murdered on the way.

The records of the District Courts were soon after stolen from Judge Stiles's office and, as he supposed at the time, destroyed. Both the Gentile Judges soon after left the Territory, reaching the States in the spring of 1857. The Mormons were now in open rebellion. Congress was not in session, but President Buchanan and War Secretary Floyd determined to send an armed force with new officials. Accordingly, a force of nearly three thousand men was sent forward from Leavenworth, under the command of Gen. W. S. Harney, who was, while on the plains, superseded by Col. Albert Sidney Johnston. At the same time new men were appointed to all the civil offices, as follows: Governor, Alexander Cumming; Chief Justice, D. R. Eckles; Associate Justices, John Cradlebaugh and Charles E. Sinclair, and Secretary, John Hartnet.

The march of the column was delayed for various reasons, and it was late in September before the army, accompanied by the officials, crossed Green River and entered the Territory. Meanwhile Captain Van Vliet, an active and discreet officer, had been sent forward to purchase provisions for the army, and assure the people of Salt Lake of the peaceful intentions of the Government. On his arrival there, he was amazed to find them preparing for war.

J

CHAPTER VI

THE BLOODY PERIOD.

Sounds of war in Utah---Popular excitement---Fears of the disaffected---Attempted flight---Murder of the Potter and Parish families---Massacre of the Aiken party---Assassination of Yates---Killing of Forbes---Brigham "Turns loose the Indians"---MOUNTAIN MEADOW MASSACRE---Horrible Barbarity of Indians and Mormons---Evidence in the case---Attempt of Judge Cradlebaugh---Progress of the "Mormon War"---Delay of the army---Treachery or inefficiency?---Mormon Legion---Lieutenant General Wells---Brigham "Commands" the National troops to withdraw---Army trains destroyed---Lot Smith, the Mormon Guerilla---The "Army of Utah" in Winter Quarters---Colonel Kane again---Negotiations with Brigham.--Governor Cumming "passed" through the Mormon lines---"Peace Commissioners"---Mormon Exodus---Weakness of Cumming---End of the War---Murders of Pike, the Jones's, Bernard, Drown, Arnold, McNeil, and others---A change at last.

WE enter now upon the black chapter in the annals of Utah—a period replete with crime and stained with innocent blood. Occasional rumors of the march of the army had reached Salt Lake early in the season, and on the 24th of July, when the entire population were collected in Cottonwood Park to celebrate "Anniversary Day," "Port" Rockwell and John Kimball appeared among them just from the plains, and announced that the column was certainly destined for Utah. Brigham turned to those nearest him and with a savage scowl remarked, "I said when we reached here that if the devils would only give us ten years I'd be ready for them. They've taken me at my word, and now they will see that I *am* ready." The news spread rapidly through the settlements, producing everywhere fierce anger or a mixture of hope and dread, according as the hearer was firm in the Mormon faith or secretly dissatisfied. The Tabernacle and Ward Assembly Rooms resounded with harangues in fierce denunciation of the Government, and Brigham Young and Heber C. Kimball vied with each other in vile language and inflammatory appeals.

Brigham repeatedly stated that "if any proved traitor, or attempted to shield his own when the day came to burn and lay waste, he should be sheared down; for judgment should be laid to the line and righteousness to the plummet." The effect of such teaching upon a fanatical people may well be imagined. A perfect reign of terror ensued. Of those devoted to Brigham, every one was a spy upon his neighbors, while the disaffected trembled at the storm, and made efforts to escape. Two men by the name of Parrish at Springville, just south of Utah Lake, had declared their intention to start for California. The night before their intended departure their stock was run off, and going to search for it they were murdered but a few hundred yards from their dwelling, and after death their bodies mutilated in a shocking manner. Two of their neighbors, by the name of Potter, were killed at the same time. One Yates, a mountaineer, passing westward was assassinated in Echo Cañon, and a party of six from California, under the command of a Mr. Aikin, were attacked west of Salt Lake, and four of them instantly killed. The other two were promised they "should be sent out of the Territory by the southern route," and, in pursuance of that promise, started south under guard. They were never again heard of, and by the testimony of an apostate woman, Alice Lamb, they were killed and their bodies thrown into a large spring near the road. She adds that one was only stunned by the first shot, when Porter Rockwell stepped up, placed a pistol to his ear, and, adding, "This never misses," literally blew out his brains. The Mormons aver that this was a party of gamblers, that they carried with them "powder to drug Mormon women," and that "they deserved death anyhow;" and in all such cases they have established the principle of assassination. In this time of excitement, suspicion was proof. About the same time Brigham Young, preaching in the Tabernacle, stated that hitherto as Governor and Indian Agent, he "had protected emigrants passing through the territory, but now he would turn the Indians loose upon them."—

This hint was as good as a letter of *marque* to the land pirates of southern Utah, and was not long in being acted upon. Early in August, and before the excitement had reached its greatest height, a large train on its way to California reached Salt Lake City. Doctor Brewer, of the United States Army, who saw this train last at O'Fallon's Bluff, on the Platte, the 11th of June preceding, describes it as " probably the finest train that had ever crossed the plains. There seemed to be forty heads of families, many women, some unmarried, and many children. They had three carriages; one very fine, in which ladies rode and to which he made several visits as he journeyed with them. There was something peculiar in the construction of the carriage, its ornaments, the blazoned stag's head upon the panels, etc." This carriage was many years afterwards in the possession of the Mormons.

In Salt Lake City several disaffected Mormons joined the train, and all proceeded by the southern route. The train was last seen entire by Jacob Hamlin, Indian sub-agent for the Pah-Utes, who lived at the upper end of the Mountain Meadow. He met them at Corn Creek, eight miles south of Fillmore, while on his way to Salt Lake City. Thenceforward no more was heard of the train; it was "lost," and a whole year had passed before any news of its fate reached the officials.

Nor was it till many years afterwards, that all the damning facts in regard to its destruction were brought to light. But when revealed, it stands forth pre-eminent in shocking barbarity above all that has occurred in American history, scarcely equalled by aught in the old world, and certainly not by anything in the history of our English race. The massacre of Glencoe pales in comparison.

Without going into detail of the witnesses examined, or the evidence of each, suffice it to give events as they occurred, and as they were fully proved in various examinations since made. Mountain Meadow is three hundred miles from Salt Lake, on the road to Los Angelos, California. The meadows are about five miles in length, and one in width, on the "divide" between the waters of the Great Basin and the Colerado. A very large spring rises near the south end, by which the emigrants camped for a few days, having been told by Hamlin that this was the best place to rest and recruit their stock before entering upon the Great Desert. Thirty four miles below the Meadow is a Mormon settlement on the Santa Clara; thirty miles north is Cedar City, and eighteen miles east of that is the town of Harmony. From the "divide" down to the Colorado, are a few Pah-Ute Indians, and north to Fillmore, a small tribe of Pah-Vents. The day after the emigrants passed Cedar City, a grand council was called there by Bishop Higbee and President J. C. Haight of that town, and Bishop John D. Lee, of Harmony. They stated that they had received a command from Salt Lake City " to follow and attack those accursed Gentiles, and let the arrows of the Almighty drink their blood."

A force of sixty men was soon raised, and joined with a much larger force of Indians, encircled the emigrants' camp before daylight. The white men had, meanwhile, painted and disguised themselves as Indians. A portion crept down a ravine near the camp, and fired upon the emigrants while at breakfast, killing ten or twelve.

The latter were completely taken by surprise, but seized their arms, shoved the waggons together, sunk the wheels in the earth, and got in condition for defence. The idea that enough of the Utes of that district could be got together to attack a train with fifty armed men is too absurd to be entertained for a moment, and the emigrants had rested in the ease of fancied security.

But their resistance was far greater than the Mormons had expected; and there for an entire week, with their women and children lying in the trenches they had dug, they maintained the siege and kept the savages, as they supposed at bay. And all of this time, as testified by Mrs. Hamlin, wife of the Agent, the shots were constantly heard at Hamlin's ranche, and parties of Mormons, bishops, elders, and laymen, were coming and going to and from the ranche eating and drinking there, and "*pitching quoits and amusing themselves in various ways.*" They had the emigrants effectually secured, and could afford to divide time and slaughter the Gentiles at their leisure. But at the end of a week they grew tired and resolved upon strategy. The firing ceased, and while the weary and heart-sick emigrants looked for relief, and hoped their savage foes had given up the attack, they saw, at the upper end of the little hollow in which they were, a waggon full of men. The latter raised a white flag, and it was perceived that they were white men. A glad shout of joy rang through the *corral* at the sight of men of their own color, their protectors, as they had every reason to believe. They held up a little girl dressed in white to answer the signal, and the party entered. The waggon contained J. C. Haight, John D. Lee, and other dignitaries. They accused the emigrants of having poisoned a spring on the road used by the Indians, which was denied. It afterwards appeared in evidence that the spring ran so strong that "a barrel of arsenic would not have poisoned it." The Mormons said they were on good terms with the Indians, but the latter were very angry, and would not let the emigrants escape. The Mormons would, however, intercede for the latter, if desired. This offer was gladly accepted, and after a few hours' absence the Mormons returned and stated that the Indians gave as an ultimatum, that the emigrants should give up all their property, *particularly their guns*, and go back the way they came. The Mormons promised in this case to guard them back to the settlements. These hard terms were acceded to, and the emigrants left their waggons and started northward on foot.

The women and children were in front, the men behind them, and a Mormon guard of forty men in the rear. A mile or so from the spring, the road runs through a thicket of scrub oaks, where are also many large rocks, and here a force of Indians lay in ambush. At an agreed signal, a sudden fire was poured into the body of emigrants, and then Mormons and Indians together rushed upon them, shooting, cutting their throats, beating them to death with stones and clubs and in a very few minutes a hundred and twenty men, women and children, Americans, Christians, Gentiles, lay dead upon the ground, the miserable, hapless victims of Mormonism. The Mormons and Indians fell upon the women, bit and tore the rings from their fingers and ears, and trampled in the faces of the dying. One young girl was dragged aside by President Haight, and kneeling implored him for life. He violated her with shameful barbarity, then beat out her brains with a club. Another young woman was taken out of the throng by John D. Lee. He afterwards stated he intended to save her life and take her to his harem; but that she struck at him with a large knife, when he immediately shot her through the head. Three men escaped. One starved to death upon the desert, another was murdered by the Indians ninety miles south, and the third was killed upon the Colorado, by whom is not known. Seventeen children were saved alive, who were supposed to be too young to remember anything about the circumstance. But two of them did, and afterwards gave important evidence.

The children were first taken to Mrs. Hamlin's and afterwards distributed among Mormon families in the neighborhood; one was shot through the arm and lost the use of it. They were all recovered two years after and returned to their friends in the States. The property was divided, the Indians getting most of the flour and ammunition; but they claim that the Mormons kept more than their share. Much of it was sold in Cedar City *at public auction ;* it was there facetiously styled, "Property taken at the siege of Sebastopol;" and there is legal proof that the clothing stripped from the corpses, spotted with blood and flesh and shredded by bullets, was placed in the cellar of the tithing office and privately sold. As late as 1862, jewelry taken at Mountain Meadow was worn in Salt Lake City, and the source it came from not denied.

Such was the Mountain Meadow Massacre; and, to the eternal disgrace of American justice, not one of the perpetrators has ever been punished according to law. But the vengeance of heaven has not spared them. Some of the young men in the Mormon party have since removed to California, and others apostatized. They earnestly insist that they were never informed that any killing was intended; that they were told the only object was to turn back the emigrants and prevent their carrying information to California; that no more than a dozen white men, besides the Bishops and President, were in the secret, and that these, with the Indians did all the killing. This is the present belief of most of the Mormons, and they add that Haight and Lee forged the order from Brigham Young, which was produced in extenuation of the crime. Two of the principal perpetrators are now insane. John D. Lee still resides in Harmony, no longer a bishop, and one can scarcely restrain a feeling of satisfaction at knowing that his life is one of misery. He is shunned and hated even by his Mormon neighbors, he seldom ventures beyond the square upon which he lives, his mind is distracted by an unceasing dread of vengeance, and his intellect disordered.

Though a too lenient Government has failed of its duty, yet, in the sufferings of a fearful mind, he anticipates the hell his crimes deserve. Some months passed away before it was even whispered in the northern district that white men were concerned in this affair; and to the credit of the Mormon people be it said, a great horror spread among them at the report. A lady, then resident at Springville, told me that the people of that place first learned of the massacre the next spring, and the complicity of white men was put beyond doubt, in her mind, by the confession of her cousin, who was in the party but claimed he did not assist at the killing. "For weeks," she added: "I and the other women could not sleep for hearing the screams and groans of the poor creatures in our ears. We thought we saw signs in the sky. We trembled in dread. We wanted to run away from the land, for we thought it was cursed—that the vengeance of God would destroy everybody in the southern district." The lady escaped to Fort Bridger, and afterwards married a Gentile. The superstitious fears, of which she speaks, still rest in many minds; nor is it difficult to believe that, in the mysterious decrees of the moral order, the fearful stain must be washed out in blood. The guilty have escaped earthly justice; but to the eye of faith an avenging Nemesis is poised upon the mountains of southern Utah, and pointing to the plains below demands "blood for blood."

One question remains: Did Brigham Young know aught of, or give command for, this massacre? The strong probability of course, is, that he did not. The majority of the Mormons, while they admit that the church officials were concerned, yet claim that they acted without Brigham's knowledge, and his own family add, that when news of the affair was brought him, he burst into tears and said, "If anything could break up and destroy this people, that one act would do it." Against these opinions there are many strong proofs; the evidence of the Mormons and Indians engaged in the affair; the failure of Brigham to give any account of it, whatever, in his next report as Indian Superindendent; the complete silence of his organ, the Church paper, on the subject; his sermon "turning loose the Indians on emigrants;" the fact that *John D. Lee is his son by Mormon "adoption," and has never been punished;* the testimony of the young Mormons who escaped from Harmony to California, and more than all else, the overwhelming certainty that no fact of great importance is entered upon without the advice and consent of Brigham Young. An attempt was made by Judge Cradlebaugh, in the autumn of 1859, to bring the murderers to justice, which failed from causes to be hereafter fully explained—Mormon courts and juries.

I resume the regular history. On the 15th of September, 1857, Brigham issued a proclamation putting the territory under martial law; all the militia and able-bodied men were ordered "to hold themselves in readiness to march at a moment's notice to repel invasion," and Lieutenant-General Daniel H. Wells was ordered with two thousand men to "occupy the passes of the Wasatch mountains, to defend their hearths and homes against the violence of the army." Echo Cañon was fortified, and orders issued to harass the Federal Army in every way, by driving off stock, burning waggons and blocking up the roads, but to take no lives till further ordered. Besides several other papers, Brigham sent to the commander of the United States forces the following remarkable document:

"GOVERNOR'S OFFICE, UTAH TERRITORY,
GREAT SALT LAKE CITY, September 29th, 1857.

"SIR: By reference to the Act of Congress, passed September 9, 1850, organizing the Territory of Utah, published in a copy of the Laws of Utah, herewith, p. 146, Chap. 7, you will find the following:

"'SEC. 2. *And be it further enacted*, That the executive power in and over said Territory of Utah shall be vested in a Governor, who shall hold his office for four years, *and until his successor shall be appointed and qualified*, unless sooner removed by the President of the United States. The Governor shall reside within said Territory, shall be Commander-in-Chief of the militia thereof,' etc., etc.

"I am still the Governor and Superintendent of Indian Affairs for this Territory, no successor having been appointed and qualified, as provided by law, nor have I been removed by the President of the United States.

"By virtue of the authority thus vested in me, I have issued and forwarded you a copy of my proclamation, forbidding the entrance of armed forces into this Territory. This you have disregarded. I now further direct that you retire forthwith from the Territory by the same route you entered. Should you deem this impracticable, and prefer to remain until spring in the vicinity of your present encampment, Black's Fork, or Green River, you can do so in peace, and unmolested, on condition that you deposit your arms and ammunition with Lewis Robinson, Quartermaster-General of the Territory, and leave in the spring, as soon as the condition of the roads will permit you to march. And should you fall short of provisions, they can be furnished you by making the proper applications therefor.

"General D. H. Wells will forward this, and receive any communications you may have to make.

"Very respectfully,
"BRIGHAM YOUNG,
"*Governor and Superintendent of Indian Affairs, Utah Territory.*

"To the Officer commanding the Forces now invading Utah Territory."

It is difficult to believe that the Federal forces were handled with any skill whatever, the official report indicating that troops and supplies were scattered without order all the way from Green River to the head of Echo Cañon; and the following extract, from the official report, will show that the Mormon forces were "obeying orders :"

"Forts Bridger and Supply were vacated and burned down. Orders were issued by Daniel H. Wells (Lieut.-General, Nauvoo Legion) to stampede the animals of the United States troops on their march, to set fire to their trains, to burn the grass and the whole country before them and on their flanks, to keep them from sleeping, by night surprises, and to block the roads by felling trees, and destroying the fords of rivers.

"On the 4th of October, 1857, the Mormons, under Captain Lot Smith, captured and burned, on Green River, three of our supply trains, consisting of seventy-five waggons, loaded with provisions and tents for the army, and carried away several hundred animals."

Late in the fall, the army halted at Fort Bridger, and wintered at a place which was called Camp Scott. November 21st, the newly-appointed Governor, Cumming, issued a proclamation, which might be summed up in a little advice to the Mormons, "to go home and obey the laws, and they would not be molested."

While matters were in *statu quo*, in January, 1858, Colonel Kane, the old friend of the Mormons, proceeded to California by sea, thence into Utah by the southern route, and reaching Salt Lake City, opened negotiations with Brigham Young. Soon after he was escorted by Porter Rockwell and Daniel Kimball through the Mormon army, and thence found his way to Fort Bridger, and had a lengthy interview with the Federal officials. The result was that Governor Cumming accompanied him on his return, and was permitted to pass through the Mormon forces to Salt Lake City. He was much flattered with his reception, particularly by an illumination in his honor of Echo Cañon, which they passed in the night. They were escorted by Kimball and Rockwell, and reached the city early in the spring; the Mormons hastened to assure him that "the rebellion in Utah was a pure invention," and the records, which were supposed to have been destroyed, were produced entire! They had only been concealed.

Such flattery and attention were bestowed upon the Governor, that he was completely captivated, and such earnest representations made, that he was soon convinced the Mormons were an innocent and much abused people, and was anxious to spare them all humiliation possible. But he could not control the army, which had orders from the Secretary of War. He reported a "respectful reception" to Washington, and on the 12th of April, Mr. Buchanan appointed L. W. Powell, of Kentucky, and Ben McCulloch, of Texas, as "Peace Commissioners," and by them sent a proclamation of pardon! But Brigham Young had given orders for a move, and early in April, 20,000 people from the city and north of it started south, they knew not where, but many supposed it was to Mexico. Governor Cumming in vain implored them to remain. Old Mormons have often described to me how he stood upon the streets, as the long trains rolled southward, with the tears streaming from his eyes, and protested, "if he followed his feelings he would rather go with them than remain with the apostates." Late that month he issued a proclamation offering "protection to all illegally restrained of their liberty in Utah," but few availed themselves of it. The latter part of May the Peace Commissioners arrived, and had an interview with the leading Mormons. The latter stipulated that the army should not be stationed within forty miles of the city; that they should protect private property; should march through the city without halting, and must not encamp till they passed the Jordan. They promised, on their part, everything that was asked, and "accepted the President's pardon."

June 26th the Federal army marched through the deserted city, led by Lieutenant-Colonel Cook, who, according to Mormon account, "rode with his head uncovered." Their permanent camp was at a point west of

Utah Lake, and forty miles south of the city, which was named Camp Floyd. Late in the season the absent Mormons returned to their homes in great poverty and destitution, and the "Mormon war" was ended. The Federal officials entered again upon their duties; courts were reopened, and attempts made to administer justice; but no grand jury would indict, and no petty jury convict, and criminals went "scot free." The following cases appear upon the record:

"During the sitting of Judge Sinclair's Court, the Mormon Grand Jury promptly found a bill of indictment against one Ralph Pike, a Sergeant in Company I, of the 10th Infantry, United States Army, for an assault with intent to kill, committed upon one Howard Spencer, the son of a Mormon bishop, at the military reserve in Rush Valley. Upon *capias* issued, Pike was arrested and brought to Great Salt Lake City. The day following, August 11, 1858, about 12 o'clock, noon, as Pike was entering the Salt Lake House, on Main Street, Spencer stepped up to him from behind, saying, 'Are you the man that struck me in Rush Valley?' at the same time drawing his pistol, and shot him through the side, inflicting a mortal wound. Spencer ran across the street, mounted his horse, and rode off, accompanied by several noted 'Danites.' Pike lingered in dreadful agony two days before he died. The 'Deseret News,' in its next issue, lauded young Spencer for his courage and bravery.

"A man by the name of Drown brought suit upon a promissory note for $480, against the 'Danite' captain, Bill Hickman. The case being submitted to the court, Drown obtained a judgment. A few days afterwards Drown, and a companion named Arnold, were stopping at the house of a friend in Salt Lake City, when Hickman, with some seven or eight of his band, rode up to the house, and called for Drown to come out. Drown suspecting foul play refused to do so, and locked the doors. The Danites thereupon dismounted from their horses, broke down the doors, and shot down both Drown and Arnold. Drown died of his wounds next morning, and Arnold a few days afterwards. Hickman and his band rode off unmolested.

"Thus, during a single term of the court held in a Mormon community, the warm life-blood of three human victims is shed upon the very threshold of the court; and although the Grand Jury is in session no prosecution is attempted, and not one of the offenders brought to justice."

Soon after, a deaf and dumb boy, named Andrew Bernard, was killed in Weber Cañon, as was pretty clearly proved by "Ephe" Hanks, a noted "Danite;" and an apostate named Forbes was found dead. The same year one Henry Jones and his mother, living near Pondtown, south of Utah Lake, were accused of horse-stealing by their neighbors. They were attacked at night, and the woman instantly killed; the young man escaped and ran some two miles, pursued by the "Danites." He was finally captured, and a pistol placed to his ear and discharged, blowing his head to pieces. Both the bodies were placed in their dwelling, a "dug-out" half under the ground; the roof was then thrown down upon them, and covered with dirt, making that their only grave. The next winter a Mormon bishop of that locality killed one of his wives for alleged infidelity; and one Franklin McNeil, who had sued Brigham Young for false imprisonment, was shot dead in his own door.

Another abomination of that bloody period was not brought to light till long after.

Early in 1858, while the army was yet at Fort Bridger, eighty discharged teamsters started through the city to California. An officer of the Nauvoo Legion was informed that he would find a "trusty force," at a certain place, with which to guard them through, and received the following order:

"SALT LAKE CITY, *April 9th*, 1858.

"The officer in command of escort is hereby ordered to see that every man is well prepared with ammunition, and have it ready at the time you see those teamsters a hundred miles from the settlements. President Young advises that they should be all killed, to prevent them from returning to Bridger to join our enemies. Every precaution should be taken, and see that not one escapes. Secrecy is required.

"By order of General Daniel H. Wells.

"JAMES FERGUSON,
"*Assistant Adjutant General.*"

The officer refused to execute the order, for which his life was threatened. He took refuge at the Federal camp, and was sent out of the Territory. The signature of Ferguson is authenticated by two Mormons, formerly merchants in Salt Lake City. Several years after, the widow of Ferguson called upon a Federal Judge, who had the writing in his possession. She stated that she had heard the rumor that there was such a paper, and desired to see it.

It was not given to her, but spread upon the desk for her inspection. She read it through, turned deadly pale, and rushed out of the room without saying a word. Through 1858 and '59 various difficulties occurred; Governor Cumming did not sustain the judiciary in their efforts, and finally an order was received from Washington, that the troops were not to be used as a posse to aid the United States Marshal in making arrests. This, of course, completely put an end even to the attempt to administer justice. But the entrance of the army had done good in a variety of ways; stage and mail lines had been established; means of intelligence had been multiplied, and a considerable Gentile influence established, and we gladly turn away from the dark period of crime and degradation, and enter upon the era in which outside influence began to produce good effects even in Utah.

CHAPTER VII.

GENTILES IN UTAH.

A New Element—Livingston and Kinkead—"Jack-Mormonism at Washington"—Judge Drummond—M. Jules Remy—Gilbert and Sons—Heavy Trade—Later Gentile Merchants—Walker Brothers—Sales at Camp Floyd—"Crushing the Mormons"—Ransohoff & Co.—Mormon Outrages again—Murders of Brassfield and Dr. Robinson—Whipping of Weston—Evidence in case of Robinson—Outrages on Lieut. Brown and Dr. Williamson—Gentiles driven from the Public Land—Territorial Surveyor—Success of General Connor's Administration—The Government Returns to the Old Policy—Murders of Potter and Wilson—Horrible Death of "Negro Tom"—The Last Witness "put out of the Way"—"Danites" again—Murder each Other—Death of Hatch---Flight of Hickman—Forty-three Murders—Another change of Officials—Doty—Durkee—Shameful Neglect of the Government—Flight of the Gentiles—Comparative Quiet Again—A better Day—The Author Arrives in Utah.

A NEW element now enters into Utah affairs, and demands attention. There had previously been Gentiles resident in Salt Lake, but before 1858, they seem to have created no special interest. The history of Gentile merchants, from the earliest times to the present, exhibits a singular record of "pluck" and enterprise, contending against the ever-varying complications of political and religious fanaticism. The first Gentile merchants to make a permanent establishment in Salt Lake were Messrs. Livingston and Kinkead, who began business there in 1850, and taking the tide of Mormon prosperity at its height, when the young colony had just realized on the California trade, their profits were immense. At the date they reached the city there were no Eastern goods in the Valley, and the first day their store was open they took in $10,000 in gold! Other merchants passed through doing some trade, but none had done so well. The custom of these early merchants was to start from the Missouri with large stocks, which they opened at Salt Lake, remaining only one autumn and winter, trading for cattle, grain and flour, which they took on to California the next season.

From 1850 till 1862, "jack-Mormonism" ruled at Washington to a considerable extent, and the Gentiles of Utah had but little help, either by protection or moral influence, from Federal appointees. Judge Kinney, who was appointed Chief Justice in 1854, came that year to the valley with his family and a large stock of goods. He kept a hotel, sold goods, speculated in various ways, and spared no pains to keep on good terms with his Mormon customers; afterwards he joined the Mormons, was baptized in the holy Jordan—it is reported that he paid the officiating priest $10 to have the job done in the night—and represented the Territory one term in Congress.

For a short time he was the colleague of Judge Drummond, the Government thus, by immorality on one side and "jack-Mormonism" on the other, playing into the hands of the Saints most effectually. Kinney had a difficulty with Brigham Young early in 1855, as reported by M. Jules Remy, who visited Salt Lake that summer, and Brigham declined the invitation of the Frenchman to dine with him at Kinney's hotel, on that account. It is a subject of curious conjecture what sort of an impression this state of affairs made on the courtly Frenchman, accustomed to see the representative of the supreme power treated with the utmost deference. Kinney left the next year, retaining, however, the office and its emoluments till 1857, and in 1860 was reappointed.

The entrance of Johnston's army, with the Government contracts thereby rendered necessary, and the more complete establishment of the overland stages, mark the beginning of a new era in Gentile history; here is a point of departure, so to speak, between the old and the new, separating ancient and modern history. Nearly all the late merchants came in with that army, or following soon after.

During the interval from 1853 to 1858, the Mormons had fallen behind, and great destitution often prevailed, particularly in the southern settlements. One year the

K

crops were short from drought, and another they were entirely destroyed by grasshoppers; during two seasons there was no surplus except a little wheat which could only be sold in barter for fifty cents per bushel; one winter thousands of the people subsisted largely upon *sego* roots, and another, of unusual severity, a third of the cattle throughout Utah died from exposure. In the period known in Mormon chronicles as "The Reformation," the Ward Teachers visited every family in their jurisdiction, and made a thorough examination of their flour barrels and meat chests, taking away the surplus, where there was any, to divide it among those who had none. In the summer of 1855, M. Jules Remy, French traveller and *savant*, and Mr. A. M. Brenchley, his English companion and botanist, journeyed from Sacramento to Salt Lake City, by the Central Nevada route and south of the lake, and spent several weeks studying Mormon institutions. Their publication, a copy of which may be found in the State Library at Sacramento, describes a condition of extreme poverty in Utah; provisions of all sorts were at premium prices, and their tour of two months, with the poorest accommodations, cost them more in gold than a first-class tour of Europe would have done. Wheat and a few other bare necessaries alone were tolerably cheap. The season of 1856-57 might be justly denominated the "Winter of Mormon discontent." And it is remarkable that during those two years were committed most of those crimes which form so black a chapter in the annals of Utah.

The entrance of Johnston's army proved a real god-send to many, and being followed by a season of unusual fruitfulness, the Mormons were again rendered prosperous. The firm of Gilbert & Sons was established in Salt Lake City about that time, though one of the firm had done business there before. This firm made large profits during the five succeeding years, their sales on one particular day amounting to $17,000 in gold. Coin was the only currency, all large payments being made in the Mormon five-dollar piece, a coin struck by the Church, which, however, contained but $4.30 in gold. Another prominent firm of that period was Ransohoff & Co., long the leading Jewish firm, who built the best stone store-house in the city. They had extensive dealings with Brigham Young, who was for a while on the best of terms with Gentile merchants, and when Johnston's army left, and the camp property was sold, Brigham borrowed $30,000 of Ransohoff to invest in army pork. Following the entrance of the army came a heavy trade with Nevada, and not long afterwards considerable with Colorado; and at this period was the rise of the firm of Walker Brothers, now, *par excellence*, the Gentile merchant princes of Utah. The Walkers, four young and middle aged gentlemen, were of Mormon parentage and reared among the Saints; having, by great industry and enterprise, secured a small stock-in-trade before the entrance of the army. The stores at Camp Floyd were sold early in 1861, with immense profits to the Saints; iron, which had retailed at a dollar per pound, became as plentiful as in the East, and Brigham Young, Walker Brothers, and other firms bought immense quantities of pork at one cent per pound, which they afterwards retailed at sixty. Thus did Buchanan "crush the Mormons." The Overland Mail service grew into greatness, furnishing another source of profit, and the Gentile merchants shared largely in the general prosperity. During 1859 and '60, though there was hostility between Camp Floyd and the Mormon heirarchy money was plenty; sufficient supplies had been forwarded to last the army ten years, and great quantities of leather, gearing, cavalry equipments, clothing, blankets and small stores were sold for one-tenth their value; Brigham was on the best of terms with the Gentile merchants; gifts and donations on both sides were common; there was for a time little or no social distinction between Mormon and Gentile, and an era of general good feeling prevailed.

The General Government soon returned to the old policy, and with the return of Kinney, Judges Flenniken and Crosby were appointed to succeed Sinclair and Cradlebaugh, removed. In 1861, Governor Cumming left Utah, and was succeeded by John W. Dawson, of Indiana, who was soon entrapped into "a base attempt on the virtue of a Mormon woman," and in consequence of many threats precipitately fled the Territory. He was waylaid, however, in Weber Canyon, and received a terrible beating, which he richly deserved for his cowardice, and, if the charge above be true, for his detestably bad taste. Notwithstanding these differences with the officials, the Mormons continued on good terms with the merchants, trade was free, and the people rather prosperous. The opening of the war signalled a sudden change; the disloyalty of the Mormons was only equalled by the disgust of the Gentiles, and the whole gist of Mormon sermons for a year or two might have been compressed into that aggravating after-prophecy, " Didn't we tell you so ?" With them it was only the realization of what Joe Smith had prophesied in 1832, and Sunday after Sunday the Tabernacle resounded with the harangues of Brigham Young and Heber Kimball, in fiendish exultation over the prospect that "the war would go on till nearly all the men, North and South, would be killed, the rest would become servants to the Saints, the women of the United States would come begging for the Mormon elders to marry them, and a general cry would go up, 'come and help us to preserve the race of man in this land.'"

Such was the stuff then preached by men who are now prating loudly of their loyalty. It was hard for an American to listen to it quietly, and but little else was heard in Salt Lake for the first two years of the war. Early in 1862, Judges Flenniken and Crosby left Salt Lake City. If they did anything while there to forward the cause of truth, to add to the dignity of the government, to increase the moral force of the Gentiles or protect the victims of Brighamism, it appears not on the record. President Lincoln was advised by telegraph of their departure, and on the 3rd of February, 1862, appointed Thomas J. Drake, of Michigan, and Chas. V. Waite, of Illinois, to succeed them. On the 31st of March following, Stephen S. Harding, an "original abolitionist," of Southern Indiana, was appointed Governor, and the new officials reached Salt Lake in July of the same year. In October following, Colonel (now General) P. Edward Connor arrived with fifteen hundred men and established Camp Douglas. This administration may well be styled the "golden age" of Gentiles in Utah. For nearly four years General Connor maintained the rights of American citizens, and protected and assisted many hundred dissenting Mormons in their escape from Utah. Their prompt action in protecting American citizens and recusant Mormons from injury, together with the anti-polygamy features of Governor Harding's first message, and the action of the Judges in asking Congress for an amendment to the Organic Act of the Territory, excited the Brighamites to great anger for a time; the hostility increased, and when an unusually large number of miners came to winter in Salt Lake, Brigham assumed entire control of Mormon trade, and flour was put up at once from $3 to $6 per hundred in gold, then equal to twice that amount in currency. Great was the indignation at this move, but the miners could not help themselves at that season and submitted, though their curses were both loud and deep. The opening of spring relieved this embargo, and the Mormons soon discovered that though Camp Douglas was something of an eye-sore, yet the presence of two regiments added materially to their trade. The triumph of the Union arms through 1864, the prompt payment of claims against the government, and the appointment of rather more acceptable officials, convinced the Mormons that loyalty " would pay " for awhile, and another era of free trade and tolerably good feeling followed. The year 1864-65 were seasons of prosperity to the Gentiles; Ransohoff & Co. cleared large sums dealing in general supplies, and Walker Brothers, who had meanwhile apostatized from Mormonism, took rank as millionaires.

The era of free trade and good feeling was short and the change sudden. In 1865 and 1866, all the California and Nevada volunteers and most of the other troops were withdrawn, and the hostility of the Church was manifested with tenfold more fierceness. All the Gentiles, who had pre-empted land west of the city, were whipped, ducked in the Jordan, or tarred and feathered, and their improvements destroyed; many were threatened and ordered out of the country; Weston, of the *Union Vedette,* was seized at night, taken to Temple Block and cruelly beaten; Brassfield was shot; Dr. Robinson assassinated, and general consternation seized upon the Gentile residents. Some of these events demand a more particular account.

Squire Newton Brassfield, formerly a citizen of California, and more lately of Nevada, while sojourning temporarily in Salt Lake City, formed the acquaintance of a woman who had been the polygamous wife of a Mormon, named Hill, but had left him, repudiated this so-called marriage and claimed that she was entitled at common law to the possession of her children by this Hill, as the offspring of an illegal marriage, or rather of no marriage at all. She and Brassfield were married in legal form by the U. S. Judge, H. P. McCurdy, on the 28th of March, 1866; a writ of *habeas corpus* was issued from the United States Court for the possession of her children, and the trial set for the night of April the 3rd, but adjourned till the 6th. Meanwhile Brassfield had taken a trunk containing her clothing from her former residence, and was arrested by the Mormon authorities on a charge of grand larceny! The ground assumed for this action was that *the clothing taken was the property of her husband.* It was also charged that he had resisted the officer attempting to make the arrest—an offence universally considered worthy of death by the Mormons. In this case also an appeal was had to the United States Court. On the evening of April 6th, about 8 o'clock, while Brassfield was passing along Second South Street, in the custody of, or in company with, United States Marshal, J. K. Hosmer, he was *shot in the back* by a *concealed* assassin; as near as could be determined, from an alley on the opposite side of the street. The assassin escaped, and no especial effort was made to arrest him. The Gentiles offered a reward of $4,500 for his apprehension; the Mormon press and speakers were either non-committal on the subject, or mildly sustained the assassin, and dared the Gentiles to publish their names to the offered reward. The possession of her two children was afterwards confirmed to Mrs. Brassfield by the United States Court, and she left the Territory with them. The following telegram was at once forwarded to General Connor, still in command of the district, but temporarily absent in New York:

GREAT SALT LAKE CITY, *April 8th*, 1866.

Brigadier-General P. E. Connor, Metropolitan Hotel, New York:—I married S. N. Brassfield to a Mormon woman, on the 28th ultimo. Brassfield was assassinated on the night of 6th instant. I have been denounced and threatened publicly. Government officials here have telegraphed to the Secretary of War to retain troops here until others are sent to relieve them. Call on Secretary of War, learn his conclusions and answer; I feel unsafe in person and property without protection,

H. P. McCURDY,
Associate Justice, Supreme Court, U. T.

A similar despatch was forwarded by Colonel C. A. Potter, who was ordered to retain troops until the regulars arrived.

Dr. Robinson was assassinated on the night of the 22nd of October. The following biography is taken from the *Union Vedette* of October 25th, 1866.

"The late Dr. J. K. Robinson, whose assassination last Monday has sent a thrill of horror to the heart of every law abiding citizen of this Territory, was a native of Calais, Maine, and was in his thirty-first year. He came to Utah from California in the spring of 1864, as an Assistant Surgeon of the United States volunteers, and, reporting to General Connor, was sent to Camp Connor at Soda Springs, Idaho; but, during the following winter, was ordered to Salt Lake, and took charge of the hospital at Camp Douglas, and remained on duty there and in this city until last winter, when he was mustered out of the service, leaving a record in the army which stands without a blemish. After leaving the service of his country, Dr. Robinson settled down in this city and engaged in the practice of his profession, in which he had taken the lead among the practising physicians of Salt Lake, and has occupied an equally prominent position in the advancement of all religious and educational schemes of the city. He was one of the most intimate friends and the roommate of the Rev. Norman McLeod, and co-operated with him in all his measures for the advancement of the social condition of the people of Utah. In this capacity he had, up to the time of his death, filled with great credit the position of superintendent in the Gentile Sunday School. On the afternoon of Mr. McLeod's departure for the East in March last, he united Dr. Robinson in the bonds of matrimony with Miss Nellie Kay, the accomplished daughter of the late Dr. Kay. No citizen of Salt Lake stood higher, morally or socially, than Dr. Robinson; we have never heard of his having a personal enemy, or that he ever infringed upon the legal or moral rights of any man living, and the only conceivable cause for his assassination is the fact that he saw fit to contest the title of a piece of land with the city in the Supreme Court. No other cause can be assigned, for had the object of the assassins been plunder, they could have obtained it, as the Doctor had upon his person a large sum of money and a valuable gold watch, *which had been untouched when* the body was found."

In common with many others, Dr. Robinson had held that the Territorial Legislature had no right to make grants of public land, and the city no right to pre-empt. He, accordingly, filed a claim upon the land surrounding the Warm Springs near the city, and erected some improvements which were torn down at mid-day by an armed force of police. He appealed his case to the U. S. Court, bringing an action of ejectment; in the course of the trial, his counsel raised the question that the city, because of the non-performance of certain acts, had no legal existence; which was argued before Chief Justice Titus, and by him decided in favor of the city. Dr. Robinson then gave notice of his intention to appeal. On the 11th of October, a bowling alley belonging to the Doctor was destroyed by a party of some twenty men with blackened faces. For this a number of persons were arrested, Chief of Police Burt and two subordinates identified and bound over by the Chief Justice. Soon after, Dr. Robinson called on Mayor Wells, in regard to the matter, was denied any answer and ordered to leave the house. This affair was thus chronicled the next morning by the *Telegraph*, then edited by the late renegade Mormon, T. B. H. Stenhouse :

"AS WELL TRAINED—The admiration for Zebra, Napoleon and Leopard, on Friday night, was snuffed out by the greater admiration for Dr. Ball-alley as he cleared from the Mayor's house yesterday afternoon. His honor had only to open the door, direct his finger and the man of pills and bluster vamoosed with a grace that fairly eclipsed little Leopard under the admirable direction of Bartholomew."

For several Sundays Brigham and other leaders had preached the most inflammatory harangues in the Tabernacle, advising the people "if any man attempted to pre-empt their land to 'send him to hell across lots," and the like. In more than one instance assassination was openly counseled and threatened, and the people were ripe for any desperate outrage. The second night after the above publication, between the hours of eleven and twelve, a man called at the house of Dr. Robinson, stated that "his brother, John Jones, had had his leg broken and required the Doctor's assistance;" the Doctor started with the man, they were joined by others, and a few steps away, at the corner of Main and Third South Street, he was struck two blows on the head, and immediately shot through the brain. One witness saw one of the assassins running down the street westward; two others saw three of them running eastward, and three was seen running southward, *making seven persons engaged in the murder*. On the investigation Mayor Wells swore that he was not informed of the murder "till ten o'clock the day after;" the policemen swore there were but eight of them on duty that night, of whom three were at the circus and "all the rest at the City Hall;" the Mormons examined swore there had been no threats made, and Stenhouse and one or two others refused to answer most of the questions asked. The investigation utterly failed to show that Dr. Robinson had a personal enemy in the world and showed that he had had difficulty with none but the city authorities. Evidence subsequently developed has fixed the guilt of this murder unmistakably upon the Mormon authorities.

The case of those Gentiles, who were driven from the public land, presents a flagrant violation of the law. The Legislature of Utah has passed an Act appointing a Territorial Surveyor; under its provisions any man can get the Surveyor to run a line round a piece of public land, then stick up stakes at the four corners, and he has a claim upon the land. It has been the custom to pay no regard whatever to the National laws, in regard to the public land. But should a Gentile attempt, under these laws, to take up a piece of land thus surveyed, he would be driven off. A number of the discharged volunteers, among them a Surgeon Williamson and Lieutenant Brown, entered upon some unoccupied land, west of the Jordan, without a sign of an improvement upon it. While erecting their cabins, some Mormons came out and claimed the land. They informed the Mormons that they did not wish to intrude on any other man's land, and if the latter would show they had taken up this land, or made any improvements upon it, they would leave it. To this reasonable request no reply was made, but that night some twenty men, with blackened faces, came to their shanties and captured both Brown and Williamson. They rolled them both up in an old tent, and carried them towards the Jordan. Lieutenant Brown, a cool and brave man, simply said: "Well, gentlemen, all I have to say is, if you intend to take my life, kill me like a man, and don't drown me like a dog." Upon this one of the crowd stepped up and remarked: "You shan't put that man in there. I know his voice; it's Lieutenant Brown, and once, when he commanded the provost guard, I had trouble with the soldiers, and he took my part and got me off. I didn't know this was the man till he spoke."

After consultation the mob tore down their shanties and released the men, on their promise to leave the country. The other settlers were ducked in the Jordan, and one of them shot through the leg while swimming the river.

The administration of General Connor had been almost a perfect success, and the American name was then respected, and Gentile safety secured in the most remote valleys of Utah; outside influences of all kinds had rapidly augmented, and a flourishing Gentile church, school and paper had been established. But Brigham and his tools had never ceased to work and intrigue at Washington for a change, and Johnson's administration proved disastrous to Utah. In a few months after General Connor was removed, and the troops withdrawn, there were three atrocious murders and numerous outrages upon Gentiles.

Soon after, three apostates, named Potter, Wilson and Walker, were arrested at Coalville, in Weber Valley, on a trumped-up charge of stealing a cow. This Potter was a brother of those murdered at Springville in 1857, and had been pursued with unrelenting hatred. Several times he had been arrested on various charges, and as often acquitted. His death was now determined upon, and one "Art" Hinckley, a "Danite" and Salt Lake policeman was sent for. Evidence, afterwards obtained, shows that he was accompanied by another policeman, and joined by parties at different points on his way. They proceeded to the school-house where the three men were confined, and took them out. Walker suspecting foul play, saw two of his guards level their guns at him, when he dodged down, and the shots only slightly wounded him in the neck. At the same instant the contents of a heavily loaded shot-gun were fired into Potter's body. Walker, being an agile man, escaped by jumping a near fence, receiving another slight wound in so doing, and made his way through cañons and ravines to Camp Douglas. Wilson also ran a little way, but was shot dead. On the evidence of Walker the assassins were arrested, but, by the connivance of Mormon officers, escaped from the Territorial Marshal, who had them in charge. The Mormon papers labored to explain the affair, stating that the prisoners were shot in attempting to escape from custody; but it is the testimony of all who saw the corpse of Potter, that the gun must have been almost touching his body when fired, and that his throat was cut after death. This was no doubt in fulfilment of the penalty in the Endowment oath. Walker remained about Camp Douglas for some time, then suddenly disappeared, and has since never been heard of. Shortly after, a colored man, generally known as "Negro Tom," who had been brought to the Territory by the Mormons as a slave, and lived many years in the family of Brigham Young and other dignitaries, called upon some Federal officials, and stated that he could give important evidence in regard to some of these murders. A few days after, his body was found upon the "bench," two miles east of the city, horribly mangled, his throat cut from ear to ear, and on his breast a large placard marked:

"LET WHITE WOMEN ALONE."

In all such cases of assassination the Mormons can command abundant evidence that the victim has "insulted a Mormon woman." Thus the last witness of these crimes was removed, and the proof put beyond the reach of earthly courts.

In the long list of murders and outrages, I have thus far particularly noted only those upon Gentiles, or in which Gentiles were specially interested. But it must be said of the Mormons, that they have always treated their own people worse than outsiders; and while they only molested those Gentiles who were particularly obnoxious, or had property to reward their assassins, they have visited apostates and dissenters with extreme vengeance. It were a wearisome and disgusting task to recount all memoirs of those who fled or attempted to flee from the Territory, and the bloody fate which has overtaken many, even of the tools of the Church, when suspected. One incident, however, is so notorious in the early annals of Utah, that, as an instance of the course often pursued, it deserves to be noted. Chief among the cut-throats of the earlier period, were three who merit an immortality of infamy, viz.: "Port" Rockwell, "Ephe" Hanks, and "Bill" Hickman. Closely associated with the last for many years was one "Ike" Hatch; but at length he grew weary of his mode of life, and, confiding in Hickman, announced his intention to escape from the Territory. Soon after Hickman and Hatch started from Salt Lake City on horseback for Provo. While crossing a small stream on the road, lined with a thick growth of willows, Hatch, who was in advance, was shot from behind, and fell from his horse. Hickman at once galloped back to the city, and reported that they had been attacked by Indians, and Hatch killed. The latter, however, had strength to climb upon his horse and reach the city before he died, and informed his father that he had been shot by Hickman. The latter had the hardihood to attend the funeral of Hatch, and actually assisted in shovelling the dirt into the grave. While in this work, the father of Hatch, overcome by sudden anger, aimed a blow at the murderer with a spade, which would certainly have ended his career, had not the blow been warded off by a friend of Hickman, who was on the watch. This murder, as well as several others by Hickman, is not even questioned among the Mormons; and yet this man was for years on friendly and even intimate terms with Brigham Young! Hickman also fell under suspicion soon after the "Morrisite war," of which an account will hereafter be given, and fled to Nevada. While there, he was taken violently ill, and sent for a "Josephite" Mormon preacher to administer absolution. It is reported that he then confessed participation in no less than forty-three deliberate murders! He recovered, and is still seen occasionally in Utah.

The vigilant administration of General Connor, and the firm position assumed by the Governor did not meet the approval of the authorities at Washington. In 1863 Harding was removed and appointed Chief Justice of Colorado, being succeeded as Governor by Hon. James Duane Doty, who had for some time been Indian Superintendent for Utah. About the same time Judge Kinney went to represent the Territory in Congress, and was succeeded as Chief Justice by Hon. John Titus, of Philadelphia. He was an able and impartial Judge; but seemed too often bound by precedents, and unwilling to disturb the order of administration which had existed from the first in the Territorial Courts, even when it was clearly proved to be contrary to a just rendering of the Organic Act. Dr. Frank Fuller, who had been Secretary of the Territory, from '61 to '63, was succeeded, in the autumn of the latter year, by Mr. Amos Reed. Judge Waite, after several ineffectual attempts to administer the law, resigned in disgust in 1864, and was succeeded by Judge McCurdy, who gave place, in 1867, *for a Mormon lawyer*, named Hoge, appointed by President Johnson. Governor Doty filled the office with all the dignity and efficiency possible to a man in such circumstances, almost without command, and entirely without the moral support of the Government. He died in 1865, and was succeeded by Hon. Charles Durkee, also of Wisconsin, who retained the office till late in 1869, and, a few weeks after his removal, died at Omaha, Nebraska. He was quite old, very feeble, without the power or energy to command, and was expressly instructed from Washington to pursue a conciliatory policy; as he once informed the writer, he "was sent out to do nothing," and it need only be added that he succeeded admirably in doing it.

The Secretary, Reed, was succeeded in the autumn of 1866 by Edward P. Higgins, of Michigan, who filled that office with marked ability till the spring of 1869. The first half of that year he acted as Governor, in the absence of Durkee, and won golden opinions for the able manner in which he performed the duties of that office. His message to the Territorial Legislature is noted as among the most able ever presented in Utah.

Soon after being relieved of his command, General Connor took up his residence in Stockton, Rush Valley, forty miles west of the city, where he has since been extensively engaged in mining.

A general stampede of Gentiles from Utah seemed likely to follow the withdrawal of all protection by the Government; and soon after Robinson's death, the Gentile merchants, with two or three exceptions, joined in a written proposal to Brigham, that they would all leave the Territory, if he or the Church would pay a nominal price for their property. To this Brigham complacently made reply that he "had not asked them to come, and did not ask them to go; they could stay as long as they pleased." This excitement subsided like the rest, and a whole year passed away without any serious outrages, or unusual threats. The influence of the approaching railroad began to be felt, resulting in another era of good feeling.

The amount of travel increased, and with it the amount of money; trade was free, with no distinction between Mormon and Gentiles; contracts on the railroad were taken by both, and little distinction made in giving employment, and in July, 1868, at a great railroad meeting, Mormon, Jew and Christian fraternized in the Tabernacle, and seemed to feel they had a common interest in the country's prosperity.

And thus stood affairs in the early autumn of 1868, when the author first entered the Territory.

CHAPTER VIII.

FIRST VIEWS IN UTAH.

The real "American Desert"—No Myth—Bitter Creek—Green River—Lone Rock—Plains of Bridger—Quaking Asp Ridge—Bear River—A Mormon Autobiography—"Pulling hair"—"Aristocracy" on the Plains—"Mule-skinners" and "Bullwhackers"—The "Bullwhackers Epic"—Cache Cave—Echo Canon—Mormon "fortifications"—Braggadocio—Storm in Weber Canon—Up the Weber—Parley's Park—A Wife-stealing Apostle—Down the Canon—Majestic Scenery—First View of the Valley—The "City of the Saints."

ON the morning of August 28th, 1868, from the heights east of Green River, then the eastern boundary of the Territory, I took my first view of Utah. I had not reached it, as I did not leave it, without tribulation. In company with a Mormon "outfit" of sixteen men, ten waggons, and sixty mules, I had made the wearisome journey from North Platte across three hundred miles of the American Desert at the dryest season of the year. The point of our departure from the railroad was too far south for us to reach the much sought Sweetwater route, and, after leaving Bridger's Pass, we struck directly for the head of Bitter Creek, down which we travelled for three days, days fixed in memory, but not dear.

A region of sand and alkali, where the white dust lay six inches deep in the road, and the whole surface of the valley looked like a mixture of dried soap and soda, this part of the American Desert is certainly no *myth*. On the 26th of August we left that stream at Point of Rocks, and travelled northward towards the upper crossing of Green River. Thirty miles on our former course would have brought us to the confluence of Bitter Creek and Green River, but it was impossible to travel longer on the former stream, the water of which resembles weak soapsuds, and has the effect upon the system of a mild infusion of aloes. The road, always bad at that season, was rendered much worse by the graders everywhere present, and at work upon the line of the railroad. The teamsters we met, whether Saxon, Mexican, or Negro, all looked of one color, a moving "pillar of cloud," and, as they shook the dust from their ears, seemed living examples of the judgment, "Dust thou art," etc.

Special notice is due the "Twenty-mile Desert," where for ten hours the train struggled wearily through a loose bed of sand and soda, enveloped by a blinding white cloud through which the driver could not see his lead mules, and naught was heard but the cracking of whips, the yells and curses of the teamsters and the "cry" of the wheels in the soda, as they seemed to be groaning out the unspeakable woes of the dumb animals. During this experience we often turned our eyes longingly toward the mountain ranges which lay so cool and invitingly before us. But a change came over the spirit of our dream, when by our new route we had reached that elevated region.

On the mornings of the 27th and 28th, we found ice a quarter of an inch thick on the water in our buckets, and the winds were so cold and piercing, that a heavy coat and two woollen wrappers seemed inadequate protection. Our route was in an irregular semi-circle, north, northwest and west; passing Lone Rock, a vast block of white and yellow stone, standing in the centre of a high, level plain, as if thrown by some convulsion of nature from a flat summit two miles distant. As we approached it up the valley from the east, at some miles distance, it bears an exact resemblance to a large steamboat coming on under full head of steam; seen from the side, it resembles a vast Gothic cathedral, with spires at the four corners, and numerous turrets, doors and windows, while the mind imagines the interior, with its ringing halls and resounding corridors. Descending to the valley by a dangerous "dugway," we forded Green River, a clear, pure stream, here fifty yards wide and three feet deep, cold as icewater, flowing rapidly southward to its junction with Grand River, where both form the Great Colorado.

From Green River, another day's travel, nearly all the way up hill, brought us upon another cold ridge, where the water froze again. The next day was Sunday, but there is no Sabbath on the plains unless a man dies, a mule gets sick, or unusually good grass and water invite to a day of rest in which case, Sunday comes any day of the week. So we thawed the ice out of our pots and buckets, took a little hot coffee, "damper," and pork, limbered up our joints and travelled on, this day crossing Ross's Fork.

Something in the air of these plains seems to furnish an exemption from the usual penalties of cold and exposure. I have often waded deep creeks or risen in the morning wet and cold, but never experienced any ill effects from it. The pure air of the region proves a perfect immunity against its exposures and hardships. From Ross's Fork we passed on to the high plains of Bridger, 7000 feet above sea level, and cold and barren in proportion. Here Johnston's army passed the winter of 1857-8, after they had lost their cattle and supplies in Echo Cañon, and here Colonel Kane, a self-constituted ambassador from the Mormons, found "the three heads of departments," Governor Cumming, Colonel Johnston and Judge Eckles, when he sought the army on his mission of peace. For the last three days we have travelled in sight of the Uintah Range; far to the south of us its snowy peaks glistened in the morning sun-light with a cloud like silvery whiteness, while lower down the dark blue green marked the timber line, which lower still faded to a dull gray, all presenting as the day advanced a varying panorama of light and shade, showing in the distance like the shadowy picture scenes of fairy land.

Our last cold night, August 31st, we spent on Quaking Asp Ridge where Boreas sent down a bitter blast, determined to punish us for intrusion into his high domains. With a double thickness of gunny-bags below our blankets and waggon-cover above we slept soundly and warmly, and while the wind whistled over my head I dreamed of the sunny valley of the Ohio, its corn ripening in the warm August night, while the yellow-brown blades rustle in the soft breeze and sigh a lament for the departing summer.

From this summit we travelled all day, constantly descending along a narrow "dugway," between ridges lined with quaking asp, or through narrow cañons where overhanging rocks nearly shut out the sun light, emerging finally into a beautiful valley with a genial climate and luxuriant grass.

The next day we crossed Bear River, finding a rich valley with some fine farms. All this valley appears capable of cultivation, while the lower hills and slopes abound in fine pasturage, and the region is evidently able to sustain a considerable population. From Bear River we moved on to Yellow Creek where we camped one night, the next day reaching Cache Cave at the head of Echo Cañon, where we made a mid-day camp of four hours.— Cache Cave is simply a hole in the rock, some fifty feet up the hill side and running back forty feet into the cliff, the inside covered with names cut, scratched and painted. Here we found the grass and water fine but no wood, not even the sage brush which had thus far served our need; so we took to the plains and gathered the fuel known to plainsmen as "bull chips," which made a very hot fire when used in sufficient quantities, and, "barrin the idee," served to cook a first-rate dinner.

As I am writing of a mode of travel now rendered entirely obsolete by the completed line of railroad, and of characters and methods of life no longer met with by the ordinary traveller, some special account of daily fare of those whose occupation has now fallen into disuse may be interesting to the general reader. In a few years more, our aggressive commercial enterprise and comprehensive civilization will have obliterated those routes along which the mule and ox trains bore the trade and immigrants to our great territories. The kind as well as routes of trade will be rapidly modified, with new agencies and a vaster scope. With the present generation will almost entirely disappear whole classes of men who were met with everywhere in the Territories. Their occupation will be gone and there will be neither demand nor school for the training of others. A hardy, brave and rough race generally, they were essential to their time, pioneers of a better day, yielding their places slowly to new routes of commerce for the world, their waggons disappearing before railroads, which are vaster than plains or mountains. With representatives of these men I was associated for the time.— Thus far we had lived rather poorly on bacon, bread, coffee without milk or sugar, and such molasses as is used in the States as a medium for fly-poison. But west of Green River we entered a region abounding in jack-rabbits and sage hens, with which our passengers kept us pretty well supplied. I had thought from its appearance that the sage hen could not be eaten, but found it rather palatable, tasting like the flesh of our domestic hen strongly flavored with sage. The jack-rabbit is about four times as large as the common "cotton tail," and two of them made an ample meal for our crowd of sixteen. For biscuits the self-rising flour is used on the plains; but our cooks are not even respectable amateurs, and half the time our bread was "Missouri-bake," *i. e.*, burnt on top and at the bottom, and raw in the middle.

The water supply was so irregular, too, that most of the way we made but one "route" per day, which implies no dinner. To aggravate the case further, we often had not enough at breakfast, and supper was our only full meal. At night all were at leisure; the mules were fed, turned out and given in charge of the night herder; the boys gathered round the fire, while the cooks took their time and prepared a bushel or more of biscuits, and we ate as long as we pleased. But in the morning all was hurry; the mules were done eating before the men began; the "waggon boss" hurried the cooks, so they did not prepare enough; at the shout of "grub-pile," every man "went for" his share in haste, and the fastest eater got the most. When we got far enough to meet Salt Lake teams with freshly dried peaches of this year's crop, we invested largely therein, and our cooks made a number of peach pies.

The materials were flour, bacon grease, peaches and the molasses above mentioned, the pies being cooked in a tin plate inside of a baking kettle. Half a dozen of them as curiosities would be a prize to a Ladies' Fair, or a rare addition to a Medical Museum. Our favorite dinner, when we could get the meat, was of fried ham and "sinkers," the latter peculiar to the plains. Here is the recipe: Flour, *ad libitum;* water, *quant. suff.;* soda, a spoonful, if you have it, if not, a pinch of ashes. Make in thin cakes, and fry rapidly in hot grease, with long handled frying pans. "Death-balls" and "Stone-blinders" are made in the same way, with the addition to the first of the molasses, and to the second plenty of saleratus.

Lady readers will give due credit for the above recipes, as I believe they are not found in "Leslie." My fellow passengers are worthy of notice. I had originally intended on leaving the States to proceed directly by railroad and stage to Salt Lake City ; but charges on the Union Pacific being then at the rate of ten cents per mile, on reaching the then terminus at North Platte, I found myself laboring temporarily under a serious attack of what Tom Hood calls "impecuniosity," and under the necessity of finding some cheaper, if less expeditious, mode of conveyance. Freight had accumulated and teamsters were in demand. So I took to the plains with the train of Naisbit and Hindley, Mormon merchants of Salt Lake City, in the capacity of a "mule skinner" for the trip, seated on the back of my "near wheeler," and wielding a whip nearly half as large as myself over the backs of three spans of mules, viz. : " Brigham " and " Sally Ann," " Ponce " and "Jule," "Kit" and Mexico." Whether the name of my "off-leader" had any reference to one of the real Brigham's numerous wives, I cannot say ; but such a reckless system of asinine nomenclature would hardly indicate a delicate respect for the Prophet on the part of these young "Saints." Of our little party of sixteen, two drivers, the night herder, and three passengers were Gentiles; the rest Mormons, or, at least, "hickory Mormons," sons of Mormon parents ; most of them tall, awkward and lank lads of eighteen or twenty, with premonitory symptoms of manhood breaking out on their chins, giving them as they never shaved, a very verdant and backwoods appearance.

For the night we joined blankets by twos, sleeping on gunny bags under the waggons. My partner was a tall, lank Mormon, a native of Mississippi,—"a tough cuss from Provo," his companions called him, who, after a few days' travel grew quite confidential and told me his whole history. He joined the Confederate army at the first call, fought till he was tired, and allowed himself to be captured in Hood's retreat from Nashville; took the amnesty oath for which his "girl, in Massassipp, wouldn't have nothin' more to say to him," when he took a huge disgust at the States, and came out and joined the Mormons in 1865. He has "a house an' lot an' two good lookin' wives in the Twentieth ward, and considers himself settled." I should think he would. As an outsider, I had kept quiet on the subject of polygamy; but one evening when reading an account of some Chicago social abomination, a young Mormon remarked, "That is the benefit of polygamy; they have nothing of that sort." "Polygamy would be all right, Bill," said another, "if they only wouldn't pull hair. But the women will pull hair any way you fix it." As the first home testimony I had received on the "peculiar institution" of Utah, this could hardly be considered favorable. In our party were two grandsons of the late Heber C. Kimball, not much of a distinction when it is remembered that worthy left some fifty children to keep his name in remembrance. I have generally found all the younger generation of Mormons to be infidels, and suspect it must be so with the youth of any religion which has in it so little of the element of spirituality; certainly with the more intelligent of them. From a gross, sensuous religion, the thinking mind glides naturally into a cold and cheerless scepticism.

Our group of sixteen stood as follows: seven infidels, mostly of Mormon parents; five "good Mormons;" two Lutherans; one Catholic, and one Methodist. Religiously, all are pretty much alike on the plains, but socially there *is* even there an "aristocracy," and considerable "class and caste" jealousy. The "mule-skinner" considers the "bull whacker" quite beneath him, and will hardly associate with him upon equal terms, while the latter, doubtless looks upon the former as "stuck up" and proud. The "bull-whackers" have to drive very late, for which reason they never seem so social and lively as the drivers in mule trains. All our work was done by dark, and gathered around the camp-fire we would spend the evening hours in lively song and merriment, varied by some with an occasional dose of "Red Jacket," which is used on the plains as an alterative, sanative, sedative and preventive. On the wild mountain side or in the deep glen, by a sage brush fire, one may imagine the roaring chorus from a dozen pairs of strong lungs, over such a choice bit of poetry as this:

"Oh, how happy is the man who has heard instruction's voice,
And turned a mule-skinner for his first and early choice," etc.

Or such a bit of history as this:

"Obadier, he dreampt a dream,
Dreampt he was drivin' a ten mule team,
But when he woke he heaved a sigh,
The lead mule kicked e-o-wt the swing mule's eye."

Compared with these bold and joyous utterances, there is quite a touch of the pathetic in

"THE BULL-WHACKER'S EPIC."

"Oh! I'm a jolly driver on the Salt Lake City line,
And I can lick the rascal that yokes an ox of mine;
He'd better turn him out, or you bet your life I'll try
To sprawl him with an ox-bow—' Root hog, or die.'

"Oh! I'll tell you how it is when you first get on the road:
You've got an awkward team and a very heavy load;
You've got to whip and hollow, (if you swear its on the sly,)—
Punch your teams along, boys—' Root hog, or die.'

"Oh! it's every day at noon there is something to do.
If there's nothing else, there will be an ox to shoe;
First with ropes you throw him, and there you make him lie
While you tack on the shoes, boys—' Root hog, or die.'

"Perhaps you'd like to know what it is we have to eat,
A little bit of bread, and a dirty piece of meat;
A little old molasses, and sugar on the sly,
Potatoes if you've got 'em—' Root hog, or die.'

"Oh! there's many strange sights to bo seen along the road.
The antelopes and deer and the great big sandy toad,
The buffalo and elk, the rabbits jump so high,
And with all the bloody Injuns—'Root hog, or die.'

"The prairie dogs in Dog-town, and the prickly pears,
And the buffalo bones that are scattered everywheres;
Now and then dead oxen from vile Alkali,
Are very thick in places, where it's 'Root hog, or die.'

"Oh! you've got to take things on the plains as you can,
They'll never try to please you, 'or any other man.'
You go it late and early, and also wet and dry,
And eat when you can get it—'Root hog, or die.'

"Oh, times on Bitter Creek, they never can be beat,
'Root hog, or die' is on every waggon sheet;
The sand within your throat, the dust within your eye,
Bend your back and stand it, to 'Root hog, or die.'

"When we arrived in Salt Lake, the 25th of June,
The people were surprised to see us come so soon;
But we are bold bull-whackers on whom you can rely,
We're tough, and we can stand it, to 'Root hog, or die.'"

It will be seen that the "sacred nine" flourish even on the American Desert.

We were two days in passing the thirty miles down Echo Cañon, our progress being slow because the roads were so badly cut up by the workmen on the railroad track. Hundreds of English, Welsh Swedes and Danes, were there at work on Brigham Young's contract, which extended sixty miles through Echo and Weber Cañons. Among them were many who had just come over, and were working out their passage money, which the Church had advanced from the Perpetual Emigration Fund. In the wildest parts of the cañon we halted for four hours of a beautiful autumn day, every moment of which was full of delight, in gazing upon the wall-like cliffs, the straw colored rocks, the deep rifts and caverns in the mountain sides, and all the sublime scenery which has made this place so noted.

The road here lay directly under a perpendicular cliff of nearly a thousand feet in height, where great rocks, of many tons weight, hung over the way; others which had fallen ages ago, and rolled to the lower plain, stood like vast table rocks in the valley's bed. Where I stood, I could view the southern slope of the hills for twenty miles, and beyond them the white peaks of the Wintah Range, bathed in clouds of clear and dazzling whiteness, through which the sun was just breaking in glorious majesty. It was the hour of morning service, and nature here seemed yielding silent worship :

> " But the sound of the church-going bell
> These valleys and rocks never heard ;
> Ne'er sighed at the sound of a knell,
> Or smiled when a Sabbath appeared."

A soft, sighing wind swept down the cañon, and mournful murmurs issued from the rocky side-crevices, which doubtless spoke often to the Indian as the spirits of his fathers, calling from the happy hunting grounds. The Greek poet would have heard in them the moanings of imprisoned souls, seeking release from their rocky dungeons ; but to the Christian the whole scene brings to solemn remembrance the time when " He stood and measured the earth ; the everlasting mountains were scattered ; the perpetual hills did bow."

Below this point we passed the remains of the fortifications, or rather stone-piles, which the Mormons erected in 1857, to stay the march of Johnston's army, and a little farther down the young Mormons pointed out a rock, rising apparently seven or eight hundred feet above the road, on the top of which a Mormon boy was shot dead by his companion below, "just on a dare, and to see if his gun would carry up that high." This was the only life lost by the Mormon forces during that memorable " war." The sight of these relics, which would have aided in checking a well-handled force about as much as the canvas forts at Pekin, caused a warm discussion to spring up among us. The " wretched awkwardness " of the Federal cavalry was contrasted very unfavorably with the " fiery valor " of the Mormon youth, who " offered to lassoo the guns, rode full tilt down a point where a blue-coat wouldn't venture, took a man prisoner, drank with him and let him go," etc., etc. "If the army had been volunteers," was the general expression, "they would have been wiped out; but we only felt pity for the low Dutch and Irish, sent out here just to keep them moving."

Something might have been deducted from this on the score of prejudice, but from other and less interested testimony, I am compelled to conclude that the army of Utah must have been "poor sticks," unless, as is probable, there was a secret understanding that they were not to force their way into the valley the first year. Of all the evils with which the "masterly inactivity" of Buchanan's Administration afflicted us, the Utah expedition of 1857, and its results, were certainly not the least. To-day three-fourths of the Mormons firmly believe that Johnston's Army was compelled to retreat by the Mormon guerilla chief, Lot Smith, and that they were only allowed to come into the valley after a treaty had been made with Brigham. When asked why the people vacated their homes and went South when the army came in the next year, if they had gained the victory, the prompt answer is: "It was the will of the Lord." This is the explanation of all difficult points in Utah, and a very convenient one it is.

On the 5th of September, we emerged from Echo into Weber Cañon, finding a pretty little settlement, in a spot of great natural beauty, where we halted for rest and feed. Scarcely had we formed *corral* and loosed our mules, when a sudden change came over the western sky, the afternoon sun was obscured by a murky haze, the Wasatch peaks were lost in sudden accumulations of dense cloud, and, in a very few minutes, the whole scene was shut out from our view by the rapidly gathering storm. For a few minutes longer, the air where we stood was in a dead calm, then a strong wind swept up the green valley of the Weber, sharp, jagged lightning ran along the mountain peaks and seemed to rebound from cliff to cliff evenly with the echoing thunder, and we had barely time to secure the fastenings of our waggon covers and take shelter within, when the storm was upon us in all its fury. Blinding clouds of dust, driven by fierce gusts of wind, were succeeded in an instant by torrents of rain, alternating again with heavy winds which threatened to hurl our waggons into the Weber. I learned with surprise that this usually dry, mild climate, was subject, during the summer and autumn, to sudden and violent wind and thunder-storms. The rain continued for an hour, sending great sluices down the mountain gulches, and lashing the placid waters of Echo Creek into a foaming, muddy torrent; then ceased as suddenly as it had risen; and issuing from our retreats, we saw the dark clouds rolling away to the south-east, over the Uintahs, and in another hour the sun was again shining brilliantly. By evening the roads were pleasantly dry, and the stormy afternoon was followed by a glorious sunset, and a night of unusual clearness. We now changed our course to the southward, following up Weber Cañon, or rather valley, for, in this part of its course, it is too wide to merit the former name. The track of the Union Pacific Railroad, which has run continuously with the old stage-road from the head of Bitter Creek, and followed down Echo Cañon for twenty miles, at the mouth of Echo turns in a direct W. N. W. course down Weber Cañon, and by that pass enters Salt Lake Valley, thirty-five miles north of the city. The stage road turns south from Echo, follows up Weber to Spring Creek, up that W. S. W. to Parley's Park, across the Park and down Parley's Cañon W. N. W. into the city.

In Weber Valley we find ourselves, for the first time in many hundred miles, in a cultivated and settled country, and the contrast is most pleasing to the eye, wearied by miles of desert and mountain, with scant growth of sage-bush, grease-wood, and desert cactus. Another Sunday's drive, the 6th of September, took us through Coalville, point of coal supply for Salt Lake City, though forty miles distant, with a high range of mountains between; a rather neat but homely looking town, with a few houses nicely built of beautiful white stone, shingled or slated, but for the most part dwellings of rough hewn logs, and pole roofs covered with dirt, and often grass and flowers growing on the top. None but Mormons live in this valley, and I soon learned that the few houses, the finish of which I admired, were the residences of the Bishops and prominent Elders. The settlements extend along the little valley of two or three miles in width, with high pastures beyond the cultivated lands, rolling back to the mountains. Vegetation showed that growth was slow, and the season late, as this valley is among the highest in the Utah. Fields of oats near the road had just been harvested, and hay-making was still in progress.

We next passed through Wanship, county-seat of Summit County, and soon after left the valley, turning to the right and following up Spring Creek Cañon, towards the summit. Nearly all day we travelled up hill, passing towards evening over a sort of summit level and then down a gentle slope into Parley's Park, a valley or mountain plateau of some ten thousand acres, 7000 feet above sea-level and entirely surrounded by rugged mountain ranges, except narrow outlets to the north and west. This tract produces fine grass both for pasturage and hay, but no grain. It was first owned by Heber C. Kimball, who had wheat sown there for seven years in succession. It grew well and headed out, but was invariably "cut off in the flower" by the frosts of early September, whereupon Kimball stated that "it was not the will of the Lord grain should grow there," and gave up the experiment. The Park received its name in honor of Parley P. Pratt, noted among the early apostles of Mormonism, and brother of Orson Pratt, scholar, historian, and astronomer, the Usman of the new faith. Parley seems to have been a radical believer in polygamy, as he was certainly thorough in its practice, having six wives some time before his death. But, not satisfied with these, he converted a Mrs. Elinor McLean, wife of Hector McLean, of Arkansas, and took her to Salt Lake City, and married her. The enraged husband sought Pratt, when on a mission in Kansas, in 1856, and literally cut him to pieces with a bowie knife. In Mormonism as in *El Islam* the wives of the infidels are lawful prey to any believer who can win them; while, at the same time, it is one of the deadliest sins in their code for any other man to entice away one of their "women," an unpardonable crime for which they openly threaten and claim the right to inflict death. To *convert* a Gentile's wife to Mormonism is

FOUR WIVES.

the highest achievement; the reverse worthy of death. There is a great deal in the way one states things; it makes all the difference between "Danite" and Damnite. Pratt was canonized among the "glorious martyrs" of the Latter-day faith, and his murder takes high rank in the long list of "persecutions" they have laid up against the Gentiles.

There is a small Mormon settlement on the south side of the Park, near where an old fort stood, but all the central portion is the property of Mr. Wm. Kimball, eldest son of Heber, formerly an ardent Mormon, but now weak in the faith, and sincerely trusting for inspiration in a more ardent *spirit*, or at least a more exhilarating one, if the testimony of his friends and nose be accepted. He has, however, "kept the faith" by taking three wives; the youngest and handsomest lives with him in a large stone hotel near the centre of the Park, on the stage road; the second wife, apparently quite old, lives in a low log house two hundred yards from the hotel, and his legal wife lives in the city, and, it is said, takes in spinning and weaving for a living. The first and second wives had each a son in our "outfit," Burton and Willie Kimball, rather bright, intelligent boys, and for the night we encamped near their father's "ranche," procuring a plentiful supply of milk, butter and eggs. I afterwards found it to be quite common for hotel-keepers on the various roads to have two or three wives; sometimes an English wife as housekeeper, a Danish wife as gardener, and if there was a third, she did the spinning and weaving for the family.

Thus all the requirements of a first-class establishment are kept up, and servants dispensed with; the "woman question," "servant-gal-ism" and "division of labor" settled by one master stroke, and profits deduced from polygamy with more certainty than polygamy from the Prophets.

From the Park we follow the stage road over a low "divide" to the head of Parley's Cañon, but made such slow progress that we were compelled to encamp for a night in the wildest part of the gorge, with barely room, and in but one place, to range the waggons in *corral* between the road and bed of the stream.

The view was one of indescribable beauty. On either hand rose the dark green sides of the cañon, apparently almost perpendicular, yet covered with masses of timber to the very summit; while down the rocky flume, in the lowest part of the cañon, dashed the clear waters of the creek, formed by melting snows but a few miles above. From where we stand the gray crest of the summit seems within pistol shot, and I am surprised to learn that it is at least one mile in a direct line from my eye, and those apparent steeps near the top are really gentle slopes covered with grass and bushes. The masses of timber which stand out so boldly towards the lower part of the cañon appear to follow up the sides gulches in rapidly lessening lines, sinking to rows of little saplings, and terminating in a mere fringe at the top like ornamental shrubbery. Yet those trifling looking poles are many of them from one to two feet thick. To one whose early life has been passed in a leveler prairie country, these mountain scenes are an ever-varying source of surprise and delight, and he only wonders why those whose home has been in the mountains should ever leave them. Nor do they often. There is a charm in the wild freedom of these heights which all must acknowledge, nor is it much less so on the plains, and though the mountaineer and plainsman may return to eastern friends and the abodes of civilization, they as often feel the irresistible longing to be back amid the untrained wildness of nature.

From this camp we made another day's travel down hill, all day by the side of the rushing stream, under numerous hanging rocks which seem to threaten destruction to all who venture beneath; now through frightful "dugways" far up the hill sides, where a variance of three feet would send team and driver to fragmentary destruction, and now far down in the deeps, where the enclosing walls above almost shut out the sunshine.

Soon after noon we passed the last stage station in a sort of open valley where a side cañon connects Emigration and Parley's, but after a few more turns we enter a deeper pass, of more wild and startling beauty. Finally we reached the Cañon gates, a narrow pass, just wide enough to afford road room, with perpendicular walls several hundred feet in height, where we emerged from the mountains and came out into a hollow with sloping sides and a freer outlook. About 4 P. M., I caught sight for the first time of the open valley and blue hills far beyond, but for an hour more we continued to wind along a "dugway," and at length emerged upon an open "bench," where I could see the distant glimmer of Jordan and the "marshes," and the mountains west of Great Salt Lake, a faint, blue, cloudy line, that in the silvery light of the declining sun appeared fading away in infinite perspective.

Slowly descending from the "bench" to the valley, I caught sight of the hill north of the city and the cañon from which issues City Creek ; then of Camp Douglass, far to the right and three miles east of the city ; then of the Arsenal, Tabernacle, Brigham's house, and the Theatre, and at last the city appeared in full view, scattered for miles over the slope, and looking in the distance and haze of evening, like a collection of villages with groves and orchards scattered among them. Night overtook us four miles out, where we formed *corral* in an open space by the "uphill canal," so called, from which place on the next morning, September 10th, we entered the city.

CHAPTER IX.

TWO WEEKS IN SALT LAKE CITY.

Views of the City—Temple Block—Brigham's Block—Theatre—Immigrants—Mormon Arguments—Reasons for Polygamy—" Book of Mormon "—First Mormon Sermon—" Old " Joe Young—His Beauty (?)
—His Sermon—Mormon Style of Preaching—Order of Services—
First impressions rather favorable—Much to learn yet.

ON first impressions Utah seems to me to have the perfection of climates, and Salt Lake City the finest natural site in the West. Nor is this feeling much lessened by longer stay. From a point on the hill just north of the city and near the Arsenal one can take in at a view the lake, the city, the mountains, and the valley for thirty miles south and south-east. From this point Jordan valley appears, nearly in the shape of a horse shoe, with the city just under the point of the northern termination of the east side, and the lake lying across the open end. But the southern point of the valley which seems to the spectator here to close, only narrows at the cañon of the Jordan, and opens beyond that to contain the Utah Lake district. Beginning north-east of the city, and extending south in the order named, are City Creek, Red Butte, Emigration, Parley's, Big Cottonwood and Little Cottonwood cañons, all breaking through the Wasatch from the east. From this point, too, every house in the city can be seen; the plat resembles the even squares of a checkerboard, the rows of trees lining all the streets, and the crystal streams of water which seem, in the distance, like threads of silver, combining to give a strange and fanciful beauty to the scene.

Salt Lake City is situated in latitude 40° 46′ north, and longitude 111° 53′ west of Greenwich, nearly 4,300 feet above sea level, and was laid out in 1847. The streets

M

are at exact right angles, running with the cardinal points, and numbered every way from Temple Block, which is, in Utah, the starting point of all measurements, calculations and principles, whether of ecclesiastical, civil, political or engineering. Its exact place is ascertained to be as above given for the city.

The street bounding it on the east is called East Temple Street, the next one First East Temple, or merely First East, the next Second East, and thus on ; the same nomenclature is maintained in all the streets, North, South and West. Each street is forty-four yards in width, with sixteen feet pavements, leaving one hundred feet clear, and each block exactly a furlong square, containing ten acres divided into eight lots of an acre and a quarter each. Nine squares are included in each ward, and there are twenty-one wards, beginning with the first on the south-east corner, and reckoned westward to the Fifth, then backward and forward, *boustrophedon*, terminating with the Twentieth on the north-east. The outer wards, however, contain large additional tracts extending the jurisdiction of the city over wide limits. The greatest length of the city proper is thus, from south-east to north-west, about four miles, and its greatest width, from north-east to south-west, a little over two miles. But a small portion, however, of this large area is thickly settled; in two-thirds of the city the scattered dwellings are mingled with orchards, gardens, small pastures or grass-plats, and even small wheat and corn fields, like a thickly settled farming country or nursery ground, rather than a city; and to this fact the place is indebted for no small share of its beauty. Nine-tenths of the buildings are of *adobes*, or sun dried brick, throughout the West, spelled and pronounced *dobies*, which material corresponds nearly with brick in the East, and, where plastered and stuccoed, makes an elegant and durable building.

The western part of the city extends to the Jordan, and the ground in that vicinity is rather low and, in winter and spring, marshy ; hence the finest residences are north and east, and all the public buildings above Third South Street. Let us note a few of them, beginning, by invariable custom, at Temple Block, which includes the usual ten acres, containing the old and new Tabernacles, the Endowment (locally known as *Ondooment*) House, and the foundation for the great Temple which is to be. The old Tabernacle is a sort of nondescript building, oblong in shape, with a third of the room underground, in the south-west corner of the block, capable of holding some 2,500 persons. The new Tabernacle is, in its way, a curiosity; there is certainly no idolatry in the reverence paid to it, for it is like nothing else in the heavens above, or the earth beneath, or probably the waters under the earth. At first sight the prevailing feeling is one of astonishment, which soon yields to curiosity as to who *could* have designed it. It is built in the form of a complete oval, the major axis of which is 250 feet in length, and the minor axis 150 feet. The lower part, or foundation for the dome, consists of a succession of forty-six pillars of red cut sand-stone, each about six feet square, and ten feet high, all around the building; along the sides there are double doors between the pillars, and at the ends a heavy partition; on this structure the dome or roof rests like the half of an egg-shell. The latter is a vast frame-work, plastered within and shingled without, raised along the centre sixty-five feet above the floor. There is not a trace of the beautiful or impressive about it; it is simply a vast pile awkwardly put together, and with twice the outlay of stone and mortar that would have sufficed to provide the same room and accommodations in some other shape. As the grand worshipping hall of the Saints it is a curiosity; as a work of art a monstrosity. The Endowment House, where the secret rites of Mormonism are performed, is an unpretentious *adobe* building, in the north-west corner of the lot. I cannot describe its interior, for the profane Gentile may not enter therein. But if the testimony of numerous witnesses may be believed, it is fitted up with various rooms, curtains, stages and scenery, for the performance of a grand drama, representing the creation, fall of man, coming of a redeemer, great apostacy and final restoration of the true priesthood through Joseph Smith.

The eastern half of Temple Block, fenced off from the western, contains only the foundation for the Temple, which is to be finished in great splendor just before the Saints return to Jackson County, Missouri. Ground was first broken for the work in February, 1853, with imposing ceremonies; in the seventeen years that have since elapsed, the edifice has reached a level with the ground, from which those familiar with the "Rule of Three" may calculate how long it will require for it to complete the proposed height of ninety-nine feet. The foundation is unsurpassed in strength and finish; of the finest mountain granite of a bright gray or white, slightly flecked with blue; a building of such material would indeed outlast the anticipated thousand years of Millennial reign. But work on it is slow, or rather it is suspended; the stone is very hard, and must be brought some twenty miles from the mountains, and only at rare intervals a workman or two is seen picking away at one of the huge masses which are scattered around by the ton. The entire square is surrounded by a wall, the base of stone, and the upper part of *adobes*, and plastered, twelve feet high, with square turrets about every ten feet, and a massive gateway under stone arches at the centre of each of the four sides. Crossing East Temple Street we reach the "Prophet's Block," two squares of ten acres each, the western containing the Deseret Store, the office of the *Deseret News*, official organ of the Church, the Tithing House and yard, the Lion House, Bee Hive House, offices and other buildings pertaining to the Prophet, Priest, Seer, Revelator, in all the world, Grand Archee, First President, and Trustee-in-trust of the Church of Jesus Christ of Latter-day Saints, all of which titles centre in and are borne by Brigham Young.

The Lion House is an oblong building of three stories, plain in style, but quite substantially built, and well finished. Its cost is reported everywhere from thirty to seventy thousand dollars. In the States it could have been built for less than the former sum. Over the pillared portico in front is a stone lion, a sad misapplication of the emblem, by the way, as that royal brute is ever content with *one mate*. The bull would have been more appropriate, but that is a matter of taste. The Bee Hive House, a large square building, just east of the former, is surmounted by a stone carving in imitation of a beehive. The entire area is surrounded by a wall eleven feet high, of boulders and cobble stones, laid in mortar, with semi-circular buttresses at equal distances, The eastern half of the enclosure contains various buildings of no special interest. Between the two lots is the main entrance to City Creek Cañon, which was "granted" to Brigham Young by the first Territorial Legislature; the entrance is by a massive stone gateway under an arch, upon which is perched an immense eagle, carved by a Mormon artist out of native wood—another perversion of a sacred emblem, the royal bird being, like his brute compeer, a *strict monogamist*.

Just north of Brigham's grounds, on the first "bench," is the block owned by the late Heber C. Kimball, containing one superior mansion, and a number of smaller dwellings, in which eleven of the Widows Kimball still reside. The other seven live in various parts of the city, with the families to which they belong. Some fourteen or sixteen of Brigham's wives reside in the Lion House and Bee Hive House; the others live in different parts of the city, or on his farms in the country.

From the cañon back of Brigham's grounds issues City Creek, which is there, by dams, diverted from its channel and carried along the upper part of the city in a main canal, from which side ditches convey the streams down both sides of every street, furnishing irrigation to the gardens, and pure water, in the upper part of the city for all other purposes. Lower down, the loose black soil and the wash of the streets render the water rather impure, though it is used, and during the season when irrigation is not in progress, is still tolerably clear. Next to Temple Block and Brigham's, the Theatre is the institution of Salt Lake City. It stands one square south of Brigham's grounds, at the corner of First South and First East streets; is built of brick and rough stone, covered with stucco in front, and its cost is variously estimated from seventy to two hundred thousand dollars. It was built while railroads were yet a thousand miles distant, probably doubling its cost. It will comfortably seat two thousand persons, and can be packed with a few hundred more; the proscenium is sixty feet deep, and the building the largest of the kind west of Chicago.

Formerly the playing was done entirely by amateurs, under the training of old London professionals turned Mormons; then they played only on alternate nights, rehearsing one night and playing the next, pursuing their ordinary calling by day. But at present there are professional players among the Mormons, receiving a regular salary, and assisted by "stars" from abroad. Just before I reached Salt Lake, one of the "leading ladies" of the home troupe, Miss Sarah Alexander, took a sudden departure for California, where she is now engaged in her profession; and quite lately another home "star," Miss Asenath Adams, born and reared among the Saints, has left to become the wife of a Gentile. Her father, a bigoted Mormon, has fully realized the text, "Train up a child and away she goes."

The Parquet is usually occupied only by Mormons and their families; for a Gentile to be seen there is apt to create a suspicion of "jack-Mormon" tendencies. The resident Gentiles and visitors occupy the first or Dress Circle, while the second and third circles are given up to miners, transients, and boys, and even Indians often find a standing "at the top of the house."

Next in interest to the theatre among public buildings, are Social Hall, the Seventies' Hall and the Court House. The last named is built entirely of *adobes*, but stuccoed with exquisite finish and in perfect imitation of variegated granite, making a building of fine and imposing appearance. On Main—East Temple—Street, the business houses are all included within two blocks; among them the stone storehouse of Ransohoff & Co., the drug store of Godbe & Co., the large building of Walker Brothers, and Masonic Hall building would take respectable rank in eastern cities the same size. The finest business house in the city is that of Wm. Jennings & Co., now devoted to the uses of "Zion's Co-operative Association." There are two well built hotels, the Revere House and Townsend, and a number of private residences of considerable taste and beauty. But it is easy to see after all, that the beauty of Salt Lake is largely by comparison. For twenty years it was the only town between the Missouri and Sacramento; to reach it, men had to plod eleven hundred weary miles, with mules or oxen, across alkali deserts, rugged mountains, and barren flats; to them it was the half-way place for rest and recruiting, and no wonder its broad well watered streets, its green, cool gardens and orchards, and its neat white *adobes*, seemed a very *terrestrial* Eden. No wonder the Mormon emigrants who had made the weary passage from Europe, broke forth into songs and shouts of glad surprise, at sight of their "Zion." But now that one can run out in three days from the well built cities of the East, the contrast is lacking, the illusion is destroyed, and early visitors are flatly accused of having "blown the Salt Lake trumpet altogether too loud."

Twenty-three years ago, this region was a desert of sage-brush, grease-wood and cactus, when on the 24th of July, 1847, the "pioneers" first entered the valley. Their material progress since shows that no human institution can be an unmixed evil.

From a ramble through the city, I went to the noted Warm Springs, just outside the city to the north-west; and without the faith of the Mormons, I can safely agree with them that this pool is "for the healing of the nations." This is the season for "the emigration" to arrive, and returning to the city I found the people excited over the arrival of a train of fifty teams, bringing a large number of new and some old converts from England, Denmark and Switzerland. The train had unloaded in the church *corral*, or tithing yard, a large walled enclosure in the Prophet's Block; I entered under an arched stone gateway and viewed the new arrivals. Old, withered-looking women, fat, clumpy-looking girls and middle-aged "vrows" composed the female portion, and all evidently of the poorest class.

Their friends, and the sisters, generally, had met them

with hearty hospitality, carrying in buckets of milk and baskets of fruit and provisions, to make a welcoming feast, and the *corral* was a scene of feasting and merriment.— But there were a few sad exceptions to the universal joy. Many who had started with this outfit had died by the way, and a few of the old people were so worn out by the long journey that it seemed they could not recover. I was particularly struck with the appearance of one group. An old English woman, whose features bore the impress of exhausting travel, while her hands indicated a lifetime of unremitting toil, was lying on a pile of bedding, evidently sinking with the weakness of fever. The young women had gathered around her with every delicacy to tempt the appetite, while a fair young Mormon girl supported the sinking head on her bosom, and presented a spoonful of ripe peach to the fevered lips. The dame smiled, while tears of weakness and joy ran from her eyes, and tried again and again to eat the proffered delicacy, but in vain. Nature was exhausted by the long voyage. The eyes that had so long and eagerly looked for "Zion," were soon to be dimmed, and the weary feet were hastening to an eternal rest.

In the universal hilarity that prevailed, the Mormon girls were selecting companions from the arrivals, and taking them to their homes for a few days' rest, the travel-worn and dusty, foreign-made garments contrasting strangely with the dress of the young Saints. Female beauty is scarce in Utah. One occasionally meets a fine looking woman, but there is four-fold the beauty in many a Gentile town of 1,000 inhabitants that I can see in all this city. Fine forms are not uncommon, and some of the younger women are quite graceful in carriage, but beauty of expression is rare, and the reason is obvious. Facial beauty is æsthetic, the result of taste, sensibility and cultivation, and, at least, a tolerable elevation of the moral faculties. It will not result from a rude and coarse existence. Beauty of the form is more purely physical, and will naturally spring up anywhere, where woman is not abused or overworked. Given a certain amount of fresh air, moderate exercise and healthy food, and the correct

MORMON TEMPLE BEING BUILT IN SALT LAKE CITY.

womanly form is the result. But beauty of the features has more of the ideal; it is the product of a higher tone of the mental and moral nature, and other things being equal, the greatest number of fine faces will be found in a virtuous and intelligent community.

The men were of the same brawny and red-faced foreign type, white haired boys, and simple looking old men, which every western man has so often seen; a low-browed, stiff-haired, ignorant and stolid race. In their faces could be seen much of the earnest, sincere and quiet; but not of the intellectual, bright or quick of comprehension. Every traveller through the rural districts of Utah, must have observed that, though individual Saints differ somewhat, as other people do, yet there are certain peculiar traits common to all. One of these is their almost total lack of the humorous faculty or principle; phrenologically speaking, they have no organ of wit and humor, or if they have it is so uncultivated that it is practically dormant.

They will laugh heartily enough at a broad joke or coarse jest, but seem quite unable to appreciate keen satire, irony, or delicate wit, or to perceive the ludicrous in odd associations of ideas. The Mormon is often terribly in earnest, but he is seldom funny. This defect is partly one of race, partly in lack of cultivation, but still more in the fact that few people who *can* understand and appreciate an absurdity would ever become Mormons. Hence we rarely see among them the genial, humorous Irishman, the keen witted Israelite, the intellectual Swiss, or the lively, and versatile Frenchman; but in their stead stolid Saxons and plodding Scandinavians. Men are, to a great extent, born to certain forms of religious belief; Boodhism is essentially Mongolian, Spiritism is of the Indian, Mahommedanism has its peculiar subjects, and, though universal in its final application, the present spirit and structure of Christianity is Gothic and European. And the most gloomy forms of error, which have sprung from a corrupt Christianity, find their devotees among the most solemnly impressive and stolid of the European races. Old residents tell me that Artemus Ward's lecture in Salt Lake was, professionally speaking, a perfect failure, simply because it was "cut too fine" for the latitude. A few laughed at his broadest jokes, then for a solid hour while he was doing his funniest the audience sat "like a bump on a log," not giving a smile. It's a wonder it did not kill the sensitive author. Mormonism might originate with keen witted Yankees, but it could not long continue without a broad basis of the North European races.

These new-comers look homely enough, but it is gratifying to observe the vast improvement even in the first generation of the native-born. Whether it is the climate, or better food, or exemption from the severe toil of the poor in Europe, most of the young girls now "coming on" in Utah exhibit a vast personal improvement over their parents, and among the very youngest, whose families have been here for twenty years, the little misses exhibit promise of the trim, graceful form, the arched instep and the light tripping step of the American girl. There are many drawbacks in the social and domestic habits of "this people," still nature is asserting her rights to some extent. She demands beauty in the female form, and even Mormonism cannot altogether prevent it. Of course, the younger generation is more quick-witted and liberal, hence the majority of young Mormons are free thinkers and anti-polygamists. It is the old story of the hen hatching swans, the vulture doves, or the caterpillar giving life to the brilliant butterfly. And this rapid improvement is notable in view of the perils of young life in Utah, of which, more anon.

In my first rambles about the city, I found the Mormons rather communicative, and quite ready to enlighten me as to the peculiar features of their faith; indeed, rather anxious to prove the superiority of their institutions over those of the Gentile world. Of course, like all new comers, I looked upon polygamy as the one great evil, if not the only evil of Utah, and our discussions most often turned upon that point. The first intelligent Mormon, who gave me his views at length, was Mr. Victor Cram, educated as a physician, in Boston, but now a builder in Salt Lake City. As an "inside view," his ideas are worthy of presentation on the venerable principle, *Audi alteram partem.* "We have," said he, "a population of 200,000, three times the population for a new State, and have had for years; but they won't admit us. The fact is, we are a little rebellious. This law of 1862 against polygamy, we don't abide by, and the people won't do so!"

"And what do you think will be the result?" I asked.

"The result? Why, it will be good when people get enlightend on this point. Then polygamy will become popular throughout the world."

"But how do you justify it, or explain this?"

"I take the ground, sir, that polygamy was absolutely necessary to purify and regenerate mankind; that such was the tendency that in no long time the world would have been depopulated, the human race become extinct, without the gracious assistance of polygamy, which inevitable destiny God foresaw, and revealed to Joseph Smith the mode of prevention."

He then proceeded in a lengthy detail of the causes which were operating to weaken the reproductive force of nature, and destroy the young before they reached a marriageable age. His views were unique and interesting, but suffice it to say that he proved, to his own satisfaction at least, that the human race was slowly and surely tending to inevitable decay and complete extinction, through the violation of a certain inter-sexual law, which violation was causing a decline among women and their offspring; that God revealed to Joseph Smith the means of cure, which necessitated the employment of polygamy, which would, in time, regenerate the human race, and restore it to primal strength and beauty.

"But how comes it," I asked, "that the Caucasian races have gone on and increased for three thousand years in single marriage?"

"Because they never run to that excess, and then this new way of killing infants before they saw the light was not known. But the present mode of living leads to excess, and America, the youngest nation, is going to lead all the rest in that excess; and when the old nations of

Europe learn these new tricks and get started on this road, they will go like a flock of sheep, and melt from the face of the earth; and without a radical corrective the race would soon be extinct.

"Mind, I say," he continued, "these are not the reasons why we practise polygamy. We do it solely because God commanded it, 'The mouth of the Lord hath spoken it,' is our sole and only warrant, which we dare not disobey (!!); but these are merely a few of the reasons why God commanded it, as we think. Or to throw aside God's ordinance, and take nature for it, these reasons are sufficient to show why polygamy is according to law and light of nature; why it is the natural order of things, and why God's chosen people were the offspring of polygamous mothers. Now, I took my second wife only last year my circumstances did not enable me to do so before, and the good effects of the arrangement are already observable in my house, particularly in the son of my second wife, which is a brighter, healthier and stronger child than either of my other eight children. And I challenge you to go to any of our schools, and pick out at random a dozen children of polygamous mothers, and then say on your honor if they are not superior to the average children of single marriages,"

This seemed like a bold offer, but one finds in time that the Saints are very much given to the "bluff" game; nor will it be thought strange that they are *not the only* people who excuse their own sins by pointing out those of others.

Without attempting to controvert his views, I accepted the loan of copies of the "Book of Mormon," "Millennial Star," and "Doctrine and Covenants," which I promised to read at my earliest leisure.

My first Sabbath in Salt Lake was bright and clear, and I determined on a visit to the Tabernacle. The early morning I devoted to the "Book of Mormon;" but two hours more than satisfied me. Of all the dull, wearisome and inconsequential books I ever dosed over, I am qualified to say that work takes the lead. It is verbose, diffuse and full of repetitions; about the size of the Old

Testament, every material fact in it could be compressed within the limits of a Tribune Almanac. The Saints aver that it was composed by the angel Moroni, and delivered to Joseph Smith. If so, I am sorry for Moroni, sorry that there were no grammars or "aids to composition" in his "sphere," that he might have given us a work somewhat worthy of criticism. The anti-Mormons, and a certain widow Davidson, now resident in New York, aver that it was written by her first husband, Solomon Spaulding, an invalid clergyman, merely for his own amusement. If so, he was easily amused. I sincerely hope, for the honor of her husband, that the good woman is mistaken, for if any scholar assisted in the production of that work, he must have been *very* invalid, in mind as well as body. I can understand how *some* people admire M. F. Tupper ; I can even, in a dim, far-off way, appreciate those who appreciate John Tyler, Junior; but that men of even average intelligence should discover literary excellence, divine philosophy or spiritual comfort in the " Book of Mormon," is beyond my powers.

That a quarter of a million of the human race should be led to stake their hopes for eternity on the divine authenticity of such a work, is one of the most melancholy evidences of the inherent weakness of the human intellect.

Service was held in the New Tabernacle which will seat eight or ten thousand people, but is quite a failure as far as hearing is concerned. The interior being a perfect oval, those in that portion nearest the stand and in the end farthest from it can hear quite well, while all is confused and indistinct in the central area, which includes nearly half the room. A canopy, or flat, some twenty feet square had been erected over the speaker's stand to serve as a sounding board, but helped the matter very little.

Brigham does not preach oftener than once or twice a month, and did not favor us with his presence this morning; his brother, Joseph Young, preached the opening sermon, and I have no hesitation in pronouncing him the most inferior-looking man I ever saw in the pulpit, and I have seen some hard specimens. He is very old, very thin, very weak-eyed, and rather sallow; his general appearance suggested that he had just slept a month, been awakened by a thunder-storm and come away without changing his clothes, washed in a mud puddle, and combed his hair by crawling through the sage brush. And yet, *he has four wives.* Let the homely take courage. The distinctive feature in Mormon sermons is their exceedingly rambling and discursive nature; touching here, there and everywhere, on everything which concerns man's moral, spiritual and material interests. The peculiar baldness of their style is made ten-fold more apparent by the homely words and phrases in which it is couched. Hints on stock raising, digging ditches, building fences and making "dobies," slip into the midst of moral disquisitions on "the whole duty of man."

I could not discover what was the special subject of Joseph Young's remarks; he took no text, as they usually do not, and fired away at all the sins of the congregation very much on the "Donnybrook Fair" principle. Before beginning his sermon proper, he called for general news from any of the settlements, gave a list of foreign letters which had arrived, and called for all returned missionaries to come into the stand and "give in their experience." No one responding, he commenced by stating that "man was a moral being;" enlarged on the troubles of the Saints; confessed his ignorance of the reason why these things were so, and began to "score" the young men for laziness and bad habits generally. From this he branched off to the necessity of giving liberally to aid the poor Saints in Europe to reach Utah: "They ought to come, the Saints ought all to be here, for the devil is watching where they are to take the spirit out of their minds, and they ought to come here, and be treated with brotherly love. But there is too much stubborness here; the brethren are all stubborn. The sisters are not quite so stubborn."

This last was news to me; but he went on to prove it by a philosophical disquisition on the peculiar difference between the masculine and feminine minds, which seemed about an equal mixture of the ideas of Plato, Tennyson, and Professor Fowler, and to have about as much relation to the subject in hand, as it had to the next Presidential election. He went on:

"Now some of you old men that come here early, feel very much broke down. You're all stiff and crippled up, and here's a lot of 'young sprouts,' as I call 'em, who'll hardly work at all. I tell you, young fellows, it won't do. You've got to stir around and labor more. And these young fellows are so strong. Why, they are as elastic as the rabbits on yon mountain! While lots of these old men can't stoop down to pick up a hoe. I tell you, as I told my folks this morning, just after family prayer, you want knowledge of how to live in this world. Take care of your bodies! Don't eat so much of this green stuff!! Keep your stomachs clean !!! And some of you men are so very inconsistent—in fact, I'm inconsistent myself sometimes. To ask God for health, and not take care of it. Why do you ask God for such a thing? Why, that's your own business. God says, 'go ahead, and take care of your stomachs and body, and I'll guarantee the rest.' One thing I've noticed here so much; nearly everybody dies so sudden, and the old people, who have died lately, almost seem as if they had just dropped dead. We have no lingering diseases among us. Come to meeting in the right spirit, and act in brotherly love and sisterly kindness. And, finally, may God bless you all, brethren and sisters, is my prayer, for Jesus' sake. Amen."

He was followed by Elder Wilford Woodruff, who gave a rather able and connected address, on the dangers of internal dissensions in states, nations, churches, and families; after which the choir sang, "Come let us anew our journey pursue," with great force and beauty, and the meeting adjourned.

In their mode of conducting prayer, singing and other services, the Saints follow the Methodist order; they, however, stand at prayer, but forbid written sermons; they have "experience meetings," and take the sacrament every Sunday, excluding, of course, all but their own people; and, finally, they immerse, repeating it after every "backsliding," interpret the Scriptures literally, preach long and loud of "one Lord, one faith, one baptism," stigmatize all others as "sectarians," and in their initial principles follow the Campbellites. My second Sunday in Salt Lake, I heard Orson Pratt deliver a rather learned discourse on the various temples erected by "the Lord's peculiar people," embodying the idea that the last and most glorious one was to be that of the Latter-day Saints, to be set up in Jackson County, Missouri, "when the fulness of time had come."

At the end of two weeks in Salt Lake City my impressions are, on the whole, rather favorable. I find the city quiet, apparently in good order, neat and pleasant to dwell in; though the people are mostly ignorant and bigoted, they did not appear contentious; I had been treated with considerable courtesy, and began to conclude the Mormons had been maligned, and often held long arguments in favor of those whom I suspected to be a much misrepresented and persecuted people. I had yet much to learn..

CHAPTER X.

TRIP TO BEAR RIVER AND RETURN.

Northward afoot—Hot Springs — " Sessions Settlement "— Polygamy again—"Ephe Roberts' young wife "—Farmington—Kaysville—Three wives, and stone walls between—" Let us have Peace "—Red Sand Ridge—Ogden—Brigham City—Into the Poor District—Scandinavian porridge--English cookery—Rural life in Utah—Bear River, North—Cache Valley and the Canon—" Professor" Barker, the "Mad Philosopher"—A New Cosmogony—Mormon Science — " Celestial Masonry "—" Adam" *redivivus*—A Modern " Eve "—Folly and Fanaticism—Mineral Springs—The country *vs.* the city Mormon.

FINE weather was running to waste, and I had seen nothing of Utah outside the city; so on the afternoon of September the 25th, I threw a few pounds of crackers, dried beef, sugar and tea, into my valise, to serve in case I should get beyond the settlements, and took my way northward on foot, determined to see Mormondom in its rural aspects. The nearest point on the Great Salt Lake is about twelve miles from the city, and this road nowhere approaches it nearer than two miles, but runs due north; with the Wasatch mountains to the east, and the lake to the west, leaving a valley with an average width of five miles. My route led me by the Warm Springs, already mentioned; three miles farther there is another, known as the Hot Springs, from being twenty-six degrees higher in temperature than the former. A stream of scalding water, as large as a man's body, boils out of a rock at the foot of the mountain, forms a hot pool two or three rods in circuit, whence the branch runs across the road, and westward into Hot Spring Lake. These springs will be more fully described in another place.

The sun was near the horizon when I reached the highest point on the road, the sky which had been hazy all day became clear, and glancing back towards the city I

N

saw her light coloured dwellings and green gardens glistening in the evening sunlight, reminding one strangely of pictures of Oriental scenes, while the gray peaks to the east, the blue mountains to the south-west, and the Lake Island hills combined to form a grand circle of beauty surrounding the modern "Zion." Seated on a projecting rock above the road, as the sun sank slowly behind the islands, I tried again and again to convey some description of the scene to paper, and as often dropped book and pencil with a mixture of delight and despair.

Ten miles out brought me to Sessions Settlement, sometimes called Bountiful, where I spent the night at the house of Mr. Perry Green Sessions, a Mormon elder and returned missionary, who entertained me with some account of his experience in England and the Eastern States "while laboring to build up Zion among those that are in darkness."

From there, I continued my journey along the stage road, now along the base of the mountains where cold springs break in jets out of the rocks, and again far out in the valley among corn and cane fields, or amid dwellings surrounded by peach orchards, where the trees were breaking under the load of ripening fruit, a sight I had not seen for many years. A larger and finer orchard than ordinary attracted my attention, and as the gate stood invitingly open, I walked forward to where two women sat beneath a tree preparing fruit for drying, and proposed to purchase a dozen or two of peaches. Fruit in plenty was offered and all pay refused, and while I took a proffered seat, the younger lady, a bright, lively, voluble woman, entered at once into conversation by asking what State I had come from.

"How do you know I am not a Utah man?" I asked.

"Oh, I knowed you was a Gentile the minute you stepped in at the gate, and you bet everybody knows it the minute they see you," was the reply.

Further conversation showed that the lady had quite a history. She told me her father came to Salt Lake City twenty-one years ago, and she was the third white child born in the place.

"But I couldn't see it in my way to marry a Saint, not much; though I was raised to believe in it, and do believe in the religion all but that."

"Is your father a Mormon?" I ventured to ask.

"Oh, yes, and got four women; only one wife, mind you, that's my mother; but four women who call themselves his wives. I never was raised to know anything else, but when I was nineteen, father married me to a Gentile, 'cause he couldn't help himself, I reckon. My husband was raised next door to me, and went to California and stayed five years, and soon as he come back we was married. I'd a stayed an old maid a thousand years before I'd take a pluralist. Plurality's all well enough for the men, but common sense shows that it don't suit women."

"Why, then, do some of them hold up for it?"

"Well, they think, they must to get salvation; it's a part of their religion, and sometimes they get along pretty well. We never had any trouble in father's family. The children all growed up just like brothers and sisters, and treated each other so. Father always taught me to respect his other women, and I always did so.

"But, law, I've seen such sights in other families. Why, I've seen our neighbor's women just pull the hair right out of each other's heads. There's so many men, when they get a young wife, will let her abuse the old one, and encourage her to do it.

"I've seen the man stand by, and say, 'Go in, kill her if you can.' Now, there is Ephe. Roberts right over there,"
—pointing to a stone house near the mountain,—"he brought a real young delicate wife from New York, now goin' on sixteen years ago, and she worked awful hard, I tell you; why I've known her to do all her own work when Ephe. had three hands and the threshin' machine at his house, and sometimes she worked out in the field, bound wheat and raked hay, which, you know, is awful hard on a delicate New York woman—'taint as if she been raised to it, like we folks, and after all, just last year, Ephe. went and married another woman, a real young one, not over twenty, and, don't you think, this spring she

knocked Maria—that's his first wife—down with the churn-dasher, and scalded her. Ephe. stood by, and just said, 'go in, Luce; kill her, if you can!' It all started about a churn, too. Both wanted to use it at once. Maria had it, and her butter was a little slow a comin', and they got mad, and Luce struck her, and then snatched the kettle right off the stove, and then poured hot water on her feet, so she fell down when she tried to run out. And what was the result, finally? Well, Maria left him; of course, she had to, or be killed. It's very nice, though, for the men. I had a dozen chances to marry old Mormons, but law! I wouldn't give that for all of 'em. Why, just turn things round, and let a woman have two or three men, and see how they'd like that! There wouldn't be any murderin' done in these parts, oh, no! And, I reckon, a woman has as fine feelin's as a man. I tell you, if my husband ever joins 'em, or tries to get another wife, that day I'll hunt another Gentile; you bet!" The testimony of "this witness," professionally speaking, was certainly plain; nor did she trouble me to cross-examine, but gave her views freely. I note one singular fact in all similar cases: During a long residence in Utah I have never, in a single instance, talked ten minutes with a young lady of polygamous family, that did not manage in some way to tell me, *she was the daughter of the first, or legal wife,* if such was the case. If silent on that point, it may safely be presumed they are of polygamous mothers. And in more than one instance, I have known them to falsely claim legitimate birth.

From this "apostate's" I journeyed on to Farmington, eighteen miles north of the city, a beautiful town and settlement of some two thousand inhabitants; the residence of the Mormon hero, Lot Smith, who commanded their guerilla force at the time it confronted Johnston's army in Echo Cañon, burned his waggons and drove off his cattle.

I spent the night with a well-to-do Mormon, who occupied a long, one-story stone house, divided into three large rooms, with a kitchen in rear of each; each room was occupied by one of his three wives and her children.

He seemed to be living at the time with the middle one, where we took supper. The partition walls must have been two feet thick, without any communication, each wife with her progeny keeping strictly to her own department. He was doubtless a "Grant man;" his motto seemed to be "Let us have peace." A "constitutional" the next morning brought me to the next settlement, Kaysville by name, where I took breakfast with a Gentile who had a Mormon wife. He was a Missourian, some fifty years old, and belonged to the Church, he told me, ten or fifteen years ago, but was "dis-fellowshipped for not payin' tithes."

He talked quite earnestly when he found I was from the States, and gave his views on the entire subject without troubling me to ask a question. "I never heard in my life," said he, "that Christ and his Apostles rode around the country in fine carriages with two span o' gray hosses, and made the people turn out provision enough to keep him up, as we've had to do for the bishop here.— Brigham Young pretends to be His successor, and at the same time makes his brags that he never touches anything he don't make money outen. Now, just look at that Deseret Telegraph line. He had all the people pay tithes and make donations for it, sayin' it would be such a nice thing for the people, and every settlement had to furnish a certain number of poles ; and now they'll charge you five dollars for sendin' ten words, be you Saint or Gentile, And here after all, he's round makin' every Saint, the poorest ov 'em, give so much to help to pay these operators that come down to teach the girls along through the Territory, how to work the wires. Now, what comes o' that money ? it goes into Brigham's pockets. But, pshaw, these people won't listen to you. Can't make my wife believe a word o' that."

The good woman retorted with a wordy defence of the Church and the Prophet, averring her firm belief in everything Mormon, to which the husband listened with a dry quizzical smile, and finally remarked : "Well, p'raps I *had* better go back. Guess I *will*, and get me another wife. Like dernation well to have a nice, trim, young creature about twenty-five."

The wife, whose waist was after the pattern of a rum barrel, and her feet models for a patent brick machine, reddened a little and was silent. I think he will convert her yet.

The Deseret Telegraph line, to which he referred, follows this road to the northern boundary of the Territory, and south of the city extends nearly to Arizona, with side branches connecting all the detached settlements; the wires centre in Brigham Young's office, and thus at a moment's notice he can send a warning of danger to five-sixths of his people, and in twenty-four hours' time the most isolated settlers could be ready to move. Whether for good or bad purposes, it is a remarkable monument of Mormon enterprise. I had intended to keep the Sabbath at this point, but falling in with a farmer returning to Cache Valley from the city, I rode some twelve miles with him, passing over the Red Sand Desert. This is a ridged piece of land jutting out from near the mouth of Weber Cañon, towards the lake, about ten miles long and eight wide, and too high for ordinary irrigation. Most of the land north of the city has one general character, a mixture of gravel and loam, or of fine red sand and " dobic earth," a peculiar whitish clay; in its natural state it is as barren as any part of the plains.

A piece of land is worthless unless water can be brought upon it; but with irrigation it produces equally with any soil in the world. Leaving the ridge we descend into Weber Valley, and in five miles reach the city of Ogden, the most important in northern Utah; containing with its vicinity a population of three or four thousand, and now the point of junction of the Union Pacific, Central Pacific and Utah Central (Brigham's) Railroads. Thence two days' sauntering, twenty-two miles, brings me through Willard Settlement to Brigham City, some sixty miles north of Salt Lake City. This is the county seat of Box Elder Co., which contains at present a Gentile population of at least a thousand.

It has a beautiful location at the foot of the Wasatch, at the mouth of a cañon, which sends out a large stream of pure, clear water, and a little north-east of the head of

Bear River Bay, the north-eastern projection of Great Salt Lake. From Brigham City, northward, the valley of Salt Lake shows much less sign of cultivation and settlement than below that point. Peach orchards entirely disappear, apple-trees and grape vines are quite rare, stone-houses and stucco-finished "dobies" are seen no more, and their place is filled by rude log-cabins, with a very uninviting exterior and interior not over clean, inhabited mostly by Welsh, Danes and Swedes.

The English inhabitants of the valley live quite well, nearly as well as the corresponding class in our Western States, though I have visited no part of America where I found them so entirely English in dialect and manner as here. Taking my meals wherever the hour overtook me, I have found rich brown coffee, golden butter and light white bread, in company with the broad English accent, and have learned to associate the "hexasperated haitch," with 'igh 'opes for a 'ungry man.

But if I stepped into a cabin and heard the Welsh or Danish guttural, I asked some trivial favor and passed on to the Britons, whom I consider the best part of the Mormon people. A traveller should not be an epicure, but I acknowledge a weakness in that respect, and while I had that glorious appetite, I hated to waste it on the suspicious looking porridge, which is a standing dish among the Scandinavian Saints.

A few of the American Mormons come up to the English standard, but in the country the majority fall below it; they constitute, however, so small a part of these people, that I do not stop with them one time in five. They are nearly all from New York and Pennsylvania, and belong to the original sect, all the late converts being foreigners. I see no Western people among them to speak of. I met one middle aged lady from Greene County, Indiana, and when she learned I was from Parke County, adjoining, she was quite overcome, got me up the best breakfast the cabin afforded, and talked and cried alternately while I was eating it. Her parents joined the Mormons while she was a young woman, and she had heard from her old home but three or four times since.

That region was attracting considerable interest, as the probable site of the "great central city of the future," the town on the railroad which *was* to be, the most convenient spot for staging and freighting to Montana, Idaho, Oregon and Washington, which would doubtless be a city of great and permanent importance. But the railroad was yet four hundred miles distant, and the location of the future city in great doubt. Many thought it would be at the last crossing on Weber River, while others were equally sanguine it would be in Curlew Valley, a hundred miles west of Bear River. Meanwhile, work was pushed forward rapidly; the Union Pacific Company had just let contracts for a hundred miles of grading north of the lake, teams were passing that way in considerable numbers, and graders' camps were thick along the route.

At the north crossing of Bear River I found a "home station" of Wells, Fargo & Co.'s stages, where their branch line to Boise City and into Oregon takes its start; also a fine hotel, bridge, store, and quite a little village. A few miles above, Bear River, which has run around a long U of three hundred miles from its source in eastern Utah, "canyons" downward a thousand feet in three miles, out of Cache into Bear River Valley.

Seventy miles up the river, in Idaho, are the noted Soda Springs; near them Camp Connor and a small settlement of "Morrisites," a sect of recusant Mormons, a little more crazy than the rest, but not quite so mean, who sought the shelter of the military in their escape from Brighamism.

My return trip from Bear River was varied by two incidents worthy of special mention—a visit to the Mineral Springs and an interview with the "mad philosopher" of Utah. This eccentric genius merits more than a passing notice. His name is J. W. Barker, generally called "Professor," an Englishman by birth, who came to this country fourteen years ago with a Mormon party. He claimed to have discovered the primitive laws, which govern the whole material universe, and that, in time, he would refute all the theories of such philosophers as Newton, La Place, and Descartes, from whom he dissented *in toto.*

True to his convictions, as soon as he had his family comfortably settled, he fell to work investigating, collecting facts, analyzing and arranging specimens, and writing the *principia* of his great work, the " Magna Charta of Universal Science," which was to annihilate all our present ideas of gravity, light, and momentum, and usher in the scientific millennium, at the same time with the moral regeneration of mankind.

For ten long, weary years, he has devoted every hour, beyond those requisite for obtaining the bare necessaries of life, to this research. He has travelled hundreds of miles among the mines and cañons, digging into drift, wash dirt, gravel, quartz, and gold gulch and bar, till he is known to the miners from Montana to Salt Lake. Night after night he has watched the moon and stars, and calculated the slightest changes of the atmosphere and mist, and every observation has been faithfully recorded, and assigned to its proper cause, in his new classification of principles. Being an unlettered man, whose only knowledge of geology was gained as an English miner, he has worked his way against difficulties which would have daunted any but a half-mad enthusiast; has surrounded himself with dictionaries and lexicons of science, and hammered his way into the first principles of more than one language, by the most exhaustive labor. I found the " Professor" in a mountain nook which might well excuse a man for going mad over the works of nature.

Directly fronting his house, three majestic grey peaks of the Wasatch range rise a mile above the level plain, while a short distance in the rear of his farm spread the azure waters of the Salt Lake, beyond which is the blue line of the mountains on the promontory.

His painfully thin and gaunt appearance showed that he had hung over his books and burned the midnight oil till the vital frame had shrunk; but his manner was earnest and his voice firm, while the corded muscles stood out on a body without an ounce of fat, and seemed to run over the bones like the wire pulleys of a metal clock. He conversed pleasantly and quite intelligently on various topics, till glancing at the mountain peaks I remarked that they must have been thrown up by some great convulsion of nature; then his eyes lighted with a strange fire as he hastily replied: "They *certainly* were *not* thrown up; they were thrown down." Then holding forth an hour on the origin of mountains, he invited me to his study. A low room half underground in the rear of his house, built of logs, had been rudely fitted up with board, chest and table, block candle-holders attached to the wall by wires, so as to bend out and in, and a few chairs. The walls were completely covered with rude maps and charts, and with long lists of words, which he stated he had to use often and did not know how to spell, all copied from the dictionary in large capitals.

Producing a seat for me, and a large bowl of water for himself, he entered on a three hours' exposition of his views. He holds that all the fluid elements of nature are resolvable into four gases; that all the grosser elements are in like manner reducible to four simple solids; and from varying proportions of these few primitives are derived all possible materials throughout the universe. He contends also that the entire Newtonian theory of gravity is erroneous and false to true science; that there is, in strictness of language, no such principle as gravity anywhere operating in creation; that the terms refraction and reflection are based on a total misconception of the nature of light; that all space outside of the atmosphere contains a material medium, and that the atmosphere is shown, by actual demonstration, to be eight thousand miles thick, instead of forty-five.

He thinks that all nature is operated upon by four simple, constant and regular laws, and that all we observe are but combinations and inter-relations of these four, which depend for their action simply on the will and moving power of God. They operate in one course through countless cycles of time, tending always to a common centre, and, having run that course, are directed in a returning course for other terms. The mental, moral and spiritual world is but a microcosmical copy of the material, consisting, too, of four subtle elements, mingled with four grosser elements, and moved upon by infinite combinations of four simple laws, directly referable to the will of God.

The mountains are remains of precipitated satellites, of which the earth has had many, the moon only remaining; but, like all the others, it is a hollow globe, destined to fall upon and give final shape to the surface of the earth. The planets inside of our orbit have now no satellites, but are hurrying on to their destiny on the face of the sun; while those outside of us have many, and are coming in more slowly. We, on the earth, are approaching the latter part of our career, and have barely time to complete the moral regeneration of the race.

It is consoling to know that the grand smash-up will not take place till after the millennium. The old gentleman has just finished his great work, and required all the information I could give him as to the cost and facilities of getting it printed in the East. It consisted of forty-six chapters, bound up in as many separate manuscript volumes. Take him all in all, he is a curious case of scientific insanity, well worthy the attention of Mr. Beck, the learned writer on the subject. The "Professor" lectures in Salt Lake City occasionally, and Orson Pratt—professor and elder, and the learned man of the city—has thought it worth while to reply to him through the press. Wild and strange as this man's ideas may appear, he is but a type of hundreds in Utah. In science, as in theology, Mormonism is at war with all existing systems; one-third of the whole people seem a little crazy on some subject or other, and the wildest, most baseless theory, the one farthest removed from natural causes, is ever the one most likely to prevail.

Having cut loose from all recognized standards in spiritual matters, they seem equally determined on the supernatural, and extra human in medicine, science, astronomy and natural history. I was once called upon by a Mormon, a little more crazy than ordinary, with an immense chart of what he called "Celestial Masonry." For the medical museum of a mad-house, it would have been a priceless treasure. A canvas, three feet square, was covered by the pictured folds of an enormous serpent, along which were drawings of the various scenes, symbols and implements of the new Masonry, divided for the various degrees, of which there are twenty-seven! All the work had been done with colored crayons; by "inspirational writing," as the Mormon averred, the spirits guiding his hand without his volition; and as a work of art, it showed remarkable style and finish.

Some three years ago, a "Josephite," or recusant Mormon, who had adopted the new Mormon doctrine of "transmission of spirits," conceived that he was Adam sent back to the flesh; his wife, a little worse crazed, was Eve; but during the six thousand years of their separation, she had fallen away and become a prostitute. To "purify her" he cut off all her hair, pulled out her teeth, and, for the better convenience of locomotion, dressed her in man's clothes, when both started on foot for the States. A year afterwards they made their appearance at a *ranche* in Colorado, nearly dead with hunger and fatigue; nor did it ever appear how they had reached here. From there they came with a returning train to the Missouri, where the authorities properly consigned them to the lunatic asylum.

There is no refuge for the insane in Utah; fortunately, perhaps, for it might require a small war to settle who should occupy it. Few are violent, but many are deranged; and the whole Territory would present a fine field for the student in the jurisprudence of insanity.

The Mineral Springs are ten miles south of Bear River Bridge, and seventy north of the city; but I defer a full description, which will be found under the proper heading.

In my trip to Bear River, and return, I journeyed nearly two hundred miles among the rural Saints, and observed their ways with all earnestness and curiosity. The country Mormon is more religious than his city brother, but less intelligent. He is a greater stickler for the small matters of his faith, but much less able to give a reason why. He is more hospitable, generous and social, but much more offensive in thrusting the unpleasant features of his faith upon you. But the greatest difference is among the women. The polygamous wife in the city is in paradise compared with her sister in the country, where farm labors and cares must be shared in common. There the condition of woman is already fast tending to what it is in other polygamous countries, and there the degeneracy is soonest manifest. While the men are enthusiastically devoted to their faith, I did not see a single woman in the country who defended polygamy, though strongly Mormon in everything else.

At least one-third the entire population of the valley is from Great Britain, one-third or more from Sweden, Norway and Denmark, while possibly one-sixth is American. As far as I know, all the posts of honor, indeed all the easy and lucrative positions, are filled by Americans, simply because the others are generally incapable. The missionaries are largely of foreign birth, each being sent back to his native country, after a few years' residence in Utah.

Little more than a year afterwards, in visiting the same section, I met with an experience in Brigham City, which, though equally novel, was nothing like so pleasant. The Saints, who had seemed indifferent on my first visit, were altogether too pointed in their attentions the last time.

But I anticipate. I reached Salt Lake City the morning of October the sixth, in time for the "fall Conference" of 1868.

CHAPTER XI.

THE CONFERENCE AND ITS RESULTS.

A Mormon mass-meeting—Faces and features—Great enthusiasm—A living "martyr"—A Mormon hymn—The Poetess—A "president" chosen—He recites the Church history—First view of Brigham—He curses the Gentiles—A "nasty sermon"—Coarseness and profanity—Bitterness of other speakers—Swearing in the pulpit—Exciting the people—Their frenzy and fanaticism—Hatred against the United States—Foolish bravado—The author gains new light on Mormonism—A subject to be studied—English and European Sects of like character—Division of the subject.

THE semi-annual conference of the Church of Jesus Christ of Latter-day Saints, convened on Tuesday morning, October 7th, in the new Tabernacle, and was, to me, an occasion of great interest. Long before the hour of meeting, indeed, from early dawn, all the roads leading into the city were thronged by crowds from distant settlements, going up to their half-yearly worship in "Zion." As I returned from Bear River, on the Sunday and Monday preceding, I was passed every hour by long trains of Saints from the northern and north-eastern parts of the Territory, and, on reaching the city, found still larger delegations from Utah Lake District, Provo, Fillmore, San Pete, and St. George.

This occasion among the Saints is every way equal to the yearly passover among the Jews, and every one who can possibly leave home makes a visit to "Zion," and esteems it an honor and a privilege to do so.

I reached the building too late on Tuesday morning, and, with many thousand others, was turned away for want of room. The Saints seemed to consider it sufficient happiness to stand around and gaze at the building, and think of what was going on inside; but I was sustained by no such enthusiasm, and consoled myself by getting an early dinner, preparatory to securing a seat as soon as the doors were opened in the afternoon. The sight was well worth the trouble. From my seat near the pulpit, and just at one side, I could overlook the whole vast sea of faces. The curtain in the rear had been removed, and the entire oval, as well as the space beside the organ, was completely filled by at least ten thousand eager auditors. The rows of high seats on either side of the pulpit were occupied by bishops and elders from distant settlements, some three hundred in all, while the four long seats constituting the pulpit, were occupied by the First Presidency, consisting of Brigham Young, Daniel H. Wells, and a vacant space for the late Heber C. Kimball; also by the Twelve Apostles, the Heads of the Quorum of Seventies, the Church Secretary, Historian and City Elders. It was the largest collection of the Saints I had yet seen, and I studied it with much interest.

Occasionally I would see a fine cast of American features, but nearly all the faces had that indescribable foreign look, which all can recognize and none portray. In companies of fifties and hundreds they had left their distant homes at the call of the missionary, had given up friends, property, country and religion, as they thought, to follow Christ; had tossed upon the waves in noisome emigrant ships, had turned their backs upon the great and fertile States, and traversed eleven hundred miles of prairie, mountain and burning sand, "to build up the kingdom of God in Deseret." And to these people, all before them to-day was a glorious reality Feeling as I did, that all this was but part of a great delusion, I could not but reverence the intense faith of these devotees.

The meeting was called to order, after which the Twentieth Ward choir sang,

" My soul is full of peace and love,
  I soon shall see Christ from above," etc.

Prayer was offered by Elder Erastus Snow, followed by a quartette by the Brigham City choir,

"Pray for the peace of Deseret,"

after which Elder John Taylor addressed the meeting. Taylor is one of the early converts to Mormonism, and enjoys a high reputation among them, having been with Joseph Smith in many trying scenes. With another brother, he was with Joseph and Hyrum at the time they were killed in Carthage jail, Hancock Co., Illinois.

According to the popular Mormon account, as the mob commenced firing, Joseph said to Taylor, "I shall pass away, but you shall live to tell the tale to children's children." At that moment Hyrum fell dead. Joseph cried, "Oh, my dear brother Hyrum!" and sprang into the window. A second volley was fired, when Joseph exclaimed, "Oh, Lord, my God!" and fell into the street. Of the same volley, four shots wounded Taylor in as many places, and a fifth—an ounce ball from a yager musket—struck him squarely in the breast, and buried in an English lever watch, which had run without interruption for ten years, stopping the hands exactly at 5 o'clock, 16 minutes, 22 seconds, P.M., which is marked among the Saints as the solemn hour of the Prophet's death. On the fall of Joseph, the mob rushed around the building, and the fourth brother, who was unhurt, carried Taylor down stairs, and to a place of safety. A Mormon tradition adds that, at the same time, a gigantic Missourian, with his face blackened, ran forward to cut off Joseph's head, for which a reward had been offered; but as he knelt, knife in hand, on the body of the Prophet, a flash of lightning darted, from the clear sky, between him and his victim, and shook the knife from his grasp. This incident, which is the subject of a sensational engraving often seen in the Mormon dwellings, rests upon the statement of one Daniels, the only witness of the assassination not connected either with the Mormons or the mob. He joined the Mormons soon after, and, at the request of the Apostles, published his account. He was afterwards "cut off" from the church, but they still cling to his testimony. The watch, which marked the hour so precisely, is kept as a sacred relic in the city. Taylor, though shot nearly all to pieces, recovered entirely, and is a healthy, venerable-looking old man of sixty years. He gave a rather able address, reciting some of the early trials, and urging the Saints to be industrious and self-sustaining.

The choir then sang the following hymn, composed by Miss Eliza R. Snow, the Mormon poetess :—

"OUR PROPHET, BRIGHAM YOUNG."

" O God of life and glory !
Hear Thou a people's prayer,
Bless, bless our Prophet Brigham ;
Let him thy fulness share.
He is Thy chosen servant—
To lead Thine Israel forth,
Till Zion, crowned with joy, shall be
A praise in all the earth.

" He draws from Christ, the fountain
Of everlasting truth,
The wise and prudent counsels
Which he gives to age and youth.
Thyself in him reflected
Through mortal agency,
He is Thy representative
To set Thy people free.

" Thou richly hast endowed him
With wisdom's bounteous store,
And Thou hast made him mighty
By Thy own Almighty power.
Oh, let his life be precious—
Bless Thou his brethren, too,
Who firmly join him side by side,
Who're true as he is true.

" Help him to found Thy kingdom
In majesty and power,
With peace in every palace
And with strength in every tower ;
And when Thy chosen Israel
Their noblest strains have sung
The swelling chorus there shall be
Our Prophet, Brigham Young."

This authoress is one of the "spiritual wives" of Brigham, which class of ladies usually retain their maidenly appellation, sometimes merely adding that of the spiritual husband. She is a very fine, intellectual-looking woman, of forty or fifty years, and, from her appearance, seems made to be loved.

On Wednesday morning Elder George A. Smith, cousin of Joseph, was chosen as First Counsellor to Brigham Young, in place of Heber C. Kimball, deceased. Daniel H. Wells is Second Counsellor, and these three constitute the First Presidency, at the head of all affairs of the Church.

President Smith then gave a lengthy account of the early history of the Church, from the time Joseph was called to take the golden plates out of the Hill of Cumorah, in western New York, to the expulsion from Nauvoo. He enlarged on their troubles in Kirkland, and journey to Missouri. "There two priests organized a mob, and the Lieutenant-Governor called out the militia. The Saints were driven from Jackson County to Clay, and from Clay to Caldwell, which they found occupied by seven persons, all hunters. Far West was built as if by magic. By August 1, 1838, they owned all of Caldwell, and parts of neighboring counties, when the mobs came upon them again. The Governor called out fifteen thousand men, but there was no law but mob law, whipping men and ravishing women. Women and children wandered for fifteen days on the burnt prairie, and could be tracked by the blood from their feet. Then the Saints went to Illinois and built the beautiful city of Nauvoo, and, while there, Joseph Smith went to see the President, Martin Van Buren, who heard his petition through, and then said: 'Your cause is just, but I can do nothing for you.' Soon after this Joseph and Hyrum were arrested and murdered. Then a combination was formed in nine counties to expel us.

"We appealed to the Governors of the States, and were told the law was on our side, but public opinion was against us, and we would have to leave. We finished our temple with the trowel in one hand and rifle in the other.

Then our city was bombarded for three days, and we retreated again. We commenced to cross the Mississippi in the month of February on the ice. While lying on the bank of the river the Lord sent quails into the camp, that they could take them with the hand, which kept the people from dying of hunger. In that condition they remained till those who had gone west could return with waggons and take them away; but, before this was done, many perished."

This history was continued at various times by all the speakers, and in the most exaggerated and inflammatory style. On Thursday morning I heard Brigham Young for the first time. He is above medium height, well proportioned, fine and portly-looking; with gray or light blue eyes, light brown or golden hair, now sprinkled with gray, clear, rosy skin, and sanguine temperament. His voice is quite clear, and his enunciation distinct, with considerable of what is termed "presence," and electric effect upon his congregation. But his style was coarse, in this instance even vulgar beyond the bounds of description. He was evidently either in an ill humor, or determined to make the people so, indulging in reminiscences both personal and public, which led him into violent denunciation of all outsiders. When he first arose I was somewhat impressed, and thought I saw one reason for his supremacy, that he was indebted for his power over an ignorant people, almost as much to his physical as to his mental superiority. But when he had closed I was utterly amazed, and it seemed incredible that one hundred people could be found, much less a thousand times that number, who should regard him as a "prophet of the Lord." Afterwards, however, I had the pleasure of hearing him when he was in a calmer mood, when he appeared, to some extent at least, the prophet, priest and king.

For the rest of the Conference, which was mainly devoted to the discussion of a general movement to prevent trade with the Gentile merchants, the speakers seemed to vie with each other in bitterness, intemperance of language, and hostility to Gentiles; and all the good opinions of the Mormons I had hitherto formed were utterly dissipated. For the first time in my life I heard the Government and people of the United States denounced, ridiculed, and cursed, and the very name of American made a hissing and a by-word; for the first time I heard professed preachers swearing in the pulpit, and such expressions as " d——d apostate" flung recklessly about by so-called apostles and priests. The Conference closed, and its bad effect was soon apparent. When I first arrived, there had been an era of good feeling; old bitterness appeared to be passing away, and I was quite convinced that much I had heard of the feud between Gentiles and Mormons was exaggerated.

In this temper of the public mind the Conference met, passed a decree of non-intercourse with the resident Gentiles, and spared no pains to inflame the public mind. The entire history of the Church was rehearsed, and in the most intemperate style; every act of "persecution," every slight and neglect was dwelt upon to the most minute particulars, and matters of comparative indifference exaggerated clear out of truthful proportion. There was not the slightest hint that the Mormons were anywhere in the wrong, that there was the least palliation for their enemies; not even the charitable assumption that some few of the latter believed themselves in the right. On the contrary, every scrap of history began and continued with the broad assumption, " We are the chosen people of God, to whom He has spoken by the mouth of His Prophet in these latter days, and, being such, of course the world hated us. There is, and must be eternal enmity between God and the devil, so there was and must be between Zion and the children of the devil, to wit, the Missourians and the Illinoisans." And these simple folks, who had come up to the Tabernacle with quiet minds, at peace with each other and all the world, left it with a burning bitterness against all Gentiles; and, as successive speakers recounted their troubles in Missouri and Illinois, they seemed wrought up to perfect frenzy. In Brigham's " sermon" he threatened dire mischiefs upon the "d——d apostates," and expressed himself as " only sorry for one thing, that God didn't tell us to fight the d——d mobocrats," to which the Tabernacle resounded with shouts of "Amen, Amen!"

Another speaker, George Q. Cannon, went much farther, and seemed to exhaust all the resources of lingual ingenuity to provoke the people to mob violence, without directly advising it. The great objects of his animosity were the *Reporter*—Gentile paper—and the grammar school of St. Mark's Associate Mission, the Gentile school of the City. Cannon stigmatized the school as one of the institutions of the devil set up in Zion, and then asked: "Shall such an institution be allowed to go on and innoculate the minds of our children with its damnable and pernicious doctrines?" Which was answered with a universal shout of "No!" "No." He hardly dared to directly advise the people to attack or destroy the *Reporter* office, but related a bit of history, with comments, which, if not intended to indicate violence, had no force that I can perceive. He said when he was a boy in Nauvoo, there was a paper published there by some "apostates" called the *Expositor*. It vilified the Saints, and scandalized their wives and daughters till the City Council declared it a nuisance. About that time the speaker was in the office of the Mormon paper there, and heard Joseph and Hyrum Smith talking about it. Hyrum said, "Rather than allow it to go on, he would lay his body in the walls of the building where it was issued." The speaker then gave a glowing account of the martyrdom of Joseph and Hyrum, and the many Saints who suffered on account of the *Expositor* till the people were wrought into a perfect frenzy. He then stated that "right here in the midst of Zion a paper was issued, so much like that, he could hardly tell them apart, and the times were so similar he almost imagined himself a boy again." Then reading some extracts from the *Reporter*, and commenting in an inflammatory style, he said: "In any other community such a paper as this would be gutted inside of five days, and its editor strung up to a telegraph pole." To which the excited congregation responded, "Hear, hear," "Here we are," etc.

I now began to understand what had at first seemed a mystery to me; that in every State where the Mormons had lived, the people who had at first welcomed them gladly, ended by hating and opposing them. Granting that all the charges against them of petty thieving, counterfeiting and trespass were untrue, such mad fanaticism could not but destroy good neighborhood, and arouse all other violent elements in opposition to their own. Mormonism, which had hitherto been to me a mere amusement or matter of passing interest, now appeared a subject worthy of serious and earnest investigation.

That a vast multitude of people should embrace a wild scheme of religion is no new thing, perhaps no great wonder; the foremost nations of Europe have witnessed greater displays of fanaticism; England had her Irvingites, Muggletonians and devotees of Joanna Southcott; Germany was compelled to slaughter fifty thousand of the fierce Anabaptists of Munster, followers of St. John of Leyden; while the convulsionists of France, and the self-mutilating sects of Russia, have shown more unnatural bigotry than the Mormons. But that a theocratic despotism should spring up in a free republic; that the cool and practical Yankee should turn Prophet, and that, after two thousand years of Christian progress, men and women should voluntarily turn back to polygamy, semi-paganism and the "dead works" of a ceremonial law—this is cause for inquiry. Let us then take a brief view of the most characteristic features of Mormonism, arranging them for convenience in the following order:

I. Mormon society and general views.
II. Analysis of Mormon theology.
III. Theoretical polygamy—its history.
IV. Practical polygamy.
V. The Mormon theocracy.

CHAPTER XII.

Difficulty at the outset—Extremes among witnesses—Prejudice on both sides—First impressions favorable—"Whited Sepulchres"—Classes of Mormons—Brigham Young; imposter or fanatic?—The dishonest class—The "earnest Mormons"—Disloyalty—Church and State—Killing men to save their souls—Slavery of woman—Brigham the government—Prophecy against the United States—"War"—"Seven women to take hold of one man"—Another war expected—Blood and thunder in store for the Gentiles—"The great tribulation" about due—Popular errors—Witchcraft—"Faith-doctoring"—Zion in Jackson County, Missouri—Comfortable prospect.

BEFORE entering upon a subject so complex as Mormon society and theology, it is necessary to warn the reader that on many of its features it is difficult to write without some warmth of feeling; and as to polygamy, quite impossible to treat thereon without coarseness. In this part of my work too, a special preface is appropriate, as our American-Saxon is particularly deficient in those delicate euphemisms which enable an author to describe that which is vile, in language which is comparatively chaste, or, at any rate, not shocking or offensive. In treating of the gross materialism and perverted sexualism of the Mormons, it has been thought best to speak plainly, that the full effects of this new Mahommedanism may be seen and read of all men.

A serious difficulty meets us at the very outset of an examination into the affairs of Utah. The fair-minded Gentile, who really desires to know the truth, must in effect, resolve himself into a perambulating jury of one, to try every fact presented by the strictest rules of legal acumen. He will find three different accounts of, three separate reasons for, and three opposite deductions from, every possible occurrence, viz.: the Mormon account wholly presumed and one-sided; the bitter anti-Mormon account which would condemn all of an opposite creed without distinction, and the account of the moderate Gentiles, who are in the best position to give a fair judgment, but being necessarily distrusted by both the other parties, are in a poor way to get at facts.

Two classes of writers have dealt with the Mormon question; the one has described in glowing terms the simple earnestness of the people, their devotion to an idea, their faithfulness to their leaders, their industry, frugality, temperance, and love of home; the other has painted, in dark colors, their horrible crimes, their lustful and debasing doctrines, their depravity, treachery, disloyalty, petty tyranny and social meanness. Paradoxical as it may appear, there is a measure of truth on both sides; thousands of the Mormon laity, ignorant, zealous and sincere, have many of the virtues claimed for them, while the gang of licentious villains who mould this pliable mass, are guilty of tenfold more crimes than the world will ever know. In all descriptions of life and manners in Utah, this distinction is to be carefully kept in mind. It is a noteworthy fact, too, that visitors who reach Salt Lake City with no decided feelings either way, nearly always form a more favorable opinion at first, than they have after a few months' residence. I was slow in arriving at the reasons for this, but there are good ones.

Men of quiet tastes arrive there from some border towns, where the offscourings of Christendom are gathered, and the apparent change strikes them with great force. They are charmed with the quiet and order and beauty that seem to prevail on every hand, and in all conversations it is carefully impressed upon their minds, that all this is the result of Brighamism and the institutions set up under it. Much more is claimed than is true, and the visitor finding things better than he expected, is led to believe them better than they really are. But as he progresses in knowledge, his views of this vaunted "quiet, and order, and beauty," begin to change. He finds that this quiet is the quiet of despotism—this order is of the kind that "reigned in Warsaw" on a certain historic occasion, when the heel of the tyrant was on fifty thousand necks, and to murmur was to be crushed.

He finds that the beauty is mostly of nature's making, and as to the boasted virtue and honesty, it is about like that of other similar communities—good, bad and indifferent. There ought to be virtue in a community where no man is introduced to a woman, until he has been thoroughly tested, and where the "dagger to the heart" is the openly avowed penalty for the slightest infraction; and yet such are the defects of their social system that, despite these dread penalties, virtue is not secured. Public prostitution is, of course, comparatively unknown, but that private immorality, and that of the most loathsome character, prevails extensively, is well known to all who care to inquire; and is often flatly acknowledged by their own speakers, one of whom said, in a public sermon, that he could not preserve his own honor, " couldn't trust his women out of his sight, and was bound to have 'em all in one house, under his own eye." The resident finally learns these facts, and learns, too, that things he considers gross crimes are practised under the name of religion.

Then a reaction begins in his mind, and anger is excited more fiercely against crimes concealed in the name of religion, than those which appear in true colors. And this is the crime of Brighamism, that a class of swindling fanatics can so put on the appearance of virtue as to deceive both those within and without, their followers and their visitors. At first, I thought I was alone in thus changing my views; but I find it to be the case, nine times out of ten, with the fair-minded Gentile. Look at the long list of visitors who have spoken or written, and it will generally be found, the shorter their stay, the more favorable their testimony. There is one point on which I long refused belief, the existence of "Danites" or "Destroying Angels." I looked upon them as rather a bug-a-boo of the Gentile mind. But the testimony is now unimpeachable. I find their existence avowed in Brigham's old sermons. I have met more than one man who had narrowly escaped from them with life. I have it from the statements of apostates, and more than all else, my personal friends, among the Mormons themselves, have avowed and defended the order. To a young Mormon woman, who was laboring for my conversion, I said, in jest: "Do you believe in these Danites? Do you sustain such a man as Bill Hickman in his murders?" and, to my surprise, the reply was: "That is his office, to cut off those who violate a sacred obligation, for which there is no forgiveness. That is the law of God."

When a man finds growing within him a sentiment of hostility to a sect claiming to be religious, he does well to consider carefully the grounds of such feeling, lest early prejudice or sectarian bias be misleading him. Charges against religious bodies are to be received with caution, and examined with more than legal distrust. We do well to remember that the crimes of religious communities have been exaggerated in every age of the world, and hence extra caution is due to them in examining their history. In this spirit I can truly say I approached Mormonism; and when compelled to radically change my views of them, while I felt a natural chagrin at having been at first deceived, it was more in sorrow than in anger that I found myself disenchanted. And this has been the experience of the great majority who have made a lengthy residence in Utah. For a few weeks all seems right; but if any man flatters himself that at the end of six weeks he has seen more than the *superficies* of Mormon society, he is wofully deceived. When the first flush of curiosity had subsided I ceased hunting for information of those so falsely called "representative men;" I began to look among the people. I talked with the young and extended my acquaintance among that class—most generally women—who have been wrecked in mind, body and estate by the maelstrom of lust and fanatical fury, which is ever raging in the Mormon capital. It is not easy to get at these facts. The witnesses will not speak while there is the slightest doubt. They know not whom to trust, and one must take a decided stand, and become himself an object of hatred and distrust to the hierarchy, before he can safely be considered a friend to its victims. But when a man has fairly cut loose from the misrepresentations of the few, and begun to get the facts from the mass, every day the odious features of Mormonism rise into clearer view, till he stands aghast to think he ever had a good opinion of the system. The Mormon Church, or rather community, may be divided into four classes.

I. First are the leaders of all ranks, from the First Presidency down through all the grades of apostles, seventies, bishops, elders, priests, evangelists, missionaries and teachers.

They are all bound to the Church by the strongest ties of self-interest, as by it they live—many of them in splendor and affluence. In such a state of facts we may well question their sincerity, especially as some of them are men of keen analytical talents, and far-reaching sagacity. But whether they think it true or false, they must stand or fall with the system. Some of them evidently believe in it with all earnestness; others, as evidently do not. Their history and unguarded expressions show that. Still a third class seem doubtful, and to this it must be confessed Brigham Young belongs. Outsiders are strangely divided in opinion regarding him. His worst enemies, while they charge him with every crime in the code, yet often admit that he is sincere in his religious belief; "but," say they, "his religion admits of the most atrocious crimes, if done to further good interests!" Others look upon him as a heartless impostor, a sensual, deceitful tyrant, and this I find to be the common view among apostates, or recusant Mormons, who have suffered from his acts. I am inclined to regard him as that strange compound of impostor and fanatic, which history has shown to be possible, as in the cases of the Florentine, Savonarola, and the Jesuit, Loyola. Incredible as it may appear to a mind and conscience yet undebauched, men may and actually do persuade themselves that they are doing God's service while committing the most heinous crimes, and

"Christians have burnt each other, quite persuaded
That all the Apostles would have done as they did."

II. The second class comprises those who have embraced Mormonism from unworthy motives, and consists generally of men with no fixed sentiments on any subject except their own self-interest. They are men who have been unfortunate or criminal in other communities, and fled to Mormonism for a refuge. Broken down merchants, professional men, without character, and the "bilks" and "dead beats" of other communities generally, who have been deceived by the representations of progress there, and expected to better themselves by casting in their fortunes with a rising sect. And from this class have originated many of the Mormon troubles, in times past. They often become dissatisfied and turbulent, and often apostatize, but have too little fixedness of sentiment, and too much dullness of moral perception to be of any value to either side. Some of them seek easy positions under the hierarchy; others, more desperate, sink lower, and become the mere tools of the leaders to do all their dirty and infamous work. Mutual guilt then makes them mutual spies, and conscious that their lives are in the power of their masters, they live as guilty and miserable slaves, with the assured knowledge that, at the slightest disloyal move, their lives will pay the forfeit. More than one of this class has met with a bloody death, from the simple fact that he knew too much, as I now know from undoubted testimony.

III. The third class consists of those who became Mormons sincerely, but from slight or insufficient motives. They united with the sect, with as much sincerity as they were capable of, but with no clear understanding of what was before them. Before embracing Mormonism, they were generally afloat on religious subjects, or dissatisfied with what they saw in their own churches, and had fallen into the dangerous habit of suspecting all men of hypocrisy who showed much zeal for morality. I have met dozens of this class who had been "lobby members" of the Methodist, Baptist, Presbyterian, and Campbellite Churches; that weak, feeble class of Christians who expect the Church to pick them up and carry them to heaven, carefully lifting them over the rough places in the road, and removing every annoying doubt which will rise in an idle or rapid brain. I have heard them speak of their churches as "stationary," or "sleepy," never dreaming that the fault was in themselves. They were the weak, discontented disciples, without the fierce vigor and aggressive spirit of the true Church; not having learned the first principle of Christianity to be zealous, unselfish laborers. In this state of mind their attention is caught and fancy captivated by the claim of a new revelation, of holding direct communion with heaven, of walking every day in new light received from without; and also at the thought of a distinctively American religion, with saints, apostles, prophets, and martyrs, all of our own race and time. This class are very enthusiastic on first reaching the new "Zion," but often grow discontented, and fall again into their doubting and querulous habits. But as they did not think their way into Mormonism, they cannot think themselves out, and so they simply float. Sometimes they apostatize, but are no loss to the Church and no gain to the Gentiles, from pure lack of intellectual vigor.

IV. The fourth class consists of those who really believe in Mormonism with all its absurdities and contradictions. They never doubt for a moment, that Joseph Smith was sent direct from God, and that Brigham Young is his successor. This class comprises about half of the whole community, and they are the really dangerous element. No miraculous story is too great for their belief, if it have the stamp of "authority," and no oppression or priestly tyranny seems to shake their faith for a moment; and, paradoxical as it may seem, in this class are found all the virtues of the Mormon community. They are industrious, frugal (often from necessity), and reasonably temperate. Their honesty, I think, has been overrated, and Brigham and other leaders often say the same. Yet, one may travel among them for weeks, as I have done, and meet with nothing but kindness and hospitality.

But in their very virtues lies the greatest danger. Their constancy to their leaders is wonderful, and their gullibility and capacity to swallow the marvelous, beyond belief; so they constitute a mass of dangerous power in the hands of corrupt and treasonable men. These are the men we ought to reach and try to save, and yet they are the very ones who are hardest to influence. They will not read our books or papers (very many of them cannot), nor listen for a moment to our arguments. They denounce everything which is not approved by the bishop, and pronounce the plainest facts of history false, if they clash with the statements of "authority." Conversing once with one such, a merchant of the city, I read the following passage from the "Book of Mormon:" "We found upon the land of promise (Central America), that there were beasts in the forest of every kind, both the cow and the *ox*, and the ass and the *horse*, and all manner of wild animals, which were for the use of men."

"Now," said I, "your Prophet says the Nephites landed in America six hundred years before Christ, and the last of them perished about A. D. 500, and all this time they had used the horse and the ass. Now, any history of America will show that the horse was completely unknown to the Indians till brought here by the Spaniards."

"O, pshaw!" was the reply, "I don't believe a word of it; it's a d—d lie, got up by some enemy of the truth."

"But," I urged, "go further back than Mormonism. Take the letters of George Washington, and you will find that he was the first man who ever imported the ass to America! Could the Nephites have had these animals, and no trace of them be found?"

"I don't believe George Washington, or any other man, knows anything about it," said he; "you examine and you will find many of the so-called facts of history are not facts. You may read every history written, and pick out every fact against that book (Mormon), and when you look into it you will find them all false."

This was the mode of reasoning adopted by a man of extra intelligence for a Mormon. I have talked with dozens of this sort, and no matter how clear on everything else, they seem to go wild in their logic when Mormonism was touched upon. "Do you actually believe," I asked an old lady, "that the earthly paradise will be in Jackson County, Missouri?" "Oh, yes," she said, "for the Lord pointed out the exact place to Joseph, and said that Zion should never be moved, and all the people of America who do not repent will be destroyed now in a few years, so there will be but one man for seven women. Those are the very words, and everything Joseph and Isaiah (!) said has turned out just exactly as they said it would."

Such are the ideas impressed upon the minds of these people. Numbers of them testify in the most positive manner to miraculous cures performed upon themselves or their friends, simply by the "laying on of hands" by an elder or bishop. They devoutly believe that Stephen A. Douglas failed politically, because he urged vigorous measures against the Mormons, and that Frank P. Blair is sinking for the same reason. The late war never would have occurred, they think, if Johnston's army had not been sent; and as to thrashing the United States, they consider it will be a mere "breakfast spell," when things get in the right fix, and Brigham gives the word. At his command they would fight the world in arms, or quietly give up their all and migrate to any part of the world he might designate. The most of this class will stick to Mormonism as long as it has an existence, but the other classes will fall away whenever it is to their interest to do so.

But with mere moral distinctions the Government and people of the United States have little to do. The patriot and statesman will ask a more important question: What is the state of public feeling among the Mormons?—how do they stand affected towards the General Government? In a full answer many influences are to be considered. It must be remembered in starting, that at least seven-eighths of all these people are foreigners, and that of the lowest and most ignorant class; that they came direct from Europe to Utah, and know absolutely nothing of the States and their people; that they merely have Mormonism grafted on to Europeanism, and cannot be expected to become nationalized like their countrymen who settle in the East. Whatever distinctively American feeling they have must, then, be looked for in the influences there and the teachings of the Church. These influences and teachings are all anti-

American. Mormonism teaches three doctrines directly opposed to the spirit of the Constitution and our institutions.

1. The union of Church and State; or rather the complete absorption of the State in the Church; that the former is a mere appendage of the latter for convenience sake, and may be dropped whenever convenience no longer calls for a state organization.

2. The shedding of a man's blood, for the remission of his sins, even his sins against the Church. This is sometimes denied and sometimes advocated, but that it is a doctrine of the Mormon Church is now beyond doubt. Brigham openly says that the only reason why it is not more generally advocated is, that it is "too strong a doctrine for the weak in faith; the people are not fully prepared for it," etc. Unwilling to leave this matter doubtful in any mind, I clip the following extracts from published sermons, the first from those of Jedediah M. Grant, delivered in the Tabernacle:

"Brethren and sisters, we want you to repent and forsake your sins. And you that have committed sins that cannot be forgiven through baptism, *let your blood be shed, and let the smoke ascend,* that the incense thereof may come up before God, as atonement for your sins, and that the sinners in Zion may be afraid." (*Deseret News,* October 1, 1856.)

"We have been trying long enough with these people, and I go in for letting the sword of the Almighty be unsheathed, not only in word but in deed." (*Ibid.*)

"I say there are men and women here, that I would advise to go to the President immediately, and ask him to appoint a committee to attend to their case, and then let a place be selected, and let that committee shed their blood." (*Deseret News,* September, 1856.)

Which was endorsed by Brigham, as follows:—

"There are sins men commit for which they cannot receive forgiveness in this world, or in that which is to come, and if they had their eyes open to see their condition, they would be perfectly willing to have their blood spilt upon the ground, that the smoke thereof might ascend to heaven as an offering for their sins ; whereas, if such is not the case, they will stick to them and remain upon them in the spirit world. I know when you hear my brethren talk about cutting people off from the earth, you consider it strong doctrine. It is to save them, not to destroy them. It is true that the blood of the Son of God was shed for our sins, but men can commit sins which it can never remit.

"As it was in ancient days, so is it in our day ; the law is precisely the same. There are sins that the blood of a lamb or a calf cannot remit, but they must be atoned for by the blood of man. That is the reason why men talk to you as they do from this stand. They understand the doctrine and throw out a few words about it." (*Deseret News*, October 1, 1856.)

This is "sound Mormon doctrine," and that many have been sacrificed under it, is well known in Utah. This is one of the features of Mormonism I was slow to believe, nor did I credit it without overwhelming proof; but to put the matter beyond doubt, more than one prominent Mormon has avowed the doctrine to me, and defended it as an ordinance of God.

Under this law, Potter and the Parish family, of Springville, were murdered when attempting to leave the Territory, and Potter and Wilson, of Weber Valley, were assassinated in jail; under the same law the Mormons claim the right to slay all who commit adultery, " or violate a sanctified oath," and for this cause Elder John Hyde was compelled to flee from the Territory, while his friends, Margetts and Cowdy, were followed several hundred miles and barbarously murdered.

3. The third anti-American feature of Mormonism is the complete subserviency and mental slavery of woman, not as to polygamy alone, though that is an outgrowth, but in everything.

Their theology teaches that, "as Eve led Adam out of Paradise, he must lead her back," and though they hesitatingly admit that she may secure "a salvation" without man's help, she cannot secure "an exaltation." She must have a husband " to lead her into the presence of God, and

P

introduce her to that husband's glory." "She will not necessarily go to hell, because she is single, but she never can rise to the first glory." Such an atrocious and un-Christian idea can have but one tendency, to make woman merely a creature for man's convenience and pleasure. Hence, all our American ideas of dower, partition, equal descent, and woman holding land in fee apart from her husband, are unknown to the laws of Utah. Everything a woman possesses at marriage becomes absolutely the property of her husband. The feminine interest is nowhere provided for, and, in looking over their laws, if they have any Common Law at all, it seems to be a transcript of that which prevailed in the time of James I. The further we pursue the investigation the more this tendency appears, till it is plain to be seen there is none of what we call Americanism there. The spirit exists neither in their birth, training nor religion. To them Brigham is the Government, and Utah is America. They know no other, and consider it the height of presumption for the United States authorities to claim the right to rule over them. True, they claim to be true Americans just as the Abyssinians claim to be true Christians, while it is evident neither understand their own words.

But there is another curious fact bearing on their views. On the 25th of December, 1852, Joseph Smith delivered a remarkable prophecy, detailing what was to happen to America for her "persecution of the Saints." It was published in *The Seer*, a Mormon periodical in Washington City, of April, 1854, from which I copy:

"WAR!

"Verily, thus saith the Lord concerning the wars that will shortly come to pass, beginning at the rebellion of South Carolina, which will eventually terminate in the death and misery of many souls. The days will come that wars will be poured out upon all nations, beginning at that place; for, behold, the Southern States shall be divided against the Northern States; and the Southern States will call upon other nations, even the nation of Great Britain, as it is called, and they shall also call upon other nations, in order to defend themselves against other nations; and thus war shall be poured out upon all nations. And it shall come to pass, after many days, slaves shall rise up against their masters, who shall be marshaled and disciplined for war. And it will come to pass, also, that the *remnant which are left of the land*† shall marshal themselves and become exceedingly angry, and shall vex the Gentiles with a sore vexation. And thus, with the sword and by bloodshed, the inhabitants of the earth shall mourn, and with famine and plague and earthquakes, and the thunder of heaven, and the fierce and vivid lightning, also, shall the inhabitants of the earth be made to feel the wrath and indignation and chastening hand of an Almighty God, until the consumption decreed hath made an end of all nations; that the cry of the Saints, and of the blood of the Saints shall cease to come up into the ears of the Lord of Sabaoth, from the earth, to be avenged of their enemies. Wherefore stand ye in holy places, and be not moved until the day of the Lord come; for, behold, it cometh quickly, saith the Lord! Amen."

It will be perceived that of the thousand predictions in relation to our civil war, Joseph's was among the most shrewd, and certainly hit on two or three very curious things. But he met with the difficulty common to all Prophets in these days; when he ran into particulars he missed it seriously. With the benevolent design of saving the country, Joseph offered himself for President, but, as he was rejected, of course the evil is bound to come.—With the Mormons this is the grand prophecy. War is to go on, they say, till nearly all the men in the Union are killed, and then the Saints are to return and set up "Zion" in Jackson County, Missouri; and the faithful, who have meanwhile gathered, are to possess the whole land, and be husbands to all the widows and fathers to all the orphans. Then is to come the time mentioned by Isaiah, when "seven women shall take hold of one man," and agree to earn their own support, if they only may "be called by his name to take away their reproach," which reproach, of course, is childlessness; or, commercially speaking,

---

† The Indians.

women will be at a heavy discount, and men at 600 per cent. premium.

As near as I can determine there have been about ten thousand commentaries written and preached on this prophecy; for the varying circumstances of every year, and almost every week, require new elucidations of the way it is all to come about. The war, of course, settled it all for awhile; but that stopped so suddenly, they maintain it must soon break out again, and several of their commentators concluded the last Presidential election would signal its re-opening. What folly for any people to pretend fealty to an institution which they claim is going to eternal smash in ten years at the most.

It is a law of mind that what we prophesy often we soon come to wish for: and, if there were no other cause, the tendency of all their preaching and prophesying is to make them look eagerly for the downfall of our Government. It is a prime principle in their creed that all mankind but themselves are on the swift road to ruin, and they are never so well pleased as in listening to statements in regard to "the great increase of crime and immorality in the States." I could not make one of them angry quicker than by persistently arguing that the highest degree of prosperity prevails in the East to-day, and my best friends were ready to knock me down at the statement that there were still more men than women in the United States.

I showed them from the census that the men were in a majority of 730,000 in 1860; that by immigration we gained several hundred thousand more men than women, and did not lose, at the outside, more than 700,000 in the war. They maintained that by authentic (?) Southern histories, we lost in battle one million rebels and two million Yankees! How easy to make men believe what they wish. All the "persecutions" these people talk so much of, were caused by Southerners and Democrats, and yet they are all rebel sympathizers and pro-slavery politicians. They talk loud and long of their loyalty, when there is anything to be gained by it; but send there a Federal judge or officer, who refuses to be Brigham's tool, and you soon hear their real feelings toward the Union. Just now they are only waiting, watching a few weeks or months, till all shall go to destruction in the State, when they will return and occupy their terrestrial heaven—Jackson County, Missouri. Thus this vast mass of ignorance has been wrought upon and moulded by a few leaders, till the people are ready for any desperate enterprise those men may direct. The common people, two-thirds of them at least, are naturally peaceable, too; but they are so terribly priest-ridden, that their best qualities are as dangerous as other men's worst.

Like the poor of all lands, they are constant in their attachments; but with the favorites they have chosen, their constancy is a vice rather than a virtue. No doubt a very large number would apostatize rather than suffer; but half of them are so rooted and grounded in their faith, that they will blindly follow their leaders, whatever course they take.

There are no free schools in Utah, and no organized systems of instruction; nevertheless the social and intellectual condition of the people is far superior to what it was ten or even five years ago. There is a general prejudice against the learned professions, particularly medicine; and a general feeling that the Saints are above the necessity of such knowledge,—which idea is summed up by Brigham Young, in these words; "Study twenty years in the world's knowledge, and God Almighty will give the poorest Saint more knowledge in five minutes than you get in all that time." In this social view, it were an endless task to mention all the thousand forms of popular error, the belief in witchcraft, dreams, *evestra*, ghostly fancies and "faith-doctrine" which prevail among them; but it is worthy of remark, that there is certainly no other place in America where retrogade ideas, as they might be called, prevail so extensively as in Utah. Nine-tenths of the Saints seem to have taken up one common wail about everything outside Utah. Whether it is to persuade themselves that they are really better than other men, or to console themselves at the thought of others' misery, it seems to be their meat and drink to denigrate the character of the rest of mankind. They take up the wailing jeremiad that there is so much more crime in the country than formerly; that people generally are so much more dishonest; that there are so few virtuous women; that the country is rapidly going to decay; that religion has lost its power; that all political action is wrong, slavery ought never to have been abolished, and nothing should have been done as it has been for the last twenty-five years. To quote history or statistics to the contrary would be no proof at all to them; they regard all such as "Gentile lies." And. thus, in the supreme belief that they alone are "in the ark of safety," they confidently wait for the "great tribulation" which is now about due; while thousands of them fully expect to live to see the time when the American nation shall be a thing of the past, and Macaulay's New Zealander shall "sit on London Bridge and muse on the decline and fall of the British Empire."

CHAPTER XIII.

ANALYSIS OF MORMON THEOLOGY.

Its origin—A theological conglomerate—Mythology, Paganism, Mohammedanism, corrupt Christianity and Philosophy run mad—"First principles of the Gospel"—The five points of variance—Materialism—No spirit—A *god* with "body, parts and passions"—Matter eternal—No "creation"—Intelligent atoms—Pre-existent souls—High Times in the Spirit Worlds—Birth of Spirits—They hunt for "Earthly Tabernacles"—The "Second Estate"—Apotheosis—The "Third Estate"—"Fourth Estate"—Men become *gods*—"Divine generation"—Earthly Families and Heavenly Kingdoms—Did man come from the Sun?—"Building up the Kingdom"—One day as a thousand years—The time of the Gentiles about out—Great events at hand—"Gog and Magog," et. al.—Gentiles, prepare to make tracks –Return to "Zion," in Missouri—Christ's earthly empire—Great destiny for Missouri—Tenets from Christianity—Baptism a "Saving Ordinance"—Baptized twelve times—Office of the Holy Ghost—Strange fanaticism—Eclectic Theology—A personal *god*—The *homoousian* and the *homoiousian*—The *Logos* and the *Aeon*—Grossness and Vulgarity.

IN their origin, the Mormons may be said to have been an offshoot from the Campbellites; Sidney Rigdon, the author of their early doctrines, having originally left the Baptists to join the former sect, from which he again seceded and founded a sect in Ohio, locally known as "Disciples." Of this band a portion went crazy as Millenarians, another part became Perfectionists, and the remainder followed Rigdon, when he joined his fortunes with those of Joe Smith, and assisted in founding Kirkland, Ohio. Under the early teachings of Brigham Young they adopted the Methodist order of services. Their missionaries, when abroad, at present, first preach principles very similar to those of the Campbellites; and what the Mormons call " the first principles of the gospel" are mainly those of that sect. But it is the smallest part of Mormon theology which has its origin in any recognized Christian system; and by the successive additions of Rigdon, Joe Smith, and Brigham Young, the laborious philosophical speculations of Orson Pratt, and the wild poetical dreams of his brother Parley P. Pratt, it may well be said there is scarcely a known system of religion, ancient or modern, but has contributed some shred of doctrine to Mormonism.

It is now beyond the power of man to invent a new religion. At this late day combination is all that is left for the innovator, and the doctrinal points of Mormonism are culled from three different sources, viz. :

I. Christianity, by a literal interpretation of the Bible, particularly the prophecies.

II. Ancient mythology and various modern forms of pagan philosophy.

III. The philosophical speculations of various schools; the whole modified and practicalized by revelation applied to events of daily occurrence.

Thus has grown up a vast and cumbrous system which is the standard Mormon theology, but of which each individual Mormon believes so much or so little as he can comprehend. It were an endless task to pursue these doctrines through all the variations, necessary to force some sort of agreement, and the lifeless application of perverted texts of Scripture. But the distinctive points in which they differ from all Christian sects, may be grouped under five heads :

I. Pure materialism; but slightly different from the atomic materialism of the Greek school.

II. The eternity of matter.

III. Pre-existence of the soul, and transmission of spirits.

IV. A plurality of *gods*.

V. A plurality of wives, or "celestial marriage."

All these are blended in various ways, and depend upon each other in a score of combinations and confused inter-relations; but, as far as possible, they are treated of separately.

I. The Mormons hold that there is no such thing as spirit distinct from matter; that spirit is only matter refined, and that spirits themselves are composed of purely material atoms, only finer than the tangible things of earth, as air is finer and more subtle than water, while both are equally material. "The purest, most refined and subtle of all, is that substance called the Holy Spirit. This substance, like all others, is one of the elements of material or physical existence, and, therefore, subject to the necessary laws which govern all other matter. Like the other elements, its whole is composed of individual particles. Each particle occupies space, possesses the power of motion, requires time to move from one part of space to another, and can in nowise occupy two places at once, in this respect differing nothing from all other matter. It is widely diffused among all the elements of space; under the control of the Great Eloheim it is the moving cause of all the intelligences, by which they act. It is omnipresent by reason of the infinitude of its particles, is the controling element of all others, and comprehends all things. By the mandate of the Almighty it performs all the wonders ever manifested in the name of the Lord. Its inherent properties embrace all the attributes of intelligence and affection. In short it is the attributes of the eternal power and Godhead."*

Gods, angels, spirits and men, the four orders of intelligent beings, are all of one species, composed of similar materials, differing not in kind, but in degree. God is a perfected man; man is an embryotic or undeveloped *god*. Orson Pratt has pursued this doctrine to its wildest ultimate, and proves, to his own satisfaction, that every original atom was endowed with a self-acting, independent intelligence, and they merely "got together" of their own volition. Thus, in the attempt to avoid the supposed mystery of an instantaneous creation by the one God, he has raised an infinity of unsolved problems, by making every atom a *god*.

II. The eternity of matter is a logical outgrowth of materialism. In this view every atom now in being has existed from all eternity past, and will exist for all eter-

---

*The quotations in this chapter are from Parley P. Pratt's "Key to Theology," a standard work among the Mormons, and by them considered as inspired.

nity to come. There never could have been a "creation," except to appropriate "matter unformed and void," and change its form, impressing new conditions upon it.

New worlds are constantly being formed of the unappropriated material of the universe, and stocked with spirits, after which faithful Saints rule over them and become *gods*.

III. Closely allied with the last principle is that of the pre-existence of souls; and here we first meet with the sexual principle which underlies all the remaining portion of Mormonism. All the sexual passions exist in full force in the different worlds, and animate the immortal *gods* as fully as their human offspring. Countless millions of spirits are thus born in the eternal worlds, and are awaiting by myriads the physical processes by which they may enter earthly tabernacles, and begin their second, or probationary state. " Wisdom inspires the *gods* to multiply their species," and as these spiritual bodies increase, fresh worlds are necessary upon which to transplant them. These spiritual bodies have all the organs of thought, speech and hearing, in exact similitude to earthly senses. But in this state they could not advance; it was necessary for them to be subject to the moral law of earth, that regeneration might go on. Hence they " seek earnestly for earthly tabernacles, haunting even the abodes of the vilest of mankind to obtain them." To bestow these tabernacles is the highest glory of woman, and her exaltation in eternity will be in exact proportion to the number she has furnished. Man may preach the gospel, may reach the highest glories of the priesthood, may, in time, even be a creator ; but woman's only road to glory is by the physical process of introducing spirits to earth. Hence, the larger her family the greater her glory; any means to prevent natural increase are, in the highest degree, sinful, and violent means an unpardonable sin.

Of these spirits it is intimated some "did not keep their first estate," and are to be thrust down and never permitted to have earthly tabernacles, or propagate their species. Those who reach this earth are in their " second estate," and if faithful Saints will pass to their " third estate," celestialized men, after which they become *gods*.

IV. There is a vast multitude of *gods*, dispersed throughout all the worlds as kingdoms, families and nations. There is, however, but one *god* regnant on each world, who is to the inhabitants of that world the "only true and living God." But each *god* having a first-born son, there is "One God and One Christ" to each world. Thus "there are lords many and gods many," but to us there is but one God, the Creator of the world, and the Father of our spirits, literally begotten. He was once a man of some world, and attained His high position by successive degrees. "He is the Father of Jesus Christ, in the only way known in nature, just as John Smith, Senior, is the father of John Smith, Junior."

All the *gods* have many wives, and become the fathers of the souls of men by divine generation. The *gods* are in the exact form of men, of material substance, but highly refined and spiritualized. A grand council of the *gods*, with a president directing, constitute the designing and creating power; but man, if faithful, will advance by degrees, till endowed with the same creative power, or strictly, *formative* will. All faithful Saints will become *gods*, and, finally, have worlds given them to people and govern. All their earthly wives and children will belong to and constitute the beginning of their heavenly kingdom, and they will rule over their increasing posterity forever.

"When the earth was prepared, there came from an upper world a Son of God, with His beloved spouse, and thus a colony from Heaven, it may be from the sun, was transplanted on our soil." Joseph Smith is one of the *gods* of this generation and now occupies a high position next to Christ, who in turn stands next to Adam. Above Adam is Jehovah and above Jehovah is Eloheim, who is the greatest *god* of whom we have any knowledge. His residence is in the planet Kolob, near the centre of our system, which revolves upon its axis once in a thousand years, which are "with the Lord as one day." There were six of our days in the first "creation" of this world, and six of the Lord's days in the great preparation or course of the world, each day lasting a thousand years. There were two of these days to each dispensation. The Patriarchal had two of these days; the Mosaic in like manner a day of rise and a day of decline; the Christian dispensation also had its two days of trial, but after St. John's death, a great apostacy began, and for eighteen hundred years the so called Christian world has been in darkness and there has been no true priesthood upon the earth. There have been no visions, revelations or miraculous gifts from the Lord enjoyed among men. The various sects knew something of the truth but not its fullness; they had the form of godliness but denied the power.

But this time of darkness is nearly completed; the dawn of the Lord's day is here, and the great Sabbath will soon be ushered in. But a few more years are given to the Gentiles, then the great contest of Gog and Magog will set in, and nearly all the Gentile world be destroyed. Those who remain will become servants to the Saints, who will return and possess the whole land; the widows will come begging the Mormon elders to marry them, and seven women will lay hold of one man. At the same the remnant left of the Indians, who are descendants of the ancient Jews, will be converted, have the curse removed and become "a fair and delightsome people." The way will be opened to the remainder of the "ten lost tribes," who are shut up somewhere near the North Pole; old Jerusalem will be rebuilt by all the Jews gathering to the Holy Land, and about the year 1890, the new Jerusalem will be let down from God out of Heaven and located in Jackson County, Missouri, with the corner-stone of the Great Temple "three hundred yards west of the old court-house in Independence," where is to be the capital of Christ's earthly kingdom. The Saints will own all the property of the country, and marry all the women they desire; the streets of their city will be paved with the gold dug by Gentiles from the Rocky Mountains; noxious insects will be banished, contagious diseases cease, the land produce abundantly of grain, flower and fruit, and everything will be lovely in the new Jerusalem!

Leaving the reader to smile or regret, as personal temperament may incline, I hasten to a consideration of the

Mormon tenets nominally derived from the Christian Bible. The Mohammedan portion of their faith and practice is reserved for the two succeeding chapters.

The Mormons steadily claim the Bible as the first foundation of their belief; that they "believe all that any Christians do, and a great deal more." Their tenets most nearly resembling those of Christian sects, and which they call the " First principles of the Gospel," are four in number, ranked in order of time as follow :

1. Faith; 2. Repentance; 3. Baptism by immersion; and 4. Laying on of hands for the remission of sins, and the gift of the Holy Ghost. They are explained at great length in the " Doctrines and Covenants," the New Testament of Mormonism. This book is made up of revelations, " selected (!) from those of Joseph Smith," and the doctrinal lectures of various elders, particularly Sidney Rigdon, with an addition containing the rules and discipline of the Church. The "Lectures on faith and repentance" contain nothing more than is familiar to every attendant on the worship of Arminian sects. Baptism the Mormons regard as "a saving ordinance," of actual and material value; and to such an extent do they carry this doctrine, that they baptize again and again, after every backsliding, and sometimes when there has been a period of " general coldness" in the Church. At the time known in Mormon annals as the "Reformation," when it was supposed the Lord had sent drought and grasshoppers to punish their backsliding, every adult member of the Church was re-baptized. Nearly all the old members have been baptized two or three times each, and Brigham Young, in one of his sermons, mentions an old reprobate who had been baptized no less than twelve times, and " cut off thirteen times for lying." Brigham himself, who was then much addicted to liquor, seems to have fallen under the power of his enemy soon after uniting with the Church, thus rendering re-baptism necessary; and a quiet joke is current among the less reverent Saints, to the effect that a noted Jew, named Seixas, then connected with the Mormons, jocosely proposed to "leave him in over night."

But the fourth tenet opens to view the whole of their divergence from Christian sects. The prime principle in their faith which marks this departure is, that the office of the Holy Ghost had been unknown on earth from the death of the last Apostle to the calling of Joseph Smith; that the "mystic power," mentioned by St. John, had warred with the Saints and overcome them; that the true priesthood was then taken from the earth, and men, blindly seeking the truth, divided into six hundred and sixty-six sects, "the number of the beast," each having a little truth, but none holding it in purity.

Joseph Smith, earnestly calling upon the Lord to know which of the sects was in the right, was told that all were alike gone astray, and was himself ordained by heavenly messengers, first to the Aaronic and afterwards to the Melchisedec priesthood. Thenceforth the Holy Ghost was to be given to all true believers; the "witness of the spirit" was to be an absolute certainty, and all who had truly embraced the new gospel were "to know for themselves, and without a shadow of doubt" that it was true. How strange and yet how natural, this constant seeking by man for certainty as to the affairs of the unseen world! Hundreds of times I have listened to the testimony of individual Mormons: " You *believe* you are right—I know this religion is true. We have a witness no other people can have—the gift of the Holy Ghost. In the old churches we always had our doubts; now we know the correctness of this doctrine." Thus for a season. But man was not made for such absolutism; it is folly to seek a perfect certainty in that which is from its very nature intangible and uncertain, and it will often be found that the wildest and most unreasoning faith has the most obstinate devotees. It is sufficient comment upon the above "testimony," to state the facts that no Church ever organized has developed so many factions in so short a time as Mormonism; that the original organization has, from time to time, given rise to twenty-five sects, of which half-a-dozen are still in existence; that of all who have ever embraced Mormonism, over seventy per cent have apostatized, and that, at the present writing, two powerful schisms are raging in the very bosom of the Church.

At the same time with the Holy Ghost, all the "gifts" of the first Church were to be restored; prophecy, healing, miracles, speaking in tongues and the interpretation of tongues were to acompany the new gospel and be its powerful witnesses among men. Hence, all the miracles which have followed the Latter-day work. The Mormons are fond of quoting that text where all power is given to the Church, and the enumeration of gifts with the statement, "These signs shall follow them that believe." They then triumphantly exclaim, "Where is the professed Christian Church which has, or even claims these gifts? We have them in their fulness, and this is our testimony that we are truly of the Lord." As far as human testimony can prove anything on such a subject, they prove numerous "miracles" in the way of healing various ailments; but I have heard of none that cannot be readily accounted for from the effects of a "fervent and fooling faith." The most common "miracle" is the cure of rheumatism and neuralgia by "laying on of hands," and anointing with holy oil. The general rule of the Church is to send for the nearest elders and bishops as soon as a Saint is taken sick; they "lay on hands," and anoint the patient with "consecrated oil," rubbing it briskly on the parts most affected. If the patient grows worse, other dignitaries are sent for, more vigorous prayers are offered up, and strenuous efforts made to arouse the "healing virtue;" but generally a physician is the last resort, a religious prejudice prevailing to some extent against the profession. A resident physician of Salt Lake City informed me that he was once called to see a woman in labor, who had been suffering for twenty-four hours, and was literally "greased from head to foot with the consecrated oil." It proved to be a very simple and by no means unusual case, which he relieved in a few minutes, at the very time the attendant women were emptying a large horn of "consecrated oil" upon the patient's head; the relief was followed by loud praises of the efficacy of the "holy oil," and the woman is now a firm witness of the "miracle."

"Speaking in tongues" is not, as one would naturally suppose, the gift of speech in the vernacular of various nations, such as attended the pentecostal season. That would be altogether too linguistic and practical for these latter days. It consists merely of uttering a rapid succession of articulate and connected sounds, not understood by the speaker himself, but which are explained by some one having the "interpretation of tongues." The mode is for the person who thinks himself endowed with this gift to "stand up, call upon the Lord in silent prayer for a few moments, then open the mouth and utter whatever words come to hand and the Lord will make them a language." An interpreter will then be provided and the hidden meaning made plain; but no person ever has both gifts.

This gift prevailed to a surprising extent among certain fanatical sects in England, and was there charitably attributed to an abnormal condition of the organs of language; but here is more naturally accounted for either by imposture or the effects of a wild fanaticism. I heard it but once, and then merely repeated by a devoted Mormon as he had heard the "gifted" deliver it, and, in a philological inquiry, I should pronounce it a cognate branch of that "dog-latin" which belongs to the erudition of school-boy days. This exercise is a little too ridiculous, even for the Mormons at present, and is rarely heard of; but in the early years of their Church it was a frequent occurrence, whole days of "speaking meetings" being devoted to it. An old apostate, who was in the Church at Nauvoo, tells me of having been present at one of those meetings where the first doubts began to rise in his mind in regard to his new faith. Having formerly been a trader among the Choctaws, he suddenly arose and delivered a lengthy speech on hunting in the language of that tribe, which the interpreter rendered in a glowing and florid account of the glories to result from the completion of the Great Temple, then in progress. Lieutenant Gunnison, in his admirable work, gives an account of one lad who had become so noted in the "interpretation of tongues" that he was generally called upon by the elders in the most difficult cases, and seems to have felt under obligation to give some sort of rendering and meaning to any speech, however crude or whimsical. On one occasion, a woman, with the "gift of tongues," suddenly rose in the meeting, and shouted " *O mela, meli, melee !*" The boy was at once pressed for an interpretation, and promptly gave the rendition, "O my leg, my thigh, my knee!" He was cited before the Council for his profanity, but stoutly maintained that his interpretation was "according to the spirit," and was released with an admonition.

Miss Eliza Snow, the Mormon poetess, was particularly "gifted" in tongues; and, according to the account of young Mormons, now apostatized, she was accustomed often during their early journeyings, to rush into the dwelling of some other woman, exclaiming: "Sister, I want to bless you!" lay her hands upon the other's head, and pour forth a strain of confused jargon, which was supposed to be a blessing in the "unknown tongue." Such are the various "gifts," and to a people less blinded by fanaticism, their practical effects among the Mormons would be sufficient to disprove the claim for their divine origin. To mention but one; it is evident to any intelligent observer that numerous deaths occur annually in Salt Lake City, simply from a disregard of hygienic laws and a lack of proper medical treatment, with a blind reliance upon treatment by "faith;" and notwithstanding their splendid climate, the death-rate of the Mormons is unusually large from those very classes of disease for which any intelligent physician can afford immediate relief. It is a remarkable fact that more women die in child-birth in Salt Lake City than in any other of the same size in America, and that for many years the death-rate of infants was only exceeded by one Southern State, Louisiana.

So much for their theology as it relates to earth; I have not been able to discover the exact source of their ideas of heaven. They hold that there are three heavens: the celestial, terrestrial, and telestial, typified by the sun, moon, and stars. The last two are of those who have neither obeyed nor disobeyed the gospel; some because they did not hear it, others from "invincible ignorance," and still others because they were morally hindered. in various ways. To one or the other of these heavens all sincere people of whatever race or creed, who have never heard the Gospel, but followed the light they had, will be admitted, and there enjoy as much happiness as they are capable of. But if they have once heard the true Gospel and refused to obey it, have persecuted the Saints or apostatized and lost the spirit of God, " this testimony will go with them through all eternity, and they can never enter a rest." Their final destiny, however, is not revealed to mortals. Woman, in and of herself, could never progress to the highest place, " As Eve led Adam out of the garden he must lead her back." If she wilfully remain single and slights the great duty imposed upon her, she is useless in the economy of creation, and therefore is condemned. But many special provisions are made for the really worthy of both sexes, by which the living may vicariously atone for the dead who never heard the Gospel. Baptism for the dead, and marriage for the dead are chief among these means. The former they found upon St. Paul's writings, and under its provisions the Saint is often baptized for some relative who died many years before in Europe, or for some eminent personage. George Washington, Benjamin Franklin and Thomas Jefferson are thus vicariously members of the Mormon Church.

The celestial heaven is theirs only who have both heard and obeyed the Gospel. In that happy state they enjoy all that made this life desirable; they eat, drink, and are merry; they are solaced by the embraces of their earthly wives, and many more will be given them; all material enjoyments will be free from the defects of earth, and pleasures will never pall. In time the most faithful will become *gods*.

" They will ever look upon the elements as their home, hence the elements will ever keep pace with them in all the degrees of progressive refinement, while room is found in infinite space:

" While there are particles of unorganized element in nature's storehouse:

"While the trees of paradise yield their fruits, or the fountain of life its river:

"While the bosoms of the *gods* glow with affection.— While eternal charity endures, or eternity itself rolls its successive ages, the heavens will multiply, and new worlds and more people be added to the Kingdom of the Fathers."

But there is still another class of persons who do not quite live up to their privileges, and yet deserve a salvation. Unmarried men and women, and those guilty of various derelictions make up this class. They will never progress, but be *angels* merely; messengers and servants to those worthy of greater glory; and "bachelor angels" only, with no families, and compelled to go through eternity without a mate.

Amusement and disgust possess us by turns as we pursue these blasphemous speculations in regard to the employment of the *gods*, or the vain attempt to supply those points of knowledge which infinite wisdom has left unrevealed. In this attempt the Mormons might well be styled eclectic theologians. They are Christians in their belief in the New Testament, and the mission of Christ; Jews in their temporal theocracy, tithing and belief in prophecy; Mahommedans in regard to the relations of the sexes, and Voudoos or Fetichists, in their witchcraft, good and evil spirits, faith doctoring and superstition. From the Boodhists they have stolen their doctrines of apotheosis and development of *god*; from the Greek mythology their loves of the immortals and spirits; they have blended the ideas of many nations of polytheists, and made the whole consistent by outdoing the materialists. In the labor of harmonizing all this with Christianity, there is scarcely a schism that has ever rent the Christian world, but has furnished some scraps of doctrine. They are Arians in making Christ a secondary being in the Godhead—"the greatest of created things and yet a creature;" they are Manicheans in their division of the universe between good and evil spirits, and Gnostics in their gross ascription of all human indulgences and enjoyments, even polygamy, to the Saviour. Of the modern sects, they have the order of service, "experience meetings" and "witness of the spirit" of the Methodists; the "first principles" of the Campbellites, and the "universal suffrage" of the Presbyterians; while their views on baptism, the "perseverance of Saints," backsliding and restoration, read like a desperate attempt to combine the doctrines of the Campbellites, Methodists, and Cumberland Presbyterians. Finally, they, are Millenarians in their speedy expectation of Christ's earthly reign; almost Universalists in the belief that a very small portion of mankind will finally fail of any heaven; Spiritualists in their faith that the unseen powers produce special and actual visible effects on earth, though by natural laws, and Communists in their system of public works. But it is in regard to the personality and life of Christ that their ideas seem most strange and blasphemous. They hold that he was the literally begotten, that he had five wives while upon earth, two of whom were Martha and Mary, and thus actually violated the law under which He lived; at the same time they vaguely unite the views of the Greek and Latin Fathers, holding Him both the *Logos* and the *Aeon*, the Mediator and the God-man.

The question which, for five centuries, agitated the early Church as to the personality of Christ, the *homoousian* and the *homoiousian*, the "same substance" or the "similar substance," can have no place in their theology; they have boldly evaded it by obliterating all distinction, either in form, substance or development, between God and man; both are alike material, and differ only in degree. Met at the outset by the difficulty of comprehending God, they simplified it by making their Deity a "perfected man." This part of their theology, then, as far as it is the result of earnest and sincere thought on the part of its devotees, merely presents itself to my mind as another one of the ten thousand schemes of man to get away from that dogma which must be received on faith, simply because it is utterly beyond the grasp of finite reason. For nearly two thousand years the Christian Church has presented for the world's acceptance a Being, not all of earth, not all of heaven, yet perfect earth and perfect heaven; has asked the world to believe in the God-Man, the Divine-Human, the humanly inexplicable mystery of "God made manifest in the flesh." But man is unable, of his own reason alone, to receive this truth; and there is an intense desire in the natural mind to know more of God and hidden things personally, to see or hear them face to face. Man would pry into the hidden mysteries of Providence, which, we are told, "the angels desired to look into, and were not able;" at the same time the carnal mind is unwilling to use the appointed means whereby only this knowledge may be obtained; to study the written Word, to do the works therein commanded, and rise to that degree of moral purity by which alone his conception of unseen things can be heightened and made harmonious. He would be gross, sensual and earthy; and, at the same time, comprehend the pure and heavenly. The two are incompatible. Hence, dissatisfied with his own condition, and without the moral energy to amend it, discontented with the truth offered, yet unwilling to take the required course to gain more truth, he seeks for some shorter, easier way, some method more consonant with a corrupt nature, to satisfy his mind, and, perhaps, quiet an awakened conscience. This natural feeling of the human mind is seized upon by imposters, sometimes "the man with a purpose," and sometimes the dupe of their own fancies; and hence from age to age the ten thousand short lived sects, diverging now to the intensely material, and again to the ultra spiritual, but still departing from the great central line of the Church.

In our own day, Spiritualism complains that the Church is too material, too earthy and secular; that man finds therein no supply for the wants of his spiritual nature, and they seek therefor a corrective; the Mormons, diverging to the opposite extreme, complain that the Church is too speculative and mystical, too much given up to the vague and intangible; that their God "without body, parts or passions" is too far removed from human sympathy, and for this they would find a corrective in the most intense materialism. And this reaction once begun, the only limit or law to filthy imagination, is the range or power of human fancy. The gross familiarity with which fanatics of all kinds speak of the Supreme Being, the Mormon claim of the office of the Holy Ghost, their polygamy, incest and blood atonement, are a necessary and logical result of this degrading conception of spiritual things. Nowhere through the long detail of their tenets is purity taught or hinted at. It is all pure selfishness, mere grossness, sexualism deified, and the domain of the senses made the empire of the universe. The Being, in whose sight "the heavens are not clean," who "puts no trust in His servants, and charged His angels with folly," who is far above all taint of earthliness, has no place in such a system. They have degraded the human conception of Deity, till He has become, in their minds, "altogether such a one as themselves." The heathen philosophers of two thousand years ago, with only the unaided light of reason, were infinitely their superiors; and Plato's Deity is as much more worthy of our adoration than Brigham's, 'as the loftiest conceptions of a refined and virtuous philosopher are above the impure imaginations of a sensualist.

CHAPTER XIV.

THEORETICAL POLYGAMY—ITS HISTORY.

Poetry of religious concubinage—Fanaticism and Sensualism—Two extremes—Origin of Polygamy—The great revelation—Its contradictions and absurdities—Mormon argument—Real origin—Beginning of Polygamy—A prostitute for religion's sake—Failures and Scandals—War in the Church—Stealing a Brother's wife—Furore in consequence—The *Expositor*—Its destruction—Death of the Smiths—Polygamy practised secretly and denied openly—Brigham's marriages—Nine years of concealment—Avowal at last—Argument in its favor—Demoralization in the English Church—A climax of unnatural obscenity—The "Reformation"—Temporary decline in Polygamy—Hostility of native Mormon girls—Outside influence—Difference of opinion—It dies hard—Spiritual wives—Mystery and abomination.

THE occasional references hitherto in regard to " Pre-existence of the soul," " Sexual resurrection," " Progress in eternity," and " Generation of the gods," have prepared the reader somewhat for special consideration of polygamy ; but it is necessary also to look into its earthly history, and the reasons urged for its origin and continuance. And in these reasons we are surprised to find how captivating a veil of religious fancy may be thrown over an institution naturally and inherently vile. Gross forms of religious error seem almost invariably to lead to sensuality, to some singular perversion of the marriage relation or the sexual instinct; probably because the same constitution of mind and temperament which gives rise to the one, powerfully predisposes toward the other, The fanatic is of logical necessity either an ascetic or a sensualist; healthy moderation is foreign alike to his speculative faith and social practice. He either gives full rein to his baser propensities under the specious name of " Christian liberty," or, with a little more conscientiousness, swings to the opposite extreme, and forbids those innocent gratifications, prompted by nature, and permitted by God. Of the former class are the Mormons, Noyseites of Oneida, the Antinomians, and the followers of St. John of Leyden; of the latter the Shakers, Harmonists, monks and nuns, and a score of orders of celibate priests.

The Mormons are particular to declare that they never would have practical polygamy, except in accordance with an express revelation from God; and though they occasionally defend it on various physiological and scriptural grounds, they always fall back upon the express command. This revelation is said to have been given at Nauvoo, Illinois, July 12, 1843. It was first published in the *Deseret News Extra*, of September 14, 1852, and next in the April number, 1853, of the *Millennial Star*, Liverpool, England; and is contained at full length in Burton's "City of the Saints," and many other publications. It is too long and discursive to quote entire, and I sectionize it for convenient reference.

1. The revelation opens with this remarkable statement, the Lord represented as speaking:

"Verily, thus saith the Lord unto you, my servant Joseph, that inasmuch as you have inquired at my hand to know wherein I, the Lord, justified my servants Abraham, Isaac and Jacob; as also Moses, David and Solomon, my servants, as touching the principle and doctrine of their having many wives and concubines; behold, and lo, I am the Lord and will answer thee as touching this matter," etc.

It will not escape notice, that as here stated Joseph had asked the Lord about the matter. We cannot but wonder whether it would have been revealed at all, without this preliminary questioning. Many good Mormons think it would not, and Mormon ladies frequently express a pious regret that the Prophet ever asked about it! The section concludes by denouncing damnation upon all who reject the new gospel.

2. This section states that, "All covenants, contracts, bonds, obligations, oaths, vows, performances, connections, associations or expectations that are not made and entered into, and sealed by the Holy Spirit of promise of him who is anointed," are void in eternity, and only good for this world.

It sets forth also with great verbosity of language, that "God's house is a house of order."

3. The same principle is applied to the marriage covenant, stating that all who are not married "and sealed according to the new and everlasting covenant," are married for this world only, and shall not be entitled to their respective partners in eternity, but shall continue "angels only, and not gods, kept as ministers to those who are worthy of a far more exceeding and eternal weight of glory."

4. Description of the future glory of those who keep the new covenant: "Then shall they be gods because they have no end; there they shall be from everlasting to everlasting, because they continue; then shall they be above all, because all things are subject unto them. Then shall they be gods, because they have all power, and the angels are subject *unto them*.

5. To such are forgiven all manner of crimes, except murder, "wherein they shed innocent blood," and blasphemy against the Holy Ghost. Apostacy, be it noted, is the worst form of the latter sin.

6. This section explains the cases of Abraham and other ancient polygamists at great length, concluding by citing David as an example of how men lose their "exaltation" by abusing their privileges: "In none of these things did he sin against me, save in the case of Uriah and his wife, and, therefore, he hath fallen from his exaltation and received his position; and he shall not inherit them out of the world, for I gave them unto another, saith the Lord."

7. Great power is conferred upon Joseph Smith to regulate all such celestial marriages, punish for adultery, and take away the wives of the guilty and give them to good men.

8. This section gives very full and explicit instructions to Emma Smith, wife of Joseph, how to conduct herself under the new dispensation; that she "receive all those that *have been given* unto my servant Joseph, who are virtuous and pure before me," and threatening her with destruction if she do not.

9. The revelation changes abruptly and gives Joseph

Smith full directions how to manage his property; particularly "let not my servant Joseph *put his property out of his hands*, lest an enemy come and destroy him," and threatening severely all who injure him.

The reader, familiar with the old Revised Statutes of Illinois, would be surprised to find the Lord talking so much like a Justice of the Peace.

10. The revelation comes, at last, to the gist of the matter and grants plurality of wives, in these words:

"And again, as pertaining to the law of the priesthood: If any man espouse a virgin and desire to espouse another, and the first give her consent; and if he espoused the second, and they are virgins, and have vowed to no other man, then is he justified; he cannot commit adultery for they are given unto him; for he cannot commit adultery with that that belongeth unto him and to none else; and, if he have ten virgins given unto him by this law, he cannot commit adultery for they belong to him and are given unto him; therefore is he justified. They are given unto him to multiply and replenish the earth according to my commandment, and to fulfil the promise which was given by my Father before the foundation of the world; and for their exaltation in the eternal worlds, that they may bear the souls of men; for herein is the work of my Father continued, that he may be glorified."

11. Heavy punishment is threatened to all women who refuse, without good cause, to give their husbands second wives; concluding as follows: "And now, as pertaining unto this law, verily, verily, I say unto you, I will reveal more unto you hereafter; therefore, let this suffice for the present. Behold, I am Alpha and Omega. Amen."

Such is the revelation. Space fails me to note all its contradictions and absurdities. One, however, is worthy of special remark. In the eighth section Emma Smith is commanded to receive lovingly "all those that have been given unto my servant Joseph." The past tense is used. Thus the first revelation authorizing polygamy implies that Joseph had already practised it. Stranger still, polygamy is expressly forbidden by the "Book of Mormon."

In the third book and second chapter of that work, the angel messenger is represented as saying to the Nephites " But the word of God burdens me because of your grosser crimes. For this people begin to wax in iniquity; they understand not the Scriptures, for they seek to excuse themselves in committing whoredoms, because of the things that were written concerning David and Solomon, his son. They, truly, had many wives and concubines which thing was abominable before me, saith the Lord, wherefore, hearken unto the word of the Lord, for there shall not any man among you have save it be one wife, and concubines he shall have none, for I, the Lord God, delighteth in the chastity of women."

It has exhausted all the ingenuity of Mormon writers to reconcile this passage with the new revelation, but they succeed in doing so sufficiently to satisfy their consciences. The Mormon history relates that when the full force of the new covenant was perceived the Prophet was filled with astonishment and dread. All the traditions of his early education were overthrown, and yet he felt that it was the work of the Lord. In vain he sought to be released from the burden of communicating the new doctrine to the world, and at length obtained permission to keep it secret, as yet, from all but the Twelve Apostles, and a few other leading men. As the hour approached when he was to meet them in council, horror and fear of what might be the result overcame him, and he hastily mounted his horse and fled from the city. But a mighty angel met him on the road, stood in the way with a drawn sword, and with awful voice and offended mien bade him return.

These pretended forebodings were fully justified by the event, for, in spite of the secresy maintained, the matter was soon bruited abroad, and there was fearful commotion in " Zion." Old Mormons have told me that when they first heard it they were horror-stricken at the thought, and for years after could not believe the report.

When the matter was first broached in secret council, William Law, First Counsellor to Joseph Smith, stood up and denounced it as from the devil, and added : " If any man preaches that doctrine in my family, I will take his life." This Law had a young and beautiful wife, for whom Joseph was already intriguing, and his final success with her and attempt to get her divorced from her husband, caused the latter to apostatize, and had no small share in bringing on the difficulties which resulted in Joseph's death.

As might be expected, the men were the first converts. Joseph and a few others began soon to act upon their new privileges. Joseph seems to have been pretty successful, and soon had half-a-dozen spiritual wives, though all was still kept secret. While soliciting ladies to become "sealed" to him, he made several unsuccessful attempts, which caused great scandal. In particular, his doings were published by Miss Martha H. Brotherton, who immediately withdrew from the Church; also by Miss Eliza Rigdon, daughter of Sidney Rigdon, Mrs. Foster, and Mrs. Sarah Pratt, first wife of Orson Pratt.

Great was the fury among the Saints at these revelations, and every epithet a vile fancy could suggest was heaped upon these ladies, for what were styled "their perjured lies to injure the Prophet." One of them was forced to sign a written retraction; another, discarded and denounced by her Mormon parents, died of a broken heart. Miss Brotherton escaped and returned to Boston, while Foster, Higbee, and a few others, whose families had been insulted, apostatized. For awhile the dissolution of the Church seemed imminent, but the mingled boldness and hypocrisy of the Prophet restored something like order, and polygamy was indignantly denounced and repudiated.

At this place in our narrative, having given the Mormon account, it may be well to give the real origin of polygamy. In the Mormon archives are a set of phrenological charts, of the various Mormon leaders at Nauvoo, taken by a prominent professor. In the chart of Joseph Smith's head, in a scale running from one to twelve, "amativeness," or sexual passion, is recorded at *eleven;* while that of Bennett, his "right hand man," is set down at "*ten—very full!*" In the propensity which these are held to indicate, was the real origin of polygamy. A prominent Mormon says that Joseph Smith informed him that, as early as 1832, he had preliminary revelations upon the subject; and it is a notorious fact, that almost from the first the Prophet had used his powers of fascination to triumph over the virtue of his female devotees, and had anticipated polygamy in accordance with revelation, by unauthorized promiscuous intercourse. His intrigues with various women had involved the rising sect in constant trouble at Kirkland and in Missouri; and by the sworn testimony of the best men who seceded from the Mormons in Missouri, the Prophet had already established a sort of polygamy.

Shortly after the settlement of Nauvoo also, Sidney Rigdon had advanced his "spiritual wife" doctrine, which regular Mormons now denounce as the great mystery of abominations, "sent by the devil to bring dishonor upon the true order of celestial marriage." Rigdon's theory of "Spiritual wifery," as reported by old Mormons, was as follows:

In the pre-existent state souls are mated, male and female, as it is divinely intended they shall fill the marriage relation in this life; or, in more poetic phrase, "marriages are made in heaven." But in the general jumble of contradictions and cross-purposes attending man in this state, many mistakes have been made in this matter; A. has got the woman first intended for B., the latter has got C's true mate, and thus on, utterly defeating the counsel of the *gods* in the pre-marriàge of the spirits. But the time had come for all this to be set right, and though they might not put aside their present wives, which would throw society somewhat out of gear, yet Smith might, in addition, exercise the privileges of husband toward Brown's wife and *vice versa*. This seems to have been merely the Mormon version of modern "free-loveism," and from recent evidence it is quite probable it also was practised to some extent in Nauvoo, thus making polygamy equally free to men and women; but it is quite different, in theory at least, from the present "spiritual wifeism" of the Mormons, as will presently appear.

But Rigdon's doctrines were both varying and dangerous, and he lacked the faculty of concealment; so he was soon condemned, and his doctrines with him.

As the first open hints of the new doctrine, in the autumn of 1843, excited so much contention, and as the indignation of the people of Illinois was justly feared, orders were given to all the travelling elders to persistently deny the doctrine. On the first of February, 1844, the *Times and Seasons*, church paper at Nauvoo, contained the following:

"NOTICE!

"As we have lately been credibly informed, that an Elder of the Church of Jesus Christ of Latter-Day Saints, by the name of Hyrum Brown, has been preaching Polygamy, and other false and corrupt doctrines, in the County of Lapeer, and State of Michigan:

"This is to notify him and the Church in general, that he has been cut off from the Church for his iniquity; and he is further notified to appear at the Special Conference, on the 6th of April next to make answer to these charges.

"JOSEPH SMITH,
"HYRUM SMITH,
" *Presidents of the Church.*"

The Gentiles appear not to have been well enough posted on the subject to pay much heed to the "Notice," but it excited no little commotion among the Mormons, who had heard or received reports from others of the doctrine; and on the day appointed a large number of the disaffected, and a few resident Gentiles, were present. Hyrum Smith arose and stated that "great reports had been bruited about of schism in Zion, and, no doubt, many were present, hoping to witness dissension; but all such hopes were vain, the Lord had healed all backslidings, there would be no charges made, and the day would be spent in prayer and other exercises;" and spent it was accordingly. Six weeks afterwards, Hyrum found it necessary to write as follows:

"NAUVOO, *March* 15, 1844.

"*To the Brethren of the Church of Jesus Christ of Latter-Day Saints, living on China Creek, in Hancock County, Greeting:*

"Whereas Brother Richard Hewett has called on me to-day, to know my views concerning some doctrines that are preached in your place, and states to me that some of your Elders say, that a man, *having a certain priesthood,* may have as many wives as he pleases, and that doctrine is taught here : I say unto you that that man teaches *false doctrine*, for there is no such doctrine taught here, neither is there any such thing practised here ; and any man that is found teaching privately or publicly any such doctrine, is culpable, and will stand a chance to be brought before the High Council, and lose his license and membership also ; therefore, he had better beware what he is about."

This letter will also be found in the 5th volume of the *Times and Seasons*, page 474. But affairs had gone too far ; a powerful schism broke out in the bosom of the Church, and William Law, Dr. Foster, Chauncy L. Higbee, Francis M. Higbee, and a number of other apostates commenced preaching openly against the Prophet, and established at Nauvoo a paper called the *Expositor*, devoted to making war upon the new system. But they only issued one number, which contained sixteen affidavits, mostly from ladies, setting forth the licentious actions of Joseph Smith and Brigham Young. Joseph was at that time not only Prophet, Priest, and Revelator, but, also, Mayor of the City and Major-General of the Nauvoo Legion.— Such a daring publication in the stronghold of his power was not to be tolerated. So he hastily convened the City Council, who, at his suggestion, declared the *Expositor* a "public nuisance," and ordered that it be "at once abated." The City Marshal and his posse forthwith attacked the office and abated it in the literal meaning of that word, and in the Mormon fashion, by breaking the press and scattering the type. The publishers fled for their lives, and, proceeding to Carthage, the county-seat of Hancock

County, procured warrants against several Mormons, under the State law of Illinois, determined to test the legality of such extensive jurisdiction by the Council. Both the Smiths were finally arrested and murdered in jail, as more fully related elsewhere.

After their death the policy of concealment was continued. In July, 1845, Parley P. Pratt, in the *Millennial Star*, Mormon publication at Liverpool, England, denounced "spiritual wifery" as a "doctrine of devils and seducing spirits; but another name for whoredom, wicked and unlawful connection, and every kind of corruption, confusion and abomination;" and in the following year, the General Conference of Europe denounced both the doctrine and practice in the strongest terms. In May, 1848, the *Millennial Star* called for the vengeance of heaven on all the liars who charged "such odious practices as spiritual wifeism and polygism" upon the Church; ending with the following:

"In all ages of the Church truth has been turned into a lie, and the grace of God converted into lasciviousness, by men who have sought to make a 'gain of godliness,' and feed their lusts on the credulity of the righteous and unsuspicious. * * * Next to the long-hackneyed and bug-a-boo whisperings of polygism is another abomination that sometimes shows its serpentine crests, which we shall call sexual resurrectionism. * * * * The doctrines of corrupt spirits are always in close affinity with each other, whether they consist in spiritual wifeism, sexual resurrection, gross lasciviousness, or the unavoidable separation of husbands and wives, or the communism of property."

In July, 1850, Elder John Taylor held a discussion at Boulogne, France, with three English clergymen. They quoted from the anti-Mormon works then just published by J. C. Bennett and J. B. Bowes, which charged polygamy as a practice of the Church; to which Taylor made the following reply: "We are accused here of polygamy, and actions the most indelicate, obscene and disgusting, such that none but a corrupt heart could have contrived. These things are too outrageous to admit of belief. Therefore, leaving the sisters of the 'white veil' and the 'black veil,' and all the other veils with those gentlemen to dispose of, together with their authors, as they think best, I shall content myself by reading our views of chastity and marriage from a work published by us, containing some of the articles of our faith." He then read from the "*Doctrines and Covenants*," which was adopted in full conference *the year after Smith's death*, the following:

"4. * * * Inasmuch as this Church of Christ has been reproached with the *crime* of fornication and polygamy; we declare that we believe that one man should have *one* wife; and one woman *but* one husband, except in case of death, when either is at liberty to marry again."

The italics are my own. As a specimen of Mormon reasoning, it may here be added, they now insist that, in the above clause, "one wife" really meant, of course, "one or more;" that the adversative "but" was added in case of the woman to cut off any such free rendering in her case, and that the clause was so worded "to specially deceive the Gentiles, and yet tell the exact truth." They further add that, "under certain circumstances, the Lord allows his priesthood to lie, in order to save His people; it would not do to give strong meat to little children; they must first be fed with milk, and when they get stronger they can have meat; so with the truth, they must be taught it little at a time."

The foreign Mormons were thus kept in perfect ignorance of the matter, and were highly indignant when the charge was made; still, as it was practised, reports of it were constantly made, and generally believed throughout the United States.

Brigham Young soon became head of the Church, and took for his second wife Lucy Decker Seely, who had previously been divorced from Doctor Seely. Not long after, at their winter quarters near Council Bluffs, Iowa, he married Harriet Cook, whose son, Oscar Young, is the first child in polygamy. He is now a young man of twenty-two or three, bright, active and intelligent, and a great favorite with his Gentile friends, though a little

R

to be dreaded sometimes on account of his savage temper when angry.

This marriage was followed by those of Clara Decker, Clara Chase, Lucy Bigelow, Harriet Bowker, and Harriet Barney. Mary Ann Angell Young, the original wife of Brigham, still lives in a house of her own, just back of the Lion House. She had five children—Brigham, Joseph, John, Alice and Luna; all are married and living in Salt Lake City. Brigham was at first a widower, and the two daughters of his first wife, now middle-aged ladies, are both married, and living in Utah. A few years after leaving Nauvoo, Brigham married Emmeline Free, who was for many years his favorite wife, and often styled, among Gentiles, "the Light of the Harem." She was finally discarded, some six years ago, for Amelia Folsom, his youngest wife, and present favorite. It is, of course, impossible to tell with exactness the number of his wives, but those best informed place them at twenty-three actual wives, and fifty-one spiritual. Miss Eliza Roxy Snow, the Mormon poetess, is one of his spiritual wives, or "proxy" women, and is married to him by proxy for Joseph Smith, of whom she claims to have been the first spiritual wife.

Meanwhile the Saints had become firmly fixed in Utah, where it seems that "Gentiles, their laws and mobs, would annoy no more;" and the necessity for concealment no longer existed. So the doctrine was more and more openly discussed, and, finally, on the 29th of August, 1852, it was publicly announced, by Brigham Young, in a meeting at Salt Lake City, where the revelation was for the first time publicly read, and pronounced valid. The sermons in its favor, by Orson Pratt and Brigham Young, were first published, together with the revelation, in the *Deseret News Extra*, of September 14th, 1852. From Young's address I extract the following:

. "You heard Brother Pratt state, this morning, that a Revelation would be read this afternoon, which was given previous to Joseph's death. It contains a doctrine a small portion of the world is opposed to; but I can deliver a prophecy upon it. Though that doctrine has not been preached by the Elders, this people have believed in it for years.

"The original copy of this Revelation was burnt up. William Clayton was the man who wrote it, from the mouth of the Prophet. In the meantime it was in Bishop Whitney's possession. He wished the privilege to copy it, which brother Joseph granted. Sister Emma (wife of Joseph Smith) burnt the original. The reason I mention this is, because that the people, who did know of the Revelation, supposed it was not now in existence.

"The Revelation will be read to you. The principle spoken upon by Brother Pratt this morning, we believe in. Many others are of the same mind. They are not ignorant of what we are doing in our social capacity. They have cried out proclaim it; but it would not do a few years ago; everything must come in its time, as there is a time for all things, I am now ready to proclaim it.

"This Revelation has been in my possession for many years; and who has known it? None but those who should know it. I keep a patent lock on my desk, and there does not anything leak out that should not."

The people of Utah were prepared for the announcement, but polygamy was too "strong doctrine" for Europe, and, when first published there, in April, 1853, it seemed that even then it would destroy the foreign Church. In England, especially, the demoralization was fearful; hundreds after hundreds apostatized, whole churches and conferences dissolved; talented knaves in many instances, finding in this the excuse for going off without surrendering the money-bags which they held. The missions entirely disappeared in many parts of Europe, and, even in America, thousands of new converts, who had not gone to "Zion," turned away and joined the Josephites, Gladdenites, Strangeites, and other sects of recusant Mormons.

The *Millenial Star* remained silent on the subject for weeks after publishing the Revelation, coming out at length with a feeble defence of the system, from the pen of J. Jaques, a leading Mormon polemic. The fact was, the people did not understand the new idea, they did not see the spiritual necessities for it; they had so far believed that Mormonism was simply an advance in Christianity, and could not feel that, " in this the fulness of time, the ancient covenant was restored with all its privileges." But in Utah a great rush was made for new wives; old men traded for young girls, and the new order was hailed as the great crowning joy and privilege of believers. Polygamy continued extending until that period known as the " Reformation," in 1855–56, when the whole Church was re-baptized, and a new point of departure taken. Then the new practice seemed, for awhile, to reach a furious climax of unnatural and degrading obscenity. The duty and importance of polygamy were presented every Sunday; hundreds of girls of only twelve or thirteen years were forced or persuaded into its practice; and, in numerous instances, even younger girls were "sealed " to old reprobates, with an agreement on the part of the latter to wait until the girls were more mature, and suited to act the part of wives. Hundreds of instances occurred which would be utterly incredible at present, were they not fully proved by many authentic witnesses. Old men met openly in the streets and traded daughters, and whole families of girls were married to the same man. This was the period when polygamy reached its worst manifestation, and, bad as it is now, gross as many of its features still are, it was ten-fold worse then. Women of my acquaintance at Salt Lake City, who were children at the time, have told me of occurrences, during that period, which would indicate an almost incredible reign of lust and fanaticism. Divorce also became so common that these marriages scarcely amounted to more than promiscuous intercourse. I met one woman who had been divorced and re-married six times, and an old Mormon once pointed out to me a woman who had once been his wife, and had been divorced and re-married nine times. In numerous instances a young girl would be married to some prominent elder, with whom she would reside a few months, after which she would be divorced and married to another, and again to another, "going the rounds," as the phrase was, of half a dozen priests.

A general demoralization seemed to seize upon the community; vulgarity of language, both in public address and private speech, became so common that thousands of Mormons were themselves disgusted, and a reaction set in against such excesses. It would seem that Brigham also became alarmed at the tendency, and, as he had been greatly annoyed by applications for divorce, commenced exacting a heavy fee for the service. The period of comparative starvation which followed, during the winters of 1856-7, may have had something to do with checking the prevailing tendency, but, certain it is, there has been no such general license since.

The entrance of Johnston's army, too, indirectly produced a great effect; stage and mail lines were fully established; Utah was brought into much closer relation with the rest of the world, a considerable Gentile influence began to manifest itself, sources of information were multiplied, and polygamy began to be unpopular with the young women of Utah. In this regard, then, Mormon history may be divided into three periods:

I. The monogamic period: from its origin till 1843, during which time all their publications and sermons were opposed to polygamy in their tone.

II. The transition period: from 1843 to 1852, when polygamy was secretly taught and extended, but openly denied and condemned.

III. The polygamic period: from 1852 to the present, in all which time polygamy has been avowed and defended as an essential part of Mormon religion. The third period might properly again be divided into an era of rise, and one of decline; for it is evident that polygamy culminated in all its worst features as early as 1856, since which time it has been slowly on the decline, and even without Government interference would hardly have endured much more than another generation. In these last statements I am aware that I differ from some, whose evidence carries the weight of authority, particularly

Judges Drake and Titus, and other United States officials, who have lately testified before the Congressional Committee on Territories. Nevertheless, such is my conclusion from a mass of evidence given by persons both in and out of the Mormon Church, and from a careful examination of the records. That polygamy has declined in the last five years is quite certain, from causes, both within and without the Church; it is now almost impossible to induce a young girl brought up in Salt Lake City, or the northern settlements, to enter that condition, and the instances of plural marriages are confined almost entirely to young women just brought from Europe.

Of their theology, as it relates to polygamy, but little need be added. It is so thoroughly grafted into and interwoven with their whole system, that at no point can one be touched without attacking the other. Polygamy is not, as recusant Mormons assert, a mere addition by Brigham Young to the original faith; it is a necessary and logical outgrowth of the system. If Mormonism be true, then polygamy is right; for "pre-existence of the soul," "progression of the gods," and all other peculiarities of the system depend, by a thousand combinations and inter-relations, upon the plurality system. A man's or woman's glory in eternity is to depend upon the size of the family; for a woman to remain childless is a sin and calamity, and she cannot secure "exaltation," as the wife of a Gentile or an apostate; her husband's rank in eternity must greatly depend upon the number of his wives, and she will share in that glory whatever it is. All this points unerringly to polygamy. Hence, also, the last feature of this complex and unnatural relationship, known as "spiritual wives," which is to be understood as follows: Any woman having an earthly husband, of whose final exaltation she is in doubt, may be "sealed for eternity" to some prominent Mormon, who will raise her and make her part of his final kingdom. In theory this gives the spiritual husband no marital rights, but, as stated by Elder John Hyde, the noted apostate, "it may well be doubted whether the woman, who can prefer another man for her pseudo-eternal husband, has not fallen low enough to sin in *deed*, as well as thought, against her earthly husband."

By "marriage for the dead," living women are sealed to dead men, and *vice versa*, some one "standing proxy" for the deceased. Thus, a widow and widower may each prefer their first partners "for eternity," but like each other well enough "for time;" in which case they are first sealed to each other "for time," then each, by proxy for the departed, "for eternity," thus requiring three separate ceremonies to settle the temporal and eternal relations of all parties, who may in turn be divorced from either by Brigham Young and the Probate Courts. So a man may have a wife "for time," who belongs to some man already dead "for eternity," in which case all the children will belong to the latter in eternity, the living man merely "raising up seed unto his dead brother." To such lengths of vain imaginings may a credulous people be led by artful imposters.

CHAATER XV.

PRACTICAL POLYGAMY.

Open evils and hidden sufferings—Miss S. E. Carmichael's testimony—Mormon sophistry—The sexual principle—Its objects—Theory and facts—Monogamist vs. Polygamist—Turk, Persian, and African vs. the Christian White—The same effects in Utah—Jealousy and Misery—Children of different wives—Cultivated indifference—Hatred among children—Brigham's idea of parental duty—Are the Mormon women happy?—Submission and silence—Degradation of women—Mormon idea of politeness—Heber C. Kimball and his "cows"—"My women"—Slavery of sex—Moses and Mohammed outdone—Incest—Marrying a whole family—Robert Sharkey—Remorse and suicide—Uncle and niece—Bishop Smith and his nieces—Mixture of blood—Horrible crimes—Half-brother and sister—The Prophet "sold"—The doctrine of incest—"Too strong now, but the people will come to it"—Now openly avowed—Brothers and sisters to marry for a "pure priesthood"—Testimony of Wm. Hepworth Dixon—Father and daughter *may* marry—Effects upon the young—Infant mortality—Large average mortality—Fatal blindness—The growing youth—Demoralization—Youthful depravity—No hope for young men and women—Sophistry and madness—Ancient sensualism to be revived.

THE worst period of polygamy has passed, but its evil effects continue in full force to the present. At the outset I meet with a difficulty in describing its greatest evils. As formerly stated, the virtues of Mormonism are all easily seen, while its vices are, as much as possible, hidden, and this is peculiarly the case with polygamy.

We can see its evils in a political point of view, in their laws, to some extent in their society, in the mixture of population, and the blood of near kindred; but who can enter into the *penetralia* of the affections, weigh and estimate woman's anguish, count the heart drops of sorrow, and say, here is so much misery, or there is so much resignation.

The last is by far the greatest evil of polygamy, and

though it may be felt, and, to some extent, seen, it can never be described.

Miss Sarah E. Carmichael, now Mrs. Williamson, who was reared at Salt Lake, says: "If I were a man, as I am a woman, I would stand in the halls of Congress, and cry aloud for the miserable women of Utah, till the world should hear and know the wrongs and miseries of polygamy." The Mormons argue that the laws of nature, physical nature, point out polygamy as the natural condition. There may be some argument in its favor in the physical organization, but when we come to the soul and mind, the mentality of woman points unerringly to monogamy as her only possible state for domestic happiness; and any system which attempts to establish unity in the household, by dividing one man's care and affection among two or three women, is founded upon a total misconception of the sexual principle. For why was that principle so deeply implanted in the human nature? The Mormons will tell us, "for the one purpose only, that men might increase." But a sound philosophy, and the history of mankind, show that this 'is but one of many reasons, though necessary and important, yet not all, either of man's duty or happiness.

In the nobler view this principle has at least three manifestations, and three objects to fulfil.

First and lowest is a mere amativeness—the feeling which the male animal has for the female—common to man with the brutes. Its object is reproduction, its nobler uses, the perpetuation of our species.

But far above this is a second division of the great principle, companionship, society, love of a congenial associate. With it is connected the admiration for beauty, grace and refinement, mutual help and protection, and the interchange of kind offices. Its public benefits are in the founding of families, and establishment of communities, and by it alone can the State be established, on aught approaching sure foundations. In this view then, marriage is not, as certain theorists would persuade us, a matter strictly between the individuals; the State has the highest interest in its regulation, and justly determines, from the experience of the past, what is best for the stability of our institutions. But he who should stop at this point in the inquiry, would have at last but a poor and mean view of the sexual principle or the marriage relation.

As man is not all animal, but also a member of a family and community, one helping and needing help, a citizen and a debtor to the public weal; so he is not all man, not all citizen, communist or worker; he is, in part, divine, he has a nature in common with the angels. And in this department of his nature, the great principle manifests itself as a high and holy affection, a pure regard for what is pure, a silent adoration for that which is divine in the human; its exercise and reward alike are in a complete intercommunion of soul, and interchange of pure affection.

And its very essence is duality; a divided affection is utterly at war with "that sweet egotism of the heart called love," that divine selfishness of choosing *one* being apart from all the world, perhaps the *only* form in which selfishness is approved of God. And the object of this principle is a higher development of the whole man, male and female; this is the most noble object of the marriage relation, and by this alone is it sanctified. Can the wildest fanaticism or most earnest sophistry claim that aught of this can be found in the polygamic order? The Mormon is but *one-third* married; he has in such unions provided for but one-third, and that the lowest, basest part of his nature. But, it may be said, this last is only a theory. Let us then briefly examine a few facts. That this indication is to be followed rather than the other, is abundantly shown by a comparative view of polygamous and monogamous nations. The Indian and native African know nothing of the softer sentiments which make life amiable and agreeable; to them woman is merely a superior beast of burden; they can purchase as many wives as their means command, and are, by nature, habit and religion, thorough-going polygamists. Coming a little higher to the partially civilized races, we find a great improvement, but nothing like Christian ideas. The Hindoo considers this such a poor world for women, that it is thought no particular harm to drown a female infant, though a heinous offence to thus dispose of a boy. The same is true, to some extent, of the Persians, Turks, and Mohammedan races, generally. Home, as understood by us, is an unknown institution; the harem takes its place, and polygamous customs have destroyed, to a great extent, the valor and energy of the men and the attractive graces of woman.

In the march of progress, these nations are fast falling behind and sinking beneath the hardy vigor of Western Christians. History scarcely records an instance where an organized nation of monogamists has fallen before polygamists.

The monogamic Greeks, with a little army of forty thousand men, overran all the proud empires of Southern Asia; the effeminate Persians and Hindoos could not stand before the hardy valor of that people, who held, as a fixed principle, that the dignity of woman is the strength of the State. Monogamic Rome completed what Greece had begun, in destroying the power of the Western Asiatics. For six hundred years the honor and dignity of the Roman matron were the subjects of unwearied praise, till Rome herself was corrupted by the nations she had conquered. The reign of the first Asiatic, who wore the Imperial purple, marks the beginning of a great decline, and Rome, in turn, fell before the hardy monogamists of Northern Europe. The Mohammedans easily overran Asia and Northern Africa, but in Europe their course was soon checked. The hosts of Abderahman melted like snow before the stout arms of the German nations, who left the plains of Poictiers covered with the corpses of three hundred thousand polygamists.

But it may be said these comparisons are unfair, as setting civilized nations against semi-barbarians. But this fact makes a better comparison impossible, that the lowest nation of monogamists is far above the highest of polygamists. The white inhabitants of Utah are the only branch of the Caucasian race that have adopted polygamy within many hundred years. Of course we would look for certain results there, and if not seen at once, many would conclude that Utah was an exception to the general rule. But it is to be remembered that polygamy has been practised among them but twenty-seven years. Nevertheless it has shown a marked and rapid tendency towards evil; and in many of its features probably worse than in any Mohammedan country.

The first result to be noted is a universal, and worse than Moslem jealousy, both among men and women. I have the testimony of dozens, brought up in the midst of the system, and several of them children of second wives, that such a thing as a harmonious family of many wives is unknown in their acquaintance. Others say there are such, but all admit they are rare. I am speaking now of the women and young people's testimony; the men will often claim the contrary, even when their own families disprove it. Among my acquaintances in Salt Lake City is a young lady, who is the daughter of a second wife, whose history illustrates this matter very forcibly. Her mother had lived in polygamy for fifteen years, and finally became convinced that it was as sinful as she had found it miserable.

The troubles of her mind brought on a mortal sickness when she called her daughter to her bedside, and told her that she had lived in misery, and was dying without hope; that she was now convinced of her sin, and only desired her daughter to escape from it.

The daughter, as required, took a solemn oath never to enter polygamy. The mother told her to be firm and her mother's spirit would protect her. Soon after she died, and, the daughter left her father's house, at the age of fourteen, to reside with a relative who had apostatized, and though twice taken back, is now permitted to live there unmolested. The father stands high in the Mormon Church, and still has four wives. During the first month of my stay in Salt Lake City, the second wife of a well known Mormon left him, and went to work in a hotel. After a short stay there, she took her child and started to Montana, when the husband took out a writ of *habeas corpus* for the child; the Sheriff overtook her thirty miles

North, when, seeing him coming, she ran for the mountains, distant half a mile. She was overtaken and the child torn away from her, and brought to the city, which of course, induced the mother to return. She was going with some emigrants who dared not assist her, for fear of Mormon vengeance.

Instances of like nature might be cited at will; and it is only too plain, that the system results in the utter destruction of domestic love and harmony. The Mormons themselves hesitatingly acknowledge that the "thing called love among the Gentiles" cannot exist under their system; but claim that they have instead, a purer feeling of respect, support and friendship.

Hence, it is quite the custom among the Mormon leaders, to speak of domestic affection and endearments with a sort of sneer, or as something to be but rarely indulged in, and rather unworthy of the manly character.

The Mormons claim that a man *may* love equally half a dozen women, as well as a mother may the same number of children, and that the women are satisfied with this divided affection; but that this is not, and never can be the case, I need say to no one who has the slightest knowledge of the female heart. For a man to love six women, equally well, is manifestly impossible; but it *is* possible for him to be equally indifferent to all. And to this does the teaching of the leaders directly tend; rather than create a jealousy, or show a marked preference for one, they are to cultivate a mere equal respect for all. Nor is it often possible for a' man, whose care and affection are divided between three or four women of varying charms and tempers, to regard equally the children of all; if he have common affection, the most affectionate child will become his favorite, and engross his attention; and thus jealousy, far from being confined to adults, rages equally in the bosoms of the young. This is seen and noticed in almost every family, and the story of Jacob's partiality, and his children's jealousy, is repeated every day in the year. So greatly do these troubles multiply in the larger families, that in spite of their inclination to secrecy, the parents are forced in bitterness of soul to make known their grievances.

In one sermon, preached while I was at Salt Lake, Brigham Young made this remark: "The women are every day complaining of what they have to suffer in plurality. If it's any harder on them than it is on the men, God help them. Many of them seem to think a man in plurality has nothing to do but listen to their troubles, and run at their beck and call. I believe I have wives that would see me damned rather than not get every little furbelow they want."

But the smaller families are happy in comparison, and it is within the walls of the larger harems, according to all reports, that the demon of jealousy reigns supreme. Female nurses of Salt Lake say that it is no uncommon thing, in the better class of polygamous households, for a child to be born to one wife and all the others to remain sullenly in their rooms, unless specially called, apparently without interest or concern for the result.

At first view it seems incredible that any woman should be indifferent under such circumstances; and yet we can readily understand that a woman would be far from pleased at the birth of a child which was her husband's but not hers. From the torment of such feelings there is no refuge but in a cultivated indifference, and such seems to be the ideal of all thorough Mormons in regard to the affections.

Brigham Young himself is personally one of the coldest of men. According to one who knows his habits, he usually sleeps alone, in a small room behind his office; and a woman who lived many years in his family, tells me she never saw him caress or pet but one of his children. In speaking to one of my Mormon acquaintances, Brigham gave the following as his idea of fatherly duty: "I pay no attention to the children, but leave that to their mothers, according to the law of nature. The bull pays no attention to his calves."

In this sentence is embodied the social perfection of polygamy, as it will be "when the Lord has healed the Saints of all their old Gentilish traditions." The question will, of course, be asked: Are the Mormon women happy? It must be remembered that only one-third or one-fourth of all the women in Utah are in polygamy, either as first or subsequent wives; and, as to the rest, there is no particular cause for unhappiness from that source, except the constant dread that their husbands will take additional wives. These exceptions noted, the testimony, as far as it can be had, is universal, that Mormonism is a "hard faith for women." Again, it may be asked: What do the women say about it? Generally, they say nothing. It is "sound Mormon doctrine," that the "first duty of a woman is submission, and the second silence;" and, certainly, the majority of Utah women would gain heaven on those conditions. The most noticeable fact to a Gentile travelling through Mormon settlements is the strangely quiet way in which women discharge their household duties.

They stand behind the guest at the way-side hotel, replenish the table and attend upon his wants, but never enter into the conversation, venture not the slightest observation or inquiry, and very rarely answer his questions in anything more than monosyllables. And those questions are few, for it is almost, if not quite, a capital crime in the Mormon code to "interfere with our *women*." Such principles and such practice can tend only to the degradation of woman; and this I note as the second great evil of polygamy. To Eastern minds it is quite impossible to convey a full comprehension of the many ways, the thousand little expressions, the tone of public and private manners, and the daily incidents in which is manifested this general lack of respect for women. This is so marked that it is a common subject of talk, even among themselves. Said a young Mormon woman, who had just married a Gentile, to me : " I don't know half a dozen men here who really respect their wives. It is a constant wonder to us, the way the Gentiles treat their women."

I have often been amused at the appearance of their young women who were attending Gentile balls for the first time. That a gentleman should bow so reverently to his partner, that he should offer a lady his arm just to cross the room, that he should esteem it a pleasure, rather than a favor, to bring a glass of water or the like, seems to excite their amazement. Social lines were closely drawn the winter of my stay in Salt Lake, and no young woman could venture to associate with the Gentiles, without losing her standing among Mormons entirely. Still, many found their way into Gentile society, though if they persisted in it, they were usually "cut off and dis-fellowshiped" by the Church authorities.

The fanaticism of the Mormons is so great that they consider a woman "lost" if she associates with Gentile men ; it is concluded at once that she can have no pure motive in so doing, and among their own people they possess the power to ruin a woman's character entirely.— An old Mormon, at whose house I visited occasionally, seldom failed to give me his views of the absurdity of our common ideas of women. His favorite style was to give me a burlesque representation of our mode of addressing ladies, and when he got warmed up on the subject, it was highly amusing to see him skip about the room, hat in hand, bowing and grimacing to the chairs, and imitating the dandified address of an exquisite. Most of the polygamists habitually speak of their wives as "my women," and in his jocular moments, while preaching, the late Heber C. Kimball often spoke of his facetiously as "my cows."

I must say, however, that all of this is not due to polygamy, but much of it to the women themselves. Nearly all of them are of foreign birth, English, Welsh, Scotch and Scandinavian, and of that class, too, among whom men have never been accustomed to respect women very highly. I am sure polygamy could not have been established in a purely American community, and the Mormons themselves say that all the trouble and opposition comes from the American or Irish wives, though there are but few of the latter.

But the vileness of Mormon polygamy, which gives it infamous pre-eminence over that of Jews, Turks, and Hindoos, is yet to be described, and consists in the grosser forms of incest, the intermarriage of near relations. In their general revolt against the ethics of Christendom, and attempt to found a society upon the most primitive models, they have disregarded alike the laws of Moses and Mohammed; and if they have any example in modern times it must be in the Utes and Shoshonees who surround them. To marry a mother and one or more of her daughters is even thought meritorious; and the Mormon authorities often advise a man to marry sisters, as they usually agree better than others.

Robert Sharkey, a merchant of Salt Lake City, married three sisters, one of whom was divorced from her first husband to marry him. They all lived in one house, and quite happily, it is said, for several years, when in some strange manner, they all became convinced that polygamy was wrong. One of the sisters started East, but soon returned and endeavoured to make some arrangement for him to put away the other two. There were difficulties in the way, and Sharkey's trouble was so great on the subject that his mind became disordered, and in August, 1868, he committed suicide by shooting himself through the head. The widowed sisters still live together, and are determined opponents of polygamy. Two of Brigham Young's favored wives, Clara Decker and Lucy Decker Seely, are sisters, the second having been the widow of Dr. Isaac Seely, of Nauvoo, Illinois. One family within my knowledge consists of two men and four women, the men's first wives being sisters, and their second wives each a sister of the other man, all living in one house. Or, to state it mathematically: A. and B. first marry sisters, then A. marries B's. sister, and B. A's sister. Here is no marriage of blood relations, and yet it looks like a terrible mixture somewhere.

The question arises for lawyers: Suppose each of the women to have children, what akin are they respectively? And which of them could lawfully marry according to Leviticus and Chancellor Kent? If polygamy continues, these mixtures are nothing to what must take place in the next generation, for without a chemical analysis no "heraldry Harvey" could ever succeed in finding the consanguineous circulation, to say nothing of the collateral. As it now is, it seems as if half the children in the city are related in some way or other to the Kimballs, the Pratts or the Youngs, and many to all three. If it stopped here, some faint excuse might be made; but the marriage of uncle and niece has occurred often enough to establish it as a Mormon custom. Bishop Smith, of Brigham City, numbers *two of his own brother's daughters* among the inmates of his harem, "sealed" to him by Brigham Young, with a full knowledge of their relationship; and in the southern settlements several such cases exist. As already stated, polygamy is but a mild affair north of Salt Lake City, compared with the southern settlements; and in the latter are found all the worst features of Mormonism. There the bishop is absolute, spiritual guide, temporal governor and social tyrant; there are collected the most ignorant and degraded of the foreign converts; the doctrines of Mormonism coincide fully with the people's natural habits of thought; respect for woman, who is practically a slave, is a thing unknown, and the marriage of near relatives is so common that to remark on it would itself be considered remarkable. The marriage of first cousins is common, but I have heard of no case of aunt and nephew. The following affair seems too horrible for belief among any people in America; but is as well proved as any fact can be by human testimony, particularly that of the woman herself who went out of the Territory with a military expedition fitted out under General Connor.

Some sixteen years ago, a young Scotchman came to Salt Lake City in company with his half sister, who commenced keeping house for him. After a time he went to Brigham and professed a desire to marry the girl, citing the example of Abraham and his half sister Sarai. Brigham owned there was something in it. Abraham was an example in favor of polygamy, and why not in this? He finally sent for the girl, and finding her handsome and lively, solved the problem by marrying her himself; the half brother yielded to the Prophet's superior claim, and all was well. But in a few short weeks the lady's delicate condition showed too plainly that the amorous half brother had anticipated marital rights, and Brigham found himself in a fair way to have an heir *de jure* that was not *de sanguine.* Here was a problem. It would never do for the Prophet to acknowledge himself "sold," so he sent for the brother, told him he had reconsidered the matter, divorced the woman from himself, and delivered her to the brother, who dutifully received her from the arms of the Prophet. She lived with her half brother a few years as his wife, and bore him three children, but finally saw the degradation of her position, and left for the States. This man still resides in Salt Lake City, is a prominent citizen, and seems to have neither blame nor shame attached to him. When I first heard of this and other instances of a like nature, and heard the horrible doctrine of incest attributed to the Mormons, I could not but think it an invention of some bitter enemy of the sect; but since then I have heard it fully avowed by the same prominent Mormon, whose testimony is given in chapter ninth. Referring to the cases above, he said: "That is the law of God under the new dispensation. Things are allowed under one dispensation which are not under others. As it was with Abel and Abraham, so it will be again. The day will soon come, when brothers and sisters will marry. Shouldn't I prefer my own blood to any other? Don't I love my own blood best?" Still another Mormon avers that "to have a pure priesthood, we may in time have to follow the *example of the doves in their nest,* as Christ meant it to be understood." This doctrine was first advanced by Brigham from the pulpit several years ago, but was received with such undisguised manifestations of surprise and disgust, that he ceased to pursue it further, closing with the remark: "Well, it's a little too strong doctrine for you now; but the time *will* be, when you will take it in fully. Since then the subject has generally been avoided at "head quarters," but cannot be altogether denied. Brigham has never favored but one Gentile with his views on the subject, viz.: Wm. Hepworth Dixon, who gives the following statement in his late work, entitled "New America."

"Perhaps it would not be too much to say that in the Mormon code there is no such crime as incest, and that a man is practically free to woo and wed any woman who may take his eye.

"We have had a very strange conversation with Young about the Mormon doctrine of incest. I asked him whether it was a common thing among the Saints to marry mother and daughter; and, if so, on what authority they acted, since that kind of union was not sanctioned, either by the command to Moses or by the 'revelation' to Smith. When he hung back from admitting that such a thing occurred at all, I named a case in one of the city wards, of which we had obtained some private knowledge.

"Apostle Cannon said that in such case, the first marriage would be only a form; that the elder female would be understood as being a mother to her husband and his younger bride, on which I named my example, and in which an elder of the Church had married an English woman, a widow, with a daughter then of twelve; in which the woman had borne four children to this husband; and in which this husband had married her daughter when she came of age.

"Young said it was not a common thing at Salt Lake.

"'But it does occur?'

"'Yes,' said Young, 'it occurs sometimes.'

"'On what ground is such a practice justified by the Church?' After a short pause, he said, with a faint and wheedling smile: 'This is a part of the question of incest. We have no sure light on it yet. I cannot tell you what the Church holds to be the actual truth; I can tell you my own opinion; but you must not publish it—you must not tell it—lest I should be misunderstood and blamed.'

"He then made to us a communication on the nature of incest, as he thinks of this offence and judges it; but what he then said I am not at liberty to print. As to the facts which came under my own eyes, I am free to speak.

"Incest, in the sense in which we use the word—marriage within the prohibited degrees—is not regarded as a crime in the Mormon Church.

"It is known that in some of these saintly harems, the female occupants stand to their lords in closer relationship of blood than the American law permits. It is a daily event in Salt Lake City for a man to wed two sisters, a brother's widow, and even a mother and daughter. In one household in Utah, may be seen the spectacle of three women, who stand toward each other in the relation of child, mother and grand-dame, living in one man's harem as his wives! I asked the President, whether, with his new lights on the virtue of breeding in and in, he saw any objection to the marriage of brother and sister. Speaking for himself, not for the Church, he said he saw none at all. What follows, I give in the actual words of the speakers:

" D.—' Does that sort of marriage ever take place ?'
" YOUNG.—' Never.'
" D.—' Is it prohibited by the Church ?'
" YOUNG.—' No ; it is prohibited by prejudice.'
" KIMBALL.—' Public opinion won't allow it.'
" YOUNG.—' I would not do it myself, nor suffer any one else, when I could help it.'
" D.—' Then you don't prohibit, and you don't practise it ?'
" YOUNG.—' My prejudices prevent me.'

" This remnant of an old feeling brought from the Gentile world, and this alone, would seem to prevent the Saints from rushing into the higher forms of incest. How long will these Gentile sentiments remain in force ?'

" ' You will find here,' said Elder Stenhouse to me, talking on another subject, ' polygamists of the third generation ; when these boys and girls grow up, and marry, you will have in these valleys the true feeling of patriarchal life.

" ' The old world is about us yet; and we are always thinking of what people may say in the Scottish hills and the Midland shires.' "

Morally, the reader may be shocked, but logically he should be prepared for all this; for if we are to restore a line of prophets and follow the example of the patriarchs, then incest and polygamy are from the same high source. The examples of Abraham and Sarai, half brother and sister ; of Lot and Judah and earlier worthies are to be repeated. As one Mormon said to me, " the world could never have been peopled without this practice, and the foremost nations of antiquity maintained it ;" and it is darkly hinted at Salt Lake that father and daughter may form an allowable union. And why not ? If "the souls in the spirit world wait earnestly for tabernacles," to furnish them in a mere mechanical act, and may be performed by one person as well as another.

Thus polygamy, incest and blood atonement grow as naturally from Mormon theology as three branches from the same stock.

The mind revolts from the pursuit of these digusting details, and to the credit of the Mormon people be it said, they are far from being universal in approval of these later doctrines.

Will it be credited after all this that the Mormons claim to be the most virtuous people in the world ? Yet such is the fact; and they never weary of pointing to the prostitution of our great cities, claiming that it is their appointed destiny to remove all such evils, and make woman universally pure. This, then, is the self-proclaimed task of Mormonism; to save a few by reducing all to a level; to abolish prostitution by legalizing concubinage; to promote conjugal purity by multiplying the husband's temptations and opportunity, and to improve the condition of woman by making her a mere life-giving machine.

Perhaps the most saddening feature of Mormon polygamy, is the effect it has had upon the young. The medico-theologians of Utah claim that polygamy tends to a more rapid increase of population, as well as to the physical and moral improvement of the species. The former claim may well be questioned, and that the latter is a serious mistake, is plain to any unprejudiced observer.

Salt Lake City already shows its bad effect on the offspring. The site is forty-three hundred feet above the level of the sea, in a dry and bracing climate, equally free from extremes of heat and cold; and consequently it should be one of the healthiest cities in the world.

Exactly the reverse is the fact. The death rate, of all ages, was for years a little more than twice that of the State of Oregon, and greater than that of New York, or any city north of the Gulf States. When we come to children, the disparity is still more frightful.

By actual statistics it is shown that the mortality among children was, for many years, greater in Salt Lake City, than any other in America, and the death rate of Utah only exceeded by that of Louisiana. The Mormons have greatly exaggerated the population of the city, which really contains a little less than eighteen thousand souls, and in this small number the sexton's report for October, 1868, the healthiest month in the year, and my first in the city, gives the interments at sixty, of which forty-four were children. Last year was unusually healthy, and yet the death rate exceeds that of any other State or Territory west of the Mississippi. The Mormons explain this by saying that their people are generally poor and exposed to hardships, but much of that poverty is directly traceable to their religion. Another sad fact is the general neglect of medical care, or rather a general tendency to run to wild and absurd schemes of doctoring. They claim that "laying on of hands and the prayer of faith," will heal the sick, and yet, no people within my knowledge are so given to "Thomsonianism," steam doctoring," "yarb medicine," and every other irregular mode of treating disease.

One day, during my residence there, three young children died in the seventeenth ward of scarlet fever. In neither case was a physician called; the Bishop came and "laid on hands with the holy anointing," and an old woman treated two of them with a mild palliative, such as is used for a sore throat. If the patient live after such treatment, it is a "miracle;" if they die, "it is the will of the Lord." Two-thirds of the polygamists do not and cannot attend properly to their children.

The bishop of one ward, the fourteenth, has thirty children living, and nearly twenty dead. Joseph Smith had a dozen spiritual wives; but three sons survived him—all of his legal wife.

When Heber Kimball was alive there were five men in the city, who had together seventy wives; they had, all told, less than a hundred and fifty children.

A Mormon grave-yard is the most melancholy sight on earth. One bishop of the city has seventeen children buried in one row, and the longest grave is not over four feet, If these men have but the common feelings of humanity, how fearfully are they punished for the crime of polygamy! Brigham's children are generally healthy, except that the girls mostly have weak eyes, and two of them are nearly blind; but they are well fed, housed and clothed. But such is the exception, and I could mention a dozen men whose houses are full of women, but their children are in the grave.

The Asiatic institution was never meant to flourish on American soil, and has resulted here in a "slaughter of the innocents," which is saddening to contemplate. As only the most hardy survive, they generally grow up robust and active; but the effects of their social bias are seen in a strange dulness of moral perception, a general ignorance and apparently inherited tendency to vice. If the testimony of Oscar Young, of the oldest son of the Elder Stenhouse, mentioned above, and of numerous other young Mormons, can be relied on, youthful demoralization certainly begins at an earlier age in Salt Lake than in any other places. In many cases of poor men in polygamy, the husband, two wives and their children, occupy the same room; in many instances the husband and two wives have but one bed, and when we consider the scenes and conversation to which these children are witnesses, it would seem that no exalted ideas of purity could ever enter their minds. Taken from school at an early age, or only permitted to enter it at all during a few winter months, they are often put, in extreme youth, to herding cattle on the "bench," or beyond Jordan; there they hear the slang of older youths, and, from hearing, learn to repeat, observe and imitate; demoralization spreads, and moral decay seizes upon the very bloom of youth.

From what they so often hear at home, they become precociously prurient and premature observers of the brute creation; and, from personal observation and the testimony of many young Mormons, I am convinced there is no part of America where youthful vice, of the peculiarly destructive and degrading kind, prevails so extensively as in Salt Lake City. And this is but a natural result; for polygamy is tenfold more unnatural with such a climate and race than in Southern Asia or Africa.

Strange and paradoxical it is that, in a barren land and temperate or harsh clime, they have succeeded in setting up a practice which social philosophy had decided to belong only in regions of abundance, in voluptuous climes, where soft airs incline to sensual indulgence.

Stranger still, in the attempt to found a purely religious community, they have begun by utterly reversing every idea which the experience of three thousand years had proved to be valuable; and in the very inception of a young society, which was to be fresh, vigorous and pure, have adopted the worst vices of an old and worn out civilization. But, to them, these arguments are idle; 'the mouth of the Lord hath commanded it;" and it is theirs not to study results, but to leave it with the Lord: so, beholding all around them the furious revenges of nature, on those who violate her most important law, they shut their eyes to these facts, and pronounce them false; and bearing in their own bodies the effects of physiological sin, impiously claim a divine sanction to violate the laws of nature.

When, leaving the mere youth we come to young men and women, we observe two curious effects of polygamy. The first is a growing tendency to single life; polygamy to some extent necessitates celibacy, for the number of the sexes being about equal, even in Utah, if one man marries two wives, some other man must do without his one. Polygamy is, in fact, the worst kind of robbery, and for the twelve young women whom Heber C. Kimball married after reaching Utah, some of them not over eighteen, twelve young men must remain single.

This tendency is now greatly on the increase, particularly among the girls, and it is a common remark with them, that they will never marry till they can leave the Territory. And this accounts, in part, for the second, a general desire among the unmarried, to get away and settle out of Utah. The world would be surprised at the constant losses to their population from this source; there has been for years a constant leak from the Territory in every direction, and, in one sermon, I heard Brigham Young enumerate a score of places in California, Nevada, Washington and Oregon, settled entirely by recusant Mormons. In spite of a steady immigration from Europe of from one to four thousand per year, it is still a debatable question whether the Mormons have gained faster than by natural increase for the last five years.

Indeed, Utah offers but few inducements for a young Mormon, if he possess more than average intelligence or enterprise; and such, it will generally be found, make their way to some other locality. Much has been claimed by the Mormons for the virtue of their young women, and more said against it by some of their opponents. From the best evidence at my command, I think their virtue will average as well, or nearly so, as that of any very poor and ignorant people; but the fatal error of the Mormons is, in allowing for no virtue except that by constraint and constant watching. No dependence whatever is placed upon the innate moral sense, and apparently no effort made to cultivate or strengthen it; it is not supposed that virtue is founded in aught but dread, and every thorough going Mormon acts as if he expected his daughters to go wrong the very first opportunity.

The jealousy of the men is even greater than that of the women. Nine-tenths of them take it for granted that a Gentile can have no good purpose in addressing a Mormon girl; and it is not uncommon to hear a Mormon say, " I will shoot any Gentile I see walking with my daughter."

It must be confessed, they have some foundation for this harsh judgment, as in former years hundreds of Gentiles merely came there to winter, and often left their wives in the spring; and it is a sad fact that of all the women who have left the Mormons, the majority have turned out badly. When the Californian volunteers left there, they took off a great many with them, of whom the majority were not married. The Mormons, of course, attribute this to the immoral character of the Gentiles;

but it is plainly attributable to their system of forced virtue, by means of constraint and constant watching. "The virtue that must be guarded is not worth the sentinel;" and these girls, who have been brought up in such strictness and seclusion, with the idea that none of their Mormon companions would dare attempt their virtue, are but poorly prepared to encounter the seductive arts we know to be common in the Gentile world. If there is such a thing as trust between the sexes in Utah, I have witnessed no manifestation of it; society has already assumed the same air of jealous distrust, so often remarked among the Moslems, while austerity and reserve are considered the noblest graces of woman.

It is gratifying to state, however, that the grossness of sentiment and language which prevailed ten years ago, is slowly yielding to something better, and, plain spoken as the Mormons now are, they would hardly listen quietly to the indecent harangues once so common from Heber C. Kimball. Though they constantly insist that they care nothing for the Gentile world, and will not be moved by its opinions, yet the Mormons are being slowly improved, in spite of themselves; they have adopted Sunday schools, daily papers, and lyceums from the Gentiles settled among them, and a more healthy sentiment is struggling weakly against the tide of corruption. But with all present mitigating features, polygamy still remains the foulest blot upon America's fame, and the Mormons still defy every law of God and man in their doctrines, and, to some extent, in their practice. Such, in brief, is Mormonism. While all the world is striving to move on to a higher, more spiritual plane of religious truth, they have turned back to the gross forms and symbols of the time when religion was in its infancy. It is as though the old mathematician should throw aside his acquired learning, and go back to the sticks and balls with which he learned to count. While the Christian world is rejoicing that Christ has freed us "from the yoke which our fathers were not able to bear," they go back two thousand years, and seek all their examples from a barbarous age and a stiff-necked and rebellious people.

And their practice is like their faith. Claiming a religion which will elevate men to *gods*, they plead for examples the base instincts of the brute creation; with snow in sight the year round, they pattern their domestic life after that of inter-tropical barbarians, and vainly hope to produce the vigor of hardy North-men from the worst practices of effeminate Asiatics.

CHAPTER XVI.

THE MORMON THEOCRACY.

Absolutism—An ancient model—Three governments in Utah—Church officials—First President—First Presidency—"The worst man in Utah"—Quorum of Apostles—"The Twelve"—A dozen men with fifty-two wives—President of Seventies—Patriarch—"A blessing for a dollar"—Bishops—Division of the City and Territory—Their magisterial capacity—High Council—Judge and Jury—Ward teachers—The confessional - The priesthood—Aaronic and Melchisedec—Evangelists—Secret police or " Danites "—Civil government only an appendage—Excessive power of the Mormon Courts—Perversions of law and justice—Organic Act defective—Federal Judges - Their weakness and disgrace—Verdict by ecclesiastical " counsel"—Verdicts dictated from the pulpit—Probate Judges really appointed by Brigham Young—Voting system—Marked ballots—"Protecting the ballot"—The Hooper-McGroarty race—Plurality of offices as well as wives—Tyranny of the Church—the Mormon *vs.* the American idea—The evils of which Gentiles complain.

IN government, as in doctrine and practice, the Mormons have adopted the most ancient model. But it was not quite possible even for them to entirely ignore the popular element, hence they have pieced out their theocracy with a shred of universal suffrage, proving themselves eclectic in politics as well as theology. Government in Utah is to be viewed in three relations, or rather, there are as many distinct governments :—

I. The recognized and openly acknowledged ecclesiastical government of the Mormon Church.

II. The secret and irresponsible government operated by a few of the leading men.

III. The Territorial government, which was for years but the mere convenient machine of the Church, and has but lately stood forth in anything like its intended character.

For the success of such an institution as Mormonism, it was absolutely necessary there should be a recognized priesthood, through which channel alone, all commands from heaven should come. If any man who "felt the moving of the Spirit" was at liberty to prophesy, prophets would soon cease to have any honor. It was necessary, too, that this priesthood should bear complete rule, and to this end an ignorant laity was necessary. These conditions have all been filled, and the Mormon Church stands forth complete as a theocratic absolutism. I present in the order of their rank, the various officers of the Church, and the duties connected with them.

FIRST PRÉSIDENT.

This officer stands at the head of all the affairs of the Church, temporal and spiritual, financial and priestly; he alone has the power of "sealing," though in some cases he may delegate it, and he only is acknowledged revelator. This office, first filled by Joseph Smith, is now held by Brigham Young, who is "Prophet, Priest, Seer, Revelator in all the world, First President and Trustee-in-trust of the Church of Jesus Christ of Latter-Day Saints," and doubtless *ex-officio* the repository of any other needed office or power.

To consider him in all these *roles** would exceed my present space; his various powers will appear more fully in the course of the work. Suffice it to say, that as Prophet, he holds the "keys of the kingdom," and without his permission *none can enter the Church or be saved;* as Revelator, he unfolds to the people the will of God concerning them; as Seer, he is warned to avoid any danger which may be in the future for him or his people, and, as Priest, he "seals" men and women for eternity. In temporal matters he is equally absolute. As President, he orders all the concerns of the Church, appoints new bishops and elders, and determines the political bearings of the community; as Trustee-in-trust, all the title to the Church

---

* Those who are curious to learn more fully of Brigham Young, and his wives and children, will find this with much other valuable information, in the ably written and only authentic work on the subject: THE MORMON PROPHET AND HIS HAREM, Written by MRS. C. V. WAITE. Printed at the *Riverside Press*, Cambridge, 1866.

property is in his name, he buys, sells, and conveys it *with no fixed system of rendering account;* as Treasurer of the Perpetual Emigrating Fund, his draft alone can be honored where the funds are on deposit. He claims and is acknowledged by his followers, to be the Supreme Pontiff of the world in all spiritual matters, and entitled to the obedience of all Mormons.

True, there are various parties now rising up among the Mormons, who claim that the President is entitled to their obedience only within certain limits; but they are generally held as heretics, " governed by an apostate spirit," and all " good Mormons" claim that they are bound by the orders of the Prophet, even to matters of life, and death. The doctrine has lately been still more authoritatively declared by the First President and his Counsellors, that " it is apostacy to differ with the Priesthood—though ever so honestly—a man may honestly differ, and go to hell for it." If there is any limit to his power, it is not apparent to the Gentile mind.

THE FIRST PRESIDENCY.

This consists of the First President and his First and Second Counsellors, George A. Smith and Daniel H. Wells. The first place was formerly filled by Heber C. Kimball, who died a short time before I entered the Territory, and at the ensuing Conference, Smith was chosen to the place. These last also have the title of President, they are the Lieutenants and Prime Ministers of the President to do all his commands, and are authorized to act in various capacities in his absence. In addition, George A. Smith is Church Historian, and Daniel H. Wells is Mayor, Justice of the Peace and Lieutenant-General of the Nauvoo Legion. He seems to bear about him less of the ecclesiastical character than his colleague, and is generally denominated 'Squire Wells; but he is probably the worst man in the Hierarchy, being both a half-crazy fanatic and a blood-thirsty bigot.

QUORUM OF APOSTLES.

The body third in importance in the Church is the College or Quorum of the Twelve Apostles. They come much nearer to the people than the First Presidency, as the whole Mormon territory is nominally divided between them, and it is their duty to inspect their various districts and see "that each stake is set in order." Individual Apostles are often put in charge of foreign missions, sent away to edit newspapers or magazines, or to preside over some newly selected "stake" of the extending settlements, in either of which cases, another Apostle is chosen in place of the absent. Thus there are sometimes as many as fifteen acting Apostles, but only the Twelve are entitled to seats in the Quorum at one time.

I present the list as it stood during my residence in Utah, and as an Apostle's dignity, like that of most other officers, depends largely upon the number of his wives, I give their number also:

ORSON HYDE,	*First Apostle,*	Five Wives.
ORSON PRATT,	*Second* "	Four "
JOHN TAYLOR,	*Third* "	Seven "
WILFORD WOODRUFF,	*Fourth* "	Three "
JOSEPH F. SMITH,	*Fifth* "	Three "
AMASA LYMAN,	*Sixth* "	Five "
EZRA BENSON,	*Seventh* "	Four "
CHARLES RICH,	*Eight* "	Seven "
LORENZO SNOW,	*Ninth* "	Four "
ERASTUS SNOW,	*Ten* "	Three "
FRANKLIN RICHARDS,	*Eleventh* "	Four "
GEORGE Q. CANNON,	*Twelfth* "	Three "

Ezra Benson died last summer, and his place had not been supplied when I left Utah. With the exception of John Taylor the Apostles are reported to be poor men; Orson Pratt particularly is in very moderate circumstances, and Orson Hyde has the reputation of being "an inveterate beggar," in an ecclesiastical way of course.

PRESIDENT OF SEVENTIES.

This office appears to rank next to that of an Apostle, and arises as follows: The great working body of male

Mormons is divided into seventy Quorums, each having nominally seventy members, though, in reality, they range everywhere from ten to seventy. Each has a President and these, collectively known as the Seventy, constitute a grand missionary board, which has the general control of all matters connected with propagating the faith. These seventy Presidents have also a President, filling the office under consideration. These offices have no special rank in the Church, as an Apostle or leading elder may be but a lay member in this order.

PATRIARCH.

I place this office fifth in rank because, though of great sanctity and honor, it is entirely spiritual, conferring no power. His business is merely to grant "blessings," written out and signed by him. The usual fee therefor is one dollar, and the "blessings," as far as I have read any of them, consist of vague and general promises that the recipient will "be blessed if faithful." The first Patriarch in the Church was "Old Father Smith," or Joseph, father of the Prophet, who was succeeded by the latter's brother Hyrum, he by "uncle" John Smith, cousin of Joe, and he in turn by William Smith, son of "Hyrum the martyr." To hold this office the only qualifications, which seem necessary, are that one should be an "uncle" and a Smith, neither of which is liable to fail for some time.

BISHOPS.

We now consider purely temporal officers, a set of men who direct municipal regulations and are, as occasion demands, either officers of the Church or Civil Magistrates. Of these the most important is the bishop. Salt Lake City is divided into twenty-one wards, each of which has a bishop, and the entire Territory is in the same manner conveniently divided into wards with a bishop over each. They hear and "determine all complaints," and as they are, under the peculiar statutes of Utah, also Probate Judges in their respective counties, they govern Gentiles in that character Thus, as spiritual guide in all matters

T

of dispute among members of his flock, and civil magistrate, in all cases where Gentiles are concerned, the bishop is equally "master of the situation," and fully apprised of whatever is going on. Hence, also, his character as informer. From his decision as Judge, the Gentile may appeal to the Superior Court, at Salt Lake City; from his episcopal adjudications the Mormon can appeal to the

HIGH COUNCIL.

This body is composed of fifteen men, chosen from the High Priests. Twelve act as a jury, of whom a majority decide the case, and the other three pass sentence, or fix the damages and costs. From this tribunal there is an appeal to the First Presidency. The bishop is assisted in his labors by the

WARD TEACHERS.

Their duty is to visit all the people in their ward, report all suspected persons, catechise every one as to personal feeling, belief, etc., to report all irregularities, heresies, false doctrine and schism, and generally to act as spies and informers. On these visitations every person is obliged to formally subscribe to all the doctrines of the Church, and many misdemeanors and even criminalities are hushed up in the ward where they occur, without the slightest knowledge thereof being made public. Hence, much of the reputation for good order, claimed by the Mormons. In one instance, which came to my knowledge an atrocious rape, committed upon a girl thirteen years old, was not known outside of the ward where it occurred until one year after, and it would probably not have been then made known, had not the father of the girl apostatized. In many cases boys of fifteen years fill the place of Teacher, and are required to report the doings of their fellows. All Mormons are solemnly sworn to keep no secrets from the Teachers, and on their monthly visits to each family these have the right to see each person alone, and hold a strict and nasty "confessional." This, with the "Danite" or secret police system, makes of Mormon society a united and tyrannized whole.

THE PRIESTHOOD.

Thus far I have treated rather of the temporal offices, but all officiating Mormons are divided into two bodies— The *Aaronic* and the *Melchisedec Priesthood*. The latter is the superior, and in many respects includes the former; it is both spiritual and temporal, while the former is exclusively temporal. A High Priest of the *Melchisedec* order may always officiate in place of an Aaronic Priest; but without special ordainment, the latter is always confined to temporal affairs. All the higher officials belong to the *Melchisedec* order. The High Priest ranks next to the Apostle, and after him some order of Elders, below whom are simple Priests and ordinary Elders. In these different ranks all Mormons are Priests of some sort, and in religious cant speak of themselves as "Kings and Priests of the most High God."

EVANGELISTS.

These, as the name implies, are propagandists. The name seems to indicate a kind of work rather than specific rank or office.

Such is the recognized ecclesiastical polity of the Church. But lest this should not prove effective in all cases, or some should grow restive under such restraint, the Church has often used an order of secret police, popularly known as "Danites." This order was first instituted during the troubles in Missouri; it was remodeled in the third or fourth year of their residence at Nauvoo, and has been continued since. By some of the Mormons its existence is denied, by others defended on the score of self-protection. That thousands of honest Mormons are ignorant of, and do not believe in, its existence, I am well aware; but that it has been, and to some extent is yet, an active working force, is as clearly proved as any fact can be. From the nature of the case but little can be known of its secret organization; its work plainly appears in the course of Mormon history.

With all their ecclesiastical organization, both public

and private, much would have remained beyond their power to compass without a civil government; and the manner in which they have used it, merely to further Church policy, is a singular comment on the forbearance of a republican government.

The most common perversion of right, and yet the most difficult to be comprehended by residents in the East, is the peculiar manner in which the laws and local courts of the Territory are made an engine of tyranny in the hands of the ruling oligarchy. Like every other territory, Utah has Federal District Courts and local Probate Courts; but unlike any other State or territory in the Union, the powers and jurisdiction of the latter are made superior to those of the former. Section 29, page 31 of the Territorial Statutes, gives the Probate Courts general jurisdiction in all matters, civil and criminal; while section 1, of an "Act in relation to Bills of Divorce and Alimony," gives the Probate Courts exclusive jurisdiction over all such cases, thus making them superior to the Federal District Courts in such matters, and equal to them in every other respect.

All this in opposition to the fact that the Organic Act of Utah gives the Legislature no power to build up such local courts, and in other territories this matter has been settled by appeal to the Supreme Court, and by its decision the Probate Courts limited to probate matters and a very limited civil jurisdiction. But the Organic Act provides that the Probate or County Courts shall have "such jurisdiction as shall be prescribed by law," and from this loose wording the Legislature claims the right to give them jurisdiction over all subjects whatever.— This anomaly in the judicial system is not without good cause. The District Judges are United States officials, and are supposed to be supporting the national authority; the Probate Judges are simply the bishops or elders in the different counties, over whom Brigham's power is absolute. In former days, Brigham divorced whomsoever he saw fit, on his own motion, and on payment of a fee of ten dollars. He boasted once in a sermon, that he made enough this way, " by their d—d foolishness, to keep him in spending money." But of late years it has been thought best to give some attention to forms of law; and now, though parties must first be divorced by Brigham, or a special deputy within the Church law, yet, after that, they must have a legal divorce in the Probate Courts. Of course, it never happens that Brigham's wishes are disregarded in the Probate. But this is their own affair; it is with their criminal jurisdiction that Gentiles have to do. A case which occurred in a southern settlement, while I was in Utah, illustrates in so forcible a manner their style of getting rid of obnoxious citizens, that I set it forth entire.

In 1860, a lad of that district, of more than ordinary intelligence, left for California, where he remained for eight years, when he returned home with a considerable amount of money, and, of course, with no disposition to submit to the exactions of Mormonism. His parents being Mormons, and that his native place, he properly belonged to the class known as "hickory Mormons" or "Come-outers." With plenty of money, and being well dressed, he went into all their dances and social parties, became a favorite with the Mormon girls, did not hesitate to express his opinion about the bishops and elders, and, in short, his example was, as the bishop said, " d—d demoralizing." One evening he accompanied a Mormon's daughter from the village to her home in the country. On their way was a narrow ravine, about half way between two houses which were just a furlong apart. They remained some minutes in this hollow, and were afterwards seen chatting for half an hour at her father's gate. One week afterwards he was arrested on a charge of rape! He was first taken before a magistrate, where he demanded a jury of twelve men, and was by them unanimously acquitted. Then the bishop of the settlement, also a Probate Judge, issued a bench warrant, pronounced all the proceedings before the magistrate void, brought the young man before himself, and, by the aid of her father, absolutely forced the girl to testify against him, and upon evidence that would have been laughed out of court in any State, pronounced him guilty, and sentenced him to the penitentiary for ten years! He was started at once for the prison in Salt Lake City, but managed to inform Judge Strickland, a lawyer of the city, who succeeded in having him brought before Chief Justice Wilson, of the District Court, by writ of *habeas corpus*, where the girl refused to testify to anything criminating him, and he was released. This atrocious perversion of legal principles is practised all over the country settlements by these bishops—judges, who are directed in their proceedings by "authority," and use their offices to drive out, or scare away all " Come-outers" or recusant Mormons. If the accused is brought to Salt Lake City, the United States officials are often able to interfere; but no matter how plain and direct the evidence, as in the case above, nine-tenths of the Mormons merely think it another case, in which a vile criminal is let loose upon them by Gentile Judges.

As might be expected, the Brighamites are very tenacious of this great power in their hands, and threaten and bluster whenever it is questioned. In a case tried before Chief Justice Wilson, the power of the Probate Courts was put in issue, and on the 20th of November, 1868, when this case was argued, Z. Snow, a Mormon lawyer, and Attorney-General for Utah, said: " If his Honor decided against such jurisdiction, blood would flow in the streets of this City." From the known character of Judge Snow, it is highly probable he never would have made such a statement but by express direction from Brigham Young. The statement was made in open court, in presence of the entire bar of the city, and a few moments after consultation with his associate counsel, also a Mormon. The plain meaning of this was, that the Brighamites intended to obey the law only when construed in their favor, but otherwise to evade it, and, when safe, try violence. Fair notice was thus given to all officials to yield, or be crushed. Judge Snow also said that, until within a few years, " United State Judges had not resided here but a very small portion of their time, though he did not know why."

This hint opens to remembrance a melancholy view of the dishonor to our Government through its officials in

Utah. Not that Brigham Young has tried violence in many cases. He is far too wary for that. Brute force is the last resort of a really astute mind, like that of Brigham. Chicane is his natural weapon, and with it he has completely circumvented the majority of the judges; assisted too often by the imbecile appointments from the time of Fillmore until Lincoln's Administration. The first Judge, Perry E. Brochus, was incautious in his attacks upon polygamy, and, having been led to believe that his life was in danger, left the Territory. Another official was detected in immorality, and resigned to avoid exposure; another disgraced his office, by taking a prostitute upon the bench with him; another impaired his efficiency by secret drinking; and still another allowed himself to be completely entrapped by two of Brigham's "decoy women." One of these delinquents was followed into Weber Cañon by a self-appointed committee of "Mormon boys," and received at their hands a severe castigation.

It is a prime principle of the Mormon faith that their affairs ought not to come before a Gentile Court at all; and if they must go there in a case where a Gentile is interested, the jury should be governed by "counsel" in making up their verdict. But there seem to have been restive spirits, even in the most palmy days of the Church government, who were often chastised from the Mormon pulpit, as witness the following from a sermon delivered in the Tabernacle, by Jedediah M. Grant, one of Brigham Young's councillors, on Sunday, March 2nd, 1856.

"Last Sunday the President chastised some of the Apostles and Bishops who were on the grand jury. Did he fully succeed in clearing away the fog that surrounded them, and in removing blindness from their eyes? No; for they could go to their room and again disagree, though to their credit be it said, a little explanation made them unanimous in their action. But how is it with the little jury? Some of them have got into the fog to suck down the words and eat the filth of a Gentile court, ostensibly a court in Utah." This extract gives a sufficiently clear idea of the jury system in Utah, and from all that has yet appeared the attempt to enforce any Federal statute by Mormon juries, would simply amount to a solemn farce. To render the matter worse, these Bishop-judges are not elected by the people, but, under the provisions of the Judiciary Act, are appointed by the Territorial Legislature, which means in effect by Brigham Young; thus the Judiciary are as completely under his management as the officers of the ecclesiastical organization. One might think there was still some chance for the people in voting, and many are inclined to ask : If there is dissatisfaction, or opposition to Brigham Young's government, can it not make itself felt in the elections? Even this outlet is effectually barred by the following Section of "An Act regulating elections," passed in January, 1853 :

"Each elector shall provide himself with a ballot containing the names of the persons he wishes elected, and the offices he would have them fill, and present it neatly folded to the judge of the election, who shall number it and deposit it in the ballot-box. The clerk shall then write the name of the elector and opposite thereto the number of his vote."

With a sarcasm which is almost amusing, the Mormon leaders call this a measure "to protect the freedom and purity of the ballot." Thus artistically do they abolish the free vote while they retain the ballot. "Thus," says the English Captain Burton, their apologist, "they retain the privilege of voting, while they avoid the evils of universal suffrage; subjecting, as it always should be, the ignorant many to the supervision of the intelligent few."

Under this system, Brigham Young's emissary can go into any precinct in the Territory and discover just how any man has voted at any election for the last fifteen years! And with this ignorant people, alive to spiritual terrors, and knowing too well what temporal trouble *may* be brought upon them, it is plain that the opposition must be in a majority before it can venture to make itself known. It cannot make a start to consolidate. It may be worthy of note here, that all the officers of the Mormon Church are proposed for re-election or rejection, twice every year, at the General Conferences, thus apparently tempering this theocratic absolutism with universal suffrage, women voting as well as men. But only three instances have been known of persons daring to vote against the known wishes of the Hierarchy ; and in each case the offenders were promptly cited before the High Council and required to explain, in default of which they were "cut off" as being in a "spirit of apostacy." Practically, one man in each settlement or ward might just as well do all the voting. The Church puts her ticket in the field, and the bishop directs the people to vote it, which they do accordingly.

On one memorable occasion, it is said, a sort of spiritual rebellion occurred in the Utah Lake district, where many American converts reside, and the opposition candidate to the Legislature was elected. On reaching Salt Lake City the successful candidate was simply "counselled" to resign, did so quietly, and the regular nominee was declared entitled to the seat. Three years ago the Jews, Gentiles, Apostates and recusant Mormons of the Thirteenth Ward, in the city, found they had a majority, as nearly all of these classes in the city lived in that ward. They elected Bishop Wooley, a good Mormon, however, for Councilman, against the regular nominee. The Bishop was at once cited before Brigham, promptly resigned according to "counsel," and the other candidate was admitted to the seat.

When the celebrated and somewhat amusing Hooper-McGroarty race, for delegate to Congress, took place, hundreds who would have voted for an available Gentile nominee, but who regarded McGroaty's candidacy as a mere burlesque, did not vote at all; consequently that gentleman received less than two hundred votes, while, as the Mormons did their best, Hooper received some fifteen thousand. It is yet a standing joke in Utah to repeat portions of McGroarty's speech, prepared to be delivered before Congress ; he employed a lawyer to write it for him, and while committing it to memory, he could never talk ten minutes with a friend without running into his speech, assuming an oratorical manner, and the plural number, as if addressing Congress.

The evils of this system of voting are numerous, besides the immense power it gives a few leaders; but one is particularly noticeable, the number and variety of offices held by the same man. In the town of Fillmore, the old capital, at one time one man held the offices of County Clerk and Recorder, Town Clerk and Justice of the Peace, Assessor and Collector of Internal Revenue, and *ex officio* Overseer of the Poor. While I was in Salt Lake City, one Robert T. Burton was Collector of Internal Revenue for the Territory, Sheriff of the County, Assessor and Collector of Territorial and County taxes, and a General in the Nauvoo Legion; besides being a prominent elder in the Church, the husband of three wives, and one of the chiefs of the secret police. This Burton is the man who led the posse to capture the Morrisites, a sect of recusant Mormons, and, according to his own account, shot four of those people after their surrender, and his continuance in the revenue office was a damning blot upon the Johnson administration in Utah. He is in appearance

"The mildest mannered man
That ever scuttled a ship or cut a throat."

But if there is truth in one-fourth the private memoirs of apostates, he is a most cruel and blood-thirsty bigot.

All the various civil officers are at the same time leading dignitaries in the Mormon Church, active agents of its will, chosen to their civil position solely on that account; they consider the latter far inferior in importance, and, in fact, subordinate in policy to their Church dignities, and knowing little, if any, law, they are guided by ecclesiastical authority and "counsel."

Let one travel wherever he will through the outer settlements, he rarely if ever hears the people speak of the Probate Judges *as* judges; it is always "the bishop decided so and so." With them he is always acting in his character as bishop, never as judge. Nor need we be surprised at this; it is the natural conflict under such a system, between the theocratic, the ecclesiastical, and the popular, the democratic and laical. The American idea is that power is derived from the people, is merely delegated to the officer, and rests upon the just consent of the governed. The Mormon idea is exactly the reverse; power and authority come from above, and operate downward through all the grades; the official is not responsible to those below him—to them he is the voice of God—but to those above him; from them he derives his authority, and to them he must render an account.

In the words of a Mormon polemic, "It is not consistent that the people of God should organize or be subject to man-made governments. If it were so, they could never be perfected. There can be but one perfect government—that organized by God; a government by apostles, prophets, priests, teachers and evangelists; the order of the original Church, of all churches acknowledged by God." I am thus minute in my statements, because so many people in the East have an idea that polygamy is the only great evil of Mormonism. There are many evils felt more than that; in fact, polygamy in itself is but a slight annoyance to the Gentile residents in Utah.

Mormonism was an unmitigated evil before they had polygamy; the priests ruled the ignorant people with spiritual terrors, and that made them dangerous neighbors and troublesome citizens wherever they lived. Probably some of these other evils grew out of or have been strengthened by polygamy, but that of itself troubles other residents very little. It is that the Territory is ruled by a Church, that civil and legal measures are carried by ecclesiastical policy rather than law; that residents, not Mormons, are subjected to all the annoyances of petty tyranny; that in their business and social life they are constantly subjected to the secret espionage of the Church; that they are hampered in business by church hostility, and the imposition of excessive taxes; that friends and fellow-countrymen have been secretly murdered, and the Church prevents them from obtaining justice; in short, they are exposed to the tyranny of an unopposed majority, and that majority controlled by a small and compact hierarchy, working out its Star-chamber decrees against liberty by secret and, to the people, irresponsible agents.

It is this that grinds the feelings of American citizens, not polygamy, though that is a great moral and social evil. The Mormon people, as a mass, are naturally disposed to deal justly, but, unfortunately, the people are ciphers, and it seems to be the policy of their leaders to keep them in a constant state of irritation and hostile feeling towards all outsiders, and to the Government of the United States.

Thus it is the union of Church and State, or rather the absolute subservience of the State to the Church, the latter merely using the outside organization to carry into effect decrees already concluded in secret council, that makes Mormonism our enemy. Missouri and Illinois found, at dear cost, that no State could tolerate a Church exercising an absolute temporal jurisdiction, within the State, but independent of and often hostile to it; dominating and directing the action of courts within its influence, subverting free institutions, and exercising a greater right over the consciences of its subjects than is claimed by the laws of the State. In short, it is not the social, immoral, or polygamic features that so chiefly concern us, but the hostile, the treasonable and the mutinous. The law against polygamy should be strictly enforced, as every other law of the Government; but it is idle to say, as so many do, that that is the only objection to the Mormons, or to the admission of Utah as a State. If polygamy were blotted out to-morrow, we could never admit Utah in her present condition. Such a State organization would be opposed to every principle of our political structure, and our Constitution was never meant to recognize the temporal government of a Church. Happily the present Administration have recognized many of the needs of Utah, and begun by removing all polygamists and Mormon sympathizers from office, filling their places with good men. Much remains to be done by the Executive and Congress, but it is gratifying to note that something of a reform has set in, and that Utah is no longer what it was through three Administrations, "the Botany Bay of worn-out politicians."

CHAPTER XVII.

RECUSANT SECTS OF MORMONS.

Repression not unity—Great break up at Nauvoo—Sidney Rigdon's Church—J. J. Strang—Cutler, Brewster, and Heddrick: "The Gatherers"—The "Truth-teller"—Lyman Wight in Texas—San Bernardino Mormons—Apostacy, Spiritualism and insanity—Brigham supreme in Utah—First Secession, the "Gladdenites"—Persecution and murders—Blood-atonement introduced—Second Secession, the "Morrisites"—War with the Sect—Massacre of the "Morrisites"—Governor Harding's adventure—General Connor protects the recusants—Soda Springs—Another Prophet—The "infant Christ"—Beginning of the Josephites—Emma and her sons—The "Re-organized Church"—First Mission—Mission of the "Smith boys"—Excitement at Salt Lake—Priestly lying—The Godbe Schism—Liberal principles—Hopeful indications—After Brigham, Who?—Orson Hyde?—Daniel H. Wells?—George A. Smith?—Probable future of the Church.

BUT all this hedging about with officials, and double-lock of civil, ecclesiastical and secret governments, has not always held the Mormons in perfect unity, or prevented schism and revolt. Perfect conformity in religion can only be secured by the rack, the stake, and the dungeon of the inquisition; Mormonism carried within its bosom the gems of disintegration, long latent though they might be, and the original organization has, from time to time, given rise to no less than twenty-five sects, *ites* and *isms*, of which six or seven, besides the main branch under Brigham, still preserve a sort of moribund existence. Like the non-juring bishops of Anglican history, secession once begun constantly repeated itself; the recusant and deposed priests in turn denounced and deposed all who questioned their prophetic right, and each of the sects solemnly points to all the others, as blind and erring apostates, whose feet are treading on the straight line to hell. During the life of Joe Smith there seem to have been no organized secessions, though many apostacies.

The living oracle could be consulted, with no dispute as to the meaning of his words; Joe Smith Mormonism was true or none was, and there was no other alternative. But his death cut off the source of infallible interpretation, and opened the way at once for a variance in doctrine. Some account has already been given of the struggle for secession, and it only remains to briefly note the course of the diverging sects, in the ever shifting phases of their pseudo-theology and protean forms of error. Of all the scattering sects no other had a leader with the executive ability, the iron nerve, and the cruel, remorseless ambition of Brigham Young; and, in consequence, as fast as they came in contact with purer faiths, most of their organizations dissolved and fell away.

Sidney Rigdon led a large colony, and that of the best material, to Pennslyvania; but there was not sufficient ignorance in the laity, or secretive cunning in the leader, and little by little they scattered among the Gentiles, a few only, with Apostle Wm. Marks at their head, returning to the Brighamite Church, from which they afterwards turned away to young Joe Smith. J. J. Strange had multitudinous revelations, that Wisconsin was to be the next "gathering place" of the Saints, and a few thousand followed him to the unsettled portion of that new State. He afterwards settled the remnant on Beaver Island, in Lake Michigan, and maintained some organization till his death; no prophet arising after him, some of his flock went "hunting for Zion" in Iowa and Missouri, some went to Salt Lake, more went back to the "re-organized Church" at Plano, Illinois, and many went crazy.

The small party which followed William Smith, only surviving brother of the Prophet, to Northern Illinois, soon dissolved. Elder Brewster took another party to Western Iowa, and Bishop Heddrick, a considerable sect into Missouri, both of which fell to pieces on the death of the leaders; but the remnants have lately got together under a new prophet, and formed the sect known as "Gatherers." They are attempting to gather and settle again in Jackson County, and are numerous enough to have an organ called "*The Truthteller*," a weakly periodical, published in Western Missouri. Bishop Cutler also led off a small party in Northern Iowa, and, after his death, most of them returned to the "Re-organized Church."

When the Church set out from Nauvoo, the Apostles issued orders to Elder Sam Brannan, then in New York, to proceed with a party by sea to their intended destination in California. He accordingly sailed soon after in the ship Brooklyn, with a body of two hundred and forty-six foreign converts, and $60,000 in gold, the property of the Church; but, arriving at San Francisco (then Yerba Buena), when the country was first attracting attention, he, and most of his party, apostatized and remained there. He invested the Church funds in real estate, and became one of San Francisco's wealthiest citizens; but has since repaid the money to the Church with interest.

Soon after, Bishop Lyman Wight led another large party to Texas, where they increased greatly, and were for some years highly prosperous. They at first acknowledged allegiance to the Twelve Apostles, but when Brigham took the reins they grew restive; when polygamy was avowed, Wight solemnly "cut-off" the Salt Lake Mormons, and no long time after, was himself cut off by death, and his flock scattered for want of a shepherd.

Soon after the founding of Salt Lake City, a large colony of Mormons was also established in San Bernardino County, California; but they were too far from headquarters, to be governed either by Apostles or "Danites," and soon became entangled in the politics and public interests of the State. Orders were issued for their return to Utah, a few obeyed, and the remainder "lost the spirit and fell into apostacy." ' But it is a fixed fact, that ninety-nine out of a hundred who have believed Mormonism for ten years, are ever after unfit for any sensible faith; apostates from Mormonism are generally infidels or visionaries, Millenarians, Adventists or Lunatics; and the San Bernardino schismatics, in a body, embraced Spiritualism. From the unseen world a revelation was received, that a youth of one of the old Mormon families would in time be called a prophet, and unite the whole Church; but unfortunately the young man died soon after, and San Bernardino was left without a prophet. A few returned to the parent organization, and a few to the "Re-organized Church;" insanity prevails to an amazing extent among the remainder, who long contributed from twelve to twenty additions, per year, to the insane asylum at Stockton; and it is reported, that institution now contains a hundred of the sect, and would have five hundred more if it were not full.

Deducting all preliminary secessions, nearly 20,000 followed the Twelve Apostles from Nauvoo, of whom less than 10,000 ever reached Utah. Throughout their Iowa pilgrimage bands and parties fell away like sparks from a flying meteor, and almost every "stake" soon became a village of recusant Mormons; Garden Grove, Mount Pisgah, Council Bluffs, Florence and Columbus were originally settled by these apostates, and considerable bodies gathered to Nebraska City, Omaha and other river towns, Dr. Isaac Galland died in extreme poverty in Iowa, and nearly all the old Nauvoo allies of Joe Smith ended their days in the gutter, the penitentiary or the poor house. But thousands of those who had honestly embraced Mormonism, and abandoned it only when convinced of the imposture, became valuable citizens among the Gentiles.

In all these branch organizations there was no isolation from the world, no repressive power, and no one man to seize the reins and drive ruthlessly forward, regardless alike of the sufferings of his people and the lives of his enemies; hence, inherent weakness increased, and they fast decayed. But in Utah Brigham was absolute; he had perfect isolation, and talent without the troublesome adjunct of a conscience, and there despotism has been a success. Nevertheless, even in Utah there have been no less than four distinct and organized attempts to throw off the yoke of Brigham, and "return to a more perfect faith." None of these bodies have professed a desire to break up the Church, only to purify it.

The first was by the sect known as "Gladdenites." It

will be remembered that Gladden Bishop was condemned at Nauvoo; but he soon after came back to the Church, and other recusants were beginning to return, when, in 1852, polygamy was avowed, and to this and other new features the Gladdenites were opposed. Their mission in Salt Lake City was headed by one Albert Smith, from Saint Louis, and seems to have made sufficient progress to stir up the Brighamites, who have left about the only history we have of the Sect in Utah. The following extract from a "sermon" by Brigham will clearly indicate how this movement was crushed:

"I will ask, What has produced your persecutions and sorrow? What has been the starting-point of all your afflictions? They began with apostates in your midst; those disaffected spirits caused others to come in, worse than they, who would run out and bring in all the devils they possibly could. That has been the starting-point and grand cause of all our difficulties, every time we were driven. I am coming to this place,—I am coming nearer home. . . . . Do we see apostates among us now? We do.

"When a man comes right out like an independent devil, and says, 'Damn Mormonism and all the Mormons,' and is off with himself to California, I say he is a gentleman by the side of a nasty, sneaking apostate, who is opposed to nothing but Christianity. I say to the former, 'Go in peace, sir, and prosper if you can.' But we have a set of spirits here, worse than such a character. When I went from meeting last Sabbath, my ears were saluted with an apostate, crying in the streets here. I want to know if any one of you who has got the spirit of Mormonism in you, the spirit that Joseph and Hyrum had, or that we have here, would say, 'Let us hear both sides of the question. Let us listen and prove all things.' What do you want to prove? Do you want to prove that an old apostate, who has been cut off from the Church thirteen times for lying, is any thing worthy of notice? I heard that a certain picture-maker in this city, when the boys would have moved away the waggon in which this apostate was standing, became violent with them, saying, 'Let this

U

man alone; these are Saints that you are persecuting." [Sneeringly.]

"We want such men to go to California, or anywhere they choose. I say to those persons, 'You must not court persecution here, lest you get so much of it you will not know what to do with it. Do NOT court persecution.' We have known Gladden Bishop for more than twenty years, and know him to be a poor, dirty curse. Here is sister Wilate Kimball, brother Heber's wife, has borne more from that man than any other woman on earth could bear; but she won't bear it again. I say again, you Gladdenites, do not court persecution, or you will get more than you want, and it will come quicker than you want it.

"I say to you, Bishops, do not allow them to preach in your wards. Who broke the roads to these valleys? Did this little nasty Smith and his wife? No. They staid in St. Louis while we did it, peddling ribbons, and kissing the Gentiles. I know what they have done here— they have asked exorbitant prices for their nasty, stinking ribbons. [Voices, 'That's true.'] We broke the roads to this country.

"Now, you Gladdenites, keep your tongues still, lest sudden destruction come upon you. I say, rather than that apostates should flourish here, I will unsheathe my bowie-knife, and conquer or die. [Great commotion in the congregation, and a simultaneous burst of feeling, assenting to the declaration.] Now, you nasty apostates, clear out, or 'judgment will be laid to the line, and righteousness to the plummet.' [Voices generally, 'Go it, go it.] If you say it is all right, raise your hands. [All hands up.] Let us call upon the Lord to assist us in this and every other good work."*

It must be remembered that all these sermons are quoted exactly as reported by the Mormons themselves and printed in the Church paper, that Brigham carefully revises them before they are printed; and that they are frequently so pared down and modified, with most of the oaths and obscenity struck out, that it is difficult for

---

* March 27, 1853. *Jour. of Dis.*, vol. i, p. 82.

the hearer to recognize the published form. In another part of the above harangue, Brigham warns the Gladdenites that they "were not playing with shadows, but were trying to fool with the voice and hand of the Almighty, and would find themselves badly mistaken." The effect of such preaching was horrible, and that some of the Gladdenites were murdered outright is beyond a doubt. But the Church authorities seem to have been fearful that a spirit of rebellion might still lurk in the minds of the people, and determined to stamp out the last traces of apostacy. To this end, the doctrine of "blood-atonement" was introduced and preached regularly for many years. This doctrine was urged particularly with a wild and savage earnestness by Jedediah M. Grant, who, it is but charity to suppose, was insane on the subject; a bloody-crazy wretch, legitimately succeeded by Daniel H. Wells. Like the latter, he was First Counsellor to Brigham, Mayor of the city and Chief of the secret police; and like him, too, he regarded murder as a holy act, if done in accordance with the rites of the Church; and there is testimony that some of these unfortunate apostates were actually sacrificed in the Endowment House, "to atone for their sins and save their souls." Young Mormons, who were children then, have often told me of hearing this J. M. Grant preach his favorite doctrine of blood-atonement, with furious mien and gestures, and actually foaming at the mouth in the intensity of frantic rage. If any should doubt the possibility of men going to such lengths in a bloody doctrine, let them peruse this extract from one of Grant's sermons, delivered March 12, 1854, *as recorded in the Mormon publication, the Deseret News;* and remember, too, that it is only the mildest possible language which is published, compared with that actually used.

"Then what ought this meek people who keep the commandments of God do unto them ? 'Why,' says one, 'they ought *to pray to the Lord to kill them.*' I want to know if you would wish the LORD *to come down and do all your dirty work?* Many of the Latter-day Saints will pray, and petition, and supplicate the Lord to do a thousand things they themselves would be ashamed to do.

* * * * * *

"*When a man prays for a thing, he ought to be willing to perform it himself.* But if the Latter-day Saints should put to death the covenant-breakers, it would try the faith of the very meek, just, and pious ones among them, and *it would cause a great deal of whining in Israel.*

"Then there was another odd commandment. The Lord God commanded them *not to pity the person whom they killed,* but to execute the law of God upon persons worthy of death. *This should be done by the entire congregation,* SHOWING NO PITY. I have thought there would have to be quite a revolution among the Mormons before such a commandment could be obeyed completely by them. For instance, if they can get a man before the tribunal administering the law of the land, and succeed in getting a rope around his neck, and having him hung up like a dead dog, it is all right. *But if the Church and Kingdom of God should step forth and execute the law of God,* O, what a burst of Mormon sympathy it would cause! *I wish we were in a situation favorable to our doing that which is justifiable before God, without any contaminating influence of Gentile amalgamation, laws, and traditions; that the People of God might lay the axe to the root of the tree, and every tree that bringeth not forth good fruit might be hewn down.*

"What! do you believe that people would do right and keep the law of God by *actually putting to death the transgressors?* Putting to death the transgressors *would exhibit the law of God, no matter* BY WHOM *it was done.* That is my opinion.

"You talk of the doings of different Governments—the United States, if you please. What do they do with traitors? What mode do they adopt to punish traitors? Do traitors to that Government forfeit their lives? Examine also the doings of other earthly Governments on this point, and you find the same practice universal. I am not aware that there are any exceptions. But people will look into books of theology, and argue that the people of God have a right to try people for fellowships, but they have no right to try them on property or life. *That makes the devil laugh,* saying : I have got them on a hook now; they can cut them off, and I will put eight or ten spirits worse than they are into their tabernacles, and send them back to mob them,"

Brigham follows up this reasoning with a plain declaration that *none can expect finally to escape,* and sooner or later the vengeance of the Church will overtake them. But he uses a different phraseology, as follows:

"There is not a man or woman who violates the covenants made with their God, that will not be required to pay the debt. The blood of Christ will never wipe that out, your own blood must atone for it; and the judgments of the Almighty will come sooner or later, and every man and woman will have to atone for breaking their covenants."

With these plain directions to an ignorant and fanatical people, from those they looked upon as the incarnate voice of God, the fate of the Gladdenites is easily foreseen. Those who could, escaped to California; the others recanted or "atoned," and we hear no more of them after 1854.

Second in order of time was the Sect known as " Morrisites," whose history is substantially as follows:

Joseph Morris was a native of Manchester, England, and came to Utah among the early converts. Like thousands of others, he thought that the pure truth delivered by Joseph Smith had been corrupted, and conceived the design of effecting a grand reformation in the Church. According to his own account, while engaged in reflection on the subject, he was one day in the pastures beyond Jordan, when he was favored with a glorious vision, and by command of Christ, Enos (son of Seth), John the Baptist, and the archangel Michael, who constitute the triune mission of Mormonism, appeared and endowed him with the holy priesthood, as the true successor of Joseph Smith.

On announcing his mission, he was at once an object of interest to all persons at South Weber, his residence, some thirty miles north of this city, and in a short time had converted to his views Bishop Cook, of Weber settlement, his brother, John Cook, and several others.

Persecution by his neighbors soon followed, and his life was frequently threatened; but little attention was paid to the matter by the regular authorities, as Morris was an exceedingly simple and illiterate man, who was thought incapable of giving the slightest trouble. Meanwhile, he continued to receive voluminous revelations, and, under the supposed influence of the Holy Spirit, composed two letters directed to Brigham Young and Heber C. Kimball, which he took to the city and delivered in person. Brigham treated the matter lightly at first, but it soon grew so serious that John Taylor and Wilford Woodruff, both apostles, were sent to Weber to investigate the matter. They called a Church meeting, in executive session, on the 11th of February, 1861, when Taylor rose and demanded whether there was a man in that ward who claimed to be a prophet, and if so, whether he had any followers? To the consternation of the Brighamites seventeen persons, with Bishop Cook at their head, arose and avowed their belief that "Joseph Morris was sent of God, and was the true priestly successor of Joseph Smith." It is to be noted that the Morrisites never denied the right of Brigham to be First President, by election, and temporal head of the Church; but they claimed that he was "neither a prophet, nor the son of a prophet."

A violent discussion followed, in which an old man named Watts said that the Morrisites "ought to be cut off under the chin and laid away in the brush," for which he was sternly rebuked by Bishop Cook. After the customary "admonition," by Taylor and Woodruff, all the adherents of Morris were formally excommunicated, and "delivered over to the buffetings of Satan for a thousand years." Morris established his church by baptizing five persons in the Weber River, on the 6th of April, 1861, exactly thirty-one years from the first baptism by Joseph Smith. Converts flocked rapidly from all parts of the Territory, and the new sect soon numbered three hundred. It never exceeded five hundred. Morris employed two scribes to take down his revealed gospel, and his followers now have six volumes of them, each containing two or three hundred manuscript pages.

The spring review of 1862 of the Nauvoo Legion, the Territorial militia, came on, and the Morrisites refused to drill, for which several of them were arrested and fined $60 and $80 each. Other troubles arose between them and the surrounding Mormons, about which there is great conflict of testimony. I have the story from those of the Morrisites now at Camp Douglas, from various Brighamites, and from official papers and testimony left by Judges Waite, Drake, and Titus. The Sect occupied a portion of the Weber Valley, with their town made in a sort of encampment in a circular hollow, below which was their cultivated land. They had all things in common, and every new convert divided his surplus property among the needy, while their common cow-herd was attended by a detailed herder among the mountain hollows. Intelligent Mormons, then resident on the Weber, tell me they took a large number of cattle from their neighbors, and committed other depredations; which the Morrisites deny, saying that they only retaliated where they had been robbed. At length one Jones seized a load of flour belonging to the Morrisites at a mile near Salt Lake, and detained it and the two boys in charge, as he alleged, in satisfaction for injuries done him.

The Morrisites sent out a strong posse, retook the load, and brought Jones and two confederates, as prisoners to their camp. Meanwhile, the Sheriff had appeared, and purposed to arrest all those who could not, or would not pay the fines assessed for refusal to drill, but he was refused admission to the settlement. Complaint was at once made to Chief Justice Kinney, who issued writs for the arrest of the leading Morrisites, and Robert T. Burton, Sheriff of Salt Lake County, attempted to serve them, but returned to the city unsuccessful. The Nauvoo Legion was at once ordered out, with several cannon, and placed under Burton's command. On their way they were joined by reinforcements from Ogden, Kaysville, and Farmington, till early on the morning of June 13, 1862, they arrived before the Morrisite Camp, with a thousand well armed men, and five pieces of artillery. They captured the Morrisites' cow-herd, killing such as they desired for beef, and sent the boys attending it into the camp, with Burton's proclamation, calling for surrender. The camp, or fort, consisted of a few houses made of willows, woven together and plastered, and covered waggons, surrounded by some rude fortifications. Morris called his men together, when they received another note to remove the women and children, as firing would begin in one hour. In about twenty minutes a cannon was fired, of which the ball entered the fort, killing two women, and carrying away the jaw of another.

Meanwhile, Morris had donned his priestly robe, and taken his divining rod, and was waiting for a revelation as to what course should be taken. After an hour or two of fanatic supplication, no revelation was received; and as the Brighamites had begun to surround the camp, the Prophet divided his forces, placed a band at each of the weak points, and assumed the responsibility of fighting. His camp was upon a knoll in the hollow of the Weber, a mile or so below the present railroad station of Uintah, while the Brighamite posse occupied the adjacent slopes. The latter soon opened a general fire upon the camp, when the Morrisites at once flew to arms and the battle began. The cannon and long range rifles of the Brighamites completely raked the fort, to which the Morrisites could only reply with their ducking-guns and a few Spanish *scopetees*, which inflicted only slight wounds. The cannon, too, were often loaded with small balls, which tore down the wicker-work and pierced the sandy hillocks, wounding the women and children who had taken refuge behind them. Still these deluded people would not surrender, and for three days, fighting with the desperate energy of religious fanaticism, maintained the unequal battle. At intervals, during that time, they often called on Morris to intercede with the Lord for their deliverance, to which he made reply : " If the Lord will, we shall be delivered and our enemies destroyed ; but let us do our duty." On the evening of the third day, some one raised a white flag; when Morris saw it, he said : "Your faith has gone, and the Lord has forsaken us. I can now do nothing more."

They threw down their arms and the Legion marched in. Amid the wildest confusion the men and women were separated, and the former placed under guard. Few of the women could speak English, and all expected nothing but destruction. Burton shot Morris, his lieutenant Banks, and two women, after the arms were given up, while the soldiers plundered the houses, took all the watches, jewellery and money, and destroyed all they could not carry away. Here, too, there is great conflict of testimony. Some of the boys who were with the Brighamite forces say that Morris ordered his men to take their arms and fight again, for which he was shot. Still others say that Banks was only slightly wounded, and called for water, when a cup was handed to him by the Brighamite surgeon, Dr. Jeter Clinton ; that he drank of it and expired in a few minutes. The Morrisites are confident he would have recovered, if he had not been poisoned, The following affidavit will give most clearly the Morrisite version of the affair :

"*United States of America, Territory of Utah, ss.*

"Alexander Dow, of said Territory, being duly sworn, says :

"In the spring of 1861, I joined the Morrisites, and was present when Joseph Morris was killed. The Morrisites had surrendered, a white flag was flying, and the arms were all grounded and guarded by a large number of the posse.

"Robert T. Burton and Judson L. Stoddard rode in among the Morrisites. Burton was much excited, and said : ' Where is the man ? I don't know him.' Stoddard replied, ' That's him,' pointing to Morris. Burton rode his horse upon Morris, and commanded him to give himself up in the name of the Lord. Morris replied: 'No; never, never.' Morris said he wanted to speak to the people.— Burton said, 'Be d—d quick about it.' Morris said,— ' Brethren, I have taught you true principles'—he had scarcely got the words out of his mouth, when Burton fired his revolver. The ball passed in his neck or shoulder.

Burton exclaimed, 'There's your Prophet.' He fired again, saying, 'What do you think of your Prophet now?' "Burton then turned suddenly and shot Banks, who was standing five or six paces distant. Banks fell. Mrs. Bowman, wife of James Bowman, came running up, crying, 'Oh! you blood-thirsty wretch!' Burton said, 'No one shall tell me that and live,' and shot her dead. A Danish woman then came running up to Morris, crying, and Burton shot her dead also. Burton could have easily taken Morris and Banks prisoners, if he had tried. I was standing but a few feet from Burton all the time. And further saith not.

"ALEXANDER DOW."

" Subscribed and sworn to before me, this 18th day of April, A.D., 1863.
"CHARLES B. WAITE,
"*Associate Justice, Utah Territory.*"

All the loose property of the Morrisites having been "confiscated," the dead bodies of Morris, Banks and eight others were thrown into a waggon, with Morris' robe, crown and rod, and succeeded by the captured Morrisites, they were guarded to the city. Young and old turned out to see them, with mingled emotions of glee and horror, and the bodies of Morris and Banks, lying for several days in the City Hall, were visited by great crowds, eager to see the noted "schismatic." The vast majority of these people regarded it simply as the proper punishment due to one who had "set himself up to teach heresy in Zion, and oppose the Lord's anointed." During the entire battle two Brighamites and ten Morrisites were killed, and a very large number wounded.

Ninety-three of the Morrisites were at once arraigned before Judge Kinney, but there was so much popular excitement, and as it was probable more would die of their wounds, he proceeded to place them all under bonds of $1,500 each, for their appearance in April, 1863. Only five of them would sign the bond; few of the rest could speak English, and those who could protested against the entire proceedings, and announced their determination "to lie in jail till the Devil's thousand years were out," before they would even by implication confess that they were treated legally.

But as the five signers still owned considerable property Judge Kinney ruled that, as in a sort of community, they could bind all the rest, as their representatives. When the April term (1863) came on, twenty of them were out of the territory, and one was dead, but most of the rest appeared. Kinney said that "their absence made no difference; he was glad to see that so many had appeared;" and proceeded to enter a fine of one hundred dollars each against the present, dead and absent. In addition, several leaders were put on trial, and sentenced to the penitentiary for from five to fifteen years each.

In June, 1862, Kinney was the only United States Judge in Utah, and the compliant tool of the Brighamites. But Governor Harding and Judges Waite and Drake had arrived in time to hear the trial of the Morrisites, and were convinced that great injustice had been done them, or even if they were guilty of resistance to legal process, the law had been strained to inflict a cruel and unusual punishment. It was known, too, as it is now, that sentence to a long imprisonment in Utah, simply means DEATH, if the keepers in charge are so instructed. Petitions began to circulate for their pardon, signed by Gentiles and some of the Mormons who relented at such severity. Quite an excitement was created by these attempts, and Governor Harding was warned by the more violent Brighamites not to interfere with the sentence of law. Bishop Woolley called upon the Governor with an earnest remonstrance against the proposed pardon, adding in conclusion, "Governor, it stands you in hand to be careful. Our people are much excited; they feel it would be an outrage to pardon these men, and if it is done they *might proceed to violence*," etc., etc.

To this truly Mormon attempt at intimidation the Governor responded with his usual firmness. While the petition, with names attached, was still in his possession, not acted upon, the Governor was aroused from sleep one night, between midnight and morning, by a furious knocking at the door; it was opened by his son, Attila, who acted as his private secretary, and there presented himself a stranger of rough aspect, who demanded peremptorily to "see the Gov'n'r." No representations of the unseasonableness of the hour appeared to move him; he insisted that his business was too important for delay; he had ridden thirty miles over bad roads, could not arrive sooner and must return at once. With precautions against surprise they admitted him to the Governor's room, and he at once began: " I understand that you have a petition for the pardon of some of the Morrisites—that you won't act on it because you don't think there are enough o' Mormon names on it—or Mormons that are well known. An' you say some Mormons want to sign it, want 'em pardoned, but are afeard to sign. Gi' me that paper an' I'll show you one Mormon that's not afeard to sign—an' one that's purty well known, too. An' I've rid thirty miles this night on purpose to sign it." The petition was procured and handed to him, and after a rapid survey of the names, he seized the pen and in broad, sprawling Roman capitals, extending entirely across the sheet, inscribed the well known name,

BILL HICKMAN.

It was indeed the redoubtable "Danite" captain. "There," said he, holding it off at arm's length, "there is a Mormon name they all know, an' they can read it without specks. Talk o' bein' afeard o' Brigham Young ! I tell you Brigham Young is a good deal more afeard o' Bill Hickman than Bill Hickman is afeard o' Brigham Young." Thus speaking he departed as unceremoniously as he came, nor did any further explanation of this singular affair ever reach the Governor. After a short imprisonment, the Morrisites were pardoned; no violence was attempted or threatened against Governor Harding, but another singular occurrence took place soon after.

One beautiful evening, while the bright sun of Utah was sinking behind the Lake island hills, into a "sea of glass, mingled with fire," tipping, with a golden glory, the gray peaks of the Wasatch, two women might have been seen descending the hill from the Morrisite settlement near Camp Douglas, and seeking the residence of the Governor. The elder was a brawny and sunburned Danish woman, of most coarse and common clay, who assisted the other's steps till they stood before the Governor. The younger woman was of a frail and delicate aspect, that indicated either long sickness and privation, or a nervous organization worn to exhaustion by excitement; her dark, sunken eyes glowed with a strange, unearthly fire, and the blue veins of her forehead stood out from a skin of marble whiteness, while her long, delicate fingers clasped and entwined with intense earnestness as she told her mission. It was the widow of Banks, the murdered Morrisite. She had, according to her faith, been in communion with the soul of her husband, and thence received knowledge of a plot against the Governor, not to take his life, but to place him in the same category with Steptoe and Dawson. She related all the particulars of the proposed attempt, with that convulsive trembling, that dilation and upward roll of the eye, and that unearthly hollow tone, so familiar to those who have investigated the phenomena of mesmerism and psychology, in their purely physical effects upon the nervous female. "Oh, Governor, Governor," she exclaimed, her thin, *spirituelle* form quivering with intense feeling, "friend and saviour of our people! Beware, beware. The spirit of the Lord and his martyred prophet is upon me, to warn you of this danger. It will come to you in the form of a beautiful woman; but be guarded, and if, within a fortnight, you are introduced to a fair woman, who presents a great temptation to you, think of this warning, and do not yield." The Governor, being gallant as well as brave, was taken somewhat aback by the fact that the *seer* had so well anticipated the temptation best calculated to overcome him; but the rest of the story is best related in his own words:

"Well, I wondered how the woman got her information, but, as the boys say, I 'wa'n't afeard,' I rather liked the idea. A few days after, the 'temptation' came.

I was called from my room to receive some company in the parlor, and was there introduced to *two* ladies, whose beauty exceeded anything I had seen in Salt Lake. They remained to tea with my landlady, after which we had a delightful evening. The youngest and most beautiful (I withhold the name given by the Governor) made herself particularly agreeable to me, and was my partner in several games at cards. When the time for starting came, it was pretty plainly intimated, by my landlady, that I was to see the lady home.

"But this was not my programme. As she stood pulling at her gloves, evidently waiting for me to 'make a break,' I stepped forward, shook hands with her, and merely said, 'Ladies, I should be pleased to act the complimentary, but I understand it is not the custom among your people for Gentiles to escort the women of the Saints. So I bid you good evening.' I then retired to my room. I afterwards learned, beyond doubt, that this was the beginning of a scheme which, if carried out, would have seriously compromised me." Whether the Governor's virtue or his astuteness enabled him to escape the evil, the writer will not pretend to say; but it is rather curious how the Morrisite woman received her first impressions of such a plot, for we cannot doubt that it was a previous mental impression acting upon her peculiar temperament which led to her dream or " vision," whichever it was.

Meanwhile, the bonds of the absent Morrisites were declared forfeited by Judge Kinney, and execution issued against the property of those still in Utah, who had any, to collect the penalty. Abraham Taylor, a prominent Morrisite, had his property in the City, worth $3,000, levied upon and announced for sale. He applied to Judge Waite, who found, on examination, that the records of the court showed no judgment against the delinquents, which fact he represented to Judge Kinney, and applied for an injunction against the officer. The application was refused by Judge Kinney, who stated that, "if there was no judgment, he could render one, as the Court *had not permanently adjourned, but only to meet again on his own motion."* Taylor's homestead was put up at once, and sold to one Joseph A. Johnson, Clerk of Judge Kinney's Court, for $200, and the family literally forced into the street. They remained a few days in the street, in front of the house, then took refuge at Camp Douglas.

After General Connor arrived with two regiments of California volunteers, and established Camp Douglas, the Morrisites gathered there ; and, in May, 1863, the General sent eighty families of them, including over 200 persons, to Soda Springs, Idaho, where they now have a flourishing settlement. Abraham Taylor, one of their leaders, remained at Camp Douglas, and, in 1866, by Major Chas. H. Hempstead, his attorney, filed a bill in the United States District Court, Judge Titus presiding, praying for restitution of his property ; and, after two years of delay and chicanery by the Mormon lawyers, and some of the hardest swearing that ever "reeked to heaven," at the October term, 1868, a decree was made in his favor by Judge Wilson, giving him possession of his old homestead, with rents for five years. The popular Mormon idea of justice may be seen from the fact, that three-fourths of the people looked upon this decree as a gross outrage on a Utah citizen by a United States Judge, and a severe act of "persecution."

Taken all in all, the Morrisites deserved a better fate. True, their religion was a wild compound of materialism, spiritism, diabolism and deism run mad, but their code was far better than that of the Brighamites.

Another prophet named Davis arose among them in Idaho, but, before his Church was well established, he had a revelation that all the rest were to deed their property to him as trustee, and practise communism, which soon weakened his prophetic hold. Not long after, they got some sort of revelation that a little child among them was to be their future Christ, and kept the child "set apart," and dressed in white, for some time ; but lately their organization has broken up, and many of them removed to Nevada.

The most successful of all the recusant and anti-polygamous sects, is that under the leadership of young Joseph

Smith, self-styled the "Re-organized Church of Latter-Day Saints," but generally known as "Josephites." It will be remembered that Joseph Smith, the Prophet, obtained gratis, from Dr. Galland, most of the land upon which Nauvoo was built. After the revelation for his people to gather there, he sold them the lots at high prices, and realized an immense fortune, reported as high as one million dollars by the best informed. With this he paid all his old debts in Ohio, lived in considerable style, supported a dozen women, and still left a considerable fortune, mostly in houses and lots, in Nauvoo. Spiritual wives having no legal rights in Illinois as in Utah, all this property was held by his widow Emma, who refused to emigrate, and remained with her three sons, Joseph, Jr., William Alexander, and David Hyrum, in Nauvoo. The oldest and youngest had been in turn blessed and dedicated to the leadership by their father, the latter before his birth; and when the Strangites organization had dissolved, Strang's successor went "hunting for Zion" in Northern Iowa, where he met the remnants of the Cutlerites, and, together, they decided that "Young Joe was the man," formed a church and made overtures to him accordingly. He responded that he had received no "call," but expected one; the Church rapidly augmented from the *debris* of the scattered sects, and, finally, in 1860, Young Smith was "called as a Prophet," and the "Re-organized Church" was set up, with head-quarters at Plano, Illinois. They number twenty or thirty thousand in the West, and have flourishing missions in Great Britain and Scandinavia. In July, 1863, E. C. Briggs and Alex. McCord, their first missionaries to Utah, reached Salt Lake, and created quite a sensation; Brigham intimated to them that their lives were in danger, and refused them the use of any public building in the city. But General Connor was then in command at Camp Douglas, with a small provost guard in the city, and the Brighamites dared not try violence; Briggs visited the people at their homes, and preached wherever Gentiles would open their houses to him, and soon had many converts. Nearly two hundred of these left the Territory in 1864, under a military escort, furnished by General Connor, and, since that time, many more have left Utah, and their missions there include over five hundred members.

But all the excitement connected with Briggs' visit was as nothing to that of last summer, when it was announced that William Alexander and David Hyrum, "sons of the Prophet and Martyr," had reached Salt Lake to advocate the reformed faith. They obtained Independence Hall, the only public building belonging to the Gentiles, for their meetings; and, on their first service, it was crowded by the Mormons, among them most of the widows of Heber C. Kimball, and the wives of Brigham Young. Unable to dispute the revelation in favor of David, the Brighamites maintain that he "is now in apostacy, and when he embraces the true faith and comes in the right way, they will receive him." This they confidently believe he will yet do. The evident absurdity of dictating to a foreordained Prophet, in just what way he shall come, does not seem to affect their views. The Brighamites were startled clear out of their propriety, abandoned their silent policy, and organized a series of meetings in opposition to the "Smith boys." But Brigham was entirely too shrewd to take the lead, and put forward Apostle Joseph F. Smith, son of "Hyrum the Martyr," to manage the opposition meetings. The writer attended most of the meetings, and fully realized the force of the maxim in regard to gleaning the truth from the disagreement of rogues. The controversy was one of that peculiar kind where both parties "know they are right," and can prove all they wish by abundant testimony.

The Brighamites can prove, beyond a doubt, that Joseph Smith practised polygamy, while the Josephites can prove, by equal personal and documentary evidence, that he denied and reprobated the doctrine till the last day of his life. Sixteen women, swore most positively, and allowed their affidavits to be published in the *Expositor*, at Nauvoo, that Joe Smith made proposals to them to become his concubines; twelve women, now in Salt Lake City, make affidavit that they were the spiritual wives of

Smith at Nauvoo; Joseph F., son of Hyrum Smith, testifies that he knew certainly of his father having more than one wife, and hundreds of old Mormons testify that Joe and Hyrum taught them the doctrine, and sealed them to extra wives.

The proof on the other side is equally clear, as already detailed,* making the question one which can never be settled by evidence, which means eternal controversy. A Gentile would find an easy way out of the dilemma, by considering Joe Smith a lying impostor; but that would never do for these sects, each of which claims to be his only true Church. The Brighamites, however, flatly acknowledge that all these denials were made; freely admit that their Prophet often found it necessary to lie to save his life, and generally state that their "religion occasionally makes it necessary for the priesthood to lie," all of which their history abundantly proves to be the case. But the "Smith boys" accomplished little in Utah. They were not the men to organize a revolution; they were in no respect shrewd enough to contend with the leading Brighamites, nor half crazy and violent enough to excite the people; they were, in fact, hopelessly mediocre. Their position was weak and untenable; their claims for their father easily disproved, and their propositions inherently absurd. The writer, from personal acquaintance with William and David, is disposed to esteem them highly as citizens, and respect them as honest in their aims; but would respectfully ask: If you "purify the Church," if you blot out polygamy, incest, blood-atonement, "Adam-worship," and "Danites," what will you have left? How much Mormonism will there be in your Church?

The "Re-organized Church" has a number of periodicals, and a lengthy "Confession of Faith," from which I extract those tenets distinguishing them from the Brighamites:

"We believe in being subject to kings, queens, presidents, rulers, and magistrates; in obeying and honoring the law.

---

*See Chapter XIV.

"We believe that the Church in Utah, under the predency of Brigham Young, have apostatized from the true order of the Gospel.

"We believe that the doctrines of polygamy, human sacrifice, or killing men to save them, Adam being God, Utah being Zion, or the gathering place for the Saints, are doctrines of devils, instituted by wicked men, for the accomplishment of their own lustful desires, and with a view to their personal aggrandizement.

"We believe in being true and loyal to the Government of the United States, and have no sympathy or fellowship for the treasonable practices or wicked abominations endorsed by Brigham Young and his followers."

Young Joe has had but two revelations, both very mild, and seems to be slow in the business of Prophet. But whoever leads off the ignorant of Utah must outbrigham Brigham, must go to greater lengths of fanaticism, and have copious revelations daily. This accounts in part for Morris' success; he was as crazy as any of his followers.

The last revolt against the power of Brigham is headed by several prominent men in Salt Lake City, among them Wm. S. Godbe, Henry Lawrence, W. H. Shearman, and —— Tullidge. This sect has been long in growing, consisting of those who supported the *Utah Magazine* as the organ of independent thought; but it was not till last autumn that the leaders boldly announced the policy of opposition to the excessive temporal government of the priesthood. The First Presidency promptly condemned the *Utah Magazine*, and Brigham issued a general order forbidding all true Saints to patronize or read it. The Editor and proprietors were cited before the *High Council*, and, refusing to recant and ask pardon, were summarily "cut off." A few who voted against this excision were called upon to explain their votes, and, failing to do so, were also "cut off." The schism increased, the new party contained some wealthy and influential men, and in a short time they had established a new weekly paper, the *Mormon Tribune*, to promulgate their views. They call their new organization the "Church of

Zion," and, at last accounts, numbered nearly five thousand in the Territory. Their platform lays down the principles, that the Priesthood are only teachers, and have no right to control the people in all their social and business relations; that the mines should be developed, and trade free and unrestricted with all classes; that tithing should consist of a tenth of all one's increase, and not a tenth of his yearly proceeds, and many other liberal principles. This is, so far, the most sensible and promising set of principles from any of the recusant sects. They still claim to be good Mormons, maintain polygamy, and every man's right to revelation. Many of the leaders are spiritualists; most are evidently honest in their views, and it is to be hoped they are sufficiently crazy to outdo Brigham in fanaticism, and carry the matter through. The present year will probably witness strange changes at Salt Lake. Granted that Mormonism is to work out its own destiny, without governmental interference, the question at once arises: After Brigham, what? Who will be his successor? There is no one in the Church who can entirely fill his place, and five or six probable aspirants, of whom one is about as well fitted as another. According to precedent, in the case of Brigham himself, Orson Hyde, President of the Twelve Apostles, would succeed; but he is a blundering and impulsive scamp, mean enough for the place, but lacking in discretion. He is, besides, rather old, and has apostatized once. Daniel H. Wells is next in rank, but his bloodthirsty fanaticism would involve the people in war in a short time. Orson Pratt is the most learned of the Apostles, but is a dreaming astronomer, quite impractical. George A. Smith is an easy going, good-natured sensualist; unscrupulous enough for the place, perhaps, but without executive ability. Should Brigham die at an early day, the strong probability is that the Church would divide into at least three bodies. Many of the English and Americans would follow David Hyrum Smith; the most enlightened and liberal would enter the "Church of Zion," and the ignorant mass would follow the lead of the Twelve Apostles as before, eventually coming under the rule of one.

Having brought down our history to near the present time, let us take a brief view of the material interests and resources of Utah. The notes in the two succeeding chapters are the result of a year's travel and residence in Utah, aided by a study of the best authorities, to which due credit is given in passing.

CHAPTER XVIII.

GEOGRAPHICAL FEATURES.

Territorial limits—"Basins"—"Sinks"—"Flats"—Rain and evaporation—Elemental action and reaction—Potamology—Jordan—Kay's Creek—Weber—Bear River—Cache Valley—Timber—Blue Creek—Promontory—Great Desert—Utah Lake—Spanish Fork—Salt Creek—Timpanogos—Sevier River—Colorado System—Fish—Thermal and Chemical Springs—Healing Waters—Hotwater plants—Analysis by Dr. Gale—Mineral Springs—Salt beds—Alkali flats—Native Salts—GREAT SALT LAKE—First accounts—FREMONT—STANSBURY—Amount of salt—Valleys—Rise of the Lake—Islands—Bear Lake—"Ginasticutis"—Utah Lake—Climate—Increase of rain—Singular phenomena—Fine air—Relief for pulmonary complaints.

UTAH is included between the 37th and 42nd parallels of North latitude, and meridians 109 and 114 west from Greenwich; deducting, however, from the north-east corner a section of one degree of latitude by two of longitude, lately attached to Wyoming. Its greatest length is thus, from north to south, five full degrees, and its width from east to west, five of the shorter meridianal degrees; the whole area divided nearly equally between two geographical sections, viz: the valley and drainage of the Colorado and its affluents, the Green and Grand rivers, and the district known as the Great or Interior Basin. This remarkable section, containing the western half of Utah, all of Nevada, and a part of southeastern California, includes all that portion of the continent extending north and south between the parallels 37 and 42, and from east to west from near the meridian 111, Greenwich, to the Sierra Nevadas, which tend northwesterly from the meridian of 116, to that of 121; an irregular parallelogram four hundred miles in extent, from north to south, and five hundred miles from east to west. The term "basin," is only applicable to the whole tract, in view of the fact, that its waters have no outlet to the ocean, for the general level of the lower tracts is as high as average mountain ranges, and the so-called valleys are little more than mountain flats; the entire section is thus composed of a succession of heights, basins, and mountain plateaus. A "succession of basins," because many of the traverse ranges are of on equal height with those on the borders; dotted also in the most level portions with detached hills and knobs, relieved at rare intervals by fertile vales, spotted again by vast deserts of sand and alkali or brackish lakes— a region

> "Now of frozen, now of fiery alps,
> Rocks, fens, bogs, dens and shades of death."

Wherever the mountains are high enough to furnish melting snow throughout the summer, large streams flow down their sides, and fertile tracts are found along their base, caused by the percolation of moisture from above; but in general at any great distance from the foot of the mountains we find barrenness, and throughout the Great Basin a large tract without mountains is invariably a desert. Most of the mountain streams sink before connecting with any other body of water, in many places among the foot-hills before reaching the plain; others spread out and supply natural irrigation to a mile or two of land, producing broad savannas of coarse, rank grass, little oases quite attractive in themselves and delightful in comparison with the sterility beyond. Along the foot of some ranges the traveller, every mile or so, crosses a considerable stream, rushing clear and strong from the mountain hollows, but two or three miles down the plain not a channel or trace of water is to be found, the thirsty soil, warm sun, and drying air, having exhausted the scant liquid; and it is only in very wet seasons that any of these streams form lakes. In other localities a more plentiful supply and the cool shadow of long ranges give rise to streams of sufficient size to be called rivers, of which the best known in Utah are the Jordan, Bear River, Sevier, Ogden and Weber; and bordering these larger streams are valleys of great fertility, comprising the agricultural wealth of the Territory. Many of the smaller streams form long, shallow lagoons or marshes near the centres or at the points of lowest depression in the basins, generally called "sinks," in which term is embodied an empirical explanation of the disappearance of the water, by those ignorant of the fact, that in nature's laboratory action and reaction are equal, and that the fall of rain and snow in an enclosed basin must be exactly counterbalanced by evaporation. In most cases the water supply is so scant that these "sinks" become entirely dry in summer, and are then known as "mud flats," of which, the most extensive are in Western Nevada. A smaller number contain some water all the year, of which a few rise to the dignity of lakes. With no outlets, and receiving all the chemical material brought down by the wash of their "feeders," they are of necessity either very saline in character, or brackish and impregnated with iron.

Throughout the Great Basin certain general features are observable; the mountain ranges mostly run north and south, and the longer valleys lie in the same direction. But in this particular man has not been able to accommodate himself to nature, and the course of civilization as well as empire has made it necessary for the roads to run east and west. One may go from Montana to Arizona, and travel in valleys nearly all the way, seldom crossing anything more than a low "divide," but from east to west each range must be crossed at certain points, for which cause the old road south of the Lake was a perfect zig-zag, selecting the most feasible valleys, avoiding the mountains wherever possible, or "canyoning" up on one side and down the other, diverging great distances from the direct line, and running to almost every point of the compass.

The "rim of the Basin" is uncontinuous, formed by various ranges. On the north are the broken chains of the Oregon system, from 8,000 to 10,000 feet high, sending out many spurs and traverse ridges. On the western border the Sierra Nevadas average 10,000 feet, and some peaks tower far above that altitude. On the south are the lower sub-ranges of the Rocky Mountains, mere "divides," separating the waters of the Basin from those of the Colorado; and on the east is the main Uintah range known by various names, with several portions rising to 9,000 or 10,000 feet. Thus the surface configuration of Utah is a great depression in a mountain land, a trough, so to speak, elevated 4,000 or 5,000 feet above sea level; subtended on all sides by mountain ranges 8,000 to 10,000 feet high, and subdivided by transverse ranges; in the geologic age, a sweet water inland sea, in aboriginal times, the home of the most abject savages—long a region of misconception and fable—then the chosen home of a strange religion, and but yesterday found to be of use and interest to the civilized world. Leaving the mountain ranges which bound the great basin, there is a general breaking down, so to speak, towards the interior; most of the transverse ranges run north and south, terminating in bold headlands towards the south, though none are of sufficient length and continuous height to constitute a well defined system. Few of these ridges present regular slopes, but are formed of acute and angular cappings, superimposed upon flatter prisons; and frequently after ascending two-thirds from the base, the upper part becomes wall-like and insurmountable. Of these interior peaks, or terminal headlands, the most noted are the Twin Peaks, south-east of Salt Lake City, ascertained by Orson Pratt and Albert Carrington to be 11,660 feet in height; Mount Nebo, 8,000 feet; the Wasatch spur, near Salt Lake City, averaging 6,000 feet, and the Oquirrh range, which terminates in a bold headland at the south end of the Lake, locally known as the West Mountain, lying twenty miles west of Salt Lake City.

The Salt Lake Basin, including many adjacent and connecting valleys, was evidently an inland sea, as shown by the "bench formation," a system of water-marks along the mountains, points of successive subsidence of the waters; while many of the detached mountain peaks were as evidently islands, similar to those now rising above the surface of the Lake. According to some, the dry land was formed by successive upheavals; according to others, by ages of evaporation. If the latter theory be correct, it must have been through a "dry cycle" of many thousand years, and if, as many suppose, the "dry cycle" has ended and the rain zones are changing so as to again include this section, we may look for a still greater rise in the Lake surface than that of the last dozen years.

The river system of Utah is curious, but unimportant as to navigation. The noted Jordan, an exact counterpart of its Eastern namesake, has its origin in Utah Lake, and by a course of fifty miles, a little west of north, discharges the surplus waters of that body into Great Salt Lake. It is quite evident, however, from mere inspection, that a much greater quantity of water is poured into Utah Lake from its many mountain affluents than flows out through the Jordan ; a small portion may escape by percolation, but at that elevation and in that drying air more is accounted for by evaporation. This stream has an average width of eight or ten rods ; through the upper part of its course and in Jordan Cañon it is swift and shallow, in the lower valley and near the City more sluggish, with a depth of ten feet or more.

Passing around the Lake eastwardly, the next stream of any note is Kay's Creek, furnishing plentiful irrigation to the farms of Kay's Ward, besides which, there are numerous streams of smaller size which break out of the Wasatch range, are diverted into irrigating canals, and by a thousand rills through the farms find their way to the marshy lands near the Lake.

The main stream from the east is the Weber, which has its rise some sixty miles east of Salt Lake City, in the highest valley of Summit County ; thence, flowing to the north, is swelled by the waters of East Branch, Silver, White, Clay and Echo Creeks, then turning northwest breaks through the Wasatch range, gives form and name to Weber Cañon, enters the valley thirty-three miles north of Salt Lake City, and forming a large U, with the bend sharply to the north, enters the Lake. Bear River rises in the same county, and but a little east and north of the Weber, and running nearly two hundred miles down a northern slope, between two spurs of the Uintah Mountains, forms a great U in Idaho, then turning southwest, "canyons" through another spur of the Uintah, into Cache Valley, the north-eastern section of the Territory and home of 10,000 Mormons; then "canyons" downward three miles, with a fall of 1000 feet, out of Cache into Bear River Valley, through which it runs to the head of Bear River Bay, the last twenty miles of its course the only navigable river in Utah.

From the mouth of Bear River Cañon to the head of the Bay, is about thirty-five miles in a direct line, the valley maintaining an average width of fifteen miles down to Corinne, where it widens imperceptibly into Salt Lake Valley.

Bear River runs through the finest lumber region in Utah, of which it is the natural outlet, and many thousand logs have been already sent down to Corinne, where a saw-mill and sash factory are now in operation.

The Malad joins Bear River a few miles above Corinne, between which place and the promontory there are a few springs breaking out of the mountains, constituting but one stream large enough to have a name, Blue Creek. West of the promontory a few springs run together in the midst of a horrible desert and form Indian Creek, which sometimes reaches the lake in wet seasons. Thence, around the head of the lake and down the entire western shore, for one hundred miles, there is no stream large enough to have a name, and but one furnishing running water in all seasons.

On the south-west a small creek from Tooelle valley reaches the lake, completing the list of affluents to that body. Next in importance are the feeders of Utah Lake, of which the principal are, Salt Creek from the south, Spanish Fork from the east, and Timpanogas from the north-east, which, with the addition of several smaller streams, furnish at least twice as much water to that "gem of the desert," as the Jordan carries off. The only other stream of any importance is the Sevier River, which rises near the southern boundary of Utah, in Fish Lake, runs a hundred and fifty miles to the north, then bends to the west around the point of Iron Mountain, receiving the small supplies of Salt Creek, San Pete, Chicken Creek, and Meadow Creek, then taking a south-west course, is lost in the "big sink" of Sevier Lake Desert. West of the

Iron Mountain range are a score of "sinking creeks," among them Pioneer, Chalk, Cove and Corn Creeks, which are fed by the melting snows of the mountains, furnish scant irrigation to a small strip of land, and are "lost" in the Great Desert of south-western Utah.

Below the "divide," the only streams of note are the Rio Virgen and its affluents, which belong to the Colorado system. Most of the larger streams abound in fish, among which mountain trout are particularly worthy of note; their waters, on issuing from hills, are of great clearness and purity, and it is only where small streams have run some distance across the plain that they are, in local phrase, "alkalied."

The rivers depend for their existence upon the mountains, and without those gorges, which supply melted snow during spring and summer, there would be no running water.

Next to the "sinking" rivers of Utah, the thermal and chemical springs constitute a remarkable feature. They are found in almost every part of the Territory, but principally along the road from Salt Lake City northward. All along the foothills of the Promontory range, in the mountains south-west of Utah Lake, and between the city and Bear River, are fountains of strong brine, discharging in many instances large volumes of water; there are sulphurous pools at the southern extremity of Salt Lake Valley; in one of the Islands in the lake are springs of every character, and in places along the Wasatch, hot, cold and chalybeate, are found side by side.

First in fame, and probably in medical value, are the Warm Springs in Salt Lake City. Issuing in large volume from the mountain side, the water is conveyed in pipes to a regular bathing house on one side, and to a plunge pool on the other, constituting, in my opinion, the most praiseworthy of Mormon institutions.

The following analysis is by Dr. Gale, assistant of Captain Stanbury, in 1850. One hundred parts of the water, whose specific gravity was 7.0112, gave solid contents of 1.068,087, divided as follows:

Sulphuretted hydrogen	0.038,182
Carbonate of lime	0.075,000
" magnesia	0.022,770
Chloride of calcium	0.005,700
Sulphate of soda	0.064,000
Chloride of sodium	0.861,600
	1,068,087

The usual temperature is 102.°

Three miles north of the city the Hot Springs boil out from a rock at the foot of the mountain, forming a hot pool two or three rods in circumference, whence the branch runs westward and forms the Hot Spring Lake, a body of sulphurous water some two miles long, and about half as wide, having an outlet into the Jordan. At several places around the margin of this singular lake, small jets of hot water boil up with great force; the air in the neighborhood is loaded with vapors, and immediately over the spring is almost stifling. Gazing into the small pool, formed by the spring, the eye is charmed by the variety of fanciful growths, the *confervae* on the rocky bottom. Every conceivable form of vegetation is to be seen; leaves, plants, flowers and fernlike stems, all of the purest emerald. But all are deceptions, mere imitations of plants formed by the chemical material on the points of stone. The temperature of this spring is 128°; its specific gravity 1.0130, and one hundred parts yield solid contents 1.0602, divided, according to Dr. Gale, as follows:

Chloride of sodium	0.8052
" magnesia	0.0288
" calcium	0.1096
Sulphate of lime	0.0806
Carbonate of lime	0.0180
Silica	0.0180
	1.0602

The most noted mineral springs are seventy miles north of Salt Lake City, near the north crossing of Bear River; they are hot and cold, impregnated with iron or with sulphur, some twenty in number, and all rising within a few feet of each other. Three springs, the first very hot and sulphurous, the second moderately warm and tasting of iron, the third of cold, pure water, rising within a space of three feet. The waters, all flowing into the same channel, do not mix at once, but run apparently in separate strata for several hundred yards, the hot metallic water often running under the clear, cold water; nor is it until the sudden bends in the channel have thrown the streams violently from side to side, that they mingle in a fluid of uniform temperature. South of Salt Lake City, along the Jordan, are found hot pools which send out very little water, and in other places are chalybeate springs, coating the earth and rocks with oxide of iron. There are also chemical springs on one or two of the Islands in the lake.

The great salt beds of the Basin are in Nevada, but in southern Utah is a peak known as the "Salt Mountain," from which that mineral can be cut in solid blocks, in its pure crystalized state.

Of the mud flats, impregnated with soda, and the alkali deposits, there is a decided surplus, particularly a man has been unable to devise any use for such a quantity of those chemicals in that shape. It is thought the presence of alkali increases the cold, nor does it seem possible to eradicate it from the soil. A slight admixture is thought to be beneficial to vegetation, but wherever there is enough to "flower out" upon the surface, it is death to all vegetation—even the hardy sage brush. Saltpetre is found, though rarely; sulphur is rather too common; borax is found in moderate amount; petroleum has lately been discovered "in paying quantities," and the native alum was analysed and pronounced good by Dr. Gale. From his report a hundred grammes of the freshly crystalized salt gave:

```
Water.................................... 70.3
Protoxide of manganese................... 08.9
Alumina.................................. 04.0
Sulphuric acid........................... 18.0
```

Of the vast chemical wealth of the Territory but little is known, and next to nothing has been utilized, but in a general view the entire Basin seems a vast laboratory of nature, where all the primitive processes have been carried out on a scale so extensive as to make man's dominion, at first sight, seem forever impossible.

First in interest among the large bodies of water, is the Great Salt Lake, the "Dead Sea of America," which lies toward the north-west corner of Utah Territory, 4,200 feet above sea-level, and twelve miles, at the nearest point from Salt Lake City. It is in the form of an irregular parallelogram, of which the major axis, running N. W. by N., is seventy miles in length, and the minor axis forty miles; the different projections, however, greatly increase the area, which is laid down by Captain Stansbury at 90 by 40 miles, in round numbers. The first mention in history of this wonderful Lake, is by Baron Hontan, French Governor of Newfoundland, who made a voyage west of the Mississippi, in the year 1690, and sailed for six weeks up a river, probably the Missouri, according to his description. Here he found a nation of Indians called the "Gnacsitares," probably one of the now extinct Mandan tribes. These Indians brought to him four captives of a "nation, far to the west, whom they called Mozeemleks," of whom the Baron says:

"The Mozeemlek nation is numerous and puissant. These four captives informed me that at a distance of one hundred and fifty leagues from where I then was, their principal river *empties itself into a salt lake* of three hundred leagues in circumference, the mouth of which is two leagues broad; that there are a hundred towns, great and small, around that sort of sea, and upon it they navigate with such boats as you see drawn on the map, which map the Mozeemlek people drew me on the bark of trees; that the people of that country made stuffs, copper axes, and several other manufactures, which the Outagamis and other interpreters could not give me to understand as being altogether unacquainted with such things," etc., etc., etc.

These captives may have been of the Ute nation, or more probably, the semi-civilized races of Mexico had colonies there at that time, as indicated by the ruins found south of the Lake. The next mention of the Lake is in a work published in America in 1772, entitled "A description of the Province of Carolana, by the Spaniards called Florida, and by the French called Louisiane," in which are recited the native accounts of "a lake many leagues west of the mountains, in which there is no living creature, but around its shore the spirits inhabit in great vapors, and *out of that lake a great river disembogues into the South Sea.*"

The "spirits" will be readily recognized in the Hot Springs, but it is singular that both accounts should give the Lake an outlet. Not long afterwards the Lake became well known to hunters and trappers, and in 1845 Colonel Fremont, then on his second expedition, made a sort of flying survey, which was scientifically completed in 1849–50, by Captain Howard Stansbury. In geologic ages the lake was doubtless an inland sea, which has declined to its present limits; but it is singular that since Stansbury's survey, the lake surface has risen at least twelve feet, of which eight feet were gained in the years 1865–66 and '67. The natural result has been to greatly weaken the saline character of the water. There is a wide-spread misapprehension on this subject, it being customary for Eastern lecturers to state that "three gallons of the water will make one of salt." The highest estimate, however, that by Fremont, only gave twenty-four per cent. of salt, and the water was taken from the north-west corner, the most saline portion of the lake. Dr. Gale found one hundred parts of the water to contain solid contents 22.282, distributed as follows:

Chloride of sodium (common salt)	20.196
Sulphate of soda	1.834
Chloride of magnesium	0.252
Chloride of calcium	a trace
	22.282

But it is quite evident that an analysis at this time would show much less, probably not more than 18 per cent. of solid matter, perhaps even less in the Eastern part, and not over 12 or 14 per cent. in Bear River Bay, the least saline arm of the Lake. Those engaged in making salt on Spring Bay, certainly the most saline, state that in 1869 it required six gallons of water to make one of salt. Even with this reduction, it has no superior but the Dead Sea water, of which one hundred parts give solid contents 24.580, while the Atlantic ocean only averages three and a half per cent. of its weight, or about half an ounce to the pound. At the spring floods the Lake often rises several feet, and retiring in the summer, leaves vast deposits of crystalized salt. In places, large bayous could easily be filled during the summer by windmills upon the Lake shore, making millions of tons of salt at a trifling outlay. Considering the area of the Lake, 90 by 40 miles, and its average depth ten feet, this would give a little over a thousand billion solid feet of water, or at the rate above mentioned, 4,800,000,000 tons of salt! Estimating the population of the earth at 1200 millions, this would be enough to supply them all, as well as domestic animals, for a thousand years. All through the slopes northwest of the lake and down the western shore, are a number of springs running pure brine, and east of the Promontory, all the wells dug within five miles of the Lake have yielded salt water at a short depth.

If any one doubts the statement that the waters of the Lake are taken up by evaporation, and inclines to the hypothesis of an underground outlet, he can easily convince himself by dipping a basin of the water and exposing it for a few moments to the action of sun and wind; the drying air and the direct rays of the sun will evaporate it in an incredibly short space of time.

Very beautiful effects are produced by taking shrubs of dwarf oak or pine, and dashing the salt water over them at intervals of a few minutes, allowing the salt to form on the leaves in thin filmy crystals. The ingenuity of man seems in a fair way to utilize even the immense saline deposits in and near the Lake. The newly discovered process of reducing native ore, in which salt is extensively used, bids fair to be generally adopted, and, as there is valuable ore all over Nevada and three-fourths of

W

Utah, the day may not be distant when we will need all of this useful preservative, which is poured out here in such profusion as to seem a waste on the part of nature. Whence comes this salt? The mountain rains and melting snows carry the washings of the "salt mountains" of southern Utah to Utah Lake, where they are imperceptible to the taste, but are carried down by the Jordan; united with the contributions of Bear River and the brine springs of Promontory, they are subjected to the condensing process of nature in Great Salt Lake. If there were an underground outlet, a few months' discharge, with the constant reception of fresh water, would make it as fresh as Utah Lake. Standing on the shore of Great Salt Lake, one may observe the whole process of nature in rain formation, he may see the mist from the lake rise to a certain height, then form in light fleecy clouds which sail away to the mountains, where they are caught by projecting peaks and higher currents of air, and forced into denser masses, and at times he may observe them pouring upon the heights, the water which will run back and mingle with the mass at his feet, completing thus the cycle of moisture which Solomon remarked in the exactly similar phenomena of the Dead Sea; " All the rivers run into the sea, yet the sea is not full; to the place whence they came, thither the waters return."

The country bordering Great Salt Lake presents almost every possible variety of soil, but little or no change in climate.

First to the south lies Jordan Valley, which is generally meant when the people speak of Salt Lake Valley, forty miles long by about twelve in breadth; all the eastern half is valuable for agriculture, and most of the western for grazing. Proceeding northward a strip of salt marsh and low pasture land, near the Lake, is bounded on the east by a strip of fertile land from one to five miles wide, back of which are considerable pastures, even some distance up the mountain side. The same is true of Bear River Valley and the eastern slope of the Promontory, the former consisting of a fertile tract from ten to fifteen miles in width; but crossing Promontory to the west the change is sudden, and we find at the north-west corner of the Lake a valley of alkali flats and salt-beds of indescribable barrenness. The entire western shore is a perfect desert; a salt and arid waste of clay and sand, of the consistency of mortar in wet weather and a bed of stifling dust in dry; not even the sage brush and greasewood find life in the poisonous soil, and near the Lake thousands of acres lie glistening in the sun, bare white with salt and alkali. Running water is found in but one place, and even the scant springs are separated by journeys of fifty miles. It is comfortable to reflect that a further rise of five feet in the Lake surface would bring it upon this desert, with an area of seventy miles square to cover, and requiring at-least ten times as much water for a rise of one foot as it did ten years ago. Along the shore the atmosphere is bluish and hazy, and Captain Stansbury observes that "it is a labor to use telescopes for geodetic purposes, and astronomical observations are very imperfect." In the body of the Lake are several islands and projecting rocks, designated in the order of their size, as follows:

1. Antelope, also called Church or Mormon Island, having been appropriated by the corporation or Church of Latter-day Saints, for their stock, a sort of consecrated cattle-*corral*, "for the Lord and Bro. Brigham."

At the nearest point it is about twenty miles northwest of Salt Lake City; for many years the channel between it and the eastern shore was fordable, and is still occasionally; it contains a number of green valleys, and some springs of pure water.

In the shape of an irregular diamond, with a sharp western projection from the northern point, it is sixteen miles long, with an extreme width of seven miles; it contains many ridges and detached peaks, the highest 3,000 feet above the lake, and, consequently, 7,200 above sealevel. Near the north-eastern coast is a rock, called Egg Island, and on the most eastern cliff, "they say" there is a cave, with remarkable blue grottoes, of which "monstrous stories" have been told.

2. Stansby Island is the second largest in the Lake,

lying south-west of Antelope, near the western shore, with which it is connected, at rare intervals of low water, by a sand-pit. It is about half the size of Antelope Island, and consists of a single ridge, twelve miles in length, and rising three thousand feet above the lake. It is of some use for grazing purposes, and is frequented by ducks, geese, plover, gulls and pelicans.

3. Carrington Island, so named from the Mormon engineer, Albert Carrington, who assisted Captain Stansbury in his survey, is an irregular circle with a single central peak; it contains no springs, but abounds in a great variety of plants and flowers. It lies a little north-west of Stansbury, and west of the north point of Antelope Island, near the western shore.

4. Fremont Island lies between Antelope and Promontory Point, nearer the last, and just below the point where Bear River Bay opens into the central part of the lake. It is shaped somewhat like a half moon—abounds in plants, particularly the wild onion, but is destitute of wood and water. Colonel Fremont named it Disappointment Island, having been led to believe, before visiting it, that it abounded in "trees and shrubbery, teeming with game of every description;" Stansbury gave it its present name, and it is sometimes locally known as "Castle Island," suggested probably by the turretted formation of its principal peak.

5. Dolphin Island lies far up towards the north-western corner, a mere rocky knoll.

6. Hat Island, south-east of Gunnison, and another small island in the vicinity, are probably part of the same reef. The deepest sounding in the Lake, forty feet, is found between Stansbury and Antelope Islands. The latter is also rich in minerals, marble of the finest quality, and roofing slate, being readily obtained in large quantities. Boats could run directly alongside of the quarries and load with the greatest convenience. A considerable boating interest will yet be built up on the Lake, in which these islands will play an important part. On the eastern shores of the Lake are cultivated farms, populous towns, mines of all valuable metals; on the island are

valuable tracts of pasturage, and, at the foot of the surrounding mountains, are medicinal springs, hot and cold, sulphur, iron and soda. The summer air of the Lake is light, saline and health-inspiring; the scenery unsurpassed, and abounding in views of memorable beauty. The romance of this *Mare Mortuum* has survived the investigations of science, and, from a region of misconception and fable, the vicinity of the Great Salt Lake has become the Switzerland of America.

Besides the noted "Dead Sea," the Great Basin is well provided with lakes, such as they are, of which those in Utah constitute an irregular chain from north to south.

Bear Lake, a mere "tarn" among the mountains, extending from Cache Valley into Idaho, is chiefly notable as the home of the "Bear Lake Monster," a nondescript, with a body half seal, half serpent, and a head somewhat like a sea lion, which has often been seen and described by Indians and Mormons, but never by white Christians, that I have heard of. It has never been properly classified or named, as it is invisible when scientific observers are at hand, but, from the description current among the latter-day Philosophers, I judge it to be a relic of that instinct species generally denominated the "Ginasticutis."

The sweetwater reservoir, Utah Lake, is fed by large streams from the western slopes of the Uintah range, its circumference, exclusive of offsets, being estimated at eighty miles. This singular analogue of the Sea of Galilee, receives the waters from the southern mountains, containing a few grains of salt to the gallon, and, after furnishing space for considerable evaporation, discharges them, by way of Jordan, into Great Salt Lake. Sevier, Preuss, Nicolet, and Little Salt Lake, in like manner, receive and furnish "sinks" for the waters from the Iron Mountain range, and the southern branch of the Wasatch, none of these lakes communicating with any other, but each dependent on a distinct water system. Only the larger streams form lakes, the smaller are either evaporated or sink in ponds and puddles of black mire; the waters in places reappear or pass underground to feed the larger lakes.

The deserts of Utah consist of alkali flats, barren sand or red earth, resulting, in most instances, merely from the lack of water, for where this can be supplied in sufficient abundance, the alkali is, in no long time, washed away; and many of the sandy districts, once thought to be irreclaimably barren, have been proved quite fertile by irrigation. It is quite evident, also, that a change has been going on for many years, reclaiming large tracts in the vicinity of the mountains. Tracts, entirely barren a score of years ago, after receiving the wash of higher lands, present a scant growth of grease-wood, which is succeeded in time by white sage-brush, and that in turn by the ranker growth of blue sage-brush, each step marking an increase of fertility in the soil. Large tracts are found entirely barren of vegetation, others that have advanced to the grease-wood stage, still others to the growth of sage-brush. In many places the transition is evident, and, from the testimony of early explorers, certain tracts have completed the entire circuit of increasing fertility within the memory of man.

Utah is in the parallel of the Mediterranean, but the elevation renders it more bleak, though not liable to sudden vicissitudes of temperature; the changes in any one winter are quite moderate, but the difference between successive winters is often much greater than in any other part of the United States. Cattle have been wintered in Cache Valley, Ogden Hole, and other sections, entirely upon the range, and without shelter; on the other hand, there have been winters in which all the settlements were isolated, when snow fell almost every day, with a high westerly wind, sometimes so high that spray was carried from the lake into the city.

The first two winters the Mormons spent in the valley were unusually mild, cattle living along the streams without feed; the third winter and that of 1854-55 were exceedingly harsh, and the people being unused to make provisions therefor, many hundred cattle perished in the snow.

Twenty years ago, rain very seldom fell between May and October; in 1860 it continued quite showery, even to the first of July, and, at present, some rain may be counted on with certainty every month in the season. The change is attributed, by one class of philosophers, to a gradual change of the rain zones; by the Mormons, to their prayers and piety, and the favor of Heaven, but is probably due to cultivation and planting. The same phenomenon is observed in western Nebraska and Kansas, and in upper Egypt. The Indians say "the pale face brings his rain with him." The summer, as marked by the thermometer, is hot, but the great elevation, the lightness and dryness of the air, the cool winds from the cañons, and the complete absence of malaria, render it delightful and wholesome.

At the north end of the lake they have the sea-breeze, the mountain air and the refreshing zephyrs from the plains. During the last summer the thermometer usually rose eight or ten degrees from sun-rise till noon; the greatest mid-day heat was not oppressive, and the mornings and evening, cooled by the mountain airs, were deliciously soft and pure.

The most disagreeable feature of this section is the dust-storms and thunder-storms, which, during the last season, though not frequent, were severe. Showers are expected when the clouds come from the west and southwest; from the east they will cling to the hills. Cultivation and irrigation giving greater facilities for evaporation, the process of nature in the cycle of moisture is quickened, the particles of water make the circuit oftener, and more frequent showers are the result. It is evident this climate of cool, dry air in the winter, moderate dryness and extreme tenuity in the summer, and stimulating rarity at all seasons, is suited to all healthy and most sickly constitutions. Paralysis is rare, consumption almost unknown—the climate lacks that humidity which developes the predisposition—asthma and phthisis meet with immediate relief, and, from my personal experience, it is evident that the air tends to expand, strengthen and give tonic force to the lungs. But rheumatism and neuralgia are by no means uncommon; as in other bracing climates, they affect the poor, and those from any cause, insufficiently fed, housed or clothed, during the winter. For all who would avoid humidity, either in soil or air; who seek relief from pulmonary diseases or dyspepsia, the climate is unsurpassed; but for inflammatory diseases the good effects of this climate are still open to debate.

CHAPTER XIX.

MATERIAL RESOURCES OF UTAH.

Amount of arable land—Its nature and location—Increased rainfall—Causes—Probable greater increase—Mode of irrigation—Aquarian Socialism—No room for competition—Alkali—Some advantages—Yield of various crops—"Beet sugar"—Sorghum syrup—Mormon improvements (?)—Grossly exaggerated—True Wealth of Utah—Mining and grazing—Bunch-grass—Mountain pastures—Sheep and goats—"Fur, fin and feather"—Trapping and hunting—Carnivora—Ruminants—Buffalo—None in the Basin—Shoshonee tradition—Game, fowl—Amphibia—"Sandy toad"—Serpents—Fish—Oysters in Salt Lake—Insects—"Mormon bedbugs"—Advantages from the dry air—Insectivora—Crickets—Grasshoppers or locusts?—Indians of Utah—Rapid extinction—"Diggers"—"Club-men"—Utes—Shoshonees—Their origin—Mormon theory—Scientific theory—Chinese annals—Tartars in America—Mormon settlers—Twenty-three years of "gathering"—Much work, slow progress—Reasons—Inherent weakness of the system—Great apostacy—Their present number—Exaggeration—Enumeration of settlements and population—Nationality—Total military force---Future of the Territory.

OF the entire area of the Great Basin, probably one half is a complete desert to begin with; one-third is of value for grazing purposes, and the remaining one-sixth agricultural land.

Most of the complete desert is in Nevada, and at least three-fourths of the fertile land in Utah. In the entire basin are numbered thirty-five considerable valleys containing cultivable land, of great, or, at least, average fertility, of which the best known are the Jordan or Salt Lake, Bear River, Sevier, Cache Tovelle, Ruby, Malad, Carson, and Humboldt Valleys. Of these, all those in Utah are fully occupied by the Mormons, except Bear River, on which they have but a few settlements, and those along the mountains eastward. The entire basin thus contains about as much good land as the State of Indiana, and three or four times as much of little or no value.

Even the most fertile valleys contain occasional desert tracts, generally of small extent, of which tracts, Bear River and Cache Valleys contain the least. The Sevier Valley is peculiar in its features; the fertile tracts are apparently richer than in the more northern valleys, but the deserts much more barren and desolate in appearance; the traveller, in places, traversing an arid waste five or ten miles in width, the bare, gray sand unrelieved even by white sage-brush, and then at a sudden turn of the road into a mountain cove, or a depression in the land, finding a few thousand acres of beauty and fertility.

Towards the upper part of its course, that valley presents a rare picture of romantic beauty. Wood and water are abundant, game plenty, and the soil very rich along the foot of the mountains. The agricultural system of Utah would present many novel features to an eastern farmer, and at first view the difficulties would seem to him insurmountable.

The most marked feature of the interior plains is the scarcity of timber; for, with the exception of a few scant willows along two or three of the streams, the whole valley of Salt Lake was originally as bare of trees as if blasted by the breath of a volcano.

The nearest timber to Salt Lake City, fit for fuel, is fifteen miles distant, and that up City Creek Cañon, which belongs to Brigham Young, by act of Territorial Legislature; and he requires every third load to be left at his *corral.* So, most of the fuel used in the city comes from cañons twenty or twenty-five miles distant, and ranges from twelve to thirty dollars per cord.

This evil has been greatly increased by their stripping the heights more bare every year, and many conjecture that this prevents the former heavy accumulations of snow, which, in turn, blows into the valley worse each winter, and may in time even lessen the source of the streams, which are chiefly supplied by the melting snow.

Planting trees, except in orchards or along the streets, has been entirely neglected. Unlike the farmers of Iowa and Nebraska, who purpose to grow their own fire-wood, there is, not to my knowledge, an artificial grove in the entire valley.

True, the trees would require occasional irrigation, but with the facilities afforded by the many little streams crossing the "bench," one man could easily attend to several thousand acres, and though his returns would be slow, they would in time be ample. The suggestion may sometime be found practicable.

The second drawback is want of water, or rather of rain, for there is plenty of the article in streams which are the source of supply.

At the first settlement of Utah there were periods of five or six months without rain, but of late years there has been a great change in that respect, and last summer rains were so frequent along the streams that many tracts required no irrigation at all. This is probably due to the same cause as the similar phenomenon in other places; but the change has probably been greater here, as irrigation, distributing the water so generally over the land in ditches and through fields, has presented a greater scope for solar evaporation, the great right hand of "cloud-compelling Jove."

This has increased the fall of rain, which must, in turn, add to the productive force of nature, till in time irrigation will be needless for the small grains and cereals.

Under the present system, each settlement becomes a sort of "socialistic community" as to its water supply.— Enough of families must make a settlement together in some convenient valley, to construct a dam further up the cañon, from which reservoir a main canal is carried through the settlement, and from this side canals and ditches convey the water among the farms, and thence into fields, and by tiny rivulets between the rows of vegetation.

The various crops are watered from one to three times per week, according to their nature, during the dry season. The greatest labor is in establishing a settlement, and opening these sources of public supply, but thereafter, the whole settlement turns out each spring, at the call of the Water-Marshal, and a few days' work gets all in order.

Hence the settlement must move as a unit in this case,

and every man claims a supply of water according to the money or labor contributed to the first construction.

For many years, in certain settlements, the Water-Marshal turned the supply to different districts at different hours, and the proprietors in each district further divided the time when each might take water; day and night during the dry season, being devoted to the work. In some settlements, and in the city, fines as high as sixty dollars were imposed for "stealing water," that is, for turning it on one's fields out of the prescribed time. But with the increase of rain and heavy dews which now water "the garden of the Lord and modern Zion," this aquatic penuriousness has ceased to be necessary, and there are but few if any localities where one may not "take water" at any hour.

The great expense is in getting the system started; after that it need not be as great as the losses attendant on waiting for rain in other regions, or having too much of it at a time. Herein also is an important politico-religious feature of the system; no Gentile can start in with a new settlement, formed as it is by a "call" from the Church authorities, and he cannot, of course, go it alone. Gentiles could only settle by entire neighborhoods together, or in some place buy out a Saint whose water-rights are already established, and run with the land. For these and other reasons, one rarely meets with a Gentile outside of the towns.

Alkali is another enemy of the Utah farmer. A moderate infusion is thought to be an advantage, but in many places it is so thick as to "flower out" like a heavy frost or light snow on the surface; there it is fatal to most crops, and many think it will not yield to the longest continued cultivation. Some crops will flourish, where it is abundant, others are ruined by the slightest sprinkle. The common pie-plant entirely loses its acidity, and the sorghum cane is completely "alkalied."

But the principle of compensation in nature applies even here, and the Utah farmer has some marked advantages. There are neither droughts nor freshets—both considerable items to an Illinois farmer; the latter are unknown, and the former of no consequence in the practice of irrigation. In the summer of 1866, there occurred a furious wind and rain storm in the locality of the writer's residence in the States, which destroyed corn, wheat and fruit, to the value of fifty thousand dollars in one township. This amount would have irrigated for many years, a tract in Utah as large as that township.

Wheat for many seasons has required but one or two waterings, and in 1867 the average yield, according to Mormon statistics, was seventeen bushels per acre. With flour at eighteen dollars per barrel, and last year it was sometimes above that, this would pay well for irrigation.

Barley and potatoes yield very heavily, and have heretofore sold at enormous prices. But the last year there has been a great decline in prices. The land produces all the small grains, especially wheat, oats and barley, in great abundance; a little Indian corn is raised, but the climate is not favorable; nearly all the fruits and vegetables of the temperate zone, pumpkins, beets and carrots—in Gentile slang, "Mormon currency"—in great size and plenty. Peaches of fine flavor, and in great quantity, are grown in almost every valley. Salt Lake Valley and the lower tracts adjacent being most favorable. But I do not fully appreciate the apples of Salt Lake; they seem insipid, stunted in some places and overgrown in others, and decidedly "pithy." The lower part of Bear River Valley and the slopes leading thereto, have all the natural indications for one of the finest fruit countries in the world, the easy changes of the winter and spring being peculiarly favorable.

Beets and onions grows to an unusual size, which suggested, in 1853, the idea of making beet sugar. The "inspired priesthood," headed by "Brother Brigham," entered into the matter with zeal; one hundred thousand dollars were expended upon the building and machinery, but the Lord must have "spoken to the Prophet with an uncertain voice;" for the experiment failed utterly; on account of the alkali, the Mormons say; for want of good management, say the perverse Gentiles, who sometimes add that the Saints made a fiery article of "Valley Tan" whiskey out of the useless material. But other sweets abound; there is great profit in sorghum, and one farmer near Kaysville reports that last year he made one hundred and five gallons from one-third of an acre, and two hundred gallons per acre throughout his field. At the low price of one dollar per gallon, this will pay for irrigation. But cane farmers must avoid the alkali lands. Of farm improvements there is little to be said. The impression prevails quite generally that the Mormons are remarkably industrious. I have impartially endeavored to find the evidence, but, with due regard for others' opinions, I fail to see it. They have built houses, barns and fences, but such as they were absolutely forced to have in order to live at all. If there is a single farm-house between Salt Lake City and Bear River, which shows an advanced idea of architecture, I do not remember it.

If there is any particular development of taste, outside a few of the cities, any adornment which shows an aspiration for the higher and more beautiful, or any improvements indicating comprehensive grasp and energy of thought, I have missed them in my travels. The Mormon converts are drawn from the most industrious races of Europe; it was impossible for even Mormonism to entirely spoil them, and they have done nearly as well, perhaps, as any other people would have done under the same circumstances.

Compared with the same races in the Western States, the Swedes, Norwegians, Danes and English, of Iowa or Minnesota, the latter have made as much progress in five years after settlement as the Mormons in ten or twenty. But on the credit side of the estimate for the latter, we must set down the fact of their great distance from civilization, the natural barrenness of much of their country, the grasshoppers, crickets, wild beasts and Indians with which they had to contend; the spiritual despotism under which they labor; their poverty and their ignorance of this mode of farming; on the debit side, the advantages from overland travel, and neighboring mining regions, which enabled them to obtain fabulous prices for their grain, the general advantages of a new country in "fur, fin and feather," the rare healthfulness of their climate, the unlimited range for stock and the benefits of unity in their labor system.

The wonder is that they settled there at all; having settled there, they have done less in the way of improvement than their countrymen in other sections in half the time.

But the true wealth of the territory is in grazing and mining. The range is practically unlimited and the mountain bunch-grass is the best in the world for cattle. This valuable and rather anomalous provision of nature seems to be indigenous to the interior plains of the Rocky Mountains. It is first found, I believe, on the western slope of the Black Hills, and extends to the eastern slope of the Sierra Nevadas. West of that boundary it gives place to other seeded grasses of the Pacific slope, and to the "wild oats" of California, which are supposed to have been introduced by the Spaniards. Millions of acres are rendered valuable by the presence of bunch-grass, which, without it, could hardly be traversed by cattle. As the name indicates it grows in clumps, and to an eastern eye would appear as if it sought the most barren spots, flourishing even upon slopes of sandy and stony hills. Like winter wheat it remains green and juicy under the snow; it usually commences growing in February or March, and continues till May or June, when it dries up and appears to die, but in the form of a light straw contains abundant nutriment. In places, during autumn and after shedding the seed, it puts forth a green shoot, apparently within the old withered stalk; with the advance of summer the best is found higher up the mountains, and it thus furnishes food the year round.

It yields a small pyriform seed, which is greedily devoured by cattle, and has remarkable fattening properties, giving an excellent flavor to the beef. It is often a subject of remark, how little food will fatten cattle upon the elevated prairies, and interior plateaus of the West; the exceeding purity, dryness and rarity of the air, by perfecting the processes of digestion and assimilation, no doubt accounts for this.

The same has been observed of the highlands of Central Asia. From the same causes cattle endure a greater degree of cold without shelter, and the plains can be made to produce abundant forage for winter. The finest, juciest, tenderest steaks of home growth, appear daily upon the tables of the Utah publicans, and there is scarcely a limit to the possible supply. By greater improvement in irrigation, and by the increase of rain, Utah will in time have great agricultural wealth, but stock raising will be her best paying interest.

Facilities for grazing are practically unbounded, the valleys supply plentiful pasturage in winter, and as spring advances and the snow line recedes up the hills, cattle will find fresh pastures.

In the valleys of Green, Grand and Colorado rivers are many thousand square miles of the finest country in the world for wool growing; on all the mountain slopes west of Bear River grass grows luxuriantly, and the higher portions of Sevier Valley contain millions of acres of grazing land, the natural home of the Merino sheep and Cashmere goat; the climate and elevation are exactly suitable for the production of the finest wools; all the facilities for manufacturing exist along the lower course of the mountain streams, and the day *will* come when the finest of shawls and other fabrics will be produced in Utah, rivalling the most famous productions from the highlands of Persia and Hindostan.

Of "fur, fin and feather," the Great Basin is rather deficient, in an economical view. There are minks, ermines, American badgers, wolverines, woodchucks, musk-rats, beavers and otters, the last two rare in other parts, but still found in such plenty on the upper tributaries of Bear River, as to make trapping profitable. The principal *carnivora* are the cougar, cat-o-mountain, large and small wolf, and a variety of foxes. Of the ruminants we find the antelope, deer, elk and Rocky Mountain sheep. The buffalo is seldom found west of Laramie plains, not at all in the Great Basin, though the Indians have a tradition that they were once very numerous even to the Sierra Nevadas, and old hunters and travellers speak of finding traces of their former existence there. The Shoshonees give the following account of their banishment: When the buffaloes herded in great numbers in these valleys, the crickets were less in number than now, but being the weakest of all the animals, they had the ear of the Great Spirit when oppressed. The buffaloes, in crowding to the rivers to drink, trampled upon the crickets and did not heed their cries, upon which the latter complained to the Great Spirit, who by a sweeping decree changed all the buffaloes to a small race of crickets, leaving nothing of the buffalo but the *milt* ! It is a singular fact that the crickets found in the basin contain a " milt " or *spleen*, exactly similar in shape to that of the bovine *genus*.

Of game birds there are several varieties: quail or partridges; two varieties of grouse, the most common called the sage-hen; the mallard duck is found in great plenty on the lower part of Bear River and Jordan, and is particularly abundant on the Sevier; while brant, curlew, plover and wild geese are much more numerous than the appearance of the country would indicate. Of useless animals and reptiles there are quite enough to give variety to animated nature. That purely western American phenomenon, half toad, half lizard, locally known as the " horned toad" or " sandy toad," scientifically ranked *Phrynosoma*, is found on all the high, dry plains. Its scaly body and inability to jump prevents its ranking strictly among " batrachians." It is found on the highest and driest ridges, is calloused on the belly like an alligator, its back is thickly studded with horny points about a quarter of an inch in length, it has legs like a common toad but runs swiftly like a lizard.

Of serpents, there are rattlesnakes, water snakes and swamp adders, and a few others, all very rare. The fishes are perch, pike, bass, chub, mountain trout, and a species of salmon trout, of which thirty-pound specimens have been caught. There are very few molluscs, periwinkles or snails. There has been much discussion of a project to plant oysters in Salt Lake at the various river mouths, but the scheme seems to have been abandoned. Probably it would not succeed, from the extreme density of the lake water, which is often driven some distance up the rivers by high winds.

In view of the desirableness of any country as a place of residence, the entomology is no inconsiderable item. Utah, in regard to insect life, is subject to great extremes. On entering the Territory from the east, the visitor's first impression would be that both animal and insect life were rare. On the road from Green River to Salt Lake City, particularly in the early part of the season, there are few stock flies, few scavengers and few large birds; troublesome insects are rare, even in the valleys, and unknown on the upland desert; but in other localities there is a surplus, and after longer residence one finds enough of them to be troublesome.

In Salt Lake City the flies are probably worse, both as to number and peculiarities, than in any other city in America, but fortunately their time is very short. During the spring and early summer they are rarely seen; in August they begin to multiply, " coming in with the emigration," according to local phrase, meaning the Mormon emigrants, who formerly completed the journey across the plains by the latter part of July.

From the middle of August till cool weather they are perfectly fearful, certainly much worse than they need be if proper cleanliness were practised; large, flat-headed, light-winged and awkward, they light and crawl over the person in the most annoying manner, not yielding, like " Gentile flies," to a light brush or switch, but requiring literally to be swept off. No other part of the Territory I have visited, is half so bad in this respect as Salt Lake City, and the southern valleys seem peculiarly free from this pest.

Fleas are, in western phrase, " tolerable bad," but bed bugs are intolerable; both in numbers and voracity those of Utah beat the world, particularly in the country towns, and among the poorer classes of foreign-born Mormons. In certain settlements their ravages are incredible, and Mormon bed bugs seem as much worse than others as their human companions. Like the latter, too, they seem to regard the Gentile as fair prey. More than once, in some secluded valley, has the writer retired to rest (intentionally) with reckless confidence, and after an hour of fierce resolution to hold out against any amount of blood letting, has risen from his couch with a full appreciation of Byron's beautiful line :

" No sleep till morn—"

I have given the worst side of affairs first, and in other respects the resident is rather free from annoyance. Mosquitoes are bad in very few places ; three-fourths of the country is entirely exempt, lacking humidity enough to produce them. With stock flies the case is much the same; in places along Bear River, and other streams where the current is sluggish they are troublesome, though such places are rare. In places around the Lake gnats are troublesome, and Captain Stansbury speaks of encountering on the western shore dense swarms of small black flies, of which he says : "An incredible number perfectly covered the white sand near the shore, changing its color completely—a fact only revealed as the swarms rose upon being disturbed by our footsteps. They, too, had apparently been driven in by the storm; for I afterwards discovered that they were as thick upon the water as the land, moving over its surface with great ease and swiftness. In the shallows left by the receding waters, I noticed also quite a number of ants (the first I had seen) drowned seemingly by the over-flow. Both of these insects furnished food for the gulls and snipes, which are almost the only birds found along this shore. Across the little bay ran a broad streak of froth or foam, formed by the meeting of counter currents, and driven in by the wind. Passing through it I found it filled with the small black flies, in the midst of which were flocks of gulls, floating upon the water and industriously engaged in picking them up, precisely as a chicken would pick up grains of corn, and with the same rapidity of motion."

With the exceptions noted, the whole of Utah is remarkably free from insects ; there are few, if any, of the thousand varieties of wood-borers, *aphides, terebræ, curculio,* weevil, wheat-fly, and the numberless insects that infest the grass and the bark of trees in lower altitudes; they are either totally wanting, or found so seldom as to be innoxious. In consequence there are very few birds of the insect-eating kinds, and no particularly dangerous reptiles. Of insects destructive to vegetation the cricket was once very troublesome, but ceased to be so at least ten years ago, though the grasshopper still makes occasional visits, as in all the Territories. The question has been raised in Utah, whether this insect, locally known as *grasshopper* is not really a locust—perhaps *the* locust mentioned in Scripture. But an examination shows it to be congeneric with the insect scientifically designated the OEDIPODA MIGRATORIA, which is certainly of the grasshopper species, though known in the East by the English name of "migratory locust."

The grasshopper of Utah is not so long and thin, light-bodied and "clipper-built" as that of Nebraska and Kansas, but fully as destructive to vegetation; though of late years its ravages have been confined to certain limited localities. Though numerous enough in Salt Lake City the past season to constitute a "visitation," they did very little damage—"poisoning the skin of apples" to a slight extent.

From grasshoppers to Indians may seems to the Eastern mind an abrupt transition; but the original inhabitants of Utah merit a brief notice. All the old accounts represent the Indians of the Great Basin as the lowest and most degraded of their race, and one is surprised in the chronicles of only thirty years ago to read of tribes, or rather bands and parts of tribes, now totally extinct.

The "Club-men," a race of savage and filthy cannibals, were once quite numerous in all the central and western valleys, but are now entirely extinct; and many of the races mentioned by M. Violet, who lived among the Shoshonees thirty-five years ago, are no longer to be found.

From these and other facts, it is very probable that all the Indians known as "diggers" were mere outcasts from other tribes, or the remnants of more noble tribes conquered in war, which had been forced into the Basin as a place of refuge.

Their tribal organization broken up; their former hunting grounds forbidden them; and themselves compelled to subsist only on the meanest and least nourishing fare, they degenerated rapidly in *morale* and physique, at the same time that they decreased in number.

They subsisted chiefly upon roots dug from the ground, the seeds of various plants indigenous to the soil, ground into a kind of flour between flat stones; and upon lizards, crickets, and fish at some seasons of the year. Thus lacking the food which furnishes proper stimulus to the brain and muscles, each succeeding generation sank lower in the scale of humanity; the generative powers declined under a regimen of exposure and scant nourishment; few children were born and fewer reared to maturity, and the kindness of nature's law forbade increase where life promised naught but exposure and misery. Of such races the numerical decline must have been steady and rapid, and their numbers only maintained by the successive additions from the superior races north and east. A little above these, in the scale of humanity, are the Utes or Utahs, inhabiting nearly all the southern part of the Great Basin, and extending into Colorado as far as the boundary of the Arapahoes, with whom they are almost continually at war. The word Ute or Utah signifies, in their language, "man," "dweller," or "resident," and by the additions of other syllables, we have the three grand divisions of that race: Pi-Utes, Gosha-Utes, Pah-Utes,. which may be freely translated "mountaineers," "valley men," and "dwellers by the water," those prefixes respectively indicating "mountain," "valley," and "water." Of all these the bravest are the mountain Utes, among whom we might include the Uintahs; but the Indians of the lower countries are rather cowardly, and dangerous only by theft or treachery. Far superior to any of these are the Shoshonees or Snakes, found all along the northern border of Utah, and extending thence north-east to the Bannacks and westward into Idaho and Nevada.

They have a complete tribal organization, and something like government and council among themselves; own horses and cattle, and display some ingenuity in their dwellings, and in the construction of fish weirs and traps of willow bushes. They feel also something like pride of race, and to call a Shoshonee a "digger," is more of an insult than to stigmatize a very light mulatto as a "nigger."

The origin of the Indians has been a subject of frequent inquiry among American antiquarians. Some forty years ago, an idea was broached, and for awhile prevailed quite extensively, that they were the descendants of the "lost tribes" of ancient Israel, and that veracious chronicle, the "Book of Mormon," has traced their descent from a Jewish family, who left Jerusalem six hundred years before Christ. But if we are to draw our arguments from any recognized human source, from language, features, customs, habits or traditions, there are no two races on earth of whose kinship there is so little proof.

The features may be greatly altered by climate, customs may change with circumstances, and two thousand years may be long enough to pervert the radical principles of a people's religion; but language, not as to single words but as to grammatical construction and derivation, has ever been considered the surest test of ethnological relationship; and every fact in the language of the Jews and those of various Indian tribes disproves the theory of a common origin. To cite but one: languages are divided into primitive, and derivative or compound; the latter showing by their combinations a derivation from older tongues, and the former maintaining their simple formation, consisting of a certain number of radical syllables.

A primitive language is never derived from a compound one, the latter is from the former.

The Indian languages are all primitive, showing no derivation from any older language, even the occasional words of similar sound being evidently accidental, and not nearly so numerous as those of the same form in the Greek and the language of the South Sea cannibals. The Hebrew, on the contrary, is a derivative language, the outgrowth of older Semetic dialects, and by its finish and complex structure, the language of the Psalms shows that mankind had even then at least two thousand years of progress and cultivation in language. Such a speech may be corrupted in the mouths of a barbarous people, but can never return to its primitive type; through a thousand variations and centuries of corruption and foreign intermixture, though constantly debased, it will become more complex and farther from its radical formation. In all other branches of the inquiry, a parallel between the Jews and Indians is found only in two, or at most, three points of their religion; both believe in *one God*, an all pervading *Spirit*, and in sacrifices; the latter belief they share with nearly all the races of men, and the former with many of them. M. Violet, a Frenchman who came to California forty years ago, and spent many years among the Shoshonees, investigated their language and traditions with much care, and came to the conclusion that they were descendants of the Mantcheux Tartars. His reasons are good, and subsequent discoveries confirm the probable truth of his theory. The lately discovered Chinese annals, which give an account of the expeditions sent out by the Tartar Kublai Khan, about the year 1280, A.D., which visited California, Mexico, Central America and Peru, show that they then recognized the fact that the country had been previously settled by men of another branch of their race. But it is not necessary to suppose all the Indians descended from one branch of the Tartars: the passage of the North Pacific being a proved fact, no doubt several different invasions of our western coast took place dating, perhaps, even as far back as the fourth generation after Noah, who, it is generally agreed, settled China, and who may be supposed to have known something about navigation.

Of the first discovery and exploration of the Great Basin, this is not the proper place to treat; but after the Indians, in the order of time, came the Mormons. They were the first white residents, and their history is the history of the Territory. Since July 24th, 1847, this has been their gathering place, the Territory of "the Lord and Brother Brigham;" a consecrated land of salt, alkali and religious concubinage ; where their morals were to be *cured*, and their spiritual interests *preserved*.

When we consider how many million people there are in the world to whom Mormonism is the natural religion, how full modern society is of the material for such a church, that it promises a heaven exactly after the natural heart of man, and with the least sacrifice of human pride, lust and passion; when we add to this their vast and comprehensive missionary system, compassing sea and land to make one proselyte ; and the still more powerful fact that Mormonism comes to the poor of the old world not merely with the attractiveness of a new religion, but with the certainty of assisted emigration to America, a land described to them as flowing with milk and honey, we would naturally expect their recruits to be numbered by tens of thousands annually.

That Utah has not filled up and overflowed half a dozen times with the scum of Europe, can only be accounted for by some inherent weakness in the system itself.

This weakness shows itself in two ways: inability to secure a class who would add real dignity and strength to a new commonwealth, and the constant loss through a steady and ever increasing apostacy. Unfettered American enterprise planted half a million people in Iowa in ten years ; the vast machinery of the Mormon emigration system, the excitement of religious fanaticism, the utmost zeal of a thousand missionaries preaching temporal prosperity and eternal salvation to an ignorant people, backed by the assurance of a speedy passage to a new country, and aided by the advantages of an organization at once ecclesiastical and secular, have succeeded in twenty-three years in fixing an uncertain population of a hundred thousand in Utah. The Mormon system of exaggerating their numbers is well known. At the death of Joe Smith, they numbered nearly 200,000 throughout the world; their own statistics showed half a million— (*Times and Seasons, Millennial Star*, etc.)

If they have half the latter number now, it is not shown by their published statistics.

Their missionaries in the Eastern States give their strength in Utah, in round numbers, at 200,000. When Brigham Young was last questioned on that point, by a well-known politician last summer, he put the number at 120,000.

A Judge of the U. S. Court who has travelled extensively through the Territory, with good opportunities for judging, estimates the total population of Utah at 85,000, probably a little too low. Tourists usually state the population of Salt Lake City in round numbers, at 25,000. There are in that city a little less than 1,800 houses, of all sizes, counting the barely habitable; allowing ten persons to the dwelling, we have 18,000, a very full estimate. Gentile communities average five persons to the dwelling, but in Utah we must double to allow for infants and extra wives. The population of the Territory may be estimated with tolerable certainty from the census of former years, and well-known facts. By reference to the U. S. census of 1860, it appears there were then in Utah 20,225 males and 20,018 females; total 40,273.

The rate of increase in ten years throughout the United States is less than forty per cent.; if we allow the excessive ratio of 150 per cent. in Utah, it would make the population this year 100,000. It will not escape observation in passing that the males slightly out-number the females, not exactly indicating polygamy as the natural law. The latest report we have at hand is that of Mr. Campbell, Mormon superintendent of common schools, for the year 1863, in which appears the following:

Number of boys between six and eighteen........3,950
Number of girls between four and sixteen........3,662
Total..7,612

We cannot suppose from any known law of population that the children between four and eighteen *were less than one-sixth* of the whole people. This would give us 46,000 nearly, for 1863, a very moderate increase over 1860. It is hardly reasonable to suppose that the Mormons have increased *more than* 100 *per cent.* in seven years. Here again we see that the boys slightly outnumber the girls, which will make it rather difficult for some of them to get wives, if polygamy lasts through that generation. From personal observation and the best information obtainable, I sum up the Mormon population of Utah, beginning on the north, as follows:

Cache and Bear Lake Valleys	13,000
Thence to Brigham City	2,000
Brigham City	2,000
West of Bear River	1,000
Thence to Ogden	1,000
Ogden and vicinity	4,000
Kaysville and vicinity	1,500
Farmington and vicinity	2,500
Centreville	1,500
Bountiful (Session's Settlement)	2,000
Weber Valley to Echo	2,500
Coalville, Wanship and Upper Weber	4,000
Total north of Salt Lake City	37,000
Salt Lake City and near vicinity	20,000
Thence to Utah Lake	7,000
Provo	4,000
Remainder of Utah Lake district	8,000
Sevier and San Pete Valleys	3,000
Provo to St. George	6,000
St. George and vicinity	3,000
Southern settlements	7,000
Tooille and Ruby Valleys	4,000
West of the last named (?)	1,000
Grand total	100,000

The population extends along an irregular line, or rather are, five hundred miles from north and south; a band fifty miles wide would include all the settlements, except a few immediately west, east and north-east of Salt Lake City; nor have I made any deduction on account of the southern settlements, now known to be in Nevada and Arizona, or the few in the southern edge of Idaho.

Of the entire population, the adult portion is made up very nearly as follows: from Great Britain, one-half; from Sweden, Norway and Denmark, one-third; a dozen or twenty each from Ireland, Italy, France and Prussia; a few Oriental; five Jews; a score or two of Kanakas; and the remaining one-seventh or eighth, American. The children, of course, are nearly all natives. While the foreigners are as seven or eight to one in the body of the Church, the Americans are about six to one in the Presidencies, Quorum of Apostles, leading Bishops and Elders, showing, pretty conclusively, the "ruling race." We are bound to say that our fellow-countrymen are smart, if they are rascally.

The entire Mormon people probably include nearly ten thousand men capable of bearing arms, of whom those in the northern settlements, and the American portion generally, know something of drill and the use of firearms; of the Scandinavians, their skill may be judged from the fact that a thousand or more of them were driven out of Sevier Valley by three hundred Mountain Utes, twenty-two of the latter, in one battle, defeating a hundred and fifty militia. But the English and American Saints in the north, displayed considerable bravery under Lot Smith, and other leaders, in 1857, when Buchanan "crushed the Mormons."

Whether they are still confident of their ability "to thrash the United States," cannot well be known. After a careful statement of its resources, Lieut. J. W. Gunnison, assistant to Capt. Stansbury, estimates that the entire Territory is capable of sustaining a population of one million persons, entirely by grazing and agriculture.

The area is but half as large as at that time, and, from my knowledge of fertile land still unoccupied, I am convinced that this estimate will apply proportionably at present. Thus, within the present limits of Utah may be developed a State, with a population of half a million engaged in agriculture, grazing, and domestic manufacture, and a quarter of a million more engaged in mining. But long before that occurs, the Territory must undergo a political and social change, and Mormonism give way to Christianity, progress and enterprise.

CHAPTER XX.

MORMON MYSTERIES—THEIR ORIGIN.

The Endowment—Actors—Scenery and dress—Pre-requisites—Adam and Eve, the Devil and Michael, Jehovah and Eloheim—A new version—Blasphemous assumptions—Terrible oaths—Barbarous penalties — Origin — Scriptures and Paradise Lost - Eleusinian mysteries — "Morgan's Free-masonry"—The witnesses—Probabilities—Their reasons—Changes.

THE ENDOWMENT.

Dramatis Personæ.

ELOHEIM, or *Head God*...............	Brigham Young,
JEHOVAH...........................	George A. Smith,
JESUS..............................	Daniel H. Wells,
MICHAEL...........................	George Q. Cannon,
SATAN.............................	W. W. Phelps,
APOSTLE PETER.....................	Joseph F. Smith,
APOSTLE JAMES.....................	John Taylor,
APOSTLE JOHN......................	Erastus Snow,
EVE...............................	Miss Eliza R. Snow.

Clerk, Washers, Attendants, Sectarians, Chorus and Endowees.

I.

THE FIRST (PRE-EXISTENT) ESTATE.

THE candidates present themselves at the Endowment House, provided with clean clothes and a lunch; they are admitted to the outer office, and their accounts with the Church verified by the clerk. Their names, ages, and the dates of their conversion and baptism are entered in the register; their tithing receipts are carefully inspected, and, if found correct, an entry thereof is made. This last is an indispensable before initiation. Evidence is also presented of faithful attendance on public service, and at the "School of the Prophets." If any husband and wife appear who have not been sealed for eternity, a

SCENES IN THE ENDOWMENT CEREMONIES.

1. Preparation—Washing and Anointing. 2. Eloheim Cursing Adam and Eve—Satan Driven out 3. Trial of Faith—The "Searching Hand." 4. Oath to Avenge the Death of Joseph Smith 5. The "Blood Atonement."

note is made of the fact, the ceremony to be performed in the initiation. They then remove their shoes and, preceded by the attendants, who wear slippers, with measured and noiseless step, enter the central ante-room, a narrow hall separated by white screens from two other rooms to the right and left; the right one is for men, and the left for women.

Deep silence prevails, the attendants communicating by mysterious signs or very low whispers; a dim light pervades the room, mellowed by heavy shades; the faint plash of pouring water behind the scenes alone is heard, and the whole scene is calculated to cast a solemn awe over the ignorant candidates, waiting with subdued but nervous expectancy for some mysterious event. After a few moments of solemn waiting, the men are led to their washing-room on the right, and the women to the left. The female candidate is stripped, placed in the bath, and washed from head to foot by a woman set apart for the purpose. Every member is mentioned, with a special blessing.

"WASHER:—*Sister*, I wash you clean from the blood of this generation, and prepare your members for lively service in the way of all true Saints. I wash your head that it may be prepared for that crown of glory awaiting you as a faithful Saint, and the fruitful wife of a priest of the Lord; that your brain may be quick in discernment, and your eyes able to perceive the truth and avoid the snares of the enemy; your mouth to show forth the praise of the immortal *gods*, and your tongue to pronounce the true name which will admit you hereafter behind the veil, and by which you will be known in the celestial kingdom. I wash your arms to labor in the cause of righteousness, and your hands to be strong in building up the kingdom of God, by all manner of profitable works. I wash your breasts that you may prove a fruitful vine, to nourish a strong race of swift witnesses, earnest in defence of Zion; your body, to present it an acceptable tabernacle when you come to pass behind the veil; your loins, that you may bring forth a numerous race, to crown you with eternal glory and strengthen the heavenly kingdom of your husband, your master and crown in the Lord. I wash your knees, on which to prostrate yourself, and humbly receive the truth from God's holy priesthood; your feet, to run swiftly in the ways of righteousness, and stand firm upon the appointed places; and now I pronounce you clean from the blood of this generation, and your body an acceptable temple for the indwelling of the Holy Spirit."

A similar washing is performed upon the male candidate in his own room, and a blessing pronounced upon his body in like manner.

He is then passed through a slit in the curtain to the next compartment forward; as he passes, an apostle whispers in his ear "a new name, by which he will be known in the celestial kingdom of God."

Reaching the second room, the candidate is anointed with oil, which has been previously blessed and consecrated by two priests, poured upon his head from a horn, or from a mahogany vessel shaped to resemble one. The oil is rubbed into his hair and beard, and upon each of his limbs, which are again blessed in order. At the same time the women are anointed in their own washing room. The candidate is then dressed in a sort of tunic, or close-fitting garment, reaching from the neck to the heels. This, or a similar one, blessed for the purpose, is always to be worn next to the body, to protect the wearer from harm and from the assaults of the devil. Many Mormons are so strenuous on this point, they remove the garment but a portion at a time when changing, partly slipping on the new before the old is entirely off. It is generally believed that Joe Smith took off his tunic the morning he went to Carthage, to avoid the charge of being in a secret society; and that he would not have been killed, if he had retained it. Over the tunic comes the ordinary underclothing, and above a robe used only for this purpose; it is made of fine linen, plaited on the shoulders, gathered around the waist with a band, and falling to the floor behind and before. On the head is placed a cap of fine linen, and on the feet light cotton shippers.

At this point begins, in the adjoining room, the preparatory debate in the grand council of the *gods*, as to whether they shall make man. Eloheim, Jehovah, Jesus and Michael intone a drama in blank verse, representing the successive steps in the creation of the world. Eloheim enumerates the works of each day, and commends them all; at the close of each, all the others unite in a responsive chorus of surprise and praise at the glory and beauty of the work, concluding:—

"*Eloheim.* Now all is done, and earth with animate life is glad. The stately elephant to browse the forest, the ramping lion in the mountain caves, gazelles, horned cattle and the fleecy flocks spread o'er the grassy vales; behemoth rolls his bulk in shady fens by river banks, among the ooze, and the great whale beneath the waters, and fowl to fly above in the open firmament of heaven. Upon the earth behold bears, ounces, tigers, pards, and every creeping thing that moves upon the ground. Each after his kind shall bring forth and multiply upon the earth; and yet there lacks the master work, the being in the form and likeness of the *gods*, erect to stand, his Maker praise, and over all the rest dominion hold."

"*Jehovah, Jesus, Michael and Eloheim.* Let us make man, in image, form and likeness as our own; and as becomes our sole complete representative on earth, to him upright, dominion give and power over all that flies, swims, creeps, or walks upon the earth."

The attendants have meanwhile placed the candidates on the floor and closed their eyes, when the *gods* enter and manipulate them limb by limb, specifying the office of each member, and pretending to create and mould. They then slap upon them to vivify and represent the creative power, breathe into their nostrils "the breath of life," and raise them to their feet. They are then supposed to be "as Adam, newly made, completely ductile, mobile in the maker's hand."

II.

SECOND ESTATE.

Men file into the next room, with paintings and scenery to represent the Garden of Eden. There are gorgeous curtains and carpets, trees and shrubs in boxes, paintings of mountains, flowers, and fountains, all shown in soft light and delicate tints, together presenting a beautiful and impressive scene. While they move around the garden to measured music, another discussion ensues between the *gods;* Michael proposes various animals, in turn, to be the intimates of man, which are successively rejected by Jehovah, Jesus and Eloheim. The men are then laid recumbent, with closed eyes, in pantomime a rib is extracted from each, out of which, in the adjoining room, their wives are supposed to be formed; the men are then commanded to awake, and see their wives for the first time since parting in the entry, dressed nearly like themselves. They walk around the garden by couples, led by the officiating Adam and Eve, when Satan enters. He is dressed in a very tight-fitting suit of black velvet, consisting of short jacket and knee-breeches, with black stockings and slippers, the last with long double points; he, also, wears a hideous mask, and pointed helmet. He approaches Eve, who is separated from Adam, and begins to praise her beauty; after which he proffers the "temptation." (Here there is a difference in the testimony. John Hyde says, the "fruit offered consisted of some raisins hanging on a shrub;" one lady states that the temptation consists of gestures and hints "not to be described;" while another young lady, after implying that Adam and Eve were nearly naked, merely adds: "I cannot mention the *nature* of the fruit, but have left more unsaid than the imagination held with the loosest possible rein would be likely to picture . . . the reality is too monstrous for human belief, and the moral and object of the whole is socially to unsex the sexes." A third lady states that the fruit consisted merely of a bunch of grapes, and adds : " Those conducting the ceremonies explained to us beforehand that this portion of the affair should be conducted with the men and women entirely naked; but that, in consequence of the prejudice existing in the minds of individuals against that method of proceeding, coupled with the fact that we were not yet sufficiently perfect and pure-minded, and that our enemies would use it as a weapon against us, it was considered necessary that we should be clothed." It is quite probable the ceremony is frequently changed.)

Eve yields and partakes of the "fruit;" soon after she

is joined by Adam, to whom she offers the same; he first hesitates, but overcome by her reproaches, also eats. They grow delirious from its effects, join hands, embrace, and dance around the room till they sink exhausted.

A loud chorus of groans and lamentations is heard behind the curtain, followed by a sudden crash as of heavy thunder; a rift opens in a curtain painted to represent a dense wood, and in the opening appears Eloheim, behind him a brilliant light; he is clothed with a gorgeous dress, bespangled with brilliants and brights stripes to dazzle the eyes.

"*Eloheim.* Where art thou, Adam,
Erst created first of all earth's tribes,
And wont to meet with joy thy coming Lord ?"

"*Adam.* Afar I heard Thy coming,
In the thunder's awful voice,
Thy footsteps shook the earth,
And dread seized all my frame,
I saw myself in naked shame,
Unfit to face Thy Majesty."

"*Eloheim.* How knew'st thou of thy shame ?
My voice thou oft has heard,
And feared it not. What hast thou done ?
Hast eaten of that tree
To thee forbid ?"

"*Adam.* Shall I accuse the partner of my life
Or on myself the total crime avow ?
But what avails concealment with earth's Lord ?
His thoughts discern my inmost hidden sense.
The woman Thou gav'st to be my help
Beguiled me with her perfect charms,
By Thee endowed, acceptable, divine,
She gave me of the fruit, and I did eat."

"*Eloheim.* Say, woman, what is this that thou hast done ?"

"*Eve.* The serpent me beguiled and I did eat."

Eloheim then pronounces a curse—literally copied from the Scripture—upon the serpent, or rather Satan, who fell upon the ground, and with many contortions wriggles out of the room. A curse is next pronounced upon Eve, and then upon Adam, paraphrased from the Scripture. They

Y.

fall upon the ground, beat their breasts, rend their clothes, and bewail their lost and sinful condition.

"*Eloheim.* Now is man fallen indeed. The accursed power which first made war in Heaven, hath practised fraud on earth. By Adam's transgression should all be under sin; the moral nature darkened, and none could know the truth. But cries of penitence have reached my ears, and Higher Power shall redeem. Upon this earth I place My holy priesthood. To them as unto Me in humble reverence bow. Man, fallen by Satan's wiles, shall by obedience rise. Behold, the Woman's Seed shall bruise the Serpent's head; from her a race proceed endowed on earth with power divine. To them shall man submit, and regain the paradise now lost through disobedience. With power divine the priesthood is endowed, but not in fulness now. Obey them as the Incarnate Voice of God, and in time's fullness Woman's Seed shall all that's lost restore to man. By woman, first fallen, Adam fell; from Woman's Seed the priesthood shall arise, redeeming man; and man in turn shall Eve exalt, restoring her to the paradise by her first lost. Meanwhile go forth, ye fallen ones, with only nature's light, and seek for truth."

The attendants now place upon each of the initiates a small square apron, of white linen or silk, with certain emblematical marks and green pieces resemblnig fig leaves, worked in and handsomely embroidered.

The candidates then kneel and join in a solemn oath, repeating it slowly after Adam : That they will preserve the secret inviolably, under penalty of being brought to the block, and having their blood spilt upon the ground in atonement for their sin; that they will obey and submit themselves to the priesthood in all things, and the men in addition, that they will take no woman unless given them by the Presidency of the Church. A grip and a key-word are then communicated, and the *First Degree* of the *Aaronic Priesthood* is conferred. Man is now supposed to have entered into life, where the light has become as darkness. They pass through a narrow opening into the next room, which is almost dark, heavy curtains shutting out all but a few rays of light. Here they stumble about, fall against blocks and furniture; persons are heard calling, "here is light," "there is light," etc., and a contest goes on among those who call themselves Methodist, Baptist, Presbyterian, Catholic, etc. The curtains are constantly agitated, and being darkly painted with hideous figures, discover a thousand chimerical shapes. The sectarians seize hold of the initiates and pull them violently about, till the latter are quite exhausted. Satan now enters, commends the sectarians, laughs, chuckles and is quite delighted; the latter recommence their struggle for the initiates, when a sudden fall of curtains throws in a full blaze of light, and Peter, James and John descend into the room. They order the devil to withdraw: he falls upon the ground, foams, hisses and wriggles out, chased and kicked by the Apostle Peter.

The initiates are then ranged in order to listen to a lecture—

"*Peter.* Brethren and Sisters, light is now come into the world, and the way is opened unto men; Satan hath desired to sift you as wheat, and great shall be his condemnation who rejects this light.—(The ceremony is explained up to this point.)—The holy priesthood is once more established upon earth, in the person of Joseph Smith and his successors. They alone have the power to seal. To this priesthood, as unto Christ, all respect is due; obedience implicit, and yielded without a murmur. He who gave life has the right to take it. His representatives the same. You are then to obey all orders of the priesthood, temporal and spiritual, in matters of life or death. Submit yourselves to the higher powers, as a tallowed rag in the hands of God's priesthood. You are now ready to enter the kingdom of God. Look forth upon the void and tell me what ye see." (Curtain is raised.)

"*Adam* and *Eve*. A human skeleton."

"*Peter.* Rightly have ye spoken. Behold all that remains of one unfaithful to these holy vows. The earth had no habitation for one so vile. The fowls of the air fed upon his accursed flesh, and the fierce elements consumed the joints and the marrow. Do ye still desire to go forward?"

"*Adam.* We do."

The initiates then join hands and kneel in a circle, slowly repeating an oath after Peter. The penalty is to have the throat cut from ear to ear, with many agonizing details. The *Second Degree* of the *Aaronic Priesthood* is then conferred, and the initiates pass into the third room in the middle of which is an altar.

III.

THIRD ESTATE.

Emblematic of celestialized men.

"*Michael.* Here all hearts are laid open, all desires revealed, and all traitors are made known. In council of the *gods* it hath been decreed that here the faithless shall die. Some enter here with evil intent; but none with evil intent go beyond this veil or return alive, if here they practise deceit. If one among you knows aught of treachery in his heart, we charge him now to speak, while yet he may and live. Brethren, an ordeal awaits you. Let the pure have no fear; the false-hearted quake. Each shall pass under the Searching Hand, and the Spirit of the Lord decide for his own."

The initiates are placed one by one upon the altar, stretched at full length upon the back, and the officiating priest passes an immense knife or keen-edged razor across their throats. It is understood that if any are false at heart, the Spirit will reveal it, to their instant death. Of course, all pass. They again clasp hands, kneel and slowly repeat after Jehovah, another oath. The penalty for its violation is to have the bowels slit across and the entrails fed to swine—with many horrifying and disgusting details. Another sign, grip and key word are given, and the *First Degree* of the *Melchizedek Priesthood* is conferred, being the third degree of the Endowment. Copies of the Bible, "Book of Mormon" and "Doctrine and Covenants" are placed upon the altar, and another lecture delivered. The initiates are now instructed that they are in a saved condition, and are to go steadily on in the way of salvation; but that temporal duties demand their first care, chief among which is a positive, immediate duty to avenge the death of the Prophet and Martyr, Joseph Smith. The account of his martyrdom is circumstantially related, after which the initiates take a solemn oath to avenge his death; that they will bear eternal hostility to the Government of the United States for the murder of the Prophet; that they renounce all allegiance they may have held to the Government, and hold themselves absolved from all oaths of fealty, past or future; that they will do all in their power towards the overthrow of that Government, and in event of failure teach their children to pursue that purpose after them. Another oath of fidelity and secresy is administered, of which the penalty is to have the heart torn out and fed to the fowls of the air. The initiates are now declared acceptable to God, taught a new form of prayer, "in an unknown tongue," and the *Second Degree* of the *Melchizedek Priesthood* is conferred. They are then passed "behind the veil," a linen curtain, to the last room.

IV.

FOURTH ESTATE.

The kingdom of the Gods.

The men enter first, and the officiating priest cuts certain marks on their garments and a slight gash just above the right knee. Then, at the command of Eloheim, they one by one introduce their women to the room. Very few instances have occurred of women being admitted to these rites before marriage. "Sealing for eternity" is then performed for all who have previously been only "married for time."

The initiated then retire, resume their regular dress, get a lunch and return to hear a lengthy address, explaining the entire allegory, and their future duties consequent on the vows they have taken. The entire ceremony and address occupy about ten hours.

Such is the Endowment, as reported by many who have passed through it. The general reader will readily recognize that portion which is paraphrased from the Scriptures and Milton's Paradise Lost. The general outline is evidently modelled upon the *Mysteries* or *Holy Dramas* of the Middle Ages, with, perhaps, an attempt to reproduce portions of the *Eleusinian Mysteries* of Ancient Greece. Much of it will be recognized as extracted from " Morgan's Free-masonry Exposé," by those familiar with that work; and the origin of this is quite curious. When Smith and Rigdon first began their work they were in great doubt what to preach; a furious religious excitement was prevalent in the West, and portions of argument in regard to all the *isms* of the day may be found in the "Book of Mormon." But Anti-Masonry was just then the great political excitement of New York, and the infant Church was easily drawn into that furious and baseless crusade, which already ranks in history as one of those unaccountable popular frenzies which occasionally disturb our politics, rising from no one knows where, and subsiding as apparently without cause. Smith's "New Translation" of the Old Testament is full of Anti-Masonry; the fifth chapter of Genesis as he has it, which is added entire to our version, is devoted entirely to the condemnation of secret societies, and sets forth particularly how they were the invention of Cain after he "fled from the presence of the Lord." But the Brighamites declare the time has not yet come to publish or circulate this Bible; and it is only quoted by the Josephites, who use this chapter to condemn the Endowment. Some years after, however, the Mormons all became Masons, and so continued till they reached Nauvoo; there Joseph Smith out-masoned Solomon himself, and declared that God had revealed to him a great key-word, which had been lost, and that he would lead Masonry to far higher degrees, and not long after their charter was revoked by the Grand Lodge. How much of Masonry proper has survived in the Endowment, the writer will not pretend to say; but the Mormons are pleased to have the outside world connect the two, and convey the impression that this is "Celestial Masonry."

But the experience of the Mormons has fully proved—if any proof were needed—that among so many ready to take vile and abominable oaths, some would be found equally ready to violate them. Of those apostate Mormons who communicated some portions of the matter to the writer, he is convinced their account is correct, and is at liberty to say no more; but it may be of interest to the reader to know how others justify the breaking of such solemn vows, even at considerable risk to themselves. John Hyde, the most noted of all apostates, and esteemed a very honourable man, gives his reasons at length, summing up as follows:

First, As no one knew what were the oaths previous to hearing them, and no one after hearing, *could refuse* to take them, they are not binding in justice. *Secondly*, As the obligations also involved other acts of obedience as well as secrecy, and as I do not intend to obey those other obligations, it can be no more improper to break the oath of secrecy than the oath of unlimited obedience. *Thirdly*, As the obligations involved treason against the United States, it becomes a duty to expose them. *Fourthly*, The promise of Endowment being a principal bait held out to the Mormons, to get them to Salt Lake, it is well they should know what it is worth. *Fifthly*, It is better to violate a bad oath, than to keep it.

In ethics Mr. Hyde's first reason is worth all the rest; the third can hardly be admitted, as he was a resident of England, unnaturalized in America, and the last would apply with equal force to any oath, and in the mouth of any man. But Elder Hyde has only exemplified the usual course of apostate Mormons; from a material and gross extreme he has blundered to the opposite ultimate of vague mysticism, and is now preaching Swedenborgianism in England. If he live twenty years, he will probably again recant, relapse into complete infidelity, or become a Millenarian, Spiritualist or lunatic.

Are we to believe the testimony of apostates, and do these things really occur?

My own opinion is, that the account is substantially correct, for many reasons: that the witnesses agree where collusion is impossible; the relation is in many instances by persons utterly incapable of inventing or constructing such a plot; apostates universally have a horror or fear of speaking about it, and never do until they are safe beyond the power of the Church; all that can be observed by outsiders corresponds with these accounts, and particularly the fact that there is a close agreement and perfect analogy between the known doctrines of the Church and the outlines of the drama.

Such is one of the means employed by the Mormon

leaders to weld their people into perfect unity; and to such a feast of blasphemy and horrors do they invite the world, in their seductive

MISSIONARY HYMN,

"Lo! the Gentile chain is broken;
Freedom's banner waves on high;
List, ye nations! by this token
Know that your redemption's nigh.

"See, on yonder distant mountain,
Zion's standard wide unfurl'd;
Far-above Missouri's fountain,
Lo! it waves for all the world.

"Freedom, peace, and full salvation
Are the blessings guaranteed;
Liberty to every nation,
Every tongue, and every creed.

"Come, ye Christian sects and Pagan,
Pope, and Protestant, and Priest;
Worshippers of God or Dagon,
Come ye to fair Freedom's feast

"Come, ye sons of doubt and wonder,
Indian, Moslem, Greek, or Jew;
All your shackles burst asunder,
Freedom's banner waves for you.

"Cease to butcher one another,
Join the covenant of peace;
Be to all a friend, a brother,
This will bring the world release.

"Lo! our King, the great Messiah,
Prince of Peace, shall come to reign?
Sound again, ye heavenly choir,
Peace on earth, good-will to men."

CHAPTER XXI.

PRESENT CONDITION AND PROSPECTS.

Co-operation—The "bull's eye" signs—Inherent weakness of the system—Immediate effects on the Gentiles—Final result to the Saints—Founding of Corinne—Its bright prospects—Trip to Sevier—The deserted city—New Silverado—Mines and mining—A new interest in Utah—Rich discoveries—Hindrances—Grant's administration in Utah—Better men in the Revenue Department—Experience of Dr. J. P. Taggart—More "persecution"—The Judges—The Governor—Congressional Legislation—"Cullom Bill"—Probable effects—Guesses at the future—Another exodus—"Zion" in Sonora.

EARLY in October, 1868, the writer took up his residence in Salt Lake City, and the latter part of the same month, took editorial control of the *Salt Lake Reporter*, the only Gentile paper in Utah. But the hostility of the Church had become so great, that the trade of Gentiles was ruined, and one by one they were forced to sell out and leave the city. As already noted, the October Conference of 1868 passed a wholesale decree of non-intercourse with resident Gentiles, forbidding any Mormon to buy of, employ, or in any way countenance them. The day of assassinations was thought to be passed, but Brigham still hoped to keep out the Gentiles, and their hated principles, by ruining their trade. But, as the Gentile merchants generally sold the cheapest, hundreds of the Saints found it impossible to distinguish one store from another, to remedy which difficulty came another "decree" from Brigham, and soon after, over every Mormon store was seen, in flaming blue and gold,

"HOLINESS TO THE LORD

(The All-seeing Eye)

ZION'S CO-OPERATIVE MERCANTILE ASSOCIATION."

This effectually "corralled" the trade for a time, but,

with that strange fatality observable in men accustomed to having their own way, which, in the very nature of things, compels them to go further and further, till they at last reach a point beyond popular endurance, Brigham determined that the Mormon firms should yield also, and the entire business of the Territory become co-operative in fact. Measures were taken to establish a store in each ward and settlement, while the entire community combined in a large wholesale establishment with a stated capital of $1,000,000. It was purposed to have an agent constantly residing in the eastern cities, with surplus cash in his safe, to be ready to watch the markets, and buy always at the best advantage. In many of the settlements co-operative stores were soon started, and, as the people there do whatever the bishops tell them, it was easy to get the scheme in operation. By their religion and habits of unreasoning obedience, without a why or wherefore, the Mormons were as well prepared for co-operation as any people could be; and it was reasonable to suppose the new scheme would be almost a perfect success, that two or three years, at least, would be required for it to wear out. But it soon developed an inherent weakness. The Mormon merchants were, of course, no better pleased than the Gentiles, to have their business ruined, and there were still a few of the laity who would not "jump as the bell wether jumped," and risk their necks in the operation. The history of co-operative movements shows that, where applied to manufacturing purposes, they have, in the majority of cases, succeeded; but in merchandizing, nine times out of ten, they have failed. And the reason is obvious. In the case of the manufacturers, a few men combine their skill and labor to create wealth; every man knows something of the business, and has an understanding eye on its management; if one can do nothing but drive pegs, he understands that, all that he has to do, and contributes his share to the success of the concern. Every member knows, at a glance, the intrinsic value of the company's articles, ready, at a moment's notice, to turn salesman, and as their business is all selling and no buying, except procuring the rude materials, they have but half the opportunity for mistakes. All these features are lacking to the merchant co-operators. Their business must be done by agents; not one in a hundred of the partners understands the principles involved. Merchandizing requires the unity and controlling energy of one directing mind; one average merchant or two can show a better set of books than a committee of fifty first-class merchants; a debating society cannot centralize its energies. They do not *create*, they only manipulate wealth; the buying of necessity equals the selling, giving twice the opportunity for mistakes. If there is but one vote to each member, a small aggregate of capital overrules a very large interest; if there is a vote to every share, the small holders are partially disfranchised, and, of course, dissatisfied; dissensions must naturally result, and a thousand men cannot reasonably be expected to have less than a dozen plans, either one of which would be good by itself. And herein the Brighamites showed their strict consistency, by maintaining that the business *must* be managed by an inspired priesthood, that there *must* be no dissension or difference of opinion, and that it "*was* apostacy to dissent," from the business plans of that priesthood; for if such a business ever becomes a success, it must be by direct inspiration from the Almighty, requiring prompt obedience, and without question; it must be "yea and amen," without an attempt to piece it out with mere human wisdom. When the Lord condescends to run a "dollar store," we may expect co-operation to be a perfect success. The end is not yet, but enough has transpired to show that co-operation in Utah is not exempt from the usual weakness.

It was on this principle of business management by the priesthood, that the Godbeites first took their stand in opposition to Brigham Young. They maintained that the priesthood should only guide in spiritual matters, while every man should manage his private business to suit himself. To this the First Presidency jointly made reply: "It is our prerogative to dictate to this people in everything, even to the ribbons the women shall wear.

It is apostacy to oppose or differ with the plans of the priesthood in temporal matters."

Of course the immediate effects of the "decree of non-intercourse" were to produce greater bitterness between Saint and Gentile. Legally it was a move which they had a sort of right to make, but it was decidedly against good neighborhood; no particular violence was for a while attempted, and both parties contented themselves with a little quiet cursing. Social ostracism seemed to be complete; the "loyal" Brighamite and the straight-out Gentile seldom met, except in enforced cases, and, when they did, either sat in sullen silence, or their conversation was a mixture of the "rile" and "knagg," both exasperating and unprofitable. During the winter of 1868-'69 the Gentile residents of Salt Lake City numbered nearly eight hundred, of all ages and sexes, among whom we include that portion of the apostates who fully associated with and were recognized as Gentiles. This estimate I make from an inspection of the subscription list of the *Daily Reporter*, the roll of membership of the Gentile (Episcopal) Church, the members of St. Mark's Grammar School and Sabbath School, the roll of the Hebrew Benevolent Society, including every Jew in the city, and the membership of the Masonic and Odd Fellow Lodges, besides having been personally acquainted with almost every one of them. Besides these, there were, one day with another, several hundred transients in the city, consisting of visitors, railroad men temporarily out of employment, teamsters, miners, and travellers, stopping from one week to three months. Early in March the number began to decrease rapidly; Gilbert and Sons departed for other points; Ransohoff and Co. sold out to the co-operative institution; Corinne was laid out on the 25th of March, and, in two months thereafter, received a large accession of Salt Lake men, and by the 1st of June there were probably less than three hundred Gentiles in the city. The arrival of the newly appointed officials, their families and deputies increased the number a little; but the general depression in business has acted upon all, and there is no encouragement for new comers either

Saint or Gentile. The Gentile power seems to have consolidated in the northern counties, along the railroad, and though the process may be slow, will eventually liberalize that section of Mormonism.

CORINNE stands forth in fame as the first and only Gentile town in Utah; though the progress of the railroad has caused settlements, of a hundred or so each, at Bear River, Wasatch, Echo City, Uintah, and Indian Creek. Corinne is sixty miles north and twelve west of Salt Lake City, occupying the same relative place on Bear River, the other does on the Jordan. It is at the railroad crossing of Bear River, midway between the Wasatch Mountains and the spur known as Promontory, some eight miles from the lake, and in the centre and richest portion of Bear River Valley. The western half of this valley, unoccupied, except by one small village of three hundred Danish Mormons, contains half a million acres of the very finest farming land; of this, one-fourth is cultivable without irrigation, and the rest could be made fruitful by moderate watering, while an extensive stock range of the richest kind extends westward and northward. The elevation is 4,300 feet above sea-level, 1,000 feet less than that of Denver, 2,000 less than Cheyenne, 3,300 greater than Omaha, surrounded north, east and west by lofty mountain ranges, and on the south by the Great Salt Lake. It is thus the central point of a beautiful valley, fifteen by twenty miles in extent, with a location unsurpassed for natural beauty.

The City was laid out March 25th, 1869, by Mr. John O'Neill, Engineer of the Union Pacific Railroad; at the first sale of lots by General J. A. Williamson, Land Agent of the Railroad Company, the sales amounted to $21,000, and in a few weeks a flourishing town had sprung up.— *Corinne* is the natural centre of the Rocky Mountains; the most convenient spot on the railroad for a point of departure to Helena and Virginia City, Montana, and the point of supply for Idaho and Northern Utah. Bear River is navigable thence to the lake for steamers of a hundred tons; and Salt Lake and Jordan equally so to within three miles of Salt Lake City. North and east of Corinne, in Utah, is already a resident population of fifteen or twenty thousand, whose natural trading point is at that place; the constant efforts of the Church authorities are directed to preventing that trade from reaching there; but it is already coming, to some extent, and must steadily increase as liberal ideas prevail in that section. Corinne is an anomaly in politics, a government within a government, a little republic in the midst of a theocracy; a free city in the territory of an absolute monarch. For a few months the town was governed by Councillors chosen without a charter; this organization was allowed to lapse, and the Mormon County authorities were acknowledged; finally, within the last few weeks, the Territorial Legislature granted a regular charter, and the city is now fully organized under it. Corinne has a little of the "wickedness" incident to new railroad towns, but thus far of a remarkably peaceful character; morally she is an exception to railroad towns; the political and religious antipodes of Salt Lake City, she is on her good behavior. A church and school have been successfully established, and this gem of the mountains, Queen city of the Lake, has started with a good reputation.

While sojourning pleasantly at Corinne, last August, rumors reached me of an immense silver district on the Sevier River, two hundred miles south of Salt Lake City. Little was known for a certainty of that region; the spot was far beyond the settlements in the edge of the Indian country, and the route thither lay through the most benighted region of Polygamia. For these and other reasons, I felt that the Sevierites needed a historian. The man was ready and the hour was propitious. Peace had been made the preceding year with the Uintahs, and the route was just safe enough to not quite destroy the spice of a slight danger. Messrs. Salisbury & Gilmer, successors in fame to Wells, Fargo & Co., had just established a tri-weekly line of coaches to Fillmore, running within a hundred miles of the new Silverado, and on the morning of September 1st, I took a seat in their best "outfit" and was soon rolling southward through the richest portion of Jordan Valley. Twenty-five miles south of the city a spur of the Wasatch juts out from the east, almost joining the West Mountain, leaving a small gap known as the "Narrows," or cañon of the Jordan; here the stage road follows a "dug-way" around the hill, several hundred feet above the river, where there is never two feet to spare between the wheels and a slope almost perpendicular. Thence we descend over a long slope, with a succession of beautiful views, into the Valley east of Utah Lake, the Galilee of modern Saints; we pass the flourishing settlements of Lehi, Battle Creek, and American Fork to the city of Provo, second oldest town in the Territory. From there a night stage brought us to Levan or Chicken Creek, a hundred and fifteen miles south of the city, where the main road bears off to the right of Iron Mountain, while to the left, a trail through a high, uninhabited valley, leads to the Sevier, near the head of which are the mines. We were now out of even Mormon civilization, and the remaining ninety-five miles were necessarily divided into two stages, thirty miles to old Fort Gunnison, now a small Mormon settlement, and sixty-five through the valley formerly settled but deserted during the Indian war. The miners have established an express over this route, making one trip per week, and the driver and myself were soon on the way, travelling for the rest of the day through a region literally alive with small game; jack-rabbits, sage-hens, and small fowl were abundant on the high plain, and ducks fairly swarmed about every pond in the lower valleys. We spent the night at Fort Gunnison, a veritable walled town and city of refuge. The place is a square of some thirty acres, surrounded by a stone wall with huge gates on the four sides; within is an awkward collection of dobie and log houses, mud huts, stone stables, "dug-outs," and willow *corrals*, inhabited by English, Danes, cattle, dogs, and fleas, the latter predominating. It may have been that the poor people could do no better on account of Indian troubles, but as I walked about this singular town it seemed to me the place rested under the curse and shadow of a barbaric superstition. The stone walls with houses built against them and towers for sentinels; the dirty children resembling Arabs more than Caucasians; the heavy gates thrown open to receive the "evening herd" of cattle, and the general air of desert life pervading the place seemed so unlike any American scene, that I almost expected to find I was in the midst of that Oriental life from which Mormonism has drawn so many of its features.

From Gunnison a few hours brought us to the noted "Salt Mountain," a series of ridges from which crystalized salt can be cut in immense blocks; around the points rise numerous springs of pure brine, and a little further on, where a stream of pure water gushes out of a rugged cañon, is the city of Salina, now completely deserted.

From this point we traversed an unbroken desert for ten miles, its bare, gray surface unrelieved save by an occasional clump of scant grease-wood or cactus. Beyond this a spur of the mountains runs out nearly to the river, and turning this point we were delighted at the sight of Glenn's Cove, a semi-circle of beauty and fertility extending back into an opening in the mountains, containing at least six miles square of land, well watered and fruitful. Moving through the low meadows where the natural grass grew to the height of a man's head, and then over a tract of farm-land, we entered the beautiful town of Glenn City. Situated in such a place, with the water of a dozen mountain springs coursing through the streets, this had evidently been a town of considerable pretensions. The streets were laid off with the cardinal points; the houses were well constructed of lumber, stone and dobies; the gardens had been enclosed with stone walls of extra finish, and the ditches lining the streets paved with that care and beauty which marks the settlements of the better English Mormons; while the cool shade and agreeable rustle of the rows of trees lining the walks, seemed to invite the desert-weary traveller to repose in coolness and comfort. But there were none to enjoy this beauty; tall "pig-weed" and rank wheat-grass filled the streets, the stone walls were broken down and overrun by wild vines, the irrigating ditches in places overflowed and rippled unchecked through front yards and gardens, and the cool winds from the cañons sighed mournfully through the deserted habitations.

Involuntarily I looked for the cemetery, for it seemed that a plague must have smitten the city; but there was no unusual record of death there. Beyond the city lay untilled fields, with ploughs in places rusting in the furrows, and still further deserted ranches and meadows, apparently sleeping in the hazy air of autumn. While the driver rested his team for an hour, I looked through the place, for it almost seemed to me the people were hidden in the houses; but when I entered the largest residence I found the floor broken through and an Indian arrow sticking in the wall. In another well built house, I observed a child's cradle, still unbroken, near the fire-place, and beside it the mildewed remnants of a dress and bonnet and baby's shoes; melancholy traces of the attack and flight when the fearful mother caught up her child and fled before the avenging arrows of the "Lamanites."

Fifteen miles further we passed Alma; a town covering thirty acres in a square; enclosed by a massive stone wall, with towers at the corners, arranged with port-holes and sentry posts. But walls and towers were useless without skilful men to man them; the savages drove away the cattle of the settlement in broad day light, and soon after the place was abandoned. The whole number of Black Hawk's band of Mountain Utes, who drove the whites out of this valley, is reported to have been less than five hundred; and though peace had been made with him for a year, the Saints were slow to return.

At Marysvale, the last town on the route, we found three returned families; and here we left the river and travelled six miles up a gulch to the westward, which brought us to Bullion City and the mines. I spent several days in this strange mountain community, consisting of some two hundred miners isolated from the world, and made a thorough examination of the district. I found an awkward condition of affairs. There are, without doubt, immense quantities of silver ore there; the facilities for working the mines, in the way of timber and water, are unequalled; but there are no placer diggings, all quartz; and the miners were men of limited means who had rushed in from Nevada, each working enough "to hold his two hundred feet," but none able to buy and bring in a quartz-mill. The various leads extend for some miles along both sides of the gulch, "cropping out" in some instances for three or four thousand feet. That there is immense mineral wealth in this district is beyond a doubt; but it is far from transportation, and no bullion returns have yet been made to convince capitalists of its richness, or create a "rush." The Mormons manage to hinder progress there in various ways, and development is slow. But I think it highly probable these will, in time, be among the most valuable mines in the West.

Gold mining has been successfully established in Bingham Cañon, twenty miles west of Salt Lake City, and in Rush Valley some farther west; within the last few months rich deposits have been discovered, and these places are attracting great attention. Other valuable discoveries have been made in Cottonwood Cañon, and with the opening of the present season the mining interests of Utah become, for the first time, important.

The accession of General Grant to the Presidency was looked forward to with great interest by the Gentiles, in the expectation that some reform would be inaugurated in Utah; nor were these hopes entirely without realization.

The new Administration hastened to remove the officers who had disgraced the Revenue Service for four years, appointing O. J. Hollister, Esq., Collector, and Dr. J. P. Taggart, Assessor, in place of Burton and Chetlaine removed. Of Burton, I have already spoken; of Chetlaine it need only be said that he was a personal friend and rather intimate associate of Brigham Young, often accompanying him in his trips about the Territory, and that he made no attempt whatever to assess the Church income. I am of opinion, however, that the serious charges against him in other respects are untrue.

Chief Justice Wilson had been appointed some time before by President Johnson, and retained his position. The Mormon Associate Justice, Hoge, was succeeded by Hon. O. F. Strickland, who had resided several years in Utah and Montana, and is eminently qualified for the position. The Judge has had great practice in the peculiar technicalities of Mormon law, and enters upon his duties endowed with valuable experience. The veteran, Judge Drake, who had served seven years in Utah, gave place to Hon. C. F. Hawley, of Illinois, as Associate Justice, who has already taken a high position among the few United States officials who have upheld the dignity and maintained the honor of the Government even in Utah.

The opinion of Associate Justices Strickland and Hawley, lately delivered, dissenting from Chief Justice Wilson, in the case of *Howard, Brannigan* and *La Valle*, has attracted great attention in the Territories, and is regarded as an authentic exposition of Federal law in Territorial courts.

But it was in the Revenue Department that the first collision arose with Brigham. The following extract from the correspondence of an Eastern Journal, exhibits the clearest view of all the facts and deductions therefrom:

"An attempt has recently been made in Salt Lake City by Dr. Taggart, the new Assessor of Internal Revenue, to assess a tax upon the income of the Mormon Church, which is known to amount to a large sum annually. In this effort he has met with the most determined and persistent opposition from Brigham and his subordinates. Singular as it may seem, the wealthy 'Church of Jesus Christ of Latter-Day Saints' has never yet paid the Government tax upon its income. The former Assessor, Chetlaine, was known by the 'Gentiles' of Salt Lake City to be the mere tool of Brigham Young.

"He accompanied Brigham upon his royal progress through the Territory, and upon one occasion, when attending an evening meeting of the Mormons, accepted an invitation to a seat upon the platform, with the Bishop and his two counsellors, known violators of the anti-Polygamy law. When, however, he is removed and a man like Dr. Taggart steps into his position, determined to discharge the duties of his office without fear or favor, the Mormons salute him with howls of rage, and threats of persecution.

"The first act of Assessor Taggart, upon assuming

office, was to assess the Government tax upon the total amount of scrip issued by the Corporation of Salt Lake City, $190,000. The Treasurer of the Corporation had made his returns regularly to the former Assessor each month, with the tax calculated at one-twelfth of one per cent. upon the circulation, as required of bankers, and General Chetlaine accepted them as proper and correct. Section 6, of the Internal Revenue Act of March 3, 1865, requires the assessment of 10 per cent. upon the issue of all corporations of cities, &c., the Act not recognizing those bodies as legitimate bankers. The tax upon $190,000 at 10 per cent. is $19,000; the tax upon $190,000 at one-twelfth of one per cent. is $158.83, leaving the sum of 18,841,69, of which the Government would be defrauded, did not the present Assessor enforce payment. The profits made upon this issue of $190,000 are really a part of the revenues of the Mormon Church, the members of the Corporation of Salt Lake City being nominated by Brigham, and their election being secured by him under the present anti-republican form of voting in Utah. In the early part of last August, Dr. Taggart forwarded to Brigham Young a set of blanks, at the same time requesting him, as Trustee of the Church, to make a proper return of its income for 1868. Brigham became greatly incensed at this, and at first flatly refused to comply, but sent in reply the following document: 'We, the Government of the United States, do not recognize any such organization as the Church of Jesus Christ of Latter-day Saints, or any such officer as the Trustee-in-Trust of said Church. We, the Government of the United States, have obliterated such church and officer from existence by legislative enactment of July 1st, 1862.' No signature was appended to this. The meaning intended to be conveyed was doubtless this: That the anti-Polygamy Act was theoretically intended to wipe the Trustee-in-Trust and 'Church of Jesus Christ of Latter-day Saints' out of existence, although practically it had failed in its object; and therefore the Government could not assess and collect a tax upon the income of that ecclesiastical corporation. This communication from Brigham was treated with the contempt which it deserved—no notice being taken of it. The Assessor declared, however, that, if proper and correct returns were not made within the time limited by law, he should proceed to make the assessment himself from the best information which he could obtain, and should also hand the affair over to the United States District Attorney. Upon the last day allowed by law, Brigham made a return stating the total income of the Church for 1864 to be $440. The return was signed by Brigham Young in his private capacity. The blank oath was filled up and purported to have been sworn to before the Deputy Assessor, a Mormon, though Brigham had been in the habit of having his private income-returns sworn to by one of his clerks, who, he said, knew more about it than he did himself.

"The papers were immediately turned over to the United States District Attorney, who prepared an elaborate opinion, demonstrating that the Mormon Church Corporation was as much liable to have its income taxed as Trinity or any church corporation, subject, of course, to the legal exemptions. The various sources of revenue of the Mormon Church were also clearly and succinctly given. The papers were then forwarded to the Commissioner at Washington to await his opinion and instructions, and there they now remain.

"The Mormon Church Corporation has dealt extensively in the buying and selling of horses and cattle. For years this business has been carried on by its agents, but no license was taken out by any of them as cattle brokers until the new Assessor informed them of his intention to prosecute, if they were not immediately obtained. The authorities own and run a distillery and a wholesale and retail liquor store, which are carried on ostensibly in the name of the Corporation of Salt Lake City, but really are part of the Church, and the profits all go into the Church treasury. By means of this distillery the Government has been defrauded of thousands of dollars, which should have been paid in the shape of $2 upon every gallon of whiskey manufactured. Brigham gives as the reason for not including the tithing in the income returns, that the payment of it is voluntary and optional, and therefore is merely a gift and not taxable. Unfortunately, however, for Brigham, the facts do not bear out his assertion. A few months past a laboring man obtained work on the grade of the Utah Central Railroad, now being built by Brigham. After earning $50 he concluded to leave work, and accordingly asked for his time, which was given to him. Upon arriving in Salt Lake City he hastened to Brigham's office to obtain his money. The clerk hunted over the Church books, and found that the man owed $48 tithing for 1868. That amount was accordingly deducted, and the balance, $2, handed over to him, notwithstanding his earnest protestations that his family were actually in need of the money to purchase food. Non-payment of tithing is visited upon the offending members with all the prosecutions which the resources of the Mormon Church enable it to employ. The Mormons estimate the total population of Utah at 130,000 souls. These figures include only the Mormons. Of this number at least 30,000 are required by the rules of the Church and undoubtedly do pay tithing. Averaging their earnings at $500 a year, a low estimate, we have $15,000,000 as the aggregate. This, of course, is not in money exclusively, but in produce. The tithing on this would be $150,000. At least five of the leading Mormon merchants pay a tithing of $10,000 each a year. The income from the whiskey distillery and liquor store cannot fall short of $100,000; the rents and profits of real estate are about $25,000 more, besides other sources of revenue not to be ascertained.

RECAPITULATION.

Tithing from 30,000 people	$150,000
Five Mormon merchants	50,000
Church distillery and liquor store	100,000
Rents and profits of real estate	25,000
Total	$325,000
Deduct exemption	50,000
	$275,000

"This leaves upward of a quarter of a million of dollar subject to the Government tax, and the probabilities are that the Church income is more than double this amount, as many sources of revenue are not stated. Out of this and other taxes upon the private incomes of the Mormon leaders, the Government has been systematically defrauded year after year, through the connivance of an Assessor who executed his duties in the interests of Brigham Young. The present officer has commenced with a determination to do his whole duty, and it is to be hoped that he will receive the support of the Government in his efforts to collect the public revenues."

Dr. Taggart proceeded to collect the evidence showing the amount of tithing, and the fact that it was a requirement of Mormon discipline and the great test of standing and fellowship in the Church ; and at the present writing, he is in Washington, to lay the whole before the Department. It now begins to look as if Brigham Young would be compelled to pay his income tax, the same as any other speculator. Of course, all this is regarded as "rank persecution" by the Mormons; as is the enforcement of any law which does not happen to suit their convenience.

It is sufficient comment on the "wonderful industry of the Mormons," of which we have heard so much, to state the plain facts, that there is no other community of a hundred thousand in America but has paid twice as much revenue as Utah ; the Territories of Colorado and Montana, with half the population, have each paid nearly twice as much to the Treasury, and added from ten to forty times as much to the national circulation, and, notwithstanding the fearful demoralization of mining camps, have, in the end, produced a better race of men and women.

General J. Wilson Shaeffer was appointed Governor, to succeed Durkee ; he was formerly the Quartermaster in General Butler's department, and is reputed in every respect well qualified for the difficult and delicate position. Thus far, however, he has not shown his administrative talents in Utah, but remains in Washington, awaiting the action of Congress in regard to Utah.

The history of "Federal relations" in Utah presents a

strange mixture of the sad and ludicrous. The first law against polygamy, that of July, 1862, was utterly inoperative, as the Act of Congress failed to provide any means of enforcing it. Two years ago, Senator Cragin introduced a much better Bill, providing for all needed reforms in the Judiciary and voting system; but it was "referred and smothered in Committee." Next was Hon. James Ashley's Bill, introduced in January, 1869, providing for a division of the Territory, and annexing half or more to Colorado, one-third to Nevada, and a small portion each to Idaho and Wyoming. This would have been the merest political quackery, a virtual backing down on the part of the Government. Nature makes the boundaries of future states in the New West, and this is peculiarly the case with Utah; it is exactly fitted for one State, and has the area and resources for the comfortable support of half a million people. Nevada is already as large as New England, and between it and the habitable valleys of Utah are interposed broad deserts and rugged mountains, forming a ten-fold greater natural boundary than the Mississippi or the Hudson. Equally plain is the natural division between Utah and Colorado, and criminals from Southern Utah, if an attempt were made to execute the law, would have to be dragged eight hundred miles, around three sides of a mountainous parallelogram, to reach the Federal court at Denver. This Bill, too, was justifiably "smothered in Committee." Last is the Bill introduced by Hon. S. M. Cullom, Chairman of the House Committee on Territories, pending before Congress as this work goes to press. It provides for giving the United States Marshal his appropriate power; for restricting the Mormon Probate Courts to Probate and a limited civil jurisdiction as in other Territories; for dividing the Territory anew into Judicial districts, and for the proper support and protection of the Courts; that only citizens of the United States shall serve as jurors, that none who uphold or practise polygamy shall sit on the trial of that crime, and for many other needed reforms. It is reasonably certain this Bill will pass both Houses, and, by the time this meets the eye of the reader, become a law.

The first effect will in all probability be, that the actual polygamists will at once retire from the northern sections and concentrate in the south; below the Utah Lake region the Bill could not probably be enforced by the courts, for many years; but the northern section would shortly be relieved of the only class who cause any trouble, for the practical polygamists there do not exceed one in six.

The writer will not attempt to forecast the future of Mormonism. It is evidently on the decline, and without interference could hardly outlast thirty years; but, with its immense local power, could do much harm in that period. On account of this decline, many have argued that the Government should take no further measures to enforce its laws in Utah; but, with due deference to their opinions, this seems to me a very unstatesman-like view of any subject. What would be thought of a court which should decide against punishing a thief or murderer, " because, if left to himself, he will die in twenty or thirty years anyhow!" If a Church is at liberty to violate the laws for religion's sake, which an individual may not do; and if the Government has no resource, in this case or any other which may arise in the future, but to wait until time and internal corruption have worn out the criminal organization, it is certainly a novel principle in political ethics.

The opportune death of BrighamYoung would simplify matters somewhat; but there is still a mass of thirty or forty thousand who would stick together under new leaders, and continue the Church for another quarter of a century. Or, in case the Government attempts to enforce its laws and the Mormon Presidency gives the command to move, at least one-third of the people would follow them into Arizona and Sonora; but the really valuable portion would remain in Utah and become first-rate citizens. The Church is constantly planting settlements further south in Arizona; they now control one county in that Territory, and are within three hundred miles of Sonora, which, it is popularly believed among them, would be their destination, if compelled to abandon Utah. The Hierarchy could take at least thirty thousand devoted followers with them, and between the Mexicans, Apaches and Mormons, we should have little to choose.

The history of all the diverging sects has clearly demonstrated one fact: wherever the Mormons have come in close contact with considerable numbers of Gentiles, it has invariably resulted in a great apostacy, a fight or an exodus. By the usual rule we should expect in Utah, first a little flurry of war, then an exodus of one-third or more of the people, and general apostacy of the rest; and to this conclusion do present indications point.

Meanwhile, various redeeming agencies are powerfully, though somewhat quietly, at work in Utah, which are of sufficient importance to merit a separate chapter.

CHAPTER XXII.

REDEEMING AGENCIES.

The Church—First attempt—Rev. Norman McLeod—Dr. J. K. Robinson—Second attempt, Father Kelley—Last attempt—The Episcopal Mission, success and progress—Sabbath School—Grammar School of St. Marks—A building needed—Mission of Rev. George W. Foote—Difficulties of the situation—Number and occupation of Gentiles—Political prospects—Gentile newspapers—The *Valley Tan*—The *Vedette*—The UTAH REPORTER—S. S. Saul, the founder—Messrs: Aulbach and Barrett—The author's experience—Principles advocated —Courtesy of the Gentiles—Conclusion.

THE Christian Church, the school and the newspaper are but just established, with fair prospects in Utah ; but already they have accomplished considerable. It is somewhat surprising that such a field for missionary labor was neglected so completely and so long. For at least fifteen years the voice of the Christian minister was never heard in Salt Lake City.

If there were Chaplains among the troops of Johnston's army, they seem to have left no record of their presence, or made any attempt to work among the Mormons. The first missionary effort was by the Rev. Norman McLeod, Chaplain of the California volunteers, at Camp Douglas. Late in 1863 he began to preach in a room on Main street, and afterwards raised money to build Independence Hall. A large part of the funds was advanced by a literary society then existing among the Gentiles, and that building has never been considered so much a church as a lecture and assembly room ; it is, however, held by trustees for " The First Congregational Church of Utah." It is still burdened, I believe, by a debt of near $2,000. Rev. McLeod established a Sabbath School, of which Dr. J. K. Robinson was for some time Superintendent ; he also delivered a series of lectures on various subjects, particularly polygamy, which excited great interest. The bent of Mr. McLeod's mind seems to have been towards controversy, and many of his lectures and sermons were highly polemic in character, exciting no little wrath among the Mormons and some discussion among the Gentiles. Whether this aggressive policy, or one more mild and persuasive, would better reach the case, is still a debatable question. In the autumn of 1866, Mr. McLeod went east to raise funds for building a church; during his absence Dr. Robinson was assassinated, and as McLeod's life was openly threatened, he deemed it best not to return. The second attempt to found a mission was by Father Kelly, a Roman Catholic, in the summer of 1866. He spent some time in Salt Lake City, managed to keep on good terms with the Mormons and from various sources raised money enough to purchase a lot, which is still owned by the Catholic Church; but he found few Catholics in the district, formed no church and left little permanent record.

The third and last missionary effort was under the auspices of Bishop Tuttle, in charge of the Diocese, including Utah. In April, 1867, at his request, Reverends George W. Foote and Thomas W. Haskins set out for Salt Lake City, where they arrived in May and commenced services at once. They found but two communicants of their own faith—Episcopal—and only twenty of all other Christian denominations. From that day to this regular services have been held in Independence Hall, and a flourishing church established. During the two and a half years of their ministry a hundred and one persons have been baptized by them, of whom thirty-four were adults, and many of Mormon antecedents. Ninety communicants have been admitted as regular members, of whom sixty-six still retain their standing in Salt Lake City; the others have either removed or died. All denominations have united to a great extent in support of this Church and Sabbath School; the Jews also attend and contribute, probably the only place in America where such is the case.

The Sabbath School was begun with a few members,

and, in consequence of orders from the authorities of the Mormon Church, some of this small number were soon after withdrawn. But others soon took their place, and, in spite of open hostility and private malice, the school increased and spread, a powerful lever for good. At different times a little over three hundred children have been instructed in the school, and the teaching, whether in the case of Mormon or Gentile youth, has been attended with marked and beneficent results. This school is still growing, and its light of Christian knowledge is a bright spot in the centre of polygamic heathenism.

The Grammar School of St. Mark's Associate Mission, the first Gentile school in Utah, was opened in July, 1867, by Rev. Thomas W. Haskins and Miss Foote, sister of the minister, with sixteen scholars. The Mormon leaders again forbade their people to allow their children to attend, but the attractions of free tuition prevailed with many; the school has steadily increased, both in numbers and scholarship, till it now has a hundred and forty pupils, and is compelled to refuse all others until enlarged accommodations can be secured. From first to last four hundred children have been instructed in the school. It is now purposed to provide more teachers, and steadily raise the grade of scholarship until young men can take a regular collegiate, or at least a regular academic, course. A fixed rate of tuition is charged, but all unable to pay are received as free pupils, of whom there are sixty in the school. This is the nearest approach to a free school at present in Utah.

As yet there is no Christian church edifice erected in Salt Lake City; but it is hoped there soon will be a building worthy of the cause, with ample accommodations for a school, and Rev. Geo. W. Foote is now in the East raising funds to that end. The mission and school have also had the assisting care of Rev. Henry Foote, who has lately removed to Boise City, Idaho. The gentlemen in charge of this mission have thought it best to raise no personal controversy. Whether it was an outgrowth of their personal disposition, or of the conservative policy of their Church, or that they hoped to avoid the bitter animosity which existed against Rev. McLeod, they have steadily refrained from aught like personal controversy or a direct attack upon the Mormon leaders, contenting themselves with "preaching Christ and Him crucified," and planting principles which should in the hearts of hearers work out in a love and desire for the truth. It was but reasonable to suppose such a policy would at least disarm personal hostility, and that men would not curse though they might not agree. But vainly would one hope by fair words to neutralize the venom of the serpent's fang; the blind adder will strike, simply because it is his nature, though charmed "never so wisely," and Mormonism when opposed flies to weapons of slander and vituperation, as well as against the persuasive reasoner as the fierce polemic. If these gentlemen hoped to be spared McLeod's experience, they have been disappointed; every epithet a vile fancy could suggest has been heaped upon them from the Mormon press and pulpit, and the madness of bigotry has not hesitated at slandering the ladies who assisted at their noble work. It was perhaps as well that this should be so; Christian ladies of such character could receive no stain from such a source, and this action merely made plain the inherent blackness of the real Mormon heart. But surely, if there be one deep, dark pit in the regions of the damned, which Divine Justice has reserved as too awful for the fate of common sinners, it is in waiting for those who have used the priestly profession to attack the reputation of woman.

Preaching was begun at Corinne early in 1869, earnest endeavors were made to secure funds for a building, which was completed and dedicated in July of the same year. Neat and unpretentious, not large but commodious, it is an ornament to the city and worthy of note as the first Christian church edifice in Utah. Sabbath School has been established and regularly continued, while a day school, as a branch of the Salt Lake Grammar School, was established last autumn and continued during the winter, to be resumed at an early day. It is taught in the Church, by Miss Nellie Wells, formerly an assistant in the Salt Lake City School; it numbers some forty scholars, and as the first entirely Gentile school in Utah, deserves a place in history.

The residence and occupation of the Gentiles are not such as to encourage either schools or churches, they being miners, herders, scattered traders, or transient residents.

The mines of Utah develop slowly, but it is reasonably certain there is mineral wealth there, if they can find it or properly get at it. Utah is in the mineral belt, there are paying mines all around it, the formation of the country corresponds exactly with those where immense wealth of gold and silver is found; some important discoveries have been made, and more will be. Sevier, Bingham, Cottonwood, Rush Valley and Stockton mines have not, altogether, developed enough as yet to create a "rush," or make any one suddenly rich ; but in several places steady industry has been found profitable, and with better facilities for transporting ore and machinery, with more experience and further discoveries, the latter will come in time.

Any present estimate of the number of Gentiles in Utah is necessarily somewhat conjectural. As they are practically disfranchised, they run no ticket and record no vote; they have but one organized church society, and very few are within reach of that; they have never held a convention *en masse*, or had an efficient organization to give us any *data;* and finally, they are scattered over half the Territory, with very imperfect understanding or communication. From the best evidence at hand, I estimate as follows:

```
Corinne................................................. 1,000
Ogden, Uintah, Echo, Wasatch and Bear River,
    (100 each).........................................   500
Salt Lake City........................................   500
Camp Douglas.........................................   400
Bingham, Cottonwood and Rush Valley (100 each)   300
Sevier mining district ..............................   300
Scattering ..............................................   500
                                                         -----
              Total........................ 3,500
```

Deducting soldiers and U.S. officials, this would leave

three thousand citizens. Of the entire number, at least two-thirds are voters, nearly all the non-voters being in Corinne and Salt Lake City. With the lowest increase we may reasonably expect in the coming summer, with the least settlement of railroad men absolutely necessary at the Junction, with no increase among the miners, and with little, perhaps very little, help from those of the Josephites, and other recusant Mormons who dare say their souls are their own, the Liberals ought to cast a vote of at least four thousand at the coming August election. They will do so, if a proper organization is effected.

As to the *legal* vote of the Mormons, it is beyond the power of Statistics to determine. At the last election of Hooper their vote amounted to 15,068; it could just as well have amounted to 1,500,068. It was only a question of a few cyphers, which do not amount to much anyhow. Deducting all those who were under age, all voted for by proxy, all unnaturalized or illegally naturalized by the Probate Court, all those disqualified by the Act of Congress of July 1st, 1862, all the double voting and false ballots, and the cypher would be moved the other way, leaving a *legal* vote of 1,568.

There have been, at different times, three Gentile papers published in Utah.

With Johnston's army came one Kirk Anderson, who soon after established a weekly paper called the *Valley Tan*. It ran through 1858 and all or nearly all of 1859, then failed for want of support. Little is known of this paper, except from the bound files still in the *Reporter* office; but it seems to have been edited a portion of its existence by Mr. Anderson, and at another time by a Mr. McGuire.

The first daily paper, the *Union Vedette,* was established at Camp Douglas late in 1863, with Gen. P. E. Connor as proprietor. At the beginning, the work was done by enlisted men of the California and Nevada volunteers, and the editing by various officers of that command. The main object of the *Vedette* seems to have been to give daily telegraphic reports from the seat of war, which were eagerly sought after by all the Gentiles. The Mormons then had but one paper, the *Weekly Deseret News*, almost as old as the Territory, but much too dull and prosy to meet the new demand for intellectual stimulus. The *Vedette* was established with the concurrence of Gen. Wright, then in command of the Department, with a view to the publication of official orders, and in the hope of disseminating more correct information on the military and civil policy of the Government among the Mormons.

In addition to the old feeling between Mormon and Gentile the *Vedette* had to deal with questions of loyalty, the volunteers being intensely devoted to American institutions, and the Mormons only differing from Southern rebels in the fact that they were not openly in arms. The paper soon become quite popular and obtained a wide circulation in Montana and Idaho, as well as Utah. In the autumn of 1865 it was removed into Salt Lake City and enlarged. Some of the officers still wrote occasionally for it, but the editorial control was in the hands of civilians, Rev. Norman McLeod and O. J. Goldrick. The controversial spirit, which was of a questionable benefit in Mr. McLeod's sermons, was much more fitting in the columns of the *Vedette*, which increased in popularity and ran well for one year. Several other persons contributed also to its pages during that time. The office then changed hands, and Mr. Shoaff, a printer from California, became nominal owner and editor. But the *Vedette* had passed the height of its prosperity and in five months was reduced one-half in size, receiving but indifferent support at that. Shoaff soon after left, handing over the paper to Judge Daniel McLaughlin and Mr. Adam Aulbach, who again enlarged it to the former size. For a short time the concern flourished, but Judge McLaughlin departed for Cheyenne, after which the paper rapidly declined and soon was compelled to suspend. During Shoaff's administration the financial embarrassment of the concern had increased to such an extent that all the surplus material was sold, and two other offices were mainly outfitted therefrom, viz: The *Utah Magazine* and the *Sweetwater Mines*.

Early in 1868 Mr. S. S. Saul arrived from California and deeming the location favorable purchased the remain-

AA

ing material, and on the 11th of May the same year, issued the first number of the *Salt Lake Reporter*, daily only. The first five months of its existence the paper was very small and but poorly supported; it was edited haphazard by several different persons, and regularly by no one. A newspaper more than any other enterprise requires the controlling energy of one directing mind; steady mediocrity is better than variable talent; above all it must have a fixed policy, and one common place worker, a mere plodder though he be, is far better than half a dozen brilliant but irregular geniuses. But it is doubtful if any newspaper could have succeeded during that period, no matter what talent might have been employed.

On the 10th of September, 1868, the writer entered Salt Lake City, and on the 19th of October took editorial charge of the *Reporter*, in which position he continued for eleven months, until September 1869. On the first of December he joined with Messrs. Adam Aulbach and John Barrett in the purchase of the entire office, which partnership continued for eight months, with real pleasure to the writer, but with little pecuniary profit. A weekly edition was commenced in February 1869, which is still continued, with increasing circulation and popularity. In the spring of 1869, the office was removed to Corinne and UTAH substituted in the title for *Salt Lake*. Early in September the writer retired, and soon after the office passed into the hands of Messrs. Huyck and Merrick, the present proprietors.

During my editorial labors I frequently had occasion to discuss the action of Mormon Courts, and particularly after our removal to Corinne. Our County Judge was the Bishop Smith, already mentioned as the husband of two of his nieces; in an article on county affairs I alluded to that fact with considerable severity, more, perhaps, than strict equity in journalism would allow. Soon after quitting the editorial position I was summoned to attend court at Brigham City, and while passing from the court room to the street received a violent blow on the back of the head, which prostrated me almost senseless upon the ground. Whether more than one took part I do not know; all I distinctly remember is a confused rush and trampling of heavy boots, and when I revived I was being raised by my friends, who were taking stock of my condition generally. My collar bone was broken in two places, and my scalp badly torn, besides minor injuries; altogether, it was a narrow escape. There were but half a dozen Gentiles present, from whom I learned that the principal assailant was a son of the Judge; but I did not see and could not now identify him. The attack was probably caused by my strictures upon his father and the Probate Courts. There was nothing to be done about it, however; it was one of those incidents to which newspaper men are liable anywhere, which are of frequent occurrence to Gentiles in Utah, and for which there is no remedy there.

Shortly before, a young apostate Mormon in Bear Lake Valley, acting as clerk for Mr. Frederick Kiesel, a Gentile merchant, was killed outright in a way that pretty clearly indicated the direction of the Church authorities; and not long after a Mr. Phelps, a young Gentile in Salt Lake City, was attacked at night by the secret police, shot through the shoulder, and narrowly escaped with his life. He had the good fortune, however, to kill one of his assailants. Such occurences are rare now, as compared with ten or fifteen years ago, still they happen often enough to make Gentiles apprehensive and not anxious to remain, which is doubtless the effect desired. The most efficient government could not altogether prevent this, but much more might be done than is.

I was wounded on the 1st of November, but in that healthful air recovered sufficiently to travel by December 1st, when, after fifteen months' residence, I left the Territory, for a short time at least. As editor for one year of the only Gentile paper in Utah, in closing these sketches a few words may be pardoned to one speaking it may be egotistically of himself, while occupying a delicate and difficult position.

Of my intercourse with the Gentiles of Utah, I have none but the most pleasant recollections. An utter stranger, quite an invalid, and in a condition where personal friendship was almost a necessity, I received from the first at their hands the most courteous and respectful attentions. My keenest sympathies were enlisted for a people, exiled as it were in the very centre of their country, claiming the name and protection of American citizens, but subject to a worse than Russian despotism; practically disfranchised and without representation in any Legislative body. My social intercourse with them has been of the most pleasant character, and if at any time I have complained of an inefficient pecuniary support for my work, I now perceive that it was due to the pressure of adverse circumstances beyond their control. It is a source of pride and deep satisfaction that my editorial management met with the hearty approval of those in whose judgment I most confided, and that the *Reporter* is now upon a footing that renders its continuance reasonably certain; for I shall ever feel a pride that I once directed its policy.

As for the Mormons, I came among them with but few ideas about them, and my first impressions were rather favorable. My first friends were all Mormons, with whom I journeyed across four hundred miles of the plains; and those persons are still my friends; they have extended me courtesies which I duly appreciate; I have "eaten their salt and warmed at their fires." But not all their kindness or personal friendship could blind me to the monstrous defects of their social system, or the odious features of a church tyranny; and if my feelings soon changed towards the hierarchy, it was only from the best of evidence. That evidence has constantly accumulated until language fails me to convey my utter detestation of their system. That the people are frugal, industrious or honest will avail them but little, while fanatically devoted to such a power. If, in the bitterness of heated controversy, injustice has inadvertantly been done to any private person, none will regret it more, or be more ready to make amends, and though some *unpleasant* experiences have fallen to my lot, I am not conscious of special animosity against the body of the people. And when a score of years shall have passed, and the principles for which we have contended are seen in their fruition, I am quite sure many who have cursed the writer will at least give him credit for sincerity; and though there still be some who dissent from the measures he has advocated, when the fierce alembic of time has proved which was correct, and the test of experience has shown what was really best for the Territory and the people, I trust they will not remember their wrath forever.

THE END.

www.ingramcontent.com/pod-product-compliance
Lightning Source LLC
Chambersburg PA
CBHW050845300426
44111CB00010B/1128